Also by
James Playsted Wood

MAGAZINES IN THE UNITED STATES

THE STORY
OF
ADVERTISING

JAMES PLAYSTED WOOD

THE RONALD PRESS COMPANY · NEW YORK

Copyright, ©, 1958, by

THE RONALD PRESS COMPANY

All Rights Reserved

2

Library of Congress Catalog Card Number: 58-8474

For

ELIZABETH CRAIG WOOD

Preface

IF ALL THE ADVERTISING ever printed were wadded into a ball, there would not be room for it. If all the advertising spoken since the beginning were likewise compressed, it would form a gaseous envelope about as large as that provided for the circling of all the planets around the sun. If all the emotions advertising has stirred, all the actions it has provoked, all the hypnotism it has exerted, and all the gullibility it has evoked could be added up, the sum would approximate the dimensions of total human nature.

This book attempts to tell some of this long and richly varied history of advertising and to appraise critically some of advertising's characteristics, accomplishments, and shortcomings. It tries to recapture some of the color, warmth, and vitality of advertising that was old a hundred years ago and to distinguish the different but equally notable qualities of me that was new yesterday. It is directed to advertisers, to vertising agencies, to the advertising media, to students of vertising as a commercial force and a pervasive and power- form of public communication, and to the consumer. ve all, it is directed to those who think people interesting, ther they find them lovable or impossible, for advertising e story of people. In firsthand actuality, advertising de- es their desires, tastes, habits, weaknesses, hopes, and pre- ons. In advertising can be seen the actuality of what e have been like in their day-to-day living through the ies and what we are like now. There can be few more e representations of a time and the people in it than the advertising amid which and, willy-nilly, by which they live.

Advertising has been lauded or castigated almost since it began. This book is neither attack nor defense. It attempts to trace and evaluate some of the significant changes that have taken place over the centuries and especially in the recent past. It describes the blatant and the subtle in advertising, the informative and the misleading, advertising that has led to material betterment of the human lot and other advertising that has distorted human values. It notes advertising up and down the scale from the insistent whine of the panhandler to the dignified statements of corporate business, which can wait with assurance for its stately institutional pronouncements to be properly heeded.

It examines advertising as sign, symbol, and arm of freedom. Advertising is a primary expression of the entire democratic concept of freedom of enterprise and consumer freedom of choice. In this way, advertising has stature and importance beyond its proven ability to distribute merchandise. Advertising is also one of the most powerful forces contributing to produce a sheeplike conformity in entire populations, helping create the compulsions to which the community responds.

My sincere thanks go to a score of friends and associates in advertising, publishing, and teaching who have answered my requests for information, offered fruitful suggestions, and stimulated through casual conversation. I am grateful to th Springfield, Massachusetts, Public Library for generous priv leges accorded and to the library of the American Philosopl cal Society for the use of its valuable files of eighteenth- a early nineteenth-century American and English materials. always, my greatest debt is to Elizabeth Craig Wood, did more than her share of independent research.

JAMES PLAYSTED WOOD

Philadelphia
April, 1958

Contents

CONTENTS

THE STORY
OF
ADVERTISING

What is Advertising?

THAT ADVERTISING EXISTS is obvious to all who can see or hear. That advertising does things is apparent on the balance sheets of corporations, in the lovely solvency of advertising agencies, in the food we eat, the clothes we wear, the kinds of houses we live in, the cars we drive, and in many of our most firmly embedded and often baseless assumptions.

Advertising has been plied for centuries. On occasion, advertising has labored and brought forth a mouse. It has also moved its various mountains. Advertising has developed and supported great industries, bulwarked entire economies, and changed a sufficient number of human habits. Yet no one seems to know surely just what advertising is and all that it entails.

Prime ministers and Presidents, professors and corporation heads, novelists, columnists, and social historians have all had a try at it. The speeches of advertising managers and advertising agency account executives are inflated with overblown definitions that do not define and platitudinous certitudes that are somewhat uncertain. Advertising has consistently eluded most attempts at confining it within the limits of useful phrase.

There are earnest essays by more and more people, using more and more impressive names for their activities, to measure and gauge, weigh and check, but the psychologists, sociologists, poll takers, and forecasters have succeeded little better than those with less esoteric vocabularies. Mercury-like, advertising slides past their gropings and, one sometimes suspects, their understanding of what they are about. Advertising

refuses to be made into a science and has never been purely
an art.

Wisely, many of those closest to advertising do not attempt to define. Like P. T. Barnum and Sir Thomas Lipton,
they simply, happily, and very profitably create it and use it.
Some of the most famous of advertising men, however, and
some of the more thoughtful have felt impelled to try.

From the beginning of his spectacular career in advertising, something in the nature of the redoubtable A. D. Lasker
made it necessary for him to know what the force he so successfully applied actually was. He decided and formulated
a working definition: "Advertising is news." That understanding worked well enough for Lasker in the 1890's. Then
he seized on another that changed his whole concept of what
he was doing and changed fundamentally much of the advertising of the next twenty years. In a Chicago saloon in 1899,
John E. Kennedy told Lasker that "Advertising is salesmanship in print." It was a revelation. Lasker immediately put
Kennedy to work for Lord & Thomas at wages commensurate with the magnitude of his vision and their combined
ability to put the revelation to practical and highly profitable
use.

In 1905 another advertising man, Earnest Elmo Calkins,
who was to become a famous copywriter, tried to put down
all of the things he thought advertising was.

Advertising [he wrote] is a great, though almost unknown, force,
a force made up of a hundred different elements, each one too intangible to be defined. It is something which, properly directed,
becomes a powerful agency in influencing human customs and manners. All the great forces that have moved the race, the eloquence
of the orator, the fervor of the religious enthusiast, superstition, panic,
terror, hypnotism—all these things are used in advertising. All the
emotions of the race are played upon, appealed to, coaxed, cultivated,
and utilized. The man who can tell most nearly what one thousand
people will think upon a given topic will come nearest to producing
successful advertising, but no human being can foretell the actual
results of any advertising that ever was planned.[1]

[1] Earnest Elmo Calkins and Ralph Holden, *Modern Advertising* (New
York: D. Appleton and Co., 1905). An unexpected witness bears testimony

Calkins was awed in 1905 at what he saw as the power of advertising. Nineteen years later, he could be briefer, but he was still awed. "Advertising," he concluded in 1924, "is the supreme flowering of a sophisticated civilization."[2] Some may find it a little difficult to distinguish between a supreme and an ordinary flowering, and there are malcontents who insist we have not yet achieved a recognizably sophisticated civilization, but it is clear that a lifetime of experience did not dim the wonder of advertising in Calkins' eyes.

"Salesmanship in print" was soon under attack as a satisfactory discipline of advertising. Its truth was denied by as eminent an authority on everything as Hearst's Arthur Brisbane. Advertising, Brisbane decided and announced, was not selling at all; it was merely "telling." He later explained, positively if somewhat ungrammatically, "A good advertisement must do five things and do them all. If it fails in one, it fails in all. It must make people see it, read it, understand it, believe it, want it."[3]

One advertising agency man agreed fully with Brisbane. Advertising was "telling." When that sounded too simple, he tried again. "Advertising is the art of making known."[4] Pretentious overstatement has seldom deterred advertising men in talking about their work or in doing it. Another agency man of this period sounded a little cynical. "Advertising is making others think as you desire. It means utilizing

---

to the latter part of Calkins' remark. Samuel Butler, satirical author of *Erewhon* and *The Way of All Flesh*, said, "Sometimes publishers, hoping to buy the Holy Ghost with a price, fee a man to read for them and advise them. This is but as the vain tossing of insomnia. God will not have any human being know what will sell." Quoted by James D. Hart in *The Popular Book* (New York: Oxford University Press, 1950), p. 288.

[2] *Louder, Please! The Autobiography of a Deaf Man* (Boston: The Atlantic Monthly Press, 1924), p. 4.

[3] Quoted by Carl Richard Greer, *Advertising and Its Mechanical Production* (New York: Tudor Publishing Co., 1940), p. 16. Greer himself comes to the conclusion that "anything is an advertisement—whether communicated by printing or otherwise to absent persons—which conveys to them knowledge where a product may be obtained, and conveys it in such a way as to cause them to desire it."

[4] Henry P. Williams, "When Advertising Can Insure Business Success," *Printers' Ink*, March, 1920.

all those forces which produce impressions and crystallize opinion. . . . The great power of advertisements is in getting into people's minds the ideas that they carry in such a way that people think they always had them."[5]

It seems a clear case of *lèse-majesté* that all argument and differences of opinion about the identity of advertising did not come to an end in 1909. In that year George Lyman Kittredge, Harvard's Chaucerian, Shakespearian, and haughty impaler of shams, made his pronouncement. "An advertisement," he wrote, and the italics are his, "is a *notification*."[6]

It is unlikely that the advertising world, little given to reverence for other than its own contributions to humanity's welfare, paid proper deference to Prof. Kittredge or was either pleased or frightened by his declaration, though some may have been awed that he paid advertising the tribute of noting its existence.

Academe had already noted the phenomenon which for centuries had been the possession and accomplishment of the vulgar. Solemn consideration of advertising seems to have crept into academic thought through a new subject which, in more conservative intellectual circles of the time, was not itself considered to be too reputable. This happened when a young theological student who had planned to become a missionary studied in Germany instead and returned to Northwestern University as an associate professor of psychology. Against the advice of his colleagues, Walter Dill Scott—he became president of Northwestern in 1920— turned his attention to advertising. Largely through this circumstance, advertising became a subject of interest to the psychologist before it became, as it did later, a major concern of the economist.

In October, 1895 *Printers' Ink* had stated editorially that eventually the advertising writer, like the teacher, would have to study psychology, for "The advertising writer and

---

[5] John Lee Mahin, *Lectures on Advertising*. Privately printed, undated; internal evidence places it before World War I.

[6] Introduction to Lawrence Lewis, *Advertisements of the Spectator* (Boston: Houghton Mifflin Co., 1909), p. viii.

the teacher have one great object in common—to influence the human mind." *Printer's Ink* had urged again in March, 1901 that the advertising writer should have a working knowledge of psychology. Scott noted both these comments in the introduction to a small book, *The Psychology of Advertising*, which, privately printed, appeared first in 1902 as *The Theory and Practice of Advertising*, but carried the better known and more accurate title in later editions.

Scott applied pre-Freudian psychology to advertising in chapters on memory suggestion, human instincts, habit, the feelings and emotions, the will, and what he called the "laws of progressive thinking." He assumed throughout that advertising's chief purpose was to attract and influence the minds of possible customers. Advertising, he thought too, was not unlike teaching. "An advertisement," he said at one point, "has not accomplished its mission till it has instructed the possible customer concerning the goods and then has caused him to forget where he received his instruction."[7]

As many have tried to do since, Scott attempted to compare the attention value of small and large space. He plunged into the "Unconscious Influence in Street Railway Advertising" and "The Psychology of Food Advertising." The human instincts, as Scott listed them in 1908, were: The Instinct to Preserve & Further the Material Possessions; Food Instincts; Clothing Instinct; Hoarding & Proprietory Instinct; The Hunting Instinct; The Constructing Instinct; The Parental Instinct; The Instincts Affecting the Social Self; The Instincts Affecting the Psychical Nature. The list seems tailor made for advertising exploitation.

Another early writer dared juxtaposition of advertising and the new social science of the spirit. In 1909 George French strained to pin down the actuality of advertising in a book which referred to pragmatism, the conscious and the unconscious mind, and generally reflected the teachings of William James. French came bravely to the not very illuminating conclusion that advertising was "personality with

[7] Walter Dill Scott, *The Psychology of Advertising* (Boston: Small, Maynard & Co., 1908), p. 221.

knowledge working upon personality with needs."[8]   Basically,
French decided, advertising was suggestion. Then, as has
happened with writers on advertising before and since, his
scientific approach broke down before his indignation.

The power of suggestion has been employed to fool and fleece
people through advertising in a most outrageous fashion. It has been
employed to sell millions of dollars worth of useless and harmful
nostrums, through suggesting ailments. The coupon advertisement
owes much of its power to suggestion. The temptation to obey the
command of the advertiser to "detach this coupon, sign and mail it
now" is one that is obeyed by a far greater number of people than
would write the advertiser if the advertisement did not contain the
specific suggestion that immediate action be taken in a specified manner. The suggestion, and the coupon, set the motor machinery of the
mind into action, and unless the will intervenes its authority, and
reverses the spontaneous impulse, there will be action of the sort the
advertiser desires.[9]

As the serious study of advertising developed, more and
more attempts were made to embalm the quickness and form-
less extravagance of advertising in the formal language of
chill abstraction.

New York University established its Advertising Division
in 1913. Two years later, four faculty members who had
helped found and develop the Division put their four heads
together and wrote a book which, they made very clear in
their preface, would embody their two years experience and,
once for all, put everything that was known about the principles, psychology, and application of advertising into its
proper place. Advertising, the four decided, "is the application of the force of publicity to the sale of commodities or
services, by increasing the public knowledge and desire for
the items specified therein."[10] It was, they added, in reality
the machine or bulk method of selling.

[8] George French, *The Art and Science of Advertising* (Boston: Sherman,
French & Co., 1909).
[9] *Ibid.,* p. 197.
[10] Harry Tipper, Harry L. Hollingsworth, Ph.D., George Burton Hotchkiss, M.A., Frank Alvah Parsons, B.S., *Advertising, Its Principles and Practice* (New York: The Ronald Press Co., 1915), p. 8.

In 1923 George French tried once more to capture the essential meaning of advertising.

The peculiar appeal that is made to people to buy something or to do something, which is called advertising, is a functioning of salesmanship and propaganda not discovered in any other use of persuasive power and language. It is something apart which cannot be defined by reference or analogy. It is in the nature of a connecting link between the spoken language and the written argument, taking on the persuasive power of the former and adding to it the descriptive qualities of the latter. . . . It is a personal appeal through impersonal mediums. . . . It is a hybrid in the field of expression, devised to effect results impossible by other methods. . . . It is a great power for good, which is often employed in attempting evil.[11]

This is more emotional than logical. It is a straining for comparisons, almost an admission of the impossibility of isolating and analyzing the essential advertising ingredient. In this way, perhaps, French came indirectly nearer the truth that advertising is basically emotional, emotional in its creation, in its operation, and in its effects.

A professor of marketing in the Harvard Graduate School of Business Administration who later became an advertising agency research director reached a definition so economical that it is almost naked. Advertising, he decided, was simply contact, ". . . the establishment of contact between one maker or vendor and thousands of actual or potential buyers."[12] A generally accepted modern description from the economic viewpoint of what advertising does rather than what it is was formulated by another student of advertising on the faculty of the Harvard Business School: "Advertising includes those activities by which visual or oral messages are addressed to the public for the purposes of informing them and influencing them either to buy merchandise or services or to act or be inclined favorably toward ideas, institutions, or persons featured."[13]

[11] George French and Harry Tipper, *Advertising Campaigns* (New York: D. Van Nostrand Co., Inc., 1923), p. 407.
[12] Paul T. Cherington, *The Consumer Looks at Advertising* (New York: Harper & Bros., 1928), p. 71.
[13] Neil H. Borden, *The Economic Effects of Advertising* (Chicago: Richard D. Irwin, Inc., 1942), p. 17.

At one point a clear-eyed businessman got somewhat impatient with all the refining and abstraction. "Advertising," he told a Williams College audience, "is nothing in the world but multiple communication about goods for sale."[14]

Advertising men are a little shocked at such ruthless dispatch just as they are somewhat chilled by the cold conclusions of the academicians. They prefer longer and more eloquent descriptions of their dedicated endeavor. Advertising to them is not just news, salesmanship in print, telling, notification, indirect selling, publicity, suggestion, "systematic instruction," appeal, contact, multiple communication, a "force," or a "something." It is a religious conviction, a "way of life," a drive, a fascination, and a mystery. Behind a protective wall of statistics, within an edifice of research where Ph.D.'s frown in conference or extrapolate alone, behind all the trappings demanded by modern advertising practice, they burn with a hard gemlike flame, trembling with the exquisite agony of creative passion. Fervor pounds in their blood. Fancy dances in their brains. It is a little like that, for advertising deals with the stuff of imagination. Yet all this they can suddenly calm almost at will and supplant with the shrewdness needed for handling the cold practicalities of their complex trade. It has been this way for a long time.

This same mingling of fervor and astuteness showed in Nath'l C. Fowler, Jr., as he signed himself, one of the prime energies in American nineteenth-century advertising, who plugged successfully for corsets, bicycles, and a hundred other commodities. Brassily, breezily, shrewdly, Fowler had his say about advertising in 1897. He said it at great length with copious illustrations in a huge "Encyclopedia of Advertising and Printing and All that Pertains to the Public-Seeing Side of Business" which he entitled *Fowler's Publicity*. Frank Presbrey quoted pages from Fowler in his comprehensive *History and Development of Advertising*. It is easy to see why. Fowler did not omit much from his 1016 folio pages. What he wrote was vivid and sensible when he wrote it. His tone

[14] Paul Hollister, "Advertising—Is It Worth What It Costs?" Speech given at Williams College, February 6, 1940.

may seem quaint today, but much that he wrote is still vivid, sensible, shrewd, and practical.

His book was unbiased, a plain statement of fact, all inclusive, and every department in it was calculated to be suggestive and beneficial to everyone of every class. Fowler said so in just those words at the very beginning. After two hundred pages of "great successes," the advertising case histories of practically every large advertiser of the 1890's, he went into every type of advertising in every medium then known, into printing, paper, layout, type selection. He even found space by the time he reached page 1013 for treatment of nudity. Fowler was for it as a man, but against it as an advertising writer and press agent. "The history of art began with nudity, and will end with it . . . but for all that, there are many who object to nudity, and so as long as they do, it is the business of business to let nudity alone."

Fowler admitted the truth of a rumor which said he had written, prepared, and suggested more advertising matter than any other man. He admitted to his book pages of axioms about advertising "which flatterers have called 'Fowlerisms.' " Here is some of the pithy advertising wisdom Nath'l C. Fowler, Jr., shared with his time.

> He who doesn't read advertisements is blind.
> He who doesn't hear advertisements is deaf.
> He who says he doesn't read advertisements and can read is a liar.
> The woman who doesn't read advertisements isn't a woman.
> Advertising connects buyer with seller.
> Advertise what you sell, not yourself, unless you are for sale.
> The good of all good is in so handling the good that the good of it does good.
> Continuous advertising stands for continuous prosperity.
> The advertiser of to-day who is not the advertiser of to-morrow may be out of business day after to-morrow.
> Appearance of success means success.
> When times are good and folks are willing to spend money, advertising suggests that they spend more money. When times are bad and folks don't want to spend money, advertising should **create** desire for and recognition of necessities.

When folks want to buy, any fool can sell them.
Invest a part of your capital in advertising. Invest a part of your
    profit in more advertising. Invest a part of your extra profit in
    much advertising.
Don't give people more than they want.
Don't print more than people will read.
Write your advertisements from the customer's standpoint. You
    can't make him appreciate your side of it.
Not what you think but what others think creates trade.
Folks must be asked.
Bait for what you would catch.
A business is judged by the advertising of it.

Fowler went on exuberantly, aphorism after axiom. At
one point in his rushing text, he called advertising a simple
announcement of something to sell, and said this:

An advertisement may be considered the same as making a request
of somebody, a request that will largely benefit the requester. More
likely than otherwise, it is not granted because the person of whom
the request is made does not discover in it any possible benefit to himself. The next day the request is repeated in a slightly different way,
and adapted to the conditions of that day. The request is again refused, but the asker is not discouraged, and continues day in and day
out, always making the same request in substance but changing the
expression of his face, voice, and words so that they may be adapted
to the conditions of the one he is addressing.[15]

Politicians, especially when they are seeking favor through
advertising, can also be eloquent about advertising and its
virtues. Calvin Coolidge paid advertising his proper little
tribute. Franklin D. Roosevelt, in a letter of June 15, 1933
to the Advertising Federation of America, described advertising as "an economic and social force of vital importance."
On another occasion he declared, "If I were starting my life
over again, I am inclined to think I would go into the advertising business in preference to almost any other."[16] Harry
Truman went dutifully through the motions of praising ad-

   [15] Nath'l C. Fowler, Jr., *Fowler's Publicity*. (New York: Publicity Publishing Co., 1897).
   [16] *Lasting Ideas* (Pleasantville, N. Y.: The Reader's Digest Association,
1956), p. 9.

vertising and its value to the United States in a signed statement. Yet the efforts of these Presidents pale beside the effusions of England's most colorful modern prime minister. In sonorous rhetoric Sir Winston Churchill declaimed:

> Advertising nourishes the consuming power of men. It creates wants for a better standard of living. It sets up before a man the goal of a better home, better clothing, better food for himself and his family. It spurs individual exertion and greater production. It brings together in fertile union those things which otherwise would never have met.[17]

Churchill had tradition and precedent behind him in taking favorable note of advertising. A famous Victorian prime minister, William Ewart Gladstone, great liberal and Christian hero, had watched it too. Sir Thomas Lipton, artful and indefatigible practitioner of advertising in a thousand forms, tells of Gladstone's uttering in a speech in Edinburgh words that influenced his whole career. What Gladstone said was: "Advertising is to business what steam is to industry —the sole propelling power. Nothing except the Mint can make money without advertising."[18] Gladstone read American magazines not for their editorial content but for their advertising. It was in American magazine advertising, he said, that he saw reflected the growth of the United States.

In assaying any or all of these definitions and attempts at definition, the rather baffled attempts to describe and explain, it is only fair to recognize the basic difficulty faced by anyone who tries to capture and bind advertising in logical terms. Advertising has no independent existence of its own. Advertising is nothing of itself, and it produces nothing, not even the smoke from one ballyhooed cigarette or the bubbles from one cake of rhapsodically described soap.

Advertising must be given an external creation, a product, service, or idea originating with some other agency, in order to exist and function. It is never an independent entity, only

---

[17] *Ibid.*

[18] Sir Thomas Lipton, *Leaves from the Lipton Logs.* (London: Hutchinson & Co., Ltd., 1931), p. 115. Though he did not credit his source, Gladstone was quoting an earlier advertising authority, Thomas Babington Macaulay.

a concomitant noise. Even when it is most successful, and transfer of a horse, a washing machine, a world cruise, a social creed, or a political prejudice is triumphantly effected, advertising achieves no actuality of its own. At its worst, advertising is an excrescence. At its best, it is a catalyst.

Awareness of the parasitic nature of their trade together with conviction of its importance and knowledge of its tremendous power, may be part of the reason for the hypersensitiveness of many advertising men to even the mildest of criticism. Often they try to forestall the criticism by loud justification before the attack is launched. There are, of course, other reasons for their defensiveness. Like poetry, and there are many ways in which advertising can be looked upon as part of the poetry of American life in the twentieth century, advertising is persuasion largely through words in printed symbols of sound, sounds that when read or spoken are symbols of meaning or, more often, of fantasy. Like poetry, the appeal of most advertising is emotional. It cannot be defended or explained by arithmetic. Unlike poetry, advertising is not disinterested art. It is sharply interested artisanship. Its purpose, as some of those whose advertising sentiments have been reviewed flatly stated, is profit, profit of some kind; and the world, while furiously engaged in the activity, charmingly persists in disdaining the pursuit.

Often the genesis of advertising is as irrational as the appeals it employs. Advertising does not always start with deliberate cupidity, market surveys, statistically forecast sales potentials, and all the other impedimenta of the modern advertising agency approach. Many times someone is fierily convinced that he has produced something that is living and beautiful. Everyone should know of it; everyone should have it. You may not be able to distinguish it from a thousand comparable objects more prosaically hatched, but he can, and he burns to educate the ignorant to appreciation.

There is another reason advertising men quail at the hint of unfriendly criticism. Standard decorum frowns on a man's boasting loudly of his prowess and possessions. Advertising men are professional boasters of the virtues of others and what they have to sell. The principal can live at peace with his modesty, looking slightly askance at the braggart antics of his hirelings. It is even a little worse than that. Advertising is a mercenary. Its services are always for hire. It has no sustained loyalties. It cannot afford them. Any good advertising agency can turn expertly from praise of one incomparable shampoo or matchless automobile to the equally deft and sincere praise of its chief competitor, which then becomes really and truly incomparable or even more matchless. Skilled advertising can unconvert, then reconvert, those it has just carefully and completely converted.

Advertising may start with the conviction that someone has some money and proceed with the determination to get it away from him before somebody else does. It may emanate from the passionate belief of someone that what he has to offer is more and better than any other benefactor ever panted to bestow upon the race. Whichever the cause and whatever the advertising means and media used, advertising has one constant upon which advertiser, agency, and medium can always depend. That constant is the enduring and endearing susceptibility of people.

From the simple announcement, which was one of the earliest forms of advertising, to the saturation bombardment repeated and continued in all media until the target is almost obliterated, no advertisement is whole until it is seen or heard. No understanding of what advertising is or does can be complete that does not take into consideration people and their response to advertising.

The response may sometimes be one of boredom. The ironist may be derisive or wryly amused. ("It must be a good such-and-whatever-it-is. It is *very* highly spoken of in the advertisements.") Theirs is still response, for response is unavoidable. The reactions of the many are more strongly marked, and usually they are pleasurable. Like other forms of mass communication, advertising is in many ways a substitute for personal communication. It is the modern counterpart of the conversation which in simpler societies could take place between the maker of an article or the creator of an

idea and the man who out of desire or idle curiosity stopped
to listen or examine. Often it was a conversation both enjoyed. Sometimes it added emotional value to the object or
idea. There was the simple fun of bargaining. Early advertising retained much of this personal flavor. It was written
by one of the parties concerned. It said what he wanted to
say in his language, language his customers understood. Modern mass advertising has necessarily destroyed something of
this personal warmth and, as it developed, changed something
of the manner as well as the actuality of the response.

There sometimes seems a convention in the conduct of
advertising almost as set as the movements in a formal dance.
The advertisement announces itself as an advertisement. Implicit in its existence is the declaration that it intends to
charm, persuade, convince, perhaps delude, sometimes to
defraud. There is an understood pretense. The advertisement pretends to offer more than it asks, while both parties
know that the greater benefits are meant to accrue to the
advertiser. Advertising in its approach must hide its confidence that it always (well, almost always) wins.

Etiquette prescribes an attitude on the part of the consumer too. He must retreat as the advertisement approaches.
He must not admit to instant interest. He must show indifference, a suspicion, sometimes a defiance, hide his willingness
to succumb. The advertisement pretends an appeal to his reason. This courteous pretense the consumer gravely accepts,
though the appeal is undisguisedly to his desires or his
dreams.

The advertising approach may be warm and impetuous,
diffident, or as subtle as a tenpenny nail through the skull.
It can scream, "Look at me!" It can assume instead a sensitive shyness—"I hope you won't notice me or will forgive
me if you do." This too is understood. An advertisement
may glow with arch innocence, shrink with modesty, or boast-
fully parade its muscles. It may provoke a cry of rage or
pain, a movement of avoidance, a whimper of delight. It
does not much matter. The challenge has been accepted.
The consumer knows that he flirts with danger, but he has

taken the dare. Surrender is inevitable. At first it may be only the surrender of a little attention, a shade of disbelief. Sooner or later, complete capitulation will come. Under stress, the man or woman may forget his own name. He will not forget the name of the car, the soap, the cigarette, the dogma, the impressions somehow received.

Advertising is a tale, a folk tale, as well as a venture in commerce. It is best known from wide experience of it by many people through the centuries. Inability to isolate logically the essence of advertising detracts not one whit from its vigor, not a decibel from its fury or a fraction from its force.

Perhaps advertising is not and has never been the stuff for limning in too tight a frame. A. D. Lasker had no definition in the end. He had lived advertising furiously and well and for a long time. It was part of him, and he was part of it. "Advertising," he breathed, "is a talent. It is born in you, like singing, or it is not. You have it or you haven't. It is conceived in the mother's womb . . ."[19]

[19] A. D. Lasker, *The Lasker Story.* (Chicago: Advertising Publications, Inc., 1953), p. 42.

Strawberries Ripe and Cherries in the Rise— Cries, Signs, and Cards

IT ALL BEGAN with street cries, with town criers and bellmen, with hawkers shouting their wares and hucksters sing-songing their chants. The first advertising was vocal; its appeal, aural. The Greeks used criers thousands of years ago to call attention to the sale of slaves and cattle as well as to intone new state edicts and make public announcements, or to chant advertising appeals like this one said to have been used in ancient Athens:

> For eyes that are shining, for cheeks like the dawn,
> For beauty that lasts after girlhood is gone,
> For prices in reason, the woman who knows
> Will buy her cosmetics of Aesclyptoe.[1]

Criers bawled Latin advertising messages in the streets of Rome. There are said to have been shop barkers even in the busy and crowded streets of Carthage, when the Phoenician city was market place for the textiles of Syria, the pottery of Greece, the incense of Arabia, African ivory, and the metals of Spain, Gaul, and Britain. As early as the third century of our own era, barkers tried to outshout each other at the fair in the English market town of Stourbridge, not far from

---

[1] Quoted in *Advertising Age*, March 17, 1952, from ABC radio documentary, "The Great Adventure."

modern Birmingham. They can be heard any Saturday afternoon now at the nearby market of Bridgnorth.

The shops of each trade were jammed together in the narrow streets and by-streets of medieval England. There was
little to distinguish the shops, each in its open stall or booth.
To snare the unwary, lure the curious, and prod the laggards,
the shopkeeper posted a man or boy, often his apprentice, at
the entrance to shout at the top of his lungs, "What d'ye lack,
sir? What d'ye lack? Mistress, what d'ye lack?"

To the cacophony of "what d'ye lack's" were added the
advertisers' pleas to "Buy!"—buy this or buy that. Buy my
roses, cranberries, rabbits, flounders, Yorkshire cakes, sage,
mint, rue, cloth, tin, dolls, mops, oysters . . . "Come, buy!
Come buy!" Shakespeare, as he so often did, was merely
using a poetic variant for a well-know popular phrase when
he gave Autolycus, rogue, peddler, and "snapper-up of un-
considered trifles," this song to sing in *The Winter's Tale:*

> Lawn as white as driven snow,
> Cyprus black as e'er was crow;
> Gloves as sweet as damask roses;
> Masks for faces and for noses;
> Bugle bracelet, necklace amber,
> Perfume for my lady's chamber;
> Golden coifs and stomachers
> For my lads to give their dears;
> Pins and poking sticks of steel,
> What maids lack from head to heel;
> Come, buy of me; come buy, come buy;
> Buy, lads, or else your lasses cry.

The cobbled streets of London resounded to the cries of
the barker and the hawker. "Hote pyes hote!" was one of
the oldest. This fourteenth-century cry was used until the
end of the eighteenth century. Elizabeth's England rang
with the lilting chants and hoarsely bawled rhythms of scores
of familiar appeals.

Come buy my whitings fine and new . . . Buy a moustrap, a
moustrap, or a tormenter for your fleas . . . Here's fine herrings, eight
a groat . . . White-hearted cabbages . . . Hot Peascods, Hot peas-

cods! . . . Strawberries ripe and Cherries in the rise . . . Lily-white vinegar . . . Hot fine Oatcake . . . Hot codlins, pies and tarts . . . Buy my Wells fleet oysters, O!

The costermonger selling *staccato fortissimo* from his stand or barrow was originally an apple vendor, the costard being a variety of English apple. The street was the market place for everything: almanacs, potatoes, pots, pans, flapping fish, clothes, knives, books, Banbury cakes, even water.

A doleful looking medieval merchant beats out advertising calls while his laden ass listens with little show of response. (Bettman Archive)

London water tasted as bad as it smelled. "Any fresh and fair spring water here! None of your pipe sludge!"
There were other ballad-like solicitations:

> One-a-penny, two-a-penny, hot cross buns!
> One-a-penny, two for tup'ence, hot cross buns!
>
> Dust, O! Dust, O! Bring it out to-day.
> Bring it out to-day! I shan't be here to-morrow!
>
> I sweep your Chimnies clean, O!
> I sweep your Chimney clean, O!

> Buy my Diddle Dumplings, hot! hot!
> Diddle, Diddle, Diddle, Dumplings, hot!
>
> Maids, I mend old Pans or Kettles,
> Mend old Pans or Kettles, O!
>
> Muffins, O! Crumpets! Muffins to-day!
> Crumpets, O! Muffins, O! Fresh to-day![2]

Joseph Addison wrote pleasantly, pleasurably too by the sound of his words, of London's street cries in No. 251 of the *Spectator.*

There is nothing which more astounds a foreigner or frightens a country 'squire than the *cries of London.* My good friend Sir Roger often declares that he cannot get them out of his head or go to sleep for them, the first week that he is in town. On the contrary, Will Honeycomb calls them the *Ramage de la ville* and prefers them to the sound of larks and nightingales, with all the music of the fields and woods.

Some chants, Addison wrote, were deep and dismal; some, light and musical. "Any old chairs to mend!" was chanted slow and sadly, but the cry of the peddlers of dill and cucumber was a pleasant air. He told of one pastryman who had so improved on the traditional cry of his trade that he was commonly known as "Colly-Molly-Puff." Addison was not sure that such radical changes should be tolerated.

In early New York a familiar peddler's cry was,

> Clams! My clams I want to sell to-day,
> The best of clams from Rockaway!

and the vendors of sweet corn sang a dozen lines of verse as they dispensed the succulent ears from their steaming kettles.

In Philadelphia in the 1840's a bonnetted and be-shawled woman used to sit before a toy shop at night as the theatre crowds moved homeward, a basket of the fragrant dried leaves and blossoms of the mint on her lap, calling musically, "Lavender! Two cents a cup! Two cents a cup for lavender! Lavender!" There were other street cries in the Philadelphia

[2] Charles Hindley, *A History of the Cries of London.* (London: Charles Hindley [The Younger], 1884).

of that and of an earlier day. "Catfish! Catfish! Buy any Catfish? Catfish!"; "Rags! Any rags? Any *wool* rags? Any rags?" After blowing his bugle, the waffleman called, "Waffles! Fresh baked Waffles! Waffles!" and then tooted his bugle again.[3]

The sounds of the German band, the organ grinder, and the postman's whistle have been silenced for some time, but many cries survived on the streets of our older cities well into the twentieth century. The cry and clanging bell of the "hokie-pokie" ice cream man have gone, but the bell of the modern vendor of ice cream confections still brings children running to his white truck. Did the "snowball man" have a cry of his own? He was usually an unwashed old man in a stained white jacket, pushing a cart with on it a cake of ice, a scraper, a spherical mold, and dusty bottles of brightly colored syrup to squirt over his frigid confections. "Rags! Any old rags?" is still the cry of the ragman, as the string of cowbells jangling on two unsteady uprights on his cart is still his flourish. "Any umbrellas to mend? Knives to sharpen!" . . . "Green beans and red tomatoes!" . . . "Bananas! Bananas!": these and many others can still be heard. The cry of the old clothes man patrolling New York neighborhood streets was always hard to make out. Did he sing *"I* cash clothes!" or *"High* cash clothes!" as he shuffled along the pavement, bundle of castoff skirts, trousers, and coats under his arm, and looked hopefully up for a tenement window to open and some housewife shrill answer to his appeal?

If advertising cries have been lessened in number and lowered in tone, they have certainly not disappeared. Vocal advertising, shouted, sung, chanted, even whispered, has simply left the street and gone into the house. The "outside talker" is now the inside talker. The pitchman has gone into the parlor where his insistent voice, mocking, ordering, insinuating, cajoling, urging, is incessant. The bleat and wheedle of, first the radio, then the television commercial is direct descendant of the more musical advertising cries of the streets.

[3] The lavender woman was shown life-size before her store front and the recorded calls were played in "Advertising in Philadelphia," exhibition in the Atwater Kent Museum, Philadelphia, 1957.

Vocal advertising came first; visual, next. According to Henry Sampson in his delightful *History of Advertising from the Earliest Times*,[4] signs over shops appear to be the earliest form of advertising that had more permanence than the spoken word.

They go back to the remotest portions of the world's history. Public notices were also posted in the first days of the children of Israel. . . . comparatively recently we have received intelligence that in Pompeii and similar places advertising by means of signs and inscriptions were quite common. "The History of Signboards". . . quotes Aristotle, refers to Lucian, Aristophanes, and others in proof of the fact that signboard advertisements were used in ancient Greece.[5]

The Romans pasted signs on the walls of forums and market places to advertise gladiatorial combats and circuses. Similar notices have been discovered on the walls of Pompeii. Usually, though, the signs of classical times were made of terra cotta and set into pilasters at the shop fronts. A goat was the sign of a dairy in Rome. A mule driving a mill designated a bakery. A boy being whipped was the all too accurate Roman sign for a school. It is probable, Sampson believed, that the various workmen of Rome used their tools as signs over their houses, for they have been found sculptured on their tombs in the catacombs. Shakespeare's assertion in the prologue to *As You Like It* that "good wine needs no bush" sprang from the ancient custom of designating a wine shop by hanging a green bush before it.

Signs in pictures that told a story were important in the Middle Ages when few people could read, and every place of business in England seems to have had its distinctive sign in those centuries. A coat of arms was the sign that came to designate an inn. The thrifty nobility had a habit of letting their houses, before which hung their coat of arms, as hostelries when they were not at home. Inns got their names in this fashion from the most prominent feature of the coat of arms —The Red Crown, The Blue Dagger, The Gold Fox, The Three Stars.

[4] (London: Chatto & Windus, 1874.)
[5] *Ibid.*, p. 19.

The London streets became a forest of signs as every shop reached out to entice customers. Signs hung on poles, against shop walls, dangled over the sidewalks, even hung across the streets. Their density was such that Charles II, annoyed by those which spanned the roadways, proclaimed that "No signs shall be hung across the streets shutting out the air and light of the heavens." Some of the worst offenders may have disappeared with the royal decree, but hundreds of swaying and creaking signs still hung over the heads of passers-by on the walks. In the time of Queen Anne, 1702-1714, there were "blue Boars, black Swans, and red Lions, not to mention flying Pigs, and Hogs in Armour, with many other Creatures more extraordinary than any in the Desarts of Africk." They were tartly described thus in No. 28 of the *Spectator*. Public sentiment was aroused against the signs when one fell in Bride Lane in 1718, killing four people. By 1762 both the City of London and the City of Westminster passed laws against overhanging signs, though all others were allowed to remain.

Each trade had its distinctive symbol. A sign of three nuns embroidering indicated a draper's. A gilt arm wielding a hammer was the sign of a gold beater. Hosiers showed a golden leg and chimney sweeps a golden pole. Other shop signs and symbols were:

    bookbinders—Bible and dove
    booksellers—authors' heads
    boot and shoemakers—golden boot
    carpenters—the carpenter's arms of three compasses
    coffin plate makers—angel and crown
    cheesemongers—dairy maid
    teamen—golden canister
    opticians—Archimedes and globe or Sir Isaac Newton's head
        or golden spectacles
    thread makers—three pigeons and sceptre
    undertaker—naked boy and coffin
    weavers—spinning wheel[6]

[6] Sir Ambrose Heal, F.S.A., *The Signboards of Old London Shops* (London: B. T. Batsford, Ltd., 1947).

The sign for a tobacconist was two black boys or sometimes a Highlander. The first cigar store Indians were carved in London from lengths of masts by ships' carpenters. Two other signs which are still familiar on our streets had their origins centuries ago. The three golden balls of the pawnbroker were byzant gold coins issued during the Crusades. Because of this circumstance, they had religious significance as well as monetary value. As moneylenders, the Lombard bankers of Italy added the three byzants to their coat of arms. The origin of the barber's red and white striped pole is less pleasant. When barbers acted as blood letters as well as hair cutters, they gave their patients a wooden pole to grip while they were being blooded into a basin. The red overflow was soaked up in towels. After surgery, the barber would place the slippery pole with the blood-soaked towels draped about it outside of his shop to dry.

The two tall jars of colored water may still be seen in some older drugstores as the symbol of the apothecary. There was also an earlier sign, the head of Galen, once surgeon to Roman gladiators, then medical doctor to Marcus Aurelius, the "prince of physicians," whom apothecaries adopted as their patron saint.

In the late eighteen century a particularly fine head of Galen hung over an apothecary's on George Street in Edinburgh. It was admired and coveted by the authors and intellectuals of the Friday Club, among them Sir Walter Scott, Professors Dugald Stewart and John Playfair of Edinburgh University, Henry Brougham, who was to become Lord Chancellor of England, Francis Jeffrey, the critic, and Sydney Smith, the cleric and wit, later canon of St. Paul's in London, who with Jeffrey founded the feared *Edinburgh Review* in 1802.

The group drank wine with their dinner one Friday night. After dinner they switched to a punch of rum, water, sugar, calves-foot jelly, lemon, and marmalade. It seemed a perfect time to pilfer the head of Galen. Playfair, Brougham, Smith, and Thomas Thompson, who was Clerk of Sessions, started out.

The sign was hung over the spiked rails of an iron fence. Brougham lurched off into the darkness and disappeared. Playfair boosted Smith up on his back, and Thompson started to climb up Smith. They teetered dangerously as Thompson stretched for the creaking sign. Their formation collapsed. They rebuilt it and tried again at the risk of impaling themselves on the spikes of the fence. Suddenly they saw the lights of the watch coming. Brougham, inspired, had gone for the police. The foiled thieves tumbled to the ground and fled without their advertising prize.[7]

Few forms of advertising, once they have been adopted and proved successful, are ever allowed to lapse. Word-of-mouth is still a potent vehicle for the advertising message. The barker still barks. The sign is everywhere. It is usually a name and a written message now, but the sidewalk clock, operative or imitative, before the jeweler's, the giant key before the locksmith's, the gold boot outside the shoe store, the gigantic gold molar of the painless dentist, and a few more, may still be seen. They provide instant notification to the interested.

While the cry and the sign were still the principal methods

[7] Hesketh Pearson, *The Smith of Smiths* (New York and London: Harper & Bros., 1934).

This was the same Sydney Smith who incurred the lasting enmity of Americans by a sneer in the January, 1820, issue of the *Edinburgh Review*. "In the four quarters of the globe," he asked, "who reads an American book? or goes to an American play? or looks at an American picture or statue?" Publication of Washington Irving's *Sketch Book* the same year was happily regarded as giving Smith a deserved rebuke.

It is not as often remembered that in the same 1820 essay Smith wrote more accurately of the United States of the mid-twentieth century. He warned the new country against the inevitable results of striving for glory: "TAXES upon every article which enters into the mouth, or covers the back, or is placed under the foot—taxes upon everything which it is pleasant to see, hear, smell, or taste—taxes upon warmth and light and locomotion—taxes on everything on earth and the waters under the earth—on everything that comes from abroad or is grown at home—taxes on the raw material—taxes on every fresh value that is added to it by the industry of man—taxes on the sauce which pampers man's appetite, and the drug that restores him to health—on the ermine which decorates the judge, and the rope which hangs the criminal—on the poor man's salt and the rich man's spice—on the brass nails of the coffin and the ribands of the bride—. . ." Smith catalogued for another half-page (without starting a new sentence) but fell far short of the actuality he prophesied.

of advertising, another made its appearance. Thanks to the early efforts of such noble spirits as Charlemagne and Alfred the Great, to the impulsion of the Renaissance and the compulsions stirred by the Reformation, people had begun learning to read and write again after the general illiteracy of the earlier Middle Ages. The Chinese invented paper, and Europe had its first paper mill by 1276. By 1438 Johann Gutenberg had developed printing from movable type. By 1500 books were being printed in Paris, London, Venice, Basel, Nuremberg, and other cities of Europe. By that time advertising had already seized on the new medium.

This, 3000 years old, discovered by an archeologist delving in the ruins of Thebes, has been held up as the first known written advertisement. Inscribed on papyrus, it read:

> The man-slave, Shem, having run away from his good master, Hapu the Weaver, all good citizens of Thebes are enjoined to help return him. He is a Hittite, 5′ 2″ tall, of ruddy complexion and brown eyes. For news of his whereabouts half a gold coin is offered. And for his return to the shop of Hapu the Weaver, where the best cloth is woven to your desires, a whole gold coin is offered.

By the end of the fifteenth century tack-up signs were in use in England. These were advertising bills headed and known as "Siquis." Public notices in Rome had been headed "Si Quis"—"If anybody"—if anybody wants, knows, etc. In England these were tacked up anywhere that crowds might gather. A principal place for posting in London was in the middle aisle of St. Paul's, which had become a place where people sought business. Attorneys sought there for clients; seamstresses went there for hire. Later, bookshops and tobacco stalls were erected in St. Paul's.

What is accepted as the first known printed advertisement in English was such a siquis, written and set by William Caxton, the English printer who had learned the art in Cologne and who with Colard Mansion had set up in Bruges, in 1474 or 1475, the first book printed in English, *The Recuyell of Historyes of Troye*. Returning to England, Caxton erected his wooden printing press at the sign of the Red Pale in the Almonry of Westminster. In 1478 he issued a handbill describing and offering for sale one of the books he printed.[8] It was the *Salisburi pye,* rules for the clergy at Easter. Caxton posted on church doors in London this black-letter notice:

> If it please ony man spirituel or temporel to bye ony
> of two and thre comemoracios of Salisburi use en-
> pryntid after the forme of this present lettre whiche
> ben wel and truly correct, late hym come to West-
> monester in to the almonestrye at the reed pale and
> he shal have them good chepe.
> Supplico stet cedula [Please let this notice stand]

The tacked-up printed notice was followed by another form of printed advertising which gave the advertiser greater circulation, thus more potential sale for his product. By the seventeenth century thousands of printed handbills were in circulation, and the number of bills and the trades using them increased vastly in the eighteenth century. Called "trades-man's cards," they were not cards at all but sheets of paper up to folio size, more accurately described as shop-bills or message-cards. They were straight-forward announcements of wares and services for sale. They gave the name of the advertiser, his place of business, and described what he had to offer. They were illustrated by woodcuts or copper en-gravings. Often the illustrations, many of which were very handsome, reproduced the sign or the door of the shop. Both the British Museum and the Victoria and Albert Museum have collections of these seventeenth- and eighteenth-century cards.

There were cards for trades of all kinds, for ballad mongers, astrologers, chimney sweeps, dog doctors, fencing masters, fishermen, lunatic keepers, nightmen, prize fighters, ventrilo-quists, oculists, musical instrument makers; for apothecaries, surgeons, mercers, tailors, drapers, bug destroyers, coopers, dentists, dancing masters, gunsmiths, hosiers, harness makers; for snuff dealers, tobacconists, wig makers, brick layers, booksellers, ship chandlers, and bun bakers.

Just as Holbein had once painted signs, William Hogarth produced tradesmen's cards. He made them for himself as

[8] "The Story of Advertising," (cartograph; New York: Standard Rate and Data Service, 1944).

an engraver, for his sisters, who moved their frock shop "from the corner of the Long Walk facing the Cloysters to ye King's Arms joyning to ye Little Britain gate near Long Walk," for boxers, fan makers, goldsmiths, inns, warehouse-men, surveyors, sign painters, tobacconists, and upholsterers.

An eighteenth-century London tradesman's card (Heal) and trade card of a merchant-jurist signer of the Declaration of Independence.

George Cordwell, his card proudly stated, was Chimney Sweeper to their Royal Highnesses, the Dukes of Gloucester and Cumberland in Berkeley Square. He flaunted the arms of both Gloucester and Cumberland to prove it.

Kenelm Dawson was a Salesman of Men's and Boys' Clothing at the Sign of the Jolly Sailor in Monmouth Street.

John Wildblood, who married the Widdow Harrington, —that John Wildblood—was a silk dyer at the Rainbow and Three Pidgens in St. Clements Lane.

W. Hogarth was an Engraver at ye Golden Ball, Corner of Chadbourne Alley, Little Newport Street.[9]

[9] Ambrose Heal, *London Tradesmen's Cards of the XVIII Century* (London: B. T. Batsford, Ltd., 1925).

3

Houghton, Addison, Steele
—Early English
Newspaper Advertising

IT IS DIFFICULT to distinguish between the first newspapers in England and the weekly newsletters and advices, the earliest of them handwritten, which preceded them. It is also difficult to determine, with any accuracy, what may be described as the first newspaper advertising.

Because it was printed and was issued with some regularity, the first newspaper or newsbook is generally conceded to have been the *Weekly Newes* ("Out of Turkey, Hungary, Silesia, Poland, Italy, Austria, Saxony, the Low-Countries, and diverse other places in the upper and lower Germany.") Published by Nicholas Bourne and Thomas Archer, the *Weekly Newes* first appeared in 1622. A rival sheet was quickly started by Nathaniel Butter, who called his more sensational paper *Newes from Most Parts of Christendom*. As so often, competition induced combination. The two papers amalgamated as *Newes of the Present Week*.

In 1625, Archer began publication of the first of the many weekly Mercuries, the *Mercurius Britannicus*. Government viewed all printing with suspicion. In 1632 the Star Chamber passed an edict against the publication of foreign news. Ten years later, the Star Chamber itself was abolished, and more newspapers sprang up to serve Cromwell's news-hungry Commonwealth: the *Mercurius Aulicus*, the *Mercurius Prag-*

maticus, the *Mercurius Politicus*, etc. Cromwell abolished all but the official *Mercurius Politicus*, published first by Marchamont Nedham, then by Henry Muddiman. When the court was in residence at Oxford during the Great Plague in 1665, Muddiman began publication of the *Oxford Gazette*. A year later this became the biweekly *London Gazette*, official organ of the English government, as it still is, and first recognized newspaper.

When press censorship was abandoned in 1693 a horde of Posts, Intelligencers, Mercuries, Courants sprang up. The *Daily Courant* was the first English newspaper to appear every day. In 1704 Daniel Defoe began publication of what was more magazine than newspaper, the *Review*. The *Review* was the forerunner of Richard Steele's *Tatler*, and the *Tatler* gave way to the *Spectator*, which Steele put out with Joseph Addison.

At one point, 1663, during the political turmoil which made the beginnings of the press in England more difficult than they might otherwise have been, Sir Roger L'Estrange was appointed surveyor of the press. Royal grant conferred on him the sole privilege of "writing, printing, and publishing all narratives, advertisements, mercuries, intelligencers, diurnals, and other books of public intelligence." It is evident from this that the word "advertising" was not yet considered to have a specialized commercial meaning distinguishing it from any other form of public notice. Only three years later a distinct meaning had accrued to the word. In June 1666 the *Gazette* announced that it would not publish advertisements. A notice in No. 62 of the paper read: "Being daily prest to the publication of Books, Medicines, and other things not properly the business of a Paper of Intelligence. This is to notifie once for all, that we will not charge the *Gazette* with Advertisements. . . ." Advertisements, the *Gazette* suggested, could be placed elsewhere in a sheet being set up for the purpose.

Henry Sampson goes away back to a German newsbook printed in 1591 and filed in the British Museum to find "the oldest newspaper paragraph approaching to an advertise-

ment." It was all the memorable occurences of 1588 and
1589, the defeat of the Spanish Armada, the murder of Henry
III of France, "and other stale matter of the same kind . . ."[1]
What many, as Sampson records, considered the first bona
fide newspaper advertisement appeared in *Several Proceedings in Parliament* in the issue dated November 28–December
6, 1650. This was an advertisement offering a reward for
the return of twelve horses stolen from a Mr. Badcraft of
Bexfield, Norfolk.[2]

The "first newspaper advertisement" in the judgment of
an anonymous writer in the *Quarterly Review,* June, 1855,
was the announcement in the *Mercurius Britannicus* of the
publication of a book, *Epithalamium Gallo-Britannicum* by
George Marceline. It appeared on the back page of the issue
for February 1, 1625.[3] The first advertisement for coffee,
and it was presented as a pleasant tasting remedy for all ills
rather than as a beverage, appeared in the *Publick Adviser,*
May 26, 1657.

> In Bartholomew Lane, on the back side of the Old Ex-
> change the drink called coffee, which is a very wholesome
> and physical drink, have many excellent vertues, closes the
> orifices of the stomach, fortifies the heat within, helpeth
> digestion, quickeneth the spirits, maketh the heart lightsum,
> is good against eye-sores, coughs, or colds, rhumes, consump-
> tions, head ache, dropsie, gout, scurvy, King's evil, and many
> others; is to be sold both in the morning and at three of the
> clock in the afternoon.

The *Quarterly* in 1855 described a dentrifice advertisement which appeared in the *Mercurius Politicus* in 1660 as the
first genuine advertisement in that it was a forthright attempt
to obtain customers for a specific brand of a product.

> Most excellent and improved Dentrifices to scour and cleanse
> the teeth, making them as white as Ivory, preserves from the
> Toothache; it fastens the Teeth, sweetens the Breath, and

---

[1] Sampson, *op. cit.,* p. 63.
[2] *Ibid.,* p. 97.
[3] Presbrey, in this instance, followed the *Quarterly* writer rather than
Sampson.

> preserves the Gums and Mouth from Cankers and Impost-
> humes. Made by Robert Turner, Gentleman, and the right
> only are to be had at Thomas Rookes, Stationer, at the Holy
> Lamb, at the East End of St. Paul's Church, near the School,
> in sealed papers, at 12d. the paper.
>
> The reader is desired to beware of Counterfeits.

There was one paper among all the spate of new publications in the late seventeenth century which advertising
historians have found of compelling interest. This was *A
Collection for the Improvement of Husbandry and Trade,*
founded in 1682 by John Houghton, an apothecary of
Bartholomew's Lane. Houghton, who sold both tea and coffee in his shop, and who was a book reviewer and fellow of
the Royal Society as well as an apothecary, believed thoroughly in advertising. He made his sheet virtually a shopper's
guide. At first he merely listed products and prices for his
readers and offered to tell callers where they could be obtained.
Later he began to give the names and addresses of those who
could supply lumber, lodgings, brimstone, whigs, servants, a
wet nurse, or a suitable school for children. Houghton solicited advertising, and he solicited customers for his advertisers.
He investigated claims personally. Like the modern advertising man, he strove to bring buyers and sellers together. "I
believe," he said in one issue, "some advertisements about
bark and timber might be of use both to buyer and seller."
In another he announced, "I know a peruke maker that pretends to make perukes extraordinary fashionable and will sell
good pennyworth. I can direct to him."

August 7, 1695, Houghton's *Collection for the Improvement of Husbandry and Trade* ran an advertisement for a
school.

> About forty miles from London is a schoolmaster has had
> much success with boys as there are almost forty ministers
> and schoolmasters that were his scholars.

Under the same roof, the master's wife kept a school for
girls. "His price is 10 pounds or 11 pounds a year, with a
pair of sheets and spoon to be restored if desired."

Houghton, Sampson says admiringly, "by untiring per-
severance and no small amount of thought and study . . .
trained his contemporaries in the art of advertising, and made
them acquainted with that valuable assistance to be derived
from a medium which, as Alexis de Tocqueville remarks,
drops the same thought into a thousand minds at almost the
same period."[4]

Certainly, Houghton's contemporaries caught on swiftly.
Advertising for services, for lost or stolen articles and for lost
or strayed people, for articles of many kinds began to appear
in profusion. If an advertisement for coffee appeared first,
one for tea, also presented as a remedy, came within less than
a year. The *Mercurius Politicus* carried this advertisement
September 30, 1658:

> The Excellent and by all Physitians approved China drink
> called by the Chineans Tcha, by other nations Tay, alias Tee
> is sold at the Sultaness Head Cophee House in Sweetings
> Rents by the Royal Exchange, London.

Dogs got lost. Some dogs got lost not once but frequently, especially if they belonged to someone known to be
able to afford an adequate reward for their return. In 1660
a royal advertiser, in an advertisement which sounds as if it
had been penned by the royal hand with the royal quill, grew
somewhat petulant in the *Mercurius Politicus*.

> We must call upon you again for a Black Dog, between a
> Greyhound and a Spaniel, no white about him onely a streak
> on his Brest, and Tayl a little bobbed. It is His Majesties own
> Dog, and doubtless was stoln, for the Dog was not born nor
> bred in *England*, and would never forsake his Master. Who-
> soever finds him may acquaint any at Whitehal, for the Dog
> was better known at Court than those who stole him. Will
> they never leave robbing His Majesty? must he not keep a
> Dog? This Dogs place (though better than some imagine)
> is the only place which nobody offers to beg.

[4] Sampson, *op. cit.*, p. 92. Sampson adds, p. 135, ". . . old Houghton,
who did much good in his time, not only for other people but for himself
as well . . . may fairly be regarded as, if not the father, certainly one of
the chief progenitors of early advertising."

Charles II had a bad time with his livestock. Next time it was a bird that flew the coop. The new loss was advertised in the official *London Gazette*, August 13, 1667.

> A Sore ger Falcon of His Majesty, lost the 13 of August, who had one Varvel of his Keeper, Roger Higs, of Westminster, Gent. Whosoever hath taken her up and give notice Sir Allan Apsley, Master of his Majesties Hawks at St. James's, shall be rewarded for his paines. Back-Stairs in Whitehall.

If dogs and birds got lost, so did people. This (with a pointing finger ornament to call attention to it) was in the *Domestic Intelligencer*, seemingly the correct medium, in March 1681:

> ☞ WHEREAS a Person in London on some discontent did early on Monday morning last retire from his dwelling-house and not yet return'd, it is the earnest request of several of his particular friends, that the said person would speedily repair to some or one of them, that he thinks most fit, it being of absolute necessity for reasons he does not yet know of.[5]

Certain other men could not be found either. They were well protected. John Dryden, who had been involved in many quarrels, some literary, some political, some both, was made England's poet laureate in 1668. A prolific writer, his famous play, *All For Love*, appeared in 1677. Dryden's talents were so well known that he was credited also with the authorship of a set of manuscript verses, called an *Essay upon Satyr*, which were circulating about London. The verses attacked a number of the socially prominent, including the Duchess of Portsmouth. That the verses had actually been written by John Sheffield, Earl of Mulgrave and Dryden's patron, did not save the poet from forceful literary criticism by the hirelings of another of his patrons and a favorite of

---

[5] Sampson, who quoted this, added, p. 142, "It is now apparent that advertising has become recognized as a means of communication not only for the convenience of trade, but for political, lovemaking, fortune-hunting, swindling, and the thousand and one other purposes which are always ready to assert themselves in a large community."

Charles II, the Earl of Rochester. An advertisement in the London Gazette for December 22, 1679 tells the rest of the story.

> WHEREAS *John Dryden,* Esq., was on Monday, the 18th instant, at night, barbarously assaulted and wounded in Rose Street in Covent Garden, by divers men unknown; if any person shall make discovery of the said offenders to the said Mr. Dryden, or to any Justice of the Peace, he shall not only receive Fifty Pounds, which is deposited in the hands of Mr. Blanchard Goldsmith, next door to Temple Bar, for the said purpose, but if he be a principal or an accessory in the said fact, his Majesty is graciously pleased to promise him pardon for the same.

A happier picture of England's social life in the closing years of the seventeenth century is painted in this charming advertisement which was inserted in the London *Flying Post,* April 22, 1699. Its language is as musical as part of the entertainment promised, and the picture it conjures up is wholly delightful. The advertiser must have been a pleasant lady.

> These may certify, all my loving masters and ladies; that on Wednesday next the 26th of this instant, April, 1699, at Dame Butterfield's at Mobbs-Hole, in the parish of Wanstead, in Essex, within a mile of the Green Man, will be a house-warming where all my loving friends shall be kindly entertained with a calf, roasted whole, and a flitch of bacon, roasted whole, and other varieties. With music. And also, being an old hunter, I shall accomodate you with six brass horns, sounding the delightful harmony of hunting. So, hoping my loving masters and ladies, friends and acquaintances will be pleased to honour me with their good company, at the time and place aforesaid and, as I am in duty bound, shall ever return you thanks and remain yours obliged to serve you. SUSANA BUTTERFIELD.

Richard Steele began publication of the *Tatler* in April, 1709. The paper, issued three times a week, was a Whig organ which carried political and foreign news, theatrical criticism, essays on what Steele saw as the follies and foibles of the day—and advertising. As Isaac Bickerstaff, the name invented by Jonathan Swift for demolition of the astrologer

Partridge, Steele turned out his humorous comments, his coffeehouse gossip, and his attacks on the Tory government. As Jenny Bickerstaff, he wrote pleasantly for his women readers. As editors of women's magazines have done since his time, he encouraged their confessions, even advertising for them in the *Tatler*, May 8, 1709.

> ANY ladies who have any particular stories of their acquaintances which they are willing privately to make public, may send 'em by the penny post to Isaac Bickerstaff, Esq., enclosed to Mr. John Morpheu, near Stationer's Hall.

In Dublin, where he had been posted as secretary to the Lord Lieutenant of Ireland, Joseph Addison recognized the handiwork of his Charterhouse schoolfellow in the *Tatler* and began to send in contributions of his own. One of these, which Steele published September 14, 1710, was on advertising. Advertising was now a commonplace, an accepted and expected part of almost all the periodicals of the day. Addison wrote of it with warmth and wit in his characteristically urbane style.

> It is my Custom in a Dearth of News to entertain my self with those Collections of Advertisements that appear at the End of all our publick Prints. These I consider as Accounts of News from the little World, in the same Manner that the foregoing Parts of the Paper are from the great. If in one we hear that a Soverign Prince is fled from his Capital City, in the other we hear of a Tradesman who hath shut up his Shop and run away. If in one we find the Victory of a General, in the other we see the Desertion of a private Soldier. I must confess, I have a certain Weakness in my Temper, that is often very much affected by these little Domestick Occurrences, and have frequently been caught with Tears in my Eyes over a melancholy Advertisement . . .
>
> But to consider this Subject in its most ridiculous Lights, Advertisements are of great Use to the Vulgar: First of all, as they are Instruments of Ambition. A Man that is by no Means big enough for the Gazette, may easily creep into the Advertisements, by which Means we often see an Apothecary in the same Paper of News with a Plenipotentiary, or a Running-Footman with an Ambassador. An Advertisement from Piccadilly goes down to Posterity with an article from Madrid; and John Bartlett of Goodman's-Fields is celebrated

in the same Paper with the Emperor of Germany. Thus the Fable
tells us, That the Wren mounted as high as the Eagle, by getting upon
his Back. . . .

A Second Use which the Sort of Writings have been turned to of
late Years, has been the Management of Controversy, insomuch that
above half the Advertisements one meets with now-a-Days are purely
Polemical. The Inventors of Strops for Razors have written against
one another this Way for several Years, and that with great Bitterness; as the whole Argument pro and con in the Case of the Morning-
Gowns is still carried on after the same Manner. I need not mention
the several Proprietors of Dr. Anderson's Pills; nor take Notice of
the many Satyrical Works of this Nature so frequently published by
Dr. Clark, who has had the Confidence to advertize upon that learned
Knight, my very worthy Friend, Sir William Read: But I shall not
interpose in their Quarrel; Sir William can give him his own in
Advertisements, that, in the Judgment of the Impartial, are as well
penned as the Doctor's.

The third and last use of these writing [Addison wrote—and it is
the use to which advertising then and now most readily admit] is
to inform the world, where they may be furnished with almost everything that is necessary for life. If a Man has pains in his head, cholic
in his bowels, or spots in his clothes, he may here meet with proper
cures and remedies. If a man would recover a wife or a horse that
is stolen or strayed; if he wants new sermons, electuaries, asses milk,
or anything else either for his body or his mind, this is the place to
look for them in.

Addison had some advice for copywriters and layout men.

The great art in writing advertising is the finding out the proper
method to catch the reader, without which a good thing may pass
over unobserved, or be lost among comissions of bankrupts. Of late
years the N. B. has been much in fashion, as also little cuts and figures,
the invention of which we must ascribe to the author of spring
trusses. . . .

Steele attacked the Tory government too forcefully. The
Tatler came to its end in 1711. Addison, thrown out of his
secretaryship by the fall of the Whigs, returned to London,
and he and Steele joined forces in the *Spectator*, which began
daily publication March 1, 1711.

The *Spectator* was a business as well as a literary venture,
and the paper's chief support came from its advertising.
There were eight advertisements in the first issue, and the

number increased as the circulation of the *Spectator* rose from 3000, which was the print order for the first issue, to 4000 and above. The circulation is said to have reached as high as 20,000, sometimes 30,000, for certain issues, but doubt has been expressed that it ever soared that high.[6] It went high enough, at any rate, for the *Spectator* to be looked upon as a sound and effective advertising medium for those who wanted to reach the carriage trade—the literate, socially well placed, sociably inclined, prosperous London market.

To reach such a public, advertisers filled the *Spectator* with their notices, claims, and appeals. The products and services they advertised and the ways in which they advertised them give colorful insight into London life under Queen Anne; and many of the advertisements, their claims, and their approach are recognizable as still characteristic of much of advertising in the mid-twentieth century.

The *Spectator* carried personals, notices of houses for sale or to let, dry goods advertising, announcements of books and plays, and advertising for financial schemes. There was always a long list of articles Lost or Stolen. Rewards were usually offered with a guarantee of no questions asked. Many were for the apprehension and return of deserters and runaway apprentices. On one occasion one hundred pounds was offered for the capture of a defaulting clerk of the Bank of England.

There was advertising for tea, coffee, chocolate, auction sales, lotteries, wigs, cosmetics, tobacco, and, discreetly, of assignations. Readers of the *Spectator* could obtain either "Famous Drops for Hypocondriak Melancolly" or "An Excellent Secret to take away Warts," or both, if they needed them.

Addison and Steele might inveigh against charlatan doctors, who rode in gilt coaches and dined from gold plate, but their indignation never waxed so unprofitably high that the promises of such men were excluded from the *Spectator*'s advertising columns. This fair specimen of patent medicine advertising appeared Friday, October 19, 1711.

[6] Lawrence Lewis, *Advertisements of The Spectator* (Boston: Houghton Mifflin Co., 1909).

Consumptions of all sorts radically Cured by a famous Elixir peculiarly invented for that Disease; its wonderful Efficacy sufficiently explodes the Erronious Opinion, that Consumptions are incurable, since it absolutely retrieves the Patient, though reduc'd to a meer Skelleton; quickly takes off all the Symptoms, as Cough, Hoarseness, Wheasing, shortness of Breath, Pain or Weight in the Breast, spitting of blood, soreness of the Stomach, Throat or Wind-pipe; also Catarrhs or Defluxions of sharp Rhume, and all Ptisical and Asthmatick Affects, Hectick Feaver, &c. perfectly cures all internal Ulcers, restores all inward Wastings, Weakness and decay of Nature, being Balsamic and Strengthning beyond Comparison; it assuredly eradicates the first Principle, or cause of Consumptions, rectifying the Disorders of Stomach and first Passages, creating an Appetite, procuring a good Digestion, reducing the vicious Ferment of the Blood and Juices, correcting the Acrid Salts that erode the Lungs, Certainly healing Ulcers therin, and infallibly curing all sorts of Consumptions, tho' never so bad, in a very short time to a Miracle. Price 3s. 6d. a Bottle with Directions. Sold only at Mr. Osborn's Toyshop at the Rose and Crown under St. Dunstan's Church, in Fleetstreet.

The modern equivalent of the following dentrifice advertisement, from the *Spectator* of October 10, 1712, with certain concessions made to the strictures of the Federal Trade Commission and censorship by the reputable media, may be heard any day by turning on the radio or television or reading a newspaper or magazine.

The Incomparable Powder for cleaning the Teeth, which has given so great Satisfaction to most of the Nobility and Gentry in England. Sold only at Mr. Halfey's, Bookseller, at the Plow and Harrow near the Royal Exchange Cornhill; and at Mr. Markham's Toyshop at the 7 Stars under St. Dunstan's Church, Fleetstreet. It at once using makes the Teeth as white as Ivory, tho' never so Black or Yellow, and effectually preserves them from Rotting or Decaying, continuing them Sound to exceeding Old Age. It wonderfully cures the Scurvy in the Gums, prevents Rheum or Defluction, kills Worms at the Roots of the Teeth, and thereby hinders the Tooth-Ach. It admirably fastens loose Teeth, being a neat cleanly Medicine, of a pleasant and grateful Scent. Price 1s. the Box. At the same Place is sold, the highly esteem'd Lip salve for Ladies, &c. of a charming Scent. Price 1s. the Box.

Thirsty? This noble quencher was offered on Friday, December 7, 1711.

> At the Green Man and Still in Grace-Church-Street, for the Accommodation of Gentlemen in Town and Country, is sold a rare Composition with which at a Minutes's Notice may be made a Bowl of the clearest and best Punch as can be drank, only by adding to it the like Quantity of Spring-Water: This Composition is of the best French Brandy, Battava-Arrack, Juice of the finest Lemons, best double re-fined Loaf-Sugar, of each an equal proportion, to answer the like Quantity of Spring-Water: This is only to save Gentlemen trouble in preparing it. It may be drank in kind: It is a noble Cordial, and will never decay, but be the better for keeping. Price but 3s. a Quart.

One of the many plays advertised in the *Spectator* was this performance of *The Tempest* in the improved version by Davenant and Dryden. It was announced January 15, 1712.

> At the Theatre Royal in Drury-Lane this present Tues-day, the 15th Day of January, will be presented the last Reviv'd Play call'd, The Tempest; or The Inchanted Island. As it was altered from Shakespear by Sir Will. D'avenant, and the late Mr. Dryden, Poets Laureat. With new Scenes, Machines, and all the Original Decorations proper to the Play. By her Majesty's Command no Persons are to be ad-mitted behind the Scenes.[7]

Dancing classes were announced in this advertisement of November 22, 1712.

> To all Ladies and Gentlemen that are Lovers of Musick and Dancing. This is to give Notice, that on Explanation of the Grounds of Dancing, and a Sett of new Courants, Minu-ets, Rigadoons, &c. All Compos'd by Mr. Fert, are to be show'd and perform'd by him, at his Dancing Room in Pater's-Yard at the upper end of Castle-street near Leicester Fields, Mondays, Wednesdays and Fridays, from five a Clock in the Afternoon till ten; where all the new Dances are taught, and if required, at Person of Quality's Houses.

Occasionally Steele had wares of his own to advertise. He inserted this notice in the issue of Thursday, November 20, 1712.

[7] No. 275, for January 15, 1712.

> A neat Pocket Edition of the 3d and 4th Vols. of Specta-
> tors, with an Index to the whole 4 Vols. Tatlers in 4 Vols.
> The Funeral, Tender Husband and Lying Lovers, Comedies
> written by Mr. Steele, Prior's Poems, Milton's Paradise Lost,
> Hudibrass, and the Christian Hero, by Mr. Steele, the last
> Edition. Printed, and Sold by Owen Lloyd near the Church
> in the Temple. N. B. All are printed with an Elzever Letter,
> and in a small Pocket Volume.

Lewis notes the interesting connection between three advertisements which appeared in the *Spectator* in a three-months
period of 1712. March 27, Addison and Steele advertised a
narrative by Captains Woodes Rogers and Edward Cooke of
their around-the-world voyage in the privateers "Duke" and
"Duchess" of Bristol, accomplished between 1708 and 1711.
The ships stopped at the uninhabited island of Juan Fernandez
and rescued the marooned Alexander Selkirk. Selkirk then
served as mate on the "Duke," later Rogers put him aboard a
prize ship as master to sail it back to England. June 17, the
Spectator carried an advertisement announcing the sale at
London auction of some of the plunder the "Duke" and the
"Duchess" had seized from the Spaniards. June 23, the *Spectator* advertised "A Crusing Voyage round the World, first
to the South Seas, then to the East Indies, and homewards by
the Cape of Good Hope . . . A most particular acct of Alexander Selkirk's living alone four Years and four Months in an
Island than has hitherto been given." The book was by
Woodes Rogers. Defoe turned the Selkirk story into *Robinson Crusoe* in 1719.

Only innocent vanity appears in this *Spectator* advertisement of Saturday, September 8, 1711.

> All Sorts of Sattin and Persian Quilted Coots, also Can-
> vass Hooped Petticoats, made by the D. of Montague's Man-
> tua-maker. To be Sold at the Gown shop at the Sign of the
> Hood and Scarf over-against Wills Coffee-house in Cornhill,
> where Gentlemen and Ladies may be fitted with great
> Variety of the Nicest Silk Gowns of All Prices, and at very
> low rates.

One may wonder pleasantly about this one of Wednesday, June 25, 1712.

> Lost or Dropt, in or near Mr. Edward Smith's House, at Iver near Uxbridge, some time last Week, a Necklace of 2 Rows of Oriental Pearls, about Sixty or Seventy Pearls in each Row, the Pearls are of a midling Size and very even. If offered to be sold or pawn'd, pray stop it and the Party, and give Notice to Mr. James Puckle, a Notary Publick in Popes head Alley in Cornhill, so as it may be had again, and you shall have 5 Guineas for your Trouble; or if the Person that has it will bring or sent it to the same place he shall have the same Reward, and no Questions ask'd.

This—it was in No. 297 of the *Spectator*—seems clear enough. It was probably very clear and the possibilities titillating to both advertiser and "Person" advertised to.

> A Person in white Cloth Suit, laced with Silver, who handed two Ladies out of the Box in the Gallery of the Play-house in Drury-Lane, on Wednesday last, is desired to come this Day, without fail, to the Abby Church in Westminster, betwixt 3 and 4 in the Afternoon.

Periodical advertising was dealt a crippling blow in England in 1712 when the Tory government imposed a dual tax on newspapers and magazines that put many of them abruptly out of business. A tax of one halfpenny was placed on every copy sold, and an additional prohibitory tax of one shilling was placed on every advertisement, long or short. If not paid within thirty days, the tax was tripled. This move by the government was not made for purposes of raising revenue but to silence the virulent criticism of the "Grub Street Journals," most of them Whig organs or, like the *Spectator*, which had eschewed open discussion of politics, Whig controlled.

The Tories were as jubilant as the papers were aghast. Jonathan Swift, whose *Examiner*, the chief Tory organ, lasted only a year (he had written earlier for Steele's *Tatler*), was delighted. August 7, 1712, he wrote Stella: "The *Observer* is fallen; the *Medleys* are jumbled together with the

Flying Post; the *Examiner* is deadly sick; the *Spectator* keeps up and doubles its price; I know not how long it will hold."

The *Spectator* managed to hold until December 6, 1712, when it was forced to surrender. Addison alone tried to revive it two years later, but, published three times a week, it lasted only six months, June 18, 1714 to December 20, 1714. The tax on periodical advertising was not to be abolished for 141 years.

Tax or no tax, London had by 1731 a newspaper which made it clear in logotype and stated purpose that its chief business was advertising. The *Daily Advertiser* put it this way.

Whereas by reasons of the great number of Newspapers daily printed and that few persons Advertise in more than one of them and that none except the most eminent Coffee-Houses take in all the daily Printed Papers, and that few Gentlemen or others who frequent these Houses read every Paper taken in, the Advertising remains unknown to great Numbers of Persons to the Prejudice and Inconvenience of the Advertiser. It is apprehended that the Publication made by this Paper will be very general and useful all the Advertisements being collected together. Persons may readily find out whatever can properly fall under the Denomination of an Advertisement, without having resource to any other Paper.

4

Benjamin Franklin, Advertising Man—Early American Advertising

JOURNALISM AND ADVERTISING were practically coeval in the American Colonies. The first number of the first successful newspaper, the *Boston News-Letter*, April 24, 1704, contained this notice.

Advertisement

> This News-Letter is to be continued Weekly, and all Persons who have Houses, Lands, Tenements, Farms, Ships, Vessels, Goods, Wares or Merchandise, &c to be Sold or Let; or Servants Run-Away, or Goods Stole or Lost; may have the same inserted at a Reasonable Rate, from *Twelve Pence* to *Five Shillings*, and not to exceed: Who may agree with John Campbel, Post-master of *Boston*.

The solicitation worked. The *Boston News-Letter*, May 1-8, 1704, carried three entries under the word "Advertising." The industry of a thief, evidently well muscled and willing to put earnest effort into the pursuit of his profession, was responsible for one of them.

> Lost on 10th of April last off Mr. Shippen's Wharf in Boston, Two Iron Anvils, weighing between 120-140 pounds each; Whoever has taken them up, and will bring or give true intelligence of them to John Campbell, Postmaster, shall have a sufficient reward.

The second advertisement offered a reward for the capture
of another thief and the return of wearing apparel, men's,
stolen from the house of James Cooper. The third advertisement was of larger space, and the copy was more detailed.

> At Oysterbay on Long Island in the province of New York
> there is a very good Fulling Mill to be Let or Sold, as also a
> Plantation, having on it a large Brick House, and other good
> house by it for a Kitchen & Workhouse, with a Barn, Stable,
> &c. a young Orchard and about 20 acres clear Land. The
> Mill is to be let with or without the Plantation: Enquire of
> Mr. William *Bradford* Printer in N. York and know further.

Other advertising followed these evildoer and real estate
notices in the *Boston News-Letter*, but periodical advertising
in the Colonies was to wait another twenty-five years before
it flowered under the skillful ministrations of the versatile
American genius of the eighteenth century.

Benjamin Franklin, wily, energetic, a showman always, is
generally credited with inventing, founding, or discovering
such disparate enterprises as the University of Pennsylvania,
lightning, the public library system, fire insurance, one of the
country's first two monthly magazines, prudential sagacity,
bifocals, and the United States Post Office. He is also, and
with sufficient reason, hailed as the father, or at least the
patron saint, of American advertising.

Advertising and public relations, especially self-advertising and publicity, were as natural to Franklin as his curiosity, restless intelligence, and practicality. Printer, politician,
philosopher, moralist, scientist, propagandist, Franklin, in all
his roles and on behalf of all his varied activities, was always
the untiring promoter. He put advertising before editorial
in the masthead of the first issue of the *Pennsylvania Gazette*
which, with Hugh Meredith as partner, he bought from his old
employer, Samuel Keimer, and began to publish October 2,
1729: "Philadelphia: Printed by B. Franklin and H. Meredith
at the New Printing Office near the Market, where Advertisements are taken in, and all Persons may be supplied with this
paper at Ten Shillings a Year."

Franklin had been a newspaper publisher in Boston when he was only sixteen years old. As he tells the story in his *Autobiography*, his half-brother James, to whom he was apprenticed at the age of twelve, had started what he described as the second newspaper in the Colonies, the *New England Courant*, in 1720 or 1721. In 1722 James Franklin was jailed by the speaker of the Massachusetts Assembly for printing liberal matter offensive to the reigning civil and church authorities. He was released only on condition that he no longer publish the *Courant*. To get around this, James, a choleric stalwart given to beating his apprentice as well as berating the theocracy, tore up his half-brother's indenture (though he drew up another in secret) and issued the *Courant* under the nominal editorship of B. Franklin.

New York's public printer, William Bradford, had got Franklin his first job in Philadelphia, and Franklin had lodged for a time with the son, Andrew Bradford, public printer in Philadelphia, but, characteristically, Franklin was not deterred by sentiment. "My hopes of success," he wrote, ". . . were founded on this, that the then only newspaper, printed by Bradford, was a paltry thing, wretchedly manag'd, no way entertaining, and yet profitable to him; I therefore thought a good paper would scarcely fail of good encouragement." It worried him a little that Bradford's *American Weekly Mercury*, started in 1719, "was thought a better distributor of advertisements than mine, and therefore had many more," but Franklin soon changed all that.[1]

The first issue of the *Pennsylvania Gazette* carried an advertisement for "choice hard soap, very reasonable." It

[1] Understandably, the Bradfords resented Franklin and some of his methods. Though indefatigable self-advertising made Franklin the more famous, the elder Bradford, who lived to be 92 years of age, was Pennsylvania's first printer, a fact proudly emblazoned on his marble monument in the burial grounds of Trinity Church in New York. The inscription reads in part: "Here lies the Body of Mr. William Bradford, Printer. He was born in Leceistershire, in Old England, in 1660; and came over to America in 1682, before the City of Philadelphia was laid out. He was Printer to this Government [the royal government of New York] for upwards of 50 years and being quite worn out with Old age and labour he left this mortal state in the lively Hopes of a blessed Immortality."

was probably boiled by Franklin's brothers in Boston. There was an advertisement for "The Psalms of David, Imitated in the Language of the New Testament, and apply'd to the Christian State and Worship by I. Watts, Y.D.M., seventh edition." Other advertisements listed books, stationery, legal forms, and the 1730 almanacs of Godfrey and Titan Leeds.[2] There were also the inevitable advertisements for the capture of runaway servants, an advertising staple in the 18th century. Most prominently displayed was this one:

> Run away on the 25th of September past, from Rice Pritchard of Whiteland in Chester County, a Servant Man named John Creswell, of a middle stature and Ruddy countenance, his hair inclining to red; He had on when he went away a little white Short Wig, an old Hat, Drugget Wastcoat, the Body lined with Linnen; Coarse Linnen breeches, gray woollen Stockings, and round toe'd shoes. Whoever shall secure the said Servant so his Master may have him again, shall have Three Pounds Reward, and Reasonable Charges paid by Rice Prichard.

The *Pennsylvania Gazette* soon had the largest circulation and the largest advertising volume of any paper in the Colonies. An early biographer, James Parton, wrote almost a century ago, "I think we must admit . . . that it was Franklin who originated the modern system of advertising. It is certain that he was the first man who used the mighty engine of publicity, as we use it now."[3]

Franklin "advertised everything," runaway servants, slaves, sales of goods of many kinds, ships' sailings, and things he sold in his own shop: books, paper, ink, quills, Spanish wine, lampblack, tea, coffee, chocolate, cheese, cloth, spectacles, com-

---

[2] In imitation of the Swift-Partridge hoax of 1708 in London, Franklin announced the death of this same Titan Leeds in his *Poor Richard's Almanac* for 1733. The fact upon which Franklin insisted was premature by five years. Like the modern advertiser, Franklin never encouraged competition.

[3] James Parton, *Life and Times of Benjamin Franklin* (New York: Mason Brothers, No. 7. Mercer Street [also Chicago, Phila., London, etc.], 1864). Parton's 1864 description of the "modern system of advertising being a mighty engine of publicity" is perhaps of even greater interest than his comment on Franklin.

passes, lumber, scales, and sundries. Shrewdly, Franklin advised others that it was always better to underestimate the merit of one's goods, so that a buyer would later say they were better than was claimed. Just as shrewdly, he always kept one- or two-line advertisements of his own in type to fill out columns with reminders of his merchandise.

The *Gazette* was so successful and profitable that Andrew Bradford, who besides all his other activities was also Philadelphia's postmaster, ordered his carriers not to deliver the paper to its subscribers. Franklin bribed the carriers to disregard Bradford's orders. He did more. He got himself appointed public printer for Pennsylvania and, in 1737, Philadelphia postmaster. Triumphantly, the *Gazette*, October 27, 1737, announced, "The Post Office of Philadelphia is now kept at B. Franklin's in Market Street." Franklin, though he denied he did it for other than strictly legal reasons, was now able to retaliate by keeping Bradford's *Mercury* out of the mails, which he did over the agonized protests of his rival. He wrote of the postermastership in his *Autobiography* with warm satisfaction, "I accepted it readily and found it of great advantage; for, tho' the salary was small, it facilitated the correspondence that improv'd my newspaper, increas'd the number demanded, as well as the advertisements to be inserted, so that it came to afford me a considerable income."

Publisher, printer, and editor of his paper, Franklin also wrote most of the copy and the advertisements. His hand is unmistakable in many of them. Among the advertisements for lotteries and panaceas in the issue for June 25-30, 1737, was this one.

> Taken out of a pew in the church [Christ Church] some months since, a Common Prayer Book, bound in red, gilt, and lettered D. F. [Deborah Franklin] on each cover. The person who took it is desired to open it and read the eighth commandment, and afterward to return it to the same pew again, upon which no further notice will be taken.

Franklin advertised in his own interest more than the goods he sold in his shop. He dealt profitably in the unexpired time of indentured servants and occasionally in slaves.

At various times he advertised: "A servant man's time for near three years, to be disposed of. He is a joiner by trade and a very good workman."—"A likely servant maid's time for four years to be disposed of. She works well with her needle."—"To be sold for her passage. A likely young woman, well clothed, can sew and do household work. Term of time as you can agree with her. *N. B.* Her passage is 8 pounds. Also a breeding Negro woman about twenty years of age. Can do any household work."—"A likely Negro wench about fifteen years old, has had the smallpox, been in this country about a year and talks English. Inquire of the printer hereof."

In the *Gazette* for June 17, 1742 Franklin advertised for the return of a strayed pony belonging to his twelve-year-old son. Any boy returning the animal would have the privilege of riding him. In February, 1739, some of Franklin's clothes were stolen. According to the advertisement in the *Gazette*, February 22 of that year, he had quite a wardrobe. Besides a partially worn coat, the stolen garments included: "four fine homespun shirts, a fine Holland shirt ruffled at the hands, a pair of black broadcloth breeches, new seated and lined with leather; two pairs of good worsted stockings, one of a dark colour and the other a lightish blue, a coarse cambric handkerchief marked with an F in red silk, a new pair of calfskin shoes."

Encouraged by the success of the *Pennsylvania Gazette*, which by this time was carrying four or five pages of advertising a week, Franklin decided to expand. He determined on publication of a monthly magazine modeled after the *Gentlemen's Magazine* of London and announced in the *Gazette*, November 13, 1740, that he would publish a magazine "in imitation of those in England." Unfortunately Andrew Bradford got wind of Franklin's intentions before his plans were fully operative. Hiring away the Philadelphia lawyer, John Webbe, whom Franklin had selected as editor and who had then gone to Bradford with information of Franklin's scheme, Bradford beat Franklin to the street with the *American Magazine, or a Monthly View of the Political States of the*

British Colonies. Franklin came out three days later, February 16, 1741, with the *General Magazine, and Historical Chronicle, for All the British Plantations in America.*

It was in the *General Magazine* that Franklin published one of the most famous of all his advertisements. It was for his stove or Pennsylvania Fireplace, as he called it, a cast-iron stove with an open firebox which heated rooms evenly and cheaply through a new arrangement for draughts. Franklin stoves are still made and sold.

> Fireplaces with small openings cause draughts of cold air to rush in at every crevice, and 'tis very uncomfortable as well as dangerous to sit against any such crevice. . . . Women, particularly from this cause (as they sit so much in the house) get cold in the head, rheums and defluxions which fall into their jaws and gums, and have destroyed early, many a fine set of teeth in these northern colonies. Great and bright fires do also very much contribute to damaging the eyes, dry and shrivel the skin, and bring on early the appearance of old age.

In bringing his newly invented stove to public notice, Franklin described not the product, but the health, comfort, and pleasure to be derived from its use. He appealed to women and their vanity. He frightened readers with what might happen to them if they did not buy what he had to sell. Were he alive, Franklin might well find his spiritual home in the modern advertising agency.

Franklin did more for advertising than write it brightly and use it effectively and profitably. He defended both advertising and press freedom in a characteristic piece of writing that he published in the *Pennsylvania Gazette*, June 10, 1731.

In the rush of business Franklin had accepted and printed an advertisement that drew severe public criticism. He was accused of malicious attack on the clergy. The advertisement itself had been innocent enough. It simply stated that such and such a ship would sail for the Barbados from such and such a wharf on a given date and that persons wishing accommodations for the voyage should make arrangements with the ship's captain. Unfortunately the advertisement bore a note at the end to which Franklin confessed in his *Apology for Printers* he had paid no attention. The note read: "*N. B.* No *Sea Hens* or *Black Gowns* will be admitted on Any Terms."

Franklin began his apology mildly enough. ". . . I request all who are angry with me on account of printing things they don't like, calmly to consider the following particulars." He then listed them under twelve heads.

> 1. That the opinions of men are almost as varied as their faces; an observation general enough to become a common proverb, *So many men, so many minds.* . . .

Franklin grew more eloquent and persuasive as he progressed: Printers, he said, print the varying opinions of different men as part of their business.

> 5. Printers are educated in the belief that when men differ in opinion, both sides ought equally to have the advantage of being heard by the public; and that when truth and error have fair play, the former is always an overmatch for the latter. Hence they chearfully serve all contending writers that pay them well, without regarding on which side they are of the question in dispute. . . .
> 8. That if all printers were determined not to print anything till they were sure it would offend no body, there would be very little printed. . . .

When he accepted the advertisement which had caused all the trouble, Franklin said, he did not know what a Sea Hen was. He professed still not to know. He did know, he confessed, that Black Gowns meant the clergy of the Church of England. "Yet I have that confidence in the generous good temper of such of them as I know as to be well satisfied such a trifling mention of their habit gives them no disturbance." Besides he had got five shillings for the advertisement, but "none who are angry with me would have given me so much to let it alone." And again besides, he had printed over a thousand advertisments without mentioning either Sea Hens or Black Gowns, "and this being a first offence, I have the

more reason to expect foregivness." Whether he was for-
given or not, B. Franklin, Printer, had no intention of changing his mind or his ways. He ended *An Apology for
Printers* with this declaration.

> I consider the Variety of Humours among Men, and despair
> of pleasing every Body; yet I shall not therefor leave off
> printing. I shall continue my business. I shall not burn my
> Press and melt my letters.

Twenty-five years later, Franklin's skill as a special pleader
secured important governmental concessions for American
advertising. The Stamp Tax on periodicals and on advertisements levied in England in 1712 was put into force in the
American Colonies in 1765. The move caused instant opposition. Newspapers appeared in mourning bands. Fifty-five
articles in all were subject to tax which was imposed on
all papers, from a bill of lading to a college diploma. The
tax on each advertisement was two shillings. Initial opposition grew to violent resistance throughout the Colonies.
Franklin saw the Stamp Tax as "the mother of mischief."
Sent to England by the Pennsylvania Assembly on other
governmental matters, he immediately became spokesman and
propagandist for all the Colonies against the Stamp Tax.

He got Edmund Burke, Pitt, and other influential politicians on his side against Grenville, whose government had
invoked enforcement of the act in the Colonies. Franklin
was summoned to appear before Commons to testify and answer questions about the issue. For ten days of February,
1766, he answered or parried with all his dialetic skill, presenting the case for the Colonies so successfully that the
House moved for repeal on the 21st of the month. The
motion was carried in the House of Lords, royal assent was
given March 8, and in the American Colonies advertising was
freed from restrictions that were enforced in England itself
all through the first half of the next century.

Benjamin Franklin appears at least once more as a force in
early American advertising. Again his advertising was suc-

cessful, though it was a deal on which in the end—it must
have been one of the very few times—Franklin lost money.

In one or another of his political roles, Franklin visited the
headquarters of General Edward Braddock in Frederick,
Maryland, when the British forces were encamped there getting ready to move against the French and Indians. Franklin
found Braddock immobilized for lack of transport, though
the British were scouring Virginia and Maryland for wagons.
Braddock asked Franklin to use his influence to procure what
he could in Pennsylvania. As soon as he got back to his own
state, Franklin published this advertisement.

Lancaster, April 26, 1755

> WHEREAS, one hundred and fifty waggons, with four
> horses to each waggon and fifteen hundred saddle or pack
> horses, are wanted for the service of his majesty's forces
> now about to rendezvous at Will's Creek, and his excellency
> General Braddock having been pleased to empower me to
> contract for the hire of the same, I hereby give notice that
> I shall attend for that purpose at Lancaster from this day to
> next Wednesday evening, and at York from next Thursday
> morning till Friday evening, where I shall be ready to agree
> for waggons and teams, or single horses on the following
> terms . . .

Detailed terms followed at some length, the advertisement
ending with a *"Note*—My son, William Franklin, is empowered to enter into like contracts with any person in Cumberland County. *B. Franklin.*"

As a result of this advertising, Franklin had 150 wagons
and 259 horses on the march for Braddock's camp within two
weeks. When Braddock's troops were ambushed and wiped
out nine miles from Fort Duquesne, their objective, "The
waggoners," Franklin reports in his *Autobiography*, "took
each a horse out of his team and scamper'd; their example
was immediately follow'd by others; so that all the waggons,
provisions, artillery, and stores were left to the enemy."
Though he tried persistently in later years, Franklin was
never able to obtain recompense from the English War Office
for his losses in the venture.

In New England, as in England, birds and beasts made popular tavern signs. This spindly federal eagle screamed in Providence, 1808. (Bettman Archive)

This handsome cigar store Indian, said to have inspired lines by Longfellow, stands now in the offices of The American Tobacco Company in New York City.

Uninhibited and unencumbered by government regulation, thanks to Franklin's efforts, advertising was able to go its ways freely in the Colonies, and it went into some strange byways. The names of other well-known figures of the time appear in many of them. In one advertisement one of the most colorful and romantic of them all appears in somewhat less romantic connection. This was Paul Revere, whose ride from Charlestown to Lexington to arouse the Minutemen on the night of April 18, 1775, Longfellow celebrated in a poem that has become part of American folklore.[4] Revere, fine silversmith, engraver, who designed both the first official seal for the Colonies and the seal still used by the Commonwealth of Massachusetts, leader of the mechanics of Boston in political and physical activity against the British, did other things as well. He manufactured gunpowder and made cannon. He also made false teeth. It was the last he advertised in the *Boston Gazette*, December 19, 1768.

WHEREAS many Persons are so unfortunate as to lose their Fore-Teeth by Accident, and otherways, to their great detriment, not only in Looks, but speaking both in Public and Private:—This is to inform all such, that they may have them re-placed with artificial Ones that looks as well as the Natural, & answers the End of Speaking to all Intents, by PAUL REVERE, Goldsmith, near the Head of Dr. Clarke's Wharf, Boston.

** All Persons who have had false Teeth fixt by Mr. John Baker, Surgeon-Dentist, and they have got loose (as they will in Time) may have them fastened by the above, who learnt the Method of fixing them from Mr. Baker.[5]

Revere's was a straightforward request for business. Some vendors in the vicinity of Boston were rather more devious

[4] Still another Revere, a lonely ancient walking the Boston streets in the Revolutionary garb he never relinquished, appears in Oliver Wendell Holmes' "The Last Leaf."

[5] Revere's claims were modest. In Philadelphia in 1784 a dentist advertised that he could transplant teeth, claiming 123 successful transplantings in six months. He offered to buy teeth for two guineas each from "persons disposed to sell their front teeth or any of them."

in their merchandising. The ingenious among them hit on a promotion approach that was evidently too successful for the taste of their competitors in the city. This advertisement, so charged with hurt disbelief, indignation, and a few well-chosen threats that it flooded over into a postscript, appeared in the *Boston Gazette* February 13, 1760.

> WHEREAS sundry evil minded Persons in some of the neighboring Towns, to discourage the Market-People coming into this Town with their Provisions, and that they may have an Opportunity to purchase at low Rates, and sell them here at an exorbitant Price, have industriously reported that the Small-Pox for some Time past has been in this Town, and now prevails here:
>
> THESE are to Inform the Public, that for near two Years past, there has been only one Person taken down in this Town with the Small-Pox, which is upwards of a Month past, who upon discovery of it was immediately removed to the Hospital, and there died, and no other Person has had it, or any Symptoms of it since.—That Yesterday there was a general Visitation of the Town by the Justices of the Peace, Selectmen and Overseers of the Poor, and upon their Report last Evening of the State and Circumstances of the Inhabitants, I hereby Certify that there is not an Infectious Distemper of any Sort, known to be in Town.—And as the above false Reports have been Propagated to the great Prejudice of this Town by those who employ themselves in Engrossing Provisions and Forestalling the Market, (many of whom are known to the Selectmen:) They are hereby particularly Notified, That unless they desist from such wicked and abusive Practices, they will be prosecuted on the Act of the Province, for making and publishing such Lyes and false Reports.—By Order of the Selectmen,
>
> Ezekiel Goldthwait, Town Clerk.
>
> Many Country-People have imagined by seeing Silks hanging on Poles, that the Small-Pox is in such Houses; but their Surmises are entirely groundless, they being hung out at the Silk Dyers for drying.

It is insinuated in this advertisement that the spiritual condition of Boston was not all it should have been in the Bay Colony.

THIS DAY PUBLISHED,

An ADDRESS to

Persons of FASHION,

Concerning frequenting of

Plays, Balls, Assemblies, Card-Tables, &c.
In which is introduced the Character of

LUCINDA.

Printed & Sold by W. McAlpine, in Marlboro'-street.
*** A Pamphlet worthy the serious Attention of
every Christian, especially at a Time when Vice and
Immorality seems to have an Ascendency over Religion,
and the Prince of the Power of the Air reigns with
almost an uncontrolled Restraint.[6]

❋❋

One reason for the Ascendency of Vice and Immorality is
indicated in another *Boston Gazette* advertisement. This in-
vitation was extended September 22, 1767.

Goods exchanged for New England rum.

Barbados Rum,	Russia Duck,
and Sugars by the	Pitch, Tar,
Hogshead or Barrel,	and
Bohea Tea,	Cordage.
Cotton Wool by the	Long & short Pipes.
Bag,	Sole Leather.
New Flour,	English Steel.
Indigo.	With,
Dumb FISH.	

A General Assortment of English Goods and
Hard Ware.

Many of the above Articles will be Exchang'd for
New England Rum,

By Samuel Allyne Otis,
At Store No. 5, South-Side of the Town-Dock.

---

[6] *Boston Gazette*, May 21, 1767. Quoted by Henry M. Brooks in *Quaint
and Curious Advertisements* (Boston: Tichknor and Co., 1886).

Morality, politics, revolutionary sentiment, and the right touch of vindictiveness all appear in a *Boston Chronicle* advertisement of March 1, 1770.

STOLEN,

From the side of the house, belonging to Richard
Silvester, now the Sign of the

BROKEN POST,

Newbury Street, Boston, about half an hour past one o'clock in the morning of the 24th ult. A Black and White Horse, with a Bridle, without a Saddle.—The Persons concerned in this Frolick, who were seen and known, are desired to replace the said Horse, in the manner and form they found him. And it is hoped, as he is a young creature, they will not corupt his morals, by teaching him any of their tricks, but return him soon, as the owner will not allow any thing for his keeping.

N. B. If he should bite or kick any that have him in possession; his former master now declares, he will not be answerable for the damages.—He was not imported from England, but manufactured in this land of liberty.

Query. Whether the persons who knocked at said Silvester's door, past three o'clock the same morning, in their return home, and cried THIEVES, were not accomplices in this glorious exploit.

Government use of advertising during wartime may be said to have started during the Revolution with broadsides issued to tempt men into the armed services. In 1776 the Continental Congress issued a broadside advertisement offering twenty dollars, a suit of clothes, and one hundred acres of land to those who would sign up to serve until the end of the war.

Another crudely printed poster advertisement with the headline "TAKE NOTICE" in large blackletter capitals, was distributed by Congress for use throughout the Colonies. Blank spaces were left for the dates, place, and the names of the recruiting officers in an appeal which did nothing to

minimize the delights and rewards of volunteering. It was
addressed:

TO ALL BRAVE, HEALTHY, ABLE-BODIED, AND WELL

DISPOSED YOUNG MEN

In this neighbourhood, who have any inclination
to join the Troops now raising under

GEORGE WASHINGTON

for the defence of the

LIBERTIES AND INDEPENDENCE

of the United States
against the hostile designs of
foreign enemies

The illustrations beneath this address show a cockaded
soldier in knee breeches going through the prescribed fourteen positions of the manual of arms. This text follows the
illustrations in one example.

THAT tuesday, Wednesday, Thursday, friday and Saturday at Spotswood in Middlesex Lieutenant Recruiting
with his music and recruiting party [indecipherable] in the
name of Major Shutes Battalion of the 11th regiment of
infantry, commanded by Lieutenant Colonel Aaron Ogden
for the purpose of receiving the enrollment of such youth
of spirit as may be willing to enter into this HONOUR-
ABLE service.

The ENCOURAGEMENT at this time to enlist, is truly
liberal and generous, namely a bounty of twelve dollars, an
annual and fully sufficient supply of good and handsome
cloathing, a daily allowance of large and ample ration of
provisions, together with SIXTY dollars a year in GOLD
and SILVER money on account of pay, the whole of which
the soldier may lay up for himself and friends, as all articles
proper to his subsistence and comfort are provided by law,
without any expence to him.

Those who may favour this recruiting party with their at-
tendance as above, will have an opportunity of hearing and
seeing in a more particular manner, the great advantages
which these brave men will have, who shall embrace this
opportunity of spending a few happy years in viewing the

different parts of this beautiful continent, in the honourable and truly respectable character of a soldier, after which he may, if he pleases return home to his friends, with his pockets FULL of money and his head covered with laurels.

GOD SAVE THE UNITED STATES

In 1777 a similar broadside was issued to recruit men for naval service under John Paul Jones.

> Any gentlemen volunteers who have a mind to make an agreeable voyage in this pleasant season of the year, may by entering on board the Ship *Ranger* Meet with every civility they can possibly expect, and for a further encouragement depend on the first opportunity being embraced to award each one agreeable to his merits.

Both before and after the Revolution fought to guarantee everyone freedom to pursue his own happiness (capture was never guaranteed) there was a brisk and profitable trade in human flesh, color immaterial. Headlined as "Bargains" in the *Pennsylvania Chronicle and Universal Advertiser*, Monday, March 2 to Monday, March 9, 1767, were these two attractions.

TO BE SOLD

> A LIKELY DUTCH BOY, who has upwards of four Years to serve. Inquire of the Printer hereof.

> A LIKELY, young Negro Wench who has had both the small-pox and measles; she is about nineteen or twenty years of age, is very strong, and is fit for country business; She is to be sold for no other fault only she wants to be married . . .

In the same column was advertised "All for Love; or, The World Well Lost." Dryden's play was running at the New Theatre in Southwark.

Chronicle advertisements offered four dollars reward for the return of a stolen kettle and opportunity with a merchant for an apprentice of about fourteen years of age "who can write tolerably well." Paul Fooks, "appt'd by His Honour the Governor as Notary and Tarbellion Public" swore he would observe secrecy and prudence in writing business letters and contracts in either French or Spanish. The Bellsize Arabian, posed in a crude woodcut, was at stud. The fee to cover a mare was four dollars and a dollar to the groom.

In the *Chronicle* for October 12-17, 1768, John Townsend advertised in almost a full column of atrocious doggerel for the return of a runaway servant. The ingrate was English and a barber. An advertisement in the *Pennsylvania Packet of the General Advertiser,* January 2, 1781, offered a huge reward for the return of a runaway slave. The reward, headlined, was "One Thousand Pounds Continental; or Twelve or Twenty-four Pounds Hard Money." The speculator could take his choice.

A wholesale lot of "likely"—it seems to have been the advertising cliché of the day—human merchandise was made available in 1768. No false social or professional distinctions were made in announcing the sale in the *Maryland Gazette; or, The Baltimore Advertiser* for May 30th of that year.

Men and Women Servants

JUST ARRIVED

In the Ship PACA, Robert Caulfield, Master in five weeks from Belfast and Cork, a number of healthy Men and Women SERVANTS. Among them are several valuable tradesmen, viz. Carpenters, Shoemakers, Coopers, Gardeners, Blacksmiths, Staymakers, Bookbinders, Clothiers, Diers, Butchers, Schoolmasters, Millwrights, and Labourers.—Their indentures are to be disposed of by the Subscribers.

BROWN and MARIS

William Wilson

The patience of purchasers was often sorely tried by the restlessness of their property. John Cochran must have realized that he was dealing with an incorrigible, a proven juvenile delinquent of the day. His advertisment for the return of a runaway ten-year-old apprentice offered no staggering reward. For his return or his being thrown into any gaol he would pay one cent and no charges.

Eighteenth-century newspaper advertising reflected some nicer things, though sometimes these were imperfect too. A Boston dancing master showed a touch of the same impatience felt by Mr. Cochran, but, of course, he minded his manners better. It was delinquent parents at whom he aimed an advertisement of March 29, 1788.

DANCING ACADEMY
CONCERT-HALL

> Mr. Turner informs the Ladies and Gentlemen in town and country that he has reduced his price for teaching, from Six Dollars entrance to One Guinea, And from Four Dollars per month to Three. Those Ladies and Gentlemen who propose sending their children to be taught, will notice, that no books will be kept, as Mr. T. has suffered much by booking. The pupils must pay monthly, if they are desirous the School should continue.

Sundry articles and services of many kinds were advertised in the newspapers of the Colonies in the eighteenth century: ships, for sale or to sail on, windows set in lead, brass skillets and table silver, land, houses, servants, slaves, books, jewelry, groceries, soap, candles, carriages, hats, liquors, sextants and compasses, wigs, umbrellas, walking sticks, whalebones, Bibles. There were always rewards offered for the capture of thieves and the return of stolen goods. Doctors, dentists, bootblacks, hatters, and publicans offered their services. Legitimate entertainment may have been hard to come by. There were a profusion of advertisements of the exhibitions of animals, for "A large Baboon, which is allowed to be the most curious Animal of its kind, ever seen in America. A Porcupine, Bear, Rackoon and Rabbit, which are also very great curiosities."; for "A Beautiful Moose"; for "A beautiful African LION"; for "THE CASSOWARY, A Bird from the East Indies. Its height is 5 feet, weighs near 100 pounds; it will eat half a peck of apples at a meal, swallowing whole eggs, also stones and apples as large as eggs, and jumps to a height,—Goldsmith says . . . it has the head of a Warrior, the eye of a Lion, the defence of a Porcupine, and the swiftness of a Courser."

Two CAMELS were advertised in the *Salem Mercury*, August 4, 1789, as on exhibition. They were billed as "being the greatest natural curiosity ever exhibited to the publick on this continent." Soon Salem had an even greater marvel. May 4, 1798, the Salem Gazette announced:

For ten days only.
MR. PINCHBECK
RESPECTFULLY informs the Inhabitants of SALEM, that he has just arrived in this town with that great natural curiosity, the

PIG OF KNOWLEDGE,

And flatters himself, after exhibiting before the President of the United States with unbounded applause, and in every principal City of the Union, to have the honour of gratifying such Ladies and Gentlemen in this place, as may favour him with their Company.

This extraordinary Animal will actually perform the following surprising particulars, viz.

He reads print or writing, spells, tells the time of day, both the hours and minutes, by any person's watch in the company, the date of the year, the day of the month, distinguishes colours, how many persons there are present, ladies or gentlemen, and to the astonishment of every spectator, will answer any question in the four first rules of Arithmetick. To conclude, any Lady or Gentleman may draw a card from a pack, and keep it concealed, and the PIG without hesitation will discover the card when drawn.

Those who doubt the truth of the above are informed in case it don't answer every expectation the advertisement can excite, and prove a real living Animal, shall have the Money returned, or be at liberty to pay after they have convinced themselves by seeing him perform.

To be seen in a convenient room under the western side of Concert-Hall, Market-Street.

Admittance, for grown persons, one Quarter of a Dollar.—Children half price.

N. B. Strict attention paid to keep the place fit for the reception of Ladies.

Sometimes a man, if he really extends himself, can be even more entertaining than a pig. This one promised to go all out.

THOMAS TOUCHWOOD, GENT.,

Proposes, on the last day of the present month, to shoot himself by subscription. His life being of no farther use to himself or his friends, he takes this method of endeavoring to turn his death to some account; and the novelty of the performance, he hopes, will merit the attention and patronage of the publick.

He will perform with two pistols, the first shot to be directed through his abdomen, to which will be added another through his brain, the whole to conclude with staggering convulsions, grinning, &c., in a manner never before publickly attempted.

The doors to be opened at eight, and the exhibition to begin precisely at nine. Particular places, for that night only, reserved for the ladies. No money to be returned, nor half price taken. Vivant Rex et Regina.

N. B. Beware of counterfeits and impostors.—The person who advertises to hang himself the same night, in opposition to Mr. Touchwood, is a taylor, who intends only to give the representation of death by dancing in a collar, an attempt infinitely inferior to Mr. T.'s original and authentic performance.[7]

Subject matter and tone of an advertisement in the *Providence Gazette* as the eighteenth century drew near a close were much more serious. Some young women in the domestic labor force seemed unaware of their proper duties and demeanor. The situation had become serious enough to

[7] Quoted by Brooks, *op. cit.*, p. 110, who attributes it merely to a Boston paper of 1789 as copied from a late London paper. "It was probably designed as a 'take-off' to some of the humbugs of the day."

warrant the expenditure of a considerable sum of money to relieve it. October 14, 1796, bearing its own evidence of the convictions and serious thought which had gone into its composition, this advertisement was printed.

Messrs. Printers,
You will oblige a number of your customers, by publishing the following advertisement in the next Gazette.

Five Hundred Dollars Reward.

Was mislaid, or taken away by mistake (soon after the formation of the Abolition of Slavery Society) from the Servant Girls of this town, all inclination to do any kind of work;—and left in lieu thereof, an impudent appearance, a strong and continued thirst for high wages, a gossiping disposition for all sorts of amusement, a leering and hankering after persons of the other sex, a desire of finery and fashion, a never ceasing trot after new places more advantageous for stealing—with number of contingent accomplishments that do not suit the wearers. Now if any person or persons will restore to the owners that degree of Honesty and Industry, which has been for some time missing, he or they shall receive the reward of Five Hundred Dollars, desire the warmest blessings of many abused and insulted.

HOUSEHOLDERS.

Colonial newspaper advertising was informed by briskness and vitality. It spoke not only of the busyness of small enterprise, the practical considerations of merchants and the purveyors of services, but also of the feelings, beliefs, and prejudices of people in New England and the Middle Colonies. The devious ways of free publicity had not yet been perfected. Men announced their attitudes and opinions in paid advertising. Public relations had not yet taught the importance of moving softly. These advertisers said what they meant and meant what they said.

Morality was freer in New England than it had been in the days of Cotton Mather, and Jonathan Edwards cried out

in vain from the wilderness of Northampton and Stock-
bridge; or else most advertising was written and inserted by
the completely unregenerate for the delectation of their
fellows.

Men and women were thirsty in the Colonies. Advertisements offered them rum. They were hungry for entertainment. Advertisements proffered wild beasts and clowns.
People danced, stole, drank, and went to war. Merchants
used foul means of competition. Men and women lost their
teeth and wanted new ones, as much for cosmetic as for
practical purposes. Goods of colonial manufacture were
often poor. Advertisements showed that products of English
make were prized for their better quality. A militant patriotism showed in some of the advertisements and an independence of spirit even in advertisements where no political
reference was intended. Some advertisements displayed wit,
but more of them a crude humor, sometimes a frontier cruelty.
Others showed avarice and credulity in equal parts. Human-
itarianism had not developed to the point where it interfered
seriously with the profitable buying and selling of slaves or
the time of the indentured.

Advertisements, many of them, were conversational, even
colloquial. It was as if the neighborhood had simply got too
big for a man to be able to talk to everyone he wished and
was forced to use printed advertising as a substitute.

It is hardly surprising to find that Benjamin Franklin was
an indefatigable advertiser, a skilled copywriter, and a pro-
ponent and defender of advertising in idea and practice. It
is more difficult to visualize the austere George Washington
as both an advertiser and a deliberate purchaser of advertised
products. It is of record that he was both.

Washington inserted this advertisement in the *Maryland
Advocate and Commercial Advertiser* for July 15, 1773, and
in the *Pennsylvania Gazette* during September of the same
year in an attempt to draw settlers to his Western lands.
The advertisement was dignified, almost legalistic in its opening paragraph, then restrained in its claims as the advertiser
described the advantages of his proposal.

Mount Vernon in Virginia, July 15, 1773

The subscriber having obtained patents for upwards of TWENTY
THOUSAND acres of Land in the *Ohio* and *Grand Kanhawa* (Ten
Thousand of which are situated on the banks of the first-mentioned
river, between the mouths of the two Kanhawas and the remainder
on the *Great Kanhawa* or New River, from the mouth or near it,
upwards in one continued survey) proposes to divide the same into
any sized tenements that may be 'desired, and lease them upon moderate terms, allowing a reasonable number of years rent free, provided
within the space of two years from next October three acres for
every fifty contained in each lot, and proportionately for a less quantity, shall be cleared, fenced, and tilled; and that by or before the
time limited for the commencement of the first rent, five acres for
every hundred, and proportionately as above, shall be enclosed and
laid down in good grass for meadow; and moreover that at least fifty
good fruit trees for every like quantity of land shall be planted on the
premises. Any persons inclined to settle on these lands may be more
fully informed of the terms by applying to the subscriber, near
Alexandria, or in his absence to Mr. LUND WASHINGTON, and
would do well in communicating their intentions before the 1st of
October next, in order that a sufficient number of lots may be laid
off to answer the demand.

As these lands are among the first which have been surveyed in
the part of the country they lie in, it is amost needless to premise that
none can exceed them in luxuriance of soil or convenience of situation, all of them lying upon the banks either of the Ohio or Kanhawa
and abounding with fine fish and wild fowl of various kinds, also in
most excellent meadows, many of which (by the bountiful hand of
nature) are, in their present state, almost fit for the scythe.

From every part of these lands water carriage is now had to Fort
Pitt, by an easy communication, and from Fort Pitt, up the Monongahela to Redstone, vessels of convenient burden, may and do pass continually; from whence, by means of Cheat River and other navigable
branches of the Monongahela, it is thought the portage to Pow-
towmack may, and will, be reduced within the compass of a few
miles, to the great ease and convenience of the settlers in transporting
the produce of their lands to market.

To which may be added that, as patents have now actually passed
the seals for the several tracts here offered to be leased, settlers on
them may cultivate and enjoy the lands in peace and safety, notwithstanding the unsettled counsels respecting a new colony on the Ohio;
and, as no right money is to be paid for these lands, and quitrent of
two shillings sterling a hundred demandable some years hence only,
it is highly presumable that they will always be held upon a more

desirable footing than where both these are laid on with a very heavy hand.

And it may not be amiss further to observe that if the scheme for establishing a new government on the Ohio, in the manner talked of, should ever be effected, these must be among the most valuable lands in it, not only on account of the goodness of the soil and the other advantages above enumerated but from their contiguity to the seat of government, which more than probably will be fixed at the mouth of the Great Kanhawa.

George Washington[8]

Washington's advertisement drew some response at the time, but he was not successful as a land developer. When ten years later, in the interval between his services as Commander-in-Chief and assuming the Presidency, he visited his Western lands, he found that squatters had settled on them

Americans !

Encourage your own Manufactories, and they will Improve.

LADIES, fave your RAGS.

AS the Subscribers have it in contemplation to erect a PAPER-MILL in *Dalton*, the ensuing spring; and the business being very beneficial to the community at large, they flatter themselves that they shall meet with due encouragement. And that every woman, who has the good of her country, and the interest of her own family at heart, will patronize them, by saving her rags, and sending them to their Manufactory, or to the nearest Storekeeper— for which the Subscribers will give a generous price.

HENRY WISWALL,
ZENAS CRANE,
JOHN WILLARD.
Worcester, Feb. 8, 1801.

First advertisement of Crane & Co., maker of all paper for U.S. Treasury currency and bonds and for some twenty other nations.

[8] *The Writings of George Washington, from the Original Manuscript Sources.* Ed. John C. Fitzpatrick (Washington: U.S. Government Printing Office, 1931), III, 144-46.

and that, ignoring his patents, land agents were selling his acreage.

Washington as convinced by an advertisement appears in a letter of January 29, 1789 to Major General Henry Knox in New York.

Mount Vernon,

My Dear Sir:

Having learnt from an Advertisement in the New York Daily Advertiser, that there were superfine American Broad Cloths to be sold at No. 44 in Water Street; I have ventured to trouble you with the Commission of purchasing enough to make me a suit of cloaths. As to the colour, I shall leave it altogether to your taste; only observing that if the dye should not appear to be well fixt & clear, or if the cloth should not really be very fine, then (in my judgment) some colour mixed in grain might be preferable to an indifferent (stained) dye. I shall have occasion to trouble you for nothing but the cloth & twist to make the button holes.

If these articles can be procured and forwarded in a package by the stage in any short time your attention will be gratefully acknowledged. Mrs. Washington would be equally thankful to you for purchasing for her use as much of what is called (in the Advertisement) London Smoke as will make her a riding habit. If the choice of these clothes should have been disposed of in New York where could they be had from Hartford in Connecticut where I perceive a Manufactory of them is established? With every sentiment of sincere friendship ·

I am always Affectionately Yrs.,
G. Washington.

Washington may have had more in mind than simply obtaining the superfine American Broad Cloths and London Smoke. He was anxious to encourage native American industry. In 1789 he visited the Hartford Woolen Manufactory, which was operated by Jeremiah Wadsworth, who had been Commissary General of the Continental Army, and ordered enough cloth called "Everlasting" for breeches for his male servants. A news item in the *Hampshire Gazette*, January 20, 1790, said proudly: "President Washington— when he addressed the two houses of Congress on the 8th instant, was dressed in a crow coloured suit of clothes of American manufacture:—This elegant fabric was from the manufactory in Hartford."

5

Dr. Johnson, the *Times*, and Mathew Carey— Eighteenth-Century England

THE TAX IMPOSED in 1712 hurt and hindered the progress of advertising in England, but the wound was not mortal. Newspaper and periodical advertising was slowed, not stopped. Outdoor advertising, untaxed, burgeoned. It would have developed anyway. Only the educated upper classes could and did read. The rest of the market still had to be reached by signs, shouts, and displays. Periodical advertising gradually recovered momentum. Advertising was necessary, and the advertiser absorbed the extra cost.

Soon the papers were rife again with thousands of eighteenth-century advertisements for silks, satins, wigs, razors, razor strops, servants, and slaves; for staples and delicacies, books, plays, and always for panaceas, elixirs, cures, and cure-alls. Quacks and charlatans sounded fanfares of themselves and flailed at their competitors. There were advertisements for goods and services commonplace or unusual; advertisements for rubbish of a hundred kinds and for still different trash of as many more.

The tax on advertisements did not deter the really serious. It was no obstacle at all to gallants who fell in love at first sight or to those, somewhat less gallant, who, with the same basic desires but rather less parade of sentiment, advertised to arrange assignations. This, one of many, is notable for its blend of acute observation, circumspect approach, and the elegance which does not hide the writer's ardor. It seems worth quoting both for its own sake and for Sampson's philosophic comment. It appeared in the *General Advertiser* in mid-century, probably 1752.

> A TALL, well-fashion'd, handsome young woman, about eighteen with a fine bloom in her countenance, a cast in one of her eyes, scarcely discernable; a well-turned nose, and dark-brown uncurled hair flowing about her neck, which seemed to be newly cut; walked last new year's day about three o'clock in the afternoon, pretty fast through Long acre, and near the turn into Drury Lane met a young gentleman, wrapped up in a blue roccelo cloak, whom she look'd at steadfastly; He believes he had formerly the pleasure of her acquaintance: If she will send a line directed to H. S. Esq. to be left at the bar of the Prince of Orange Coffeehouse, the corner of Pall Mall, intimating where she can be spoken with, she will be inform'd of something greatly to her advantage. She walked in a dark coloured undressed gown, black hat and capuchin; a low, middle-aged woman, plainly dressed, and a footman following close behind, seemed to attend her.

"It is to be presumed," Samson remarked, "that the hair and not the neck, is referred to as being newly cut, though at this distance of date it certainly does not matter much which, except for the purpose of discovering probable fresh peculiarities among our very peculiar ancestors."[1]

Another mid-eighteenth-century advertisement proved, if it has ever been doubted, the truth that "advertising pays." At least it proved the effectiveness of advertising and that one of advertising's chief assets is always human credulity.

The Duke of Montague, Lord Portman, the Earl of Chesterfield, and a few other noblemen were amusedly discussing the gullibility of the populace. Montague was convinced that he could fill a London playhouse simply by advertising the most impossible thing in the world. He was so convinced that he offered to lay a wager on it. Chester-

---

[1] Sampson, *op. cit.*, p. 194.

field was willing. He said no one would believe it if a man said he would jump into a quart bottle.

The following advertisement appeared in several London papers the first week of January, 1749:

At the New Theatre in the Hay market, on Monday next, the 12th instant, is to be seen a Person who performs the several most surprising things following, viz.—1st. He takes a common walking Cane from any of the Spectators, and thereon plays the music of every Instrument now in use, and likewise sings to surprising perfection.—2dly. He presents you with a common Wine Bottle, which any of the Spectators may first examine; this Bottle is placed on a Table in the middle of the Stage, and he (without any equivocation) goes into it, in the sight of all the Spectators, and sings in it; during his stay in the bottle, any Person may handle it, and see plainly that it does not exceed a common Tavern Bottle.—Those on the Stage, or in the Boxes, may come in masked habits (if agreeable to them); and the Performer, if desired, will inform them who they are.—Stage, 7s. 7d. Boxes, 5s, Pit, 3s. Gallery, 2s. Tickets to be had at the Theatre: To begin at half an hour after six o'clock. The performance continues about two hours and a half.

Note.—If any Gentlemen or Ladies (after the above Performance) either single or in company, in or out of mask, is desirous of seeing a representation of any deceased Person, such as Husband or Wife, Sister or Brother, or any intimate Friend of either sex, upon making a gratuity to the performer, shall be gratified by seeing and conversing with them for some minutes, as if alive; likewise, if desired, he will tell you your most secret thoughts in your past Life, and give you a full view of persons who have injured you, either dead or alive. For those Gentlemen or Ladies who are desirous of seeing this last part, there is a private Room provided.

These performances have been seen by most of the crowned Heads of Asia, Africa, and Europe, and never appeared public anywhere but once; but will wait upon any at their Houses, and perform as above for five Pounds each time. A proper guard is appointed to prevent disorder.

At half an hour after six o'clock on Monday the 12th inst. the Haymarket was jammed and the crowd growing

impatient. The catcalls and stamping from the gallery grew
louder. Flirtatious ladies in masks twitched their fans nerv-
ously. Scented dandies fiddled with their swords. Gentlemen on stage tried to look disdainfuly imperturbable, but
they too were getting restless. Finally an agent of one of
the noble plotters appeared onstage and promised that if the
performer, who seemed to be detained, did not appear within
fifteen minutes, all entrance money would be refunded. A
disapproving roar went up. The threats and laughter grew
even louder. A man in the gallery shouted that for twice the
money he would jump into a *pint* bottle.

That did it. The audience arose en masse. While ladies
and gentlemen rushed shouting and screaming for the doors,
those who were really annoyed or simply pleased with the
idea began to tear up the benches. Others leaped to help
them. Delighted with their efforts, they tore loose everything
else that would give way before combined assault. Wigs,
hats, swords, gloves, and dresses were lost in the magnificent
confusion. Smashed benches and splintered woodwork were
lugged out of the mob-gutted theatre, and a huge bonfire was
built outside. The theatre curtain was ripped down, tied to a
pole, and marched gloriously down the street.

A day or two later the Duke of Cumberland advertised
for his sword, lost in the melée. An answering advertisement
appeared immediately. The sword had been found "entangled in the slit of a Lady's demolished smock Petticoat . . .
supposed to have been stolen from the plump side of a Great
General, in his precipitate retreat from the Battle of Bottle-
Noodles." An *N.B.* to the advertisement said that nothing it
contained was true.

Possibly it was advertisements such as these, probably
it was the more prosaic run of general advertising, that led
Samuel Johnson to devote No. XI of the *Idler*, Saturday,
January 20, 1759, to an essay on the "Art of Advertising."

It was a tolerant but provocative essay, as perceptive as
Addison's a half century before. ". . . whatever is common,"
Johnson wrote, "is despised. Advertisements are now so
numerous that they are very negligently perused, and it is

therefore become necessary to gain attention by magnificence of promise and by eloquence sometimes sublime and sometimes ridiculous. . . . Promise, large promise, is the soul of an advertisement."

As instances of the absurdities proposed in advertisements, Johnson mentioned a washball (ball of toilet soap) that it was claimed gave an exquisite edge to a razor; a down bed covering that "is warmer than four or five blankets and lighter than one"; a lotion "that repels pimples, washes away freckles, smooths the skin, and plumps the flesh"; though Johnson admitted that the advertiser of the last did not promise the complexion of fifteen to the woman of fifty.

"The trade of advertising," Johnson announced, "is now so near perfection that it is not easy to propose any improvement."[2]

The sentence has been ironically quoted to show how ridiculous and short-sighted the sage Dr. Johnson really was. Seldom quoted is the sentence which followed immediately in the original. "But as every art ought to be exercised in due subordination to the public good, I cannot but propose it as a moral question to these masters of the public ear, Whether they do not sometimes play too wantonly with our passions?"

Johnson made another suggestion before he concluded his essay. "In an advertisement it is allowed to every man to speak well of himself, but I do not know why he should assume the privilege of censuring his neighbor. He may pro-

[2] Addison had found at least one advertisement in 1710 that he felt approached perfection. The *Tatler* had been paid five shillings to insert it as an advertisement, but Addison thought it such a pattern of good advertising, he said, that he inserted it in the body of his *Tatler* essay, September 14, 1710:

"The highest compounded spirit of lavender, the most glorious, if the expression may be used, enlivening scent and flavour that can possibly be, which so enraptures the spirits, delights the gust, and gives such airs to the countenance, as are not to be imagined but by those that have tried it. The meanest sort of thing is admired by most gentlemen and ladies; but this far more, as by far it exceeds it, to the gaining among all a more than common esteem. It is sold in neat flint bottles fit for the pocket, only at the Golden key in Wharton's-court near Holbourn-bars for three shillings and sixpence, with directions."

claim his own virtue or skill, but ought not to exclude others from the same pretensions."

Sampson agreed with Dr. Johnson's belief that the art of advertising had reached nearly to perfection in the eighteenth century. He thought, and said in 1874, that by 1800 the skill of advertisers and the development of advertising had reached their peak. Advertising of 1800 was just about what he saw around him when he was writing his history seventy-odd years later. Sampson acted on this conclusion when he reached the end of the eighteenth century in his chronological account and devoted most of the remainder of his book, nearly four hundred more pages, to curious and eccentric advertisements, lottery advertising, swindles and hoaxes, quacks and impostures, drawing most of his examples from the seventeenth and eighteenth centuries.

Both Dr. Johnson and Sampson were right. Advertising arose the first time a man wanted to trade something he had or was for something possessed by another. It began with the original impulse to compete for attention and rewards. It may have been done by signs and grunts before the barker began to brag of his merchandise or the criers followed after bell, pipe, or drum to hawk the wares of their patrons in the Middle Ages. Signs, then printed media, permitted refinements, but the advertising had the same basic motivation, the attraction of customers for profit. It was cupidity appealing to curiosity, excitement, avarice, and dozens of other emotions and desires and gradations of emotions and desires; the appeals ranging up and down the register from simple notices to impassioned demands. Advertisers shouted until the veins stood out on their necks, or simpered delicately of insinuated delights. Hysterical denunciation of rival peddlers choked some with indignation. Other advertisers ignored their competition. The purpose, matter, manner, approach, tone, often the product, has changed little since the eighteenth century. There are new products, new services, new media, larger campaigns, fantastic expenditures, but advertisers use these as their forebears used the only methods available to them, to say the same things, make the same kinds of appeals, to about the same kinds of people.

The London newspapers were charged with advertising in the late eighteenth century. There were fifty-three news-papers in London alone by 1776, and many of them were vigorous advertising media. The *Times, or Daily Universal Register* was founded by John Walter in 1788, and "The Thunderer" was a strong advertising sheet from the begin-ning. January 1, 1788, the newspaper appeared for the first time as simply the *Times*, with "logographically printed" lettered under the Royal coat of arms in the middle of the logotype. The whole of the front page of this first issue of the *Times* was advertising. Prominently displayed was A CAUTION to PREVENT IMPOSITION. It advertised SHARP's CON-CAVE RAZORS. (They were the best and all imitations were inferior.) Music, opera, snuff, plays, books, kitchen furnish-ings, lectures in midwifery and on anatomy, perfumes, furs, diamonds and watches, auction notices and shipping notices covered the front and back pages of the four-page paper. Advertisements inside the fold were for books, gifts, lodgings, the English state lottery, help wanted, and the "Refined Liquoric for Coughs, Colds, Asthmas, and Defluxions of the Lungs."

John Walter made his position regarding advertisements clear They would be inserted in the *Times*, without fail, the day after receipt. Though he promised to carry nothing which would "wound the ear of delicacy or corrupt the heart," he also felt that "A News-Paper in this particular ought to resemble an Inn, where the proprietor is obliged to give the use of his house to all travellers who are ready to pay for it and against whose person there is no legal or moral objection." Still it is rather startling to find this advertise-ment on page one of the staid *Times* for Monday, August 2, 1790.

> A YOUNG WOMAN, who has been tenderly brought up, and received a genteel Education, but left destitute of Fortune and Friends, will think her-self happy could she meet with a single Gentleman,

> of benevolent disposition to take her under his
> ONLY protection and friendship. Such a gentle-
> man might be sure of meeting a heart full of grati-
> tude and sincerity for such friendly aid by calling
> personally or addressing a line to H. G. at Mr. Ray-
> burn's, Grocer, No. 30 John-street, Howland-street.

People asked for what they wanted in those days without
false modesty. Among the *Times* advertisements in this
same issue for Hewter's Restorative Balsam, Brownwood's
Sylvanus Peronia, Mr. Greenough's Tincture for the Teeth,
La Blache's Military Drops, and the sales by Mr. Christie "At
his Great Room in the Pall-Mall," was one for "A sinecure of
One Hundred Pounds per Annum."

Another gentleman requested a sinecure and stated his
terms in *The Oracle, Bell's New World,* January 11, 1789.

> ### WANTED
> A place under GOVERNMENT, with an income
> of 500 l. per annum, for which an adequate pre-
> mium will be given. A line addressed to T. A. at
> No. 12 Warwick-street, Goldensquare, will be duly
> attended to.—None but principals will be treated
> with.

Stephen Williams wanted to be a director of the East
India Company. He put forward his claims in an advertise-
ment in the *Diary; or, Woodfall's Register,* February 15,
1790, addressed "To the Proprietors of East-India Stock."
He asked for election in the place of a lately deceased direc-
tor, Joseph Sparkes. Thomas Cheap wanted to be an East
India director, too, and advertised in a subsequent issue of the
Diary.

A cautious soldier thought the *Morning Herald* a better
medium for obtaining what he wanted. This appeared in the
Herald, December 16, 1789.

> An officer would be happy to meet with a Single
> Lady or Widow on honourable terms.
> No letters will be received but what are post paid
> with real name and place of abode.
> Direct to H. B. to be left at Mr. Dunn's, Hatter,
> Shug-lane, near the Haymarket.

A lady simply wanted money. She simply asked for it in the *Morning Chronicle and London Advertiser*, January 7, 1791

An Address to the Feeling Heart

A LADY of QUALITY, a WIDOW of an officer in the French service, is, for the immediate want of a few pounds, in the utmost Distress—The Truth of her critical situation may be known and the smallest sums thankfully received by Mr. de Mondezer, No. 13 Queen-street, Soho.

Another advertiser in the *Chronicle*, May 6, 1791, knew exactly what he wanted, exactly why he should have it, and how he and his family would feel if and when he got it.

To the Right Honourable the LORD MAYOR, the Worshipful COURT OF ALDERMEN, and the COMMON COUNCIL of the CITY of LONDON.

The Office of COMMON CRYER to the City of London having become vacant by the death of Mr. Bishop, I seize the earliest opportunity most fervently to entreat your votes and interest as a Candidate for that Office.

The situation of my family, consisting of a Wife and Nine children, induces me to offer myself on this occasion, to your countenance and support. I was born a Freeman of your City; have been upon the Livery of CLOTHWORKERS over twenty years; have served all Ward and Parish offices in St. Martin's Ludgate; and have been engaged in the business of Woolen Draper for more than twenty-three years, without an imputation, I trust, on the fairness of my character as a Trader, or my integrity as a man.

These circumstances, will, I flatter myself, now operate in my favor; and should my hopes, by your kindness, be eventually crowned with success, my gratitude will speak in the feelings of my happy family, and, on my part, by the most unremitted assiduities to the duties of the Office. I am,

My Lord and Gentlemen,
Your devoted humble Servant,
THOMAS JAMES LAWRENCE

No. 2 Cheapside
May 3, 1791

The advertising in the London papers of the day gives a colorful picture of the city's life. Advertisements for plays and books filled the front pages. *As You Like It* was playing at Drury Lane in 1790; *Richard The Third* at the Theatre Royal, Covent Garden. *The Beggars Opera* and *The Rivals* were both playing in 1790. Sadler's Wells was a daily advertiser. Ranelagh, "by the desire and patronage of the Prince of Wales," was putting on a magnificent display of fireworks and a masquerade for the "QUEEN'S BIRTH-DAY," May 21, 1791. In June, Vauxhall put on a comparable fete for "the birthday of HIS MAJESTY."

A justifiably irate gentleman advertised a reward of £150 for capture of the man who set fire to his house. A reward of five guineas was offered in the *Chronicle,* January 7, 1791, for the discovery of a coachman who had urged his horses and equipage past a disabled coach, knocking down and severely injuring the coachman of the stranded vehicle and stampeding its horses. Tontine insurance was offered by various coffeehouses. Money lenders were generous in offering "the nobility and gentry" loans on freeholds, leaseholds, jointures, and expectancies.

The *Morning Herald* was the popular want-ad medium. Its advertising columns were classified by "Want Places," "Sales by Auction," "To Be Sold," "To Be Lett." Cooks, upper servants, housemaids, teachers, coachmen, ladies' maids all offered their services in short advertisements, each with a three-line initial capital. Mr. Christie used the back page of the *Morning Post and Daily Advertiser* almost daily for long listings of estates, houses, furniture, plate, paintings, leaseholds, libraries, and other properties at sales to be held always "at his Great Room." Christie advertised daily in the *Post,* the *Times,* the *Oracle,* and other papers as well. He had discovered early the values of frequency, continuity, and diffusion in advertising.[3]

[3] In 1843 the *Edinburgh Review* described him as Christie "of hanging wood notoriety." He had described one charming old estate as having a "hanging wood." The surprised purchaser found this to be an old gallows. Another real estate auctioneer, George Robins, went one better than

A fight was called off, but another would go on, the fighter promised in the *Diary*, February 27, 1790.

> D. MENDOZA respectfully acquaints the public in general that he is extremely sorry to have disappointed them on Saturday last, in consequence of a severe indisposition, but that being now recovered, he means again to exhibit the Art of Boxing, THIS Day at the Lyceum in the Strand.

One suspects more than meets the eye here in an advertisement in the *Diary*, April 19, 1791. What fears prompted the advertiser to insert this notice?

> Several most scandalous and malicious reports having been circulated that PETER OWEN, a joiner, who was very lately in my service, had been so ill-treated at Mr. Holland's, that his life was in danger, I think it right to inform the public that such reports are totally false and groundless, the said PETER OWEN never having been in the least danger and being as well now as he ever was in his life.
>
> JOHN WEST
>
> April 16, 1791
> No. 5 Wood-street, Westminster

The *Times*, the *Oracle*, the *Morning Herald*, the *Diary*, the *Westminster Evening Herald*, the *World*, the *Public Advertiser*, the *Morning Post and Daily Advertiser*, virtually all the London newspapers, were crammed with advertising and heavy on patent medicines . . . Dr. Steele's Opodeloc (for chilblains) . . . Essence of Coltsfoot . . . The Alternative American Syrup, an absolute specific cure . . . Peppermint lozenges . . . cures for corns. Advertisers had discovered the virtues of the testimonial, the more awesome the names the better. For "Saintsbury's Chemical Fluid for the Obliteration of Marks of the Skin" testimonials were offered by The Right Honourable the Countess Dowager of Spencer, The Right Honour-

---

Christie. He confessed in his advertisement that there were two drawbacks to a choice property. These were "the litter of the rose leaves and the noise of the nightingales."

able the Countess Dowager of Jersey. The Right Honourable the Countess of Falmouth, The Right Honourable Viscount Grimster, and Mrs. Poyntz.

The newspapers vied with each other in competition for advertising. Publishers claimed virtues for their own paper which no other possessed. Daniel Stuart, co-proprietor of the *Morning Post* claimed toward the end of the period that his paper led both the *Times* and the *Herald* in arousing the attention of the public. He boasted of his success and explained it.

> Advertisements flowed in beyond bounds. I encouraged the small, miscellaneous advertisements in the front page, preferring them to any others, upon the rule that the more numerous the customers, the more independent and permanent the custom. . . . I interest numerous and varied readers looking out for employment, servants, sales, and purchasers, etc. Advertisements act and react. They attract readers, promote circulation, and circulation attracts advertisements.

Stuart's complacent remarks sound like publisher's promotion today. He was even, Stuart says, embarrassed by the amount of advertising thrust on him and by the demands for position. The booksellers crowded into the *Post* and each demanded that his "cloud of advertisements" be inserted at once on the front page. Unwilling to cut down on his profitable miscellaneous advertisements, Stuart did his best to satisfy their demands, then placed the overflow on his back page. Affronted, the booksellers began publication of their own papers, the *British Press* in the morning and the *Globe* in the evening.

In England there were no dailies outside London at this time, but Dublin had an active newspaper press in which advertising throve. It was in Dublin that Mathew Carey, later to become well known as a newspaper, magazine, and book publisher in the early United States, got into difficulties for his political sentiments, and in one issue of his radical newspaper broke all precedent by using a two-column spread on his front page to talk about advertising.

In the 1780's the front pages of *Saunder's News-Letter and Daily Advertiser*, of the *Dublin Morning Post*, and of the

Evening Chronicle were solid advertising, and generally the back pages too, with more inside. The *Dublin Journal* had no advertising on its front page, but pages three and four and part of page two were all advertising of linens for sale, lodgings, notices of benefits, annuity advertising, auctions, seeds, land for sale, and patent medicines. A section of T. T. Faulkner's *Dublin Journal* was given over to "Decrees," proclamations and orders issued from Dublin Castle "By the LORD LIEUTENANT and COUNCIL of IRELAND." One clever advertiser of patent medicine managed to get his product notice inserted into this section by heading it "By Authority." The advertisement, January 20, 1785, was for "Keyser's only ORIGINAL and GENUINE Pills that are universally allowed to be the only cure for a certain Disorder . . . N. B. The above pills may be had of all the Country Booksellers, but as there are Counterfeits now circulating, it is requested that such as stand in Need will be careful for their Health's sake."

The *Dublin Journal* bore a clean and modern look, for its real estate advertising was classified by counties: Monahan, Kildare, Dublin and Wicklow, Meath, Down, Langford, etc., offering sufficient evidence that the *Journal* had a sound circulation outside of Dublin itself.

On April 21, 1784, the *Evening Chronicle* had its usual array of front-page advertising for ladders, miniature painting, books, pamphlets, gun, ammunition, tea, and furniture. Buried on page three was a news item which said that certain men had refused to go bail for Mathew Carey, "the supposed printer of the *Volunteers Journal* when he was taken out of prison and brought up for hearing." The *Chronicle* railed at the proceedings and ended its item with: "The virtues of Ireland shall soon triumph over the enemies of liberty. There are FIFTEEN THOUSAND PATRIOTS armed in Ulster ready for the onset. The Province of CONNAUGHT is also in array, and in LEINSTER and MUNSTER the bands of Freedom will not be tardy."

Mathew Carey, at twenty, had published a seditious pamphlet "Letter to the Catholics of Ireland." His father shipped him to France to avoid prosecution. There he worked for almost a year in Benjamin Franklin's print shop in Passy. Returning to Ireland in 1783, he began publication in Dublin of the *Volunteers Journal; Or, Irish Herald.* Years later, a distinguished resident of Philadelphia, Carey called his Dublin newspaper "enthusiastic and violent." It was at least that. Under the *Volunteers'* logotype in large letters Carey ran this quotation: "When the Men of Ireland forget their destructive religious prejudices, and embrace each other with the warmth of genuine philanthropy, then, and not till then, will they eradicate the baneful English influence, and destroy the aristocratic tyrannies of the land . . . O'NIAL." The paper went on from there, and in 1784 Carey was arrested.

He was freed but was under indictment for libel while his militant, anti-English *Volunteers Journal* was soliciting and getting its share of advertising. It was in these circumstances that Mathew Carey spread his two-column "To the Public" across the front page of the *Journal* for April 7, 1784. In it he wrote:

A word or two to advertisers—The Dublin Circulation of the *Volunteers Journal,* though in its infancy, is much superior to many papers whose existence reckons as many years as the VOL. JOURNAL can weeks—In several parts of the kingdom there is a large correspondence already established; and such measures are pursuing, as can hardly fail to render this Paper in point of country circulation, as it is ALREADY ALLOWED TO BE, with respect to intrinsic merit, THE FIRST IN THE KINGDOM; the point to be considered by advertisers, being first, the *most extensive circulation,* and then *moderate terms,* it may be presumed they will find it peculiarly their interest to give a *Decided* Preference to the *Volunteers Journal.*

Local and national circulation, impact, economy—Mathew Carey in 1784 was using just about the same presentation, in much the same words, that press advertising media blazon in their full-page metropolitan newspaper advertising today. He spoke the same arguments that salesmen of advertising space use in confronting advertisers and the media buyers in the modern advertising agency.

Again, there is little essential difference between the advertising of 1759, when Dr. Johnson indited his opinions about advertising, the advertising of 1874, when Henry Sampson agreed with him, and advertising of the present. Surface differences lie in the more numerous and complex advertising vehicles and in the broader markets the advertiser attempts to exploit. The advertising Dr. Johnson knew in the eighteenth century and that Henry Sampson examined in the nineteenth was primarily local. It was not designed, as so much of major advertising has been designed since the closing years of the nineteenth century, to make whole countries and continents perform as the advertiser wishes.

It took an industrial revolution and the development of national advertising media to make this expansion possible and economically necessary. Advertising has mass production to support, instead of the output, sold in a single shop, of one artisan or an artisan and his family and perhaps an apprentice or two. Advertising uses mass magazines, radio, television, sky writing, and all the rest, as well as scores of newspapers and the newspaper supplements. The print is larger, the noise is louder, the spectaculars are more spectacular, but the advertising message is essentially the same. The large promises are larger and more pretentious, but they are still the soul of the advertising messages. The advertiser still speaks well of himself and as ill as he dares of his competitors. The appeal is still both *"Buy* my lavender!" and "Buy *my* lavender!"—or soap, cigarettes, automobiles, corporate philosophy, economic beliefs, Presidential candidate, chewing gum, concept of charity, education, or racial and religious tolerance.

Not only were advertising and advertising promotion thoroughly established and, to a degree, set in modern patterns by the end of the eighteenth century, but in both Great Britain and the United States, the newspaper press, then the only general means of public communication, had established itself as an advertising medium. What magazines there were carried no advertising, or little of any account, and were not to run advertising for another half century. Magazines did not become major advertising media until the late years of the nineteenth century. Advertising supported the newspapers, making them profitable, thus possible. Publishers got little of their support from subscribers. They were continually dunning readers for payment. In the United States even the postriders who delivered the newspapers had to run notices begging or threatening subscribers who were in arrears to them for copies received.

As already indicated, there was newspaper advertising in America almost from the very beginning. The *Boston News-Letter*, the first Colonial paper (except for *Publick Occurrences*, only one issue of which was published, September 25, 1690) carried advertisements from the year of its founding in 1704.[4] Franklin capitalized on advertising as Bradford had tried to do. Well before 1800 most English and American newspapers were not only supported by advertising but they were, even primarily, vehicles for the dissemination of advertising.

The front pages of almost all the four-page Boston, New York, and Philadelphia newspapers were generally solid advertising, and the back page as well, often with two or three columns of additional advertisements on page three. In the 1780's the *Pennsylvania Packet, or The General Advertiser* had only one and one-half pages of editorial matter; all the rest was varied advertising.[5] In the 1790's *Dunlap and Claypoole's American Daily Advertiser* in Philadelphia was a busy commercial journal with five columns of advertising across the front page and only enough editorial text, mostly reprints, to hold the paper together. In New York, the *New York Daily Advertiser*, started by Francis Childs in 1785 in imitation of Dunlap's Philadelphia success, was doing just as well. The *American Apollo*, Boston, which, June 5, 1794, carried an advertisement by a Samuel Adams of building materials for sale, was crammed with advertising. The *Providence Gazette* was mostly advertising on page one, completely ad-

---

[4] Unaccountably, Isaiah Thomas, in his invaluable *History of Printing in America*, 1810, says that in this country as in Europe there were few advertisements in the first newspapers.

[5] In 1788, Stephen Girard, later merchant, financier, and philanthropist, was using the *Packet* to advertise his Brandy, Malaga Wine, Frontignac, Hermitage, and other liquors.

vertising on page three. Philadelphia's *General Advertiser* in 1794 spilled over with advertising.

The *Democratic Press* in Philadelphia, then the social and commercial metropolis of the country, was filled with advertising around the turn of the century, as was the Philadelphia *Mercantile Advertiser* and the *Aurora for the Country*. A good three-quarters of the oversize *Political and Commercial Register* was advertising. The *Independent Chronicle and The Commercial Advertiser* of Boston was rich in advertising. The *Gazette of the United States* and *Daily Evening Advertiser* carried its full share. The *Maryland Journal* ran more advertising than editorial matter.

Then, as often now, as much of the news of immediate and compelling interest was in the advertisements as in the editorial text of the daily press.

6

New York, Philadelphia, and New England— American Newspapers After 1800

BENJAMIN FRANKLIN, in his *Autobiography*, said that there were only two newspapers in the American colonies in 1721. By 1771, according to Franklin, there were at least 25. Actually, there were 31, for a population of 2,205,000. There were 37 newspapers when the Revolution began.[1] By the end of the war there were 43. By 1790 there were 106 newspapers; and in 1800, 260 newspapers for some 5,308,000 people in the United States. By 1820, when the population of the country had risen to 9,638,000, there were 532 papers, and already over a thousand newspapers had been born and died.[2]

Practically all these newspapers were weeklies, with three or four columns of news, some other editorial content, and most of the remaining space filled with advertising. The first daily newspaper was the *Pennsylvania Packet*; the second, the *New York Daily Advertiser*. There were 27 dailies

[1] One of these, the *Evening Post* of Philadelphia was the first to publish the Declaration of Independence, July 6, 1776. Other papers copied from the *Post*.

[2] Harry B. Weiss, "A Graphic Summary of the Growth of Newspapers in New York and Other States, 1704-1820," *Bulletin of the New York Public Library*, Vol. 52, No. 4, April, 1948.

in 1810. Philadelphia and New York were the newspaper publishing centers, New York passing Philadelphia in number of newspapers in 1800 as it began to pass Philadelphia in population and commercial importance.

Isaiah Thomas, who knew of only 150 newspapers in 1800 but counted 360 when he was writing in 1810, said there were then more newspapers published in the United States than in the United Kingdom of Great Britain and Ireland.[3]

From 1800 to roughly the mid-century, advertising in these newspapers reflected war and the pursuits of peace, the changing life of the new country, the growing commercialism. Newspaper advertising grew in volume and insistence. Patent medicine advertisements increased in number and in the exaggeration of their claims. With the advertising increase, in particular the mounting number and transparent fraudulence of the nostrum advertisements, rose public protest which forced many editors and publishers into explanation and defense of their advertising policies. The period saw greater use of crude illustration and advertising display, and the first advertising of several present-day national advertisers appeared. Settlers were pushing into the West, and advertising moved with them. Some of the changes can be seen through an examination of Thomas' own famous newspaper.

Isaiah Thomas was printer, publisher, and editor of a newspaper which, though interrupted for several years during the Revolution, lasted from 1770 to 1904. The printer, whom Franklin called "The Baskerville of America," began publication of the *Massachusetts Spy* in Boston but, a Son of Liberty who rode with Paul Revere, fled the city with his press when Boston was occupied by the British. After an interval in Salem, he re-established his paper in Worcester in 1778 as the *Massachusetts Spy, or Worcester Gazette*. While publishing the *Spy*, Thomas founded and edited two im-

3 Isaiah Thomas, LL.D., *The History of Printing in America with a Biography of Printers and an Account of Newspapers*. (2d ed., 2 vols.; Albany, New York: Joel Munsell, Printer, 1874).

portant early American magazines, the *Royal American Magazine*, which ran for only two years, 1786–88, and later, for seven years, the *Massachusetts Magazine*, and he became the leading book publisher of the United States, issuing some four hundred titles and printing tens of thousands of children's books, including the first American edition of *Mother Goose's Melody*.

His advertising policy in the *Spy* was conservative, and he did not approve of some of the pretentious innovations he saw in other papers. In *The History of Printing* he points out that advertisements were not separated from the editorial matter by lines in the earliest papers, and were not even begun with a two-line letter.

> . . . when the two line letters were introduced, it was some time before one advertisement was separated from another by a line or rule . . . After it became usual to separate advertisements, some printers used lines or metal rules; others lines of flowers irregularly placed. I have seen in some New York papers great primer flowers between advertisements. At length it became customary to "set off" advertisements, and for using types not larger than those with which the news were printed, types of the size of French canon have often been used for names, especially of those who advertised English goods.[4]

Thomas's *Spy*, beautifully printed on a large-size four-page fold, carried no advertising at all on the front page, which was all news and essays. Page two was devoted to editorial matter. There were usually a few advertisements on page three, and page four was completely given over to advertising.

Every column of the *Spy* for Wednesday, January 1, 1800, was bordered in black. The lead news column on the front page, with heading in Old English black face type read: "On Saturday the 14th Instant died suddenly at his SEAT in VIRGINIA *The Illustrious* Gen. George Washington." Isaiah Thomas had revered Washington. January 8, 1800 he issued an extra, again with black borders about each column,

[4] *Ibid.,* p. 10.

filled with eulogies. Among the advertisements in this issue
was one which read:

MASONIC NOTICE

The several LODGES of the Ancient Fraternity of
Free and Accepted Masons and the Brethren at
large, in this County, are invited and affectionately
requested to attend the funeral ceremonies at Oxford, on the 15th instant, to be performed in consequence of the Death of our worthy and illustrious
brother

GEORGE WASHINGTON

Isaiah Thomas was master of the Grand Lodge of Massachusetts.

Advertisements in the *Spy* were brief, brisk, and modest.
They were for books, dry goods, real estate, sundries, but
not, in 1800, for patent medicines. There were many for
rags for the growing paper industry, for apprentices, press-
men, and other skilled labor. Thomas was running his own
advertising, at this time for his newly published *Young Ladies
and Gentlemen's Spelling Book*. Advertisements not exceeding twelve lines were run in the *Spy* for three weeks for one
dollar and continued three weeks longer for fifty cents. Perhaps Thomas discounted this one which Abraham White,
Postrider from Worcester to Northampton, ran for weeks.
Mr. White "informs his customers that he is in great want of
CASH, and hopes that all those who are indebted to him for
the MASSACHUSETTS SPY, for the last year, will make an immediate settlement."

Thomas turned over management of the *Spy* to his son in
1802, but for years no basic changes were apparent in the
appearance or evident policies of the paper. Neither was
there any change in the difficulties of the postriders. In 1811
there was this advertisement.

Money!

IMPERIOUS necessity obliges the Subscriber to
call on all persons indebted to him for newspapers to make payment on or before the fifth
of April next without fail.   Jonathan Peirce

Another man, who had quit postriding in disgust was running
"Positively the Last Notice!"

The *Spy* had more advertising by 1811, but there was
still none on the front page. There was still continual advertising for books published by Thomas, and a few patent
medicine advertisements had begun to appear. By 1830, the
Spy had gone to a larger size sheet, much smaller type, and
in many issues half the front page was in miscellaneous advertisements studded with small cuts. The *Spy* had given in to
the customs of the times. Most colonial and early American
newspapers were well and legibly printed on good paper.
The discovery of ways to make bad newsprint had not yet
been made, and the papers were printed by men proud of
their craft. By the 1830's and through the middle years of
the nineteenth century, the newspapers even in New York
and Philadelphia had gone into small type, very difficult to
read, and composition that completely lacked the cleanness
of earlier typographic production. The changed appearance
of the *Spy* in the 1830's was matched by the changes on the
front page. Featured there now were Tyler's Remedy for
the Piles, and Byanis Celebrated Genuine Physical Drops. Advertised under a large head with reverse lettering on the back
page was "Embrocation; or, Whitwell's Original Opodeldoc."
Albion Corn Plaster and Dr. Reefe's Pills for Debilitated
Females had large space on page four.

Where the advertising in the *Spy* was conservative in the
first years of the nineteenth century, that in many other
newspapers was not. In Philadelphia all through the first
quarter of the century the front page of *Poulson's American
Daily Advertiser* was solid advertising. Many advertisements
were mundane and prosaic, but occasionally one was lyrical.
An artist who advertised in 1801, with all the rhapsodic elo-

quence achieved by modern copywriters addressing themselves
to women, stated his terms with discretion and delicacy.

To the Ladies

Ladies,

As it is under the warmth and effulgent rays of your power-
fully creative influence that all the arts, and especially the
FINE ARTS, have received their birth and acquired their
present degree of perfection, it is reasonable to expect that
considering them as your darling offsprings, you will continue to feel for them that tenderness and interest without
which they must certainly die away; they have a natural
and undisputable claim to your immediate protection; and
among them that of MINIATURE PAINTING being intirely
[sic] devoted to you, has an exclusive right to your foster-
ing solicitude. . . .

   . . . his price is moderate, and he waives it occasionally on
particular considerations.

Your very humble and obedient
Servant
THE PAINTER

At least three-quarters of the *Political and Commercial
Register* of Philadelphia, printed on sheets larger than those
of a modern newspaper, consisted of advertising in 1804.
Many advertisements were mere notices, and there were no
patent medicines, but five years later they overran the sheet.
Dr. Robertson dominated the back pages, June 5, 1809, with
columns broken by reverse lettering in script against black
blocks. Almost a column in small type listed remarkable
cures by his panaceas. Names were listed of people who had
been cured of colds, dysentery, flux, influenza, "deep decline,"
asthma, and consumption. Mrs. Brown was cured of a pain
in her stomach; Mrs. Wild of a pain in her breast; Mr.
Thomas W. Oliver "of a nervous complaint occasioned by a
long residence in the West Indies;" Capt. Walker of "a deplorable debility;" Mrs. Ripley's son of worms; others, of
gout, rheumatism, or any other disease the advertiser could
spell.

Another Philadelphia paper, *Aurora for the Country*, carried advertising which gave its pages the kind of local color in which the antiquarian delights. It was evidently a sheet of sound local circulation. Among the advertisements in 1804 for books, plays, and dry goods, were always the orders of the Washington Blues and notices of the meetings of various lodges and societies. One which seemed strangely out of place in Philadelphia were notices of the meetings of the Tammany Society, or Columbian Order at their great Wigwam, sign of Columbus.

A small history of at least one aspect of the War of 1812 was given in three advertisements on the front page of a New England paper. The first of these advertisements, prominently displayed in the *American Mercury* of Hartford, September 20, 1814, was this one.

124

Dollars BOUNTY

Fifty paid on Enlistment, Fifty as soon as mustered for service, Twenty-four when honourably discharged, and ONE HUNDRED AND SIXTY ACRES OF LAND—and NINETY-SIX Dollars per year, sixteen paid at the end of every two months.

> 1 Coat
> 1 Vest
> 4 Pairs Pantaloons
> 4 Shirts
> 4 Pair Stockings
> 1 Cap and Stock and Blanket

Will be given yearly to every robust Man between 16 and 46 years of age, who will enroll himself in the 25th U. States Infantry during the present war or five years, any young Gentleman who wishes to distinguish himself in the honourable service of his country and avenge its wrongs, can have an opportunity by calling on the Subscribers, near the Little Bridge in Hartford Con. where a Rendevous is now open.

> John G. Munn, 1st Lieut.
> 25th U. S. Infantry

The second advertisement offered more elegant equipage to a different social and military class.

MILITARY GOODS

Silver, gilt, and plated swords; Silver plated and gilt Epaulets, Silk and Worsted Sashes; word Knotts; Red, White, and black Plumes; silver vellum Lace, Prussian Binding; Gold, silver, plated and worsted Cord; Priming Wires and Brushes, etc.

There was less gold lace, martial music and glory in the third advertisement. The sailor, perhaps, had gone back to sea.

FIFTY DOLLARS

REWARD

Deserted from the Rendezvous in Kent on the Ist. inst. WILLIAM EVEN, a soldier in the 37th Regt. U. S. Infantry— born in Famington, County of Hartford, State of Connecticut, aged 30 years, 5 feet, 3 1-2 inches high, grey [sic] eyes, gray [sic] hair, the hair on the top of his head very thin and very white, and by profession a seaman. He had on when he went away a butnut [sic] colored coat, and blue striped trousers. Whoever will apprehend said deserter and return him to the rendezvous in Kent or secure him at any military post in the U. S. shall receive fifty dollars.

EBENEZER FISK
Lieut. 37th Regt. U. S. Inf.

If there were such stories of the War of 1812 in American newspaper advertising, there were tragic reminders of the larger conflicts in Europe advertised in the British press. Among the front page advertisements for books, silks, razor strops, and Tunbridge Wells in *The Courier*, London, April 2, 1812, was this plea.

Lloyd's, March 28, 1812

SUBSCRIPTION for the RELIEF of the WIDOWS and
FAMILIES of the OFFICERS and MEN lately lost
in his Majesty's Ships

> ST. GEORGE, of 98 guns
> HERO, of 74 guns,
> DEFENCE, of 74 guns,
> SALDHANA, of 36 guns,
> FANCY, of 12 guns

The Committee chosen for the Management of
this Subscription, in order to make known the extraordinary claims and magnitude of the calamity
requiring relief, beg to state, that the number of
lives lost in the above-mentioned Ships, amounts to
upwards of 2300, and much exceed the number of
those in either of the Great Battles of the Nile,
Copenhagen, or Trafalgar.

A long list followed of those who had already subscribed,
together with the amounts donated. The officers and crews
of scores of naval ships, dozens of nobleman, and the Rev.
Richard Raikes, Gloucester, had come forward. So had the
Bank of Ireland, The Corporation of the City of London, the
Emmanuel College Combination Room, the Order of the
Friendly Brothers of St. Patrick, the Forum of Edinburgh,
and "the proceeds of a play performed at Rye." When calamity calls forth charity, this formal type of advertisement still
appears in England.

The *Providence Gazette* in the first decade of the nineteenth century was mostly advertising on page one, all advertising on page four. In 1805 there seemed more than usual
of the many notices inserted by indignant husbands that they
would pay no more bills contracted by erring wives, and one
advertisement that ran for many issues, indicating either that
the advertiser had got what he wanted or was letting his advertisement run in order to extract his full money's worth
from it, was: "Wanted, two or three families with children,

Males or Females from 7 to 18 Years of Age, to whom constant Employment will be given."

In Philadelphia by 1818, Zachary Poulson's *American Daily Advertiser* had a much more ornate logotype, and the advertising showed greater variety and use of illustration. Woodcuts of smudged craft under way embellished ship advertising, a post chaise for a coach line showed a coach and four, driver on his seat, whip snaking out over the horses. Cuts of houses were used in the real estate columns. All advertising was still in single columns but some bore 24-point heads. A corkscrew and bottle illustration was used in an advertisement for porter, and one hauler advertising his services ran a cut of a loaded dray with a man, presumably himself, mounted on one horse of his team.

In 1821 there was a dashing cut used in the advertising of the Philadelphia to Reading mail stage. May 26, 1824, a blurred woodcut of a full-grown African lion and another cut of a female elephant, somewhat smaller, were used in the advertising of an exhibition. The first page of the *Daily Advertiser* was further enlivened with pictures in the advertising of men's hats and women's bonnets, shoes, ships, and an open book. There were heavy type and ornaments used in the advertising of various lotteries. On the back page was another innovation. Among all the more staid advertisements there was a shout, in large type of "Look Here—Bargains!" The other Philadelphia daily newspapers, too, were beginning to use cuts and display type in their advertising.

A consistent user of newspaper space in Philadelphia was the same Mathew Carey who had published the *Volunteers Journal* in Dublin. Dressed as a woman, Carey had fled from Ireland to the United States, landing in Philadelphia in the autumn of 1784. On January 25, 1785, with four hundred dollars borrowed from LaFayette, who was then visiting in Virginia, he started *Carey's Pennsylvania Evening Herald*. His anti-Federalist newspaper was quickly a success, due largely to his shorthand reporting of the speeches of delegates in the Pennsylvania Assembly—enough of a success so that he was forced to fight a duel (which Carey won) with Col. Eleazar Oswald, editor and publisher of the Federalist *Inde-*

pendent Gazeteer. Like Isaiah Thomas in Worcester, Carey founded two magazines, first the short-lived monthly *Columbian,* and then, in 1787, *The American Museum,* which lasted for thirteen years. Again like Thomas, he became a book publisher, and his book press in Philadelphia rivaled that of Thomas in New England. Carey reprinted Scott's Waverley novels as they came out and hired a large force of book agents to peddle his wares in what was then the West. Chief of these agents was Parson Weems, famed as the early biographer of Washington.

Carey believed what he had written about advertising in Dublin. He plied the influential Philadelphia newspapers with advertising of his books, scattering his advertising in different positions in the paper. One issue of the *Democratic Press* in 1808 carried long advertisements for Carey as bookseller and publisher in three different places.

Lotteries were a staple in the advertising of the day. Cities, states, churches, and the national government all ran lottery advertisements. In the *National Intelligencer,* Washington, in 1829, John F. Webb, Stock Broker, Washington City, was advertising drawings of the Grand Consolidated Lottery, the Union Canal Lottery, No. 10, and the Washington City Lottery, No. 14. First prize in the last was $10,000.

In Boston by 1821 there was quite modern looking display advertising in the *Boston Intelligencer and Evening Gazette* which claimed an encompassing devotion to "News —Commerce—Agriculture—Manufacturing—Literature— Piety—Arts & Sciences—etc., etc." There were double-column advertisements, another departure, for wines and liquors and for furniture; and in a paper obviously largely meant to appeal to women readers and consumers, a plenitude of patent medicine and cosmetic advertising. The paper, as domestic and genteel as the *Transcript* was to become in later years, had columns of advertising for "Rowland's Alsana Extract, or, the Abyssinian Botanical Specific," "Essence of Tyre for changing Red or Grey Hair, Whiskers, or Eyebrows to most brown or black," and a Genuine Macassar Oil "for promoting the growth of Hair, restoring it in bald places, etc." Feminine readers were titillated with further advertising for

Canton silks, parasols, preserves, mandarin oranges, young
ladies' school books, strained oil for family use, Leghorn
straws and bonnets, sheetings, dining ware, Indian Muslins,
mantles, and dresses.

The Saturday Evening Post in that day boasted "circulation through Pennsylvania and all the other States of the
Union, rising 7,000 papers every publication." The *Post*,
which advertised its own job printing services, illustrating
its advertisements with a cut of a hand press, was heavy
with patent medicine advertising, but in one issue had something even more spectacular to present. This, illustrated by
a large cut, was "The Greatest Natural Living CURIOSITY
Ever Exhibited in America. The *Unicorn* or One-Horned
RHINOCEROS."

Already there was some advertising by companies whose
names and products, nationally distributed for many years,
are familiar in the mid-twentieth century. As early as 1789
Peter and George Lorillard were advertising their snuff and
tobacco in the *New York Daily Advertiser*. Pierre Lorillard
had opened his tobacco manufactory in 1760 at Chatham
Street near Tyron Row where he made both pipe tobacco and
snuff from puddings of cured leaves from Virginia. After his
sons entered the business, the Lorillards built a new snuff and
tobacco mill on a gorge of the Bronx River in the Westchester
woods, growing their own roses to perfume the snuff. The
Lorillard mill, a fieldstone structure of 1800 which replaced
the original wooden building, still stands in what is now the
New York Botanical Garden. The Lorillards advertised
continuously, both their "segars, pigtail, and plug tobacco"
and their "macaboy, rappee, Strasburgh, and Curracao" snuffs
—even, about 1790 another mill site on part of the Bronx
estate. By 1830 they had seized on another advertising idea.
They printed broadsides listing wholesale prices of all their
snuffs and tobaccos and sent them to all the postmasters in the
United States.

In 1801 an advertisement appeared in Worcester which
announced the planned erection of a paper mill in Dalton,
Massachusetts, and pled for support of a native American
industry.

One of the three signers of this advertisement was Zenas Crane. Crane & Company, Inc., makers of fine papers, have been consistent advertisers ever since, running full schedules in a selective list of national magazines. Since 1879, with the exception of two years during which another firm received a small part of the contract, Crane & Co. has made at its "Government Mill" in Dalton all the paper used for currency by the United States Treasury, paper for Treasury bonds, and currency paper for about twenty foreign countries, most of them in South America.

By January 1817, William Colgate & Company, which operated a soap and candle manufactory in New York, was advertising that it had "for sale on the best terms a constant supply of Soap, Mould and Dipt Candles of the first quality." A. T. Stewart, who became New York's first merchant prince and one of the first to conceive of and operate a department store, was advertising in the *New York Enquirer* in 1828.

Even before the advent of the penny newspapers, the New York dailies had become strong advertising media. When in 1829 the *New York Enquirer* was combined with the *Morning Courier*, the *Courier & Enquirer* was compelled to issue a two-page supplement on some days and on Saturdays a four-page supplement to accommodate all their advertisers. Fifty out of the 56 columns in the Saturday supplement were given over to advertising. Five out of New York's eight morning papers were exclusively commercial in content.[5]

The literary *New York Evening Post*, founded in 1801 as a Federalist organ which boasted Joseph Rodman Drake and Fitz-Green Halleck as early contributors and was edited for almost fifty years by William Cullen Bryant, stated flatly in its issue for December 1, 1803, the importance which advertising had to the newspaper publisher," . . . It is the advertiser who provides the paper for the subscriber. It is not to be disputed, that the publisher of a newspaper in this country, without a very exhaustive advertising support, receives a less reward for his labour than the humblest mechanic."

[5] William Grosvenor Bleyer, *Main Currents in the History of American Journalism* (Boston: Houghton Mifflin Co., 1927), p. 146.

The sentiments expressed by the *Post* were emphasized in other newspapers. In 1824 Samuel Bowles founded in Springfield, Massachusetts, what became perhaps the best American newspaper published outside New York, Philadelphia or Boston. Honest, unbiased, politically independent, the *Springfield Republican* became a daily in 1844 and achieved national reputation and influence under Samuel Bowles II. Benjamin H. Day, who founded the New York *Sun* in 1833, had worked on the *Republican*. Josiah Gilbert Holland, founding editor of *Scribner's Monthly* in 1870, spent years as a *Republican* editor. The *Republican* was the only publication to print any of Emily Dickinson's verse while she was still alive. The *Springfield Republican* was only two years old when, November 1, 1826, Samuel Bowles ran this piece as a reprint from the *Providence Journal*. Note the head he placed on the story.

> *Advantage of Advertising*—In November last, Mr. Caleb Raffe lost a valuable diamond (such as is used by glaziers for cutting glass) and advertised the same in the *Journal*, offering a reward to the person who should return it. Several months had elapsed and he gave it up for lost, but a short time since a man from the country called on him to know if he had lost a diamond, and on presenting the same to him, related the circumstance of his finding it, & the manner he discovered the name of the owner, several months after he had found it, by purchasing an article at a store in this town done up in a part of the Journal containing Mr. Raffe's advertisement, which was discovered by his children in perusing it, after it was taken from the article purchased.

Samuel Bowles obviously picked up the *Journal* story and reprinted it as a bit of useful promotion and a reminder to advertisers and potential advertisers in the *Springfield Republican* of the value of his paper. A few years later he ran an editorial which was much more specific.

Seemingly, adverse criticism of advertising began with advertising itself. In London in 1729 coffeehouse proprietors were already complaining that there was too much advertising in the papers and that publishers were making too much money from advertising. One hundred years later American newspaper readers were complaining too, especially about the patent medicine advertising that the newspapers carried in such volume.

Samuel Bowles went at it like a man who intended to dispose of a troublesome problem once and for all. He did not, but he made a forthright and sensible attempt, ending on a note of tart Yankee humor, in the *Republican,* September 14, 1831.

Advertising—We frequently hear complaints from our subscribers that they do not want to see the paper occupied so much with advertisements and especially with disgusting nostrums, promising to cure every evil that "flesh is heir to"—Now we confess we do not like the sight of these nostrums any better than the most fastidious of our readers and have perhaps as little confidence in their efficacy. But we ask the professional man if everything he is obliged to do in the way of his profession, is agreeable to his own feelings, and whether were it not for the means of support, he would do and say many things he does now? We ask the farmer if he does not cultivate and bring to market those things which will best advance his interest, whether they are wanted in his own family or not? He does not ask himself which is the most agreeable crop to cultivate, but which is the most profitable. We ask the mechanic if every job he is employed upon, and from which he derives his means of support, is executed according to his own taste, and views of necessity and propriety? And then we ask why we are found fault with for taking all the advertisements we can get, when *too, the very existance* [sic] *of the paper depends upon this advertising patronage.* There is not a newspaper in the country which would be published a single month, at the present low prices, without its advertising patronage. The same may be said of hundreds in the country. It is in consequence of advertising patronage, more than from any other fact, that newspapers are so numerous, and so freely and widely diffused. If our readers will agree to give us three dollars instead of two a year for their paper, we will agree to give them one free from advertisements. The quantity of reading matter we now afford, independent of advertisements (which no one is obliged to read) is greater for the money, than is afforded in any book or periodical, except newspaper. This may be said of newspapers generally. To conclude, this craving for more reading matter in a cheap newspaper, reminds us of the group of boys around a butcher, all calling for beef's liver, when one seeing he was not likely to get a slice, says, "Mr. can't you kill an ox next time that's all liver?"

Bowles made one very practical point in his sensible editorial that is reminiscent of Benjamin Franklin's *Apology for
Printers* a hundred years before. The cheaper newspapers
ran more patent medicine advertising than the earlier more
expensive papers because they needed the additional income
for their support. The penny newspapers, the first of which
appeared in New York in 1833, also appealed to a wider, less
educated reading public than the earlier sixpenny papers.
The *Journal of Commerce*, established in New York in 1827,
might be able to exclude advertisements of theatres, lotteries,
and "business to be transacted on the Sabbath" from its columns, but many segments of the popular press could not
afford the moral luxury.

Twenty-three-year-old Benjamin H. Day, who had learned
his trade on the *Springfield Republican*, was a job printer in
New York when he began publication of the paper that under
Moses Y. Beach and later C. A. Dana was to become and remain for many years the best-written and most colorful
newspaper in New York, the "newspaperman's newspaper."
Even in the five years it was under Day's control, the New
York *Sun* took on some of its characteristics in featuring
human interest stories and local news. It also took all the
patent medicine advertising it could get, all the advertising
of any kind it could get, as did the other penny papers soon
started, the *Transcript*, 1834, and the long sensational *New
York Herald* with which James Gordon Bennett hit the
streets in 1835.[6]

Day not only got all the advertising of whatever kind
he could into the *Sun*, but he established a policy which
Bennett adopted and which became standard newspaper practice where, mostly in the larger cities, the publishers could

[6] One eager publisher of another of the penny papers quickly established
when the success of the *Sun, Transcript,* and *Herald* was apparent was too
far in advance of his time. William Newell established the *Ladies' Morning
Star* as a penny paper for women, a "moral daily paper." New York
merchants saw no profit in a paper addressed exclusively to women and
failed to patronize it. Newell could attract neither advertisers nor circulation, and his paper, despite change of name to merely the *Morning Star*,
quickly failed.

enforce it. He would publish no advertising, except that contracted for on a yearly basis, that was not paid for in advance.

The *Herald*, which was to become notorious in the latter half of the nineteenth century for its advertising, particularly its "personals," was early under attack for the quantity and quality of its patent medicine advertising. Bennett, as was to be expected, showed none of the restraint of Samuel Bowles in answering his critics. The following diatribe was directed against a broker who had rashly aired his complaints. Dr. Brandeth was a famous or infamous advertiser of his pills. It was Brandeth's advertising to which the broker had taken exception. "Send us more advertisements than Dr. Brandeth," Bennett retorted in the *Herald* in the summer of 1836, "—give us higher prices—we'll cut Dr. Brandeth dead. Business is business—money is money—and Dr. Brandeth is no more to us than Mr. 'Money Broker!' If he does not like this proposition, he may cut and run. We permit no blockheads to interfere with our business."

Though more readers objected, Bennett continued to run the advertisements for Brandeth's Pills. Then he had a disagreement with Brandeth, as later he was to have a more famous row with P. T. Barnum. He threw the Brandeth advertising out of the *Herald* and, March 25, 1837, wrote, "Our purpose is to warn the public throughout the whole country from being any longer deceived and cheated by the quackeries of this most impudent charlatan Brandeth." Four days later the *Herald* emphasized the point, ". . . without a doubt Brandeth is the most superlative quack that ever appeared in the world." Bennett's wrath did Dr. Brandeth little damage. His pills were still being advertised when the *Herald* disappeared in 1924 through merger with the *New York Tribune*.

While Bennett was exploding in New York, the publisher of a Boston newspaper had an idea which was more than a hundred years in advance of his time. The *Boston Daily Times* had the effrontery to suggest that political parties use paid advertising space to air their ideas. The *Times*, October

22, 1838, proposed that "if either or both parties wish to obtain the use of our advertising columns in order to disseminate their political doctrines or dogmas, they can have them by paying the customary fee." When shocked readers rebuked the newspaper, the editor defended the idea. "We advertise for individuals and associations of every kind, and why not a political party?"

Bennett soon had a much more formidable opponent than Dr. Brandeth. In 1841, Horace Greeley founded his *New-York Tribune*, destined to become one of the great and influential penny newspapers of New York. Greeley, a Whig who became a Free Soiler, then a Republican, briefly a member of Congress and finally a Presidential candidate, fought hard for labor, the protective tariff, and other reforms. On the break-up of Brook Farm, the Transcendentalist community in which he was sympathetically interested, he hired Charles A. Dana, whom he used as foreign correspondent, then for many years as managing editor, Margaret Fuller to do book reviews, and later George Ripley. One of his *Tribune* staff was Henry J. Raymond who ten years later founded *The New York Times*. Eccentric, difficult, forceful, capable of loosing just as much shrill abuse as the next newspaper editor in those years of political journalism, Greeley lost no time at all in attacking editorially the unsavory advertising in both Bennett's *Herald* and Beach's *Sun*. In April, 1841, he railed at both for accepting the advertising of a notorious woman abortionist. Soon he had to defend advertising of his own in the *Tribune*.

December 20, 1841, Greeley wrote: "A friend writes us to complain of the ingenuity of our advertisers in writing commendations of their medicines. He should complain to our advertisers themselves, who are not responsible to us for the style or language (if decent) of their advertisements, nor have we any control over them." Like the other penny papers, the *Tribune* depended on advertising.

The *Tribune*, the *Herald*, and the *Sun* were read by the burgeoning population of what had become an exciting and busy metropolis. Washington Irving, America's first man of letters, had spent much of his life abroad as writer and minister to England and Spain. He returned to the United States in 1846 and a city he hardly recognized. New York, he wrote his sister, was now one of the most racketing cities in the world. It was like Frankfort on fair day, only in New York every day was fair day.

Changes and excitement were manifest everywhere in the country. "Manifest Destiny" was the phrase. John L. Sullivan had used it first in the United States News and Democratic Review in an editorial of 1845: ". . . our manifest destiny to overspread the continent allotted by Providence for the free development of our yearly multiplying millions." Polk gave the phrase practical meaning in the Mexican War which started in 1846. Bryant upheld the idea and the effort in the *Post;* Greeley thundered against it in the *Tribune.* The industrial north with factories springing up everywhere was largely against it, the agrarian south almost wholly for it. The abolitionists and anti-slavery men were violently opposed. They saw the war merely as another attempt to expand slave territory. James Russell Lowell satirized it in the first series of the *Bigelow Papers* which were being published in the *Boston Courier* and the *Anti-Slavery Standard.*

General Zachary Taylor met and defeated the Mexican Santa Anna at the battle of Buena Vista. One of the great and most spectacular of all advertisers seized his opportunity. In the *Tribune* and other New York papers, P. T. Barnum was soon advertising another compelling attraction at his American Museum on Broadway—Santa Anna's wooden leg, taken, so he claimed, by the American army in Mexico.

By 1847 Europe was aflame with revolutions which Charles A. Dana was there reporting for Greeley. More millions of immigrants, Germans, and Irish starved out by the potato famines, were pouring into New York. Five million immigrants entered the north between 1820 and 1860. Thousands were landing in New York every month. Whether its critics liked it or not, Manifest Destiny was on. Texas had been made a state in 1845. The Mexican Cession after the war gave the country the territories of Utah, Arizona, and New Mexico. The seizure of California was confirmed. Brigham Young and his twelve thousand followers, harried from place to place, reached Salt Lake in 1846. New Yorker, Philip Hone, traveling west in 1847 exclaimed over Chicago, calling it "the wonder city of the Western World." Cincinnati too was fast becoming a metropolis, though neither of the western cities could rival Boston, New York, Philadelphia, Baltimore, or New Orleans; and the important cities of the east were already joined by magnetic telegraph. The country was growing with undreamed of rapidity. "Manifest Destiny"—but what the United States really needed, said Walt Whitman, editor of the Brooklyn *Eagle*, was more theatres and better plays. What is *really* needed, Henry Thoreau was writing in Concord, was less growth, less industrialism, less interference with the individual, and more civil disobedience. "Some say that government is best which governs least. I say that government is best which governs not at all," was the way he began.

General Taylor, hero of the Mexican War, was elected President. Enthusiasm at the Whig Convention in the Chinese Museum in Philadelphia where he was nominated was so great that one politician exclaimed the party could elect Old Zach President and his charger, Whitey, Vice President.

Barnum added new attractions to Santa Anna's wooden leg. In 1848 he was advertising in the *Tribune*,

SPLENDID PERFORMANCES every afternoon at 3 o'clock, and every evening at 7½ o'clock. The manager is happy to announce the English giant, ROBERT HALE, the largest man on earth, the tallest and the heaviest, being over eight feet high, and weighing over a quarter of a ton. In addition and in contrast with the above, he has engaged the SMALLEST HUMAN PAIR that ever was seen alive, MAJOR LITTLEFINGER and his petite sweetheart, TITANIA, THE FAIRY QUEEN, both being much smaller than GENERAL TOM THUMB. He is also happy to announce for another week, THE BURLESQUE OPERA, written especially for the American Museum, entitled THE SLEEP WALKER. Also the SABLE BROTHERS, GREAT WESTERN, the Yankee comedian. THE WORSTED HOMESTEAD, THE HIGHLAND MAMMOTH BROTHERS, LIVING OURANGOUTANG! WAX SCRIPTURAL STATUARY, MADAME ROCKWELL, the Fortune-Teller. Admission 25 cents; children under ten years of age, 12½ cents.

Chinese Junk, a play satirizing the American Museum, was playing at the Olympia and advertising in the penny papers.

Soon Horace Greeley had something even more exciting than a Barnum production or a burlesque on it to advertise. Westward expansion, new factories everywhere, the slavery–abolitionist controversy with Clay's compromise and the other patchwork arguments wearing thinner and thinner gave Greeley plenty of political news. The discovery of the use of sulphuric ether to produce unconsciousness by Dr. William T. G. Morton, a Boston dentist (Dr. Oliver Wendell Holmes, professor of anatomy and physiology at the Harvard Medical School, named the new process "anaesthesia"), and the magnetic telegraph gave him scientific miracles to publicize. The triumph of the Mexican War gave a segment of the population patriotic glory to enjoy to the full. All this and then, in January of 1848, the discovery of gold at Sutter's Mill in California.

The *San Francisco Californian* announced the discovery May 15. Three-quarters of the population of San Francisco abandoned their homes and ordinary pursuits to scramble for the gold. The *Baltimore Sun* broke it in the east September 20. Crews deserted ships touching on the California coast. Farmers flung their hoes. Shopkeepers shut up shop. As the news traveled east, the gold fever struck everywhere. By the middle of November, 1848, hordes were racing to California by any route—long or short, overland in covered wagons or around the Horn by ship—over which they could obtain any kind of transport. Daily the *Tribune* ran columns of advertising "For California," announcing ships' sailings and offering for sale equipment men would need on the voyage and at the mines. Between mid-December 1848 and mid-January 1849 sixty-one ships cleared New York, Boston, Philadelphia, and Baltimore for the gold fields. By 1850, 76,000 Americans, mostly from New England, New York, and Pennsylvania, had scrambled into California. San Francisco leaped from a total population of 459 in 1847 to a city of 35,000. The territory, which Fremont had seized for the United States in 1846, became a state in 1850.

With the movement of people west, with the expansion of trade and commerce down the rivers and across the land, went the newspapers. Every center had to have at least one of its own. With the newspapers went advertising, and the advertising in the frontier newspapers vividly reflected the life of these settlements.

Minnesota was established as a territory in 1849. The *Minnesota Pioneer*, now the *Pioneer Press*, was established in St. Paul in the same year. Its early issues were rich in advertising for furniture, tools, sperm, tallow, star candles by the box or by the pound and, in that cold climate, muffs, gloves, and shawls. Sartorial niceties found a market on the frontier too. General stores advertised Gent's cravats, lace, muslin, and what the advertisements always called "&c, &c." April 28, 1849, the firm of Fuller & Brother was breezy but insistent in the *Pioneer:*

> Examine, if you please, Ladies and Gentlemen, the prime staple and firm texture of these woolen goods! here is a "jam up" article of Sheep's Gray for pantaloons; or, if you want something finer, look at this Kerseymere. Here are Satinetts, which are warranted to wear like buckskin and which we could sell for all wool if we were not too honest. Here are Vestings hard to beat, especially, when on the back of a fighting man. Examine the bolt of Fustian, so firm that it seems like anything but "all Fustian."[7]

The doctor was also the druggist in St. Paul then, and he advertised that he did not use calomel or the steam treatment. Another versatile gentleman described himself in his advertising as jeweler, dentist, and gunsmith. The same 1849 issue of the *Pioneer* carried two conflicting advertisements. One was for "Whiskey—50 bbls old rectified Whiskey, for sale cheap for cash." The other was a notice of a meeting of The Sons of Temperance, Cataract Division, No. 2. Another 1849 advertisement announced that there was A Splendid Bowling Saloon in St. Paul.

[7] Quoted by Theodore C. Blegen, "Minnesota's Pioneer Life As Revealed in Newspaper Advertisements," *Minnesota History*, Vol. 7, No. 2, June, 1926.

Lawyers advertised in the *Pioneer* that they specialized in preemption claims and military warrants. Railroads, stage lines, and river steamboats were regular advertisers. An enterprising magazine dealer ran this advertisement February 20, 1850.

> St. Valentine; St. Valentine! Now is the time
> to subscribe to the Magazines; Graham, Godey
> or Sartain. A copy of either is certainly the
> neatest Valentine a Gentleman can send a Lady.

The newspapers of the eighteenth century had always their advertisements for runaway slaves or servants. This in the *Pioneer*, April 17, 1850, was a little different.

RUN AWAY

> From St. Paul, without paying his honest debts, a
> person in the shape of a man, calling himself DR.
> SNOW and formerly of Prarie du Chien. This is to
> warn all persons against this man's rascality.
> Prarie du Chien Patriot please copy.

The patent medicines followed the settlers. One druggist advertised them all: "Anti-bilious, cathartic, vegetable, and ague pills. Coxe's hive syrup, Stoughton's bitters, Burgundy pitch, Liniment—volatile, nerve and bone, poor man's and anodyne; Am., apodeldoc, paregoric, castor oil without taste or smell, rheumatic drops, together with every article in the Drug Line for sale cheap for cash."

Other advertisers in the early years of the territory and of the *Minnesota Press* pressed their claims and asked for cash, credit being a risky commodity on the frontier as elsewhere, but none matched in eloquence or literary elegance the barber who ran this advertisement May 30, 1850.

ABSOLOM LOST HIS LIFE FOR WANT OF A BARBER

> William Armstrong, a Castilian by birth, continues to
> smooth the countenance of the male public at the Central
> House, amputating the beard with the utmost facility upon
> new and scientific principles. He also performs the opera-
> tions of hair-cutting and hair dressing in the latest fashion

and most approved style of the art. Shampooing in the
Asiatic method, as taught in Constantinople, is also his forte.
It will be his delight to render these operations as agreeable
as possible without the use of chloroform.[8]

People in the west used newspaper advertising to buy and
sell, but also to complain and to make requests, sometimes for
odd services. Editors had the same difficulties in satisfying
advertisers that editors endured in England or in the east.
One was so driven that he used some of his space to express
his despair in an advertisement of his own.

> Wanted—At this office, an Editor who can please
> every body; also, a Foreman who can so arrange the
> paper as to allow every man's advertisement to head
> the column.[9]

Money was hard to come by and harder to loose. A bookseller went whimsical to avoid becoming lachrymose in this
Alabama newspaper advertisement.

> NOTICE—Persons indebted to the Tuscaloosa Book Store
> are respectfully solicited to pay their last years accounts
> forthwith. It is of no use to honey; payments must be made
> at least once a year, or I shall run down at heel. Every body
> says, How well that man Woodruff is going on in the world,
> when the fact is I have not positively spare change enough to
> buy myself a shirt or a spare pair of breeches. My wife is
> now actually engaged in turning an old pair wrong side out,

[8] Perhaps the advertisement a New Jersey barber ran in the *True American* September 8, 1827, will serve to contrast the more restrained advertising
of the settled east with the informal approach of the west. "DON CARLOS
HALL, professor of shaving and hair dressing, respectfully informs the public that he intends to make Trenton his place of abode, and therefore hopes
the gentlemen of the cities and others, from a distance, will not be scrupu-
lous but will give him a portion of their custom. He returns his warmest
thanks for their very liberal patronage, since he has opened his establishment in Market Street, and hopes by assidoous attention to business to
merit (not demerit) their patronage. RECOMMENDATION—From a gentleman
in Trenton, forwarded to my shop, dated Sunday, Aug. 19, 1827. Sir: You
are justly entitled to the name of Professor. I recommend you highly to
the citizens of Trenton as a man of Principle. (Signed) P. E. Thomas,
President, Mechanic's Bank."

[9] Quoted from *The Culpepper Observer* in "Newspaper Advertisements,"
Harper's New Monthly Magazine, November, 1866.

and trying to make a new shirt out of two old ones. She declares that in Virginia, where she was raised, they never do such things; and that it is, moreover, a downright vulgar piece of business altogether. Come, come, pay up, friends! Keep peace in the family and enable me to wear my breeches right side out. You can hardly imagine how much it will oblige, dear Sirs, the public's most obedient, most obliged, and most humble servant. [10]

Another advertiser had problems of a different kind, and he was desperate about them, desperate enough to add threat to his petition.

Whereas, at particular times, I may importune my friends and others to let me have liquor, which is hurtful to me and detrimental to society: This is, therefore, to forbid any persons selling me liquor, or letting me have any on any account or pretense; for if they do, I will promptly prosecute them, notwithstanding any promise I may make to the contrary at the time they let me have it.

John Holmes[11]

[10] *Blegen, op. cit.*
[11] *Ibid.*

7

Nineteenth-Century English Advertising and its Magazine Critics

OBVIOUSLY, THE FIRST American newspapers were started in imitation of those already being published in England. By their own boast, the first American magazines were hopefully patterned after English models. The unbridled advertising of patent medicines was a staple of the English press long before American newspapers adopted and successfully adapted the practice. Likewise, the penny newspapers of New York were fashioned after the daily newspapers of London.

The dual taxation of newspapers through most of the eighteenth century and the first half of the nineteenth century acted restrictively on advertising in the English press. The taxes first levied in 1714 were increased at various times, so that by 1804 the newspaper tax was threepence, and the tax on every advertisement inserted in a newspaper was three shillings and sixpence. The principal effect of these "taxes on knowledge" was to keep the news from the many and to keep the products of British manufacturers, multiplying under the stimulus of the industrial revolution which overtook England between 1760 and 1800, from reaching wide domestic markets.

In 1814 the taxes were increased yet once more. This seemed the signal for concerted opposition. Largely through the efforts of Bulwer-Lytton, novelist–politician, then of

Milner-Gibson and Richard Cobden, leaders of the fight which brought about repeal of the Corn Laws under Peel, some reduction was effected in 1836. Unshackling of the press was a necessary concomitant of the rebellion against social and economic conditions brought on by the industrial revolution and of forwarding all of the liberal movements whose first major victory was the Reform Act of 1832. In that year the advertising tax brought the government £170,649. The next year the tax on advertisements was lowered to one shilling and sixpence. In 1836 the tax on newspapers was reduced to one penny. Newsdealers, who had been acting more like librarians, lending out the *Times* at a penny an hour, were now able to sell their papers at the lower prices made possible through the tax reductions.

The *Times*, so influential in politics that it was described as almost another arm of government, was equally powerful as an advertising medium. In both spheres its position was assured and its attitude sometimes arrogant. Greville has described its influence in politics on more than one occasion. February 27, 1833 Greville recorded:

Yesterday there appeared an article in the *Times* about the Irish Bill in a style of lofty reproof and severe admonition, which was no doubt as appalling as it was meant to be. The article made what is called a sensation; always struggling, as this paper does, to take the lead in public opinion and watching all its turns and shifts with perpetual anxiety, it is at once regarded as undoubted evidence of its direction and dreaded for the influence which its powerful writing and extensive sale have placed in its hands. It is no small homage to the power of the press that an article like this makes as much noise as the declaration of a powerful Minister or a leader of Opposition could do in either House of Parliament.[1]

At a time of political crisis in November, 1834, the Duke of Wellington himself was compelled to accede to the terms on which Thomas Barnes, editor of the *Times*, would offer his paper's support to a new government. Barnes stated his conditions, which were that there would be no mutilation of

---

[1] *The Greville Memoirs*, ed. Henry Reeve (New York: D. Appleton and Co., 1875), II, 151.

the Reform Bill and no change in foreign policy. Greville, acting as intermediary, drew up a statement of the Duke's position. Lyndhurst, Lord Chancellor under the new government, rewrote the statement. Barnes was graciously pleased to approve the Duke of Wellington's policy, and The Thunderer came out in his favor. "Why, Barnes," Lyndhurst exclaimed, "is the most powerful man in the country."[2]

A newspaper of such proven power was a magnet to the advertiser. The *Times* had been a powerful advertising medium from the start. The theatres got the lead position among its front page advertisements, the royal theatres first. Their advertising was followed by that of the booksellers, shipping notices, and other commercial announcements. The back page was given over to advertisements for auction sales, real estate, and notices of horses and carriages and the like for sale. The *Times* ran not only straightforward advertisements but advertisements disguised as news. Notices of dancing lessons (Louvre, Cotillions, Hornpipe, Devonshire Minuet) had little to distinguish them from the editorial matter they followed.

The *Times* charged more for longer advertisements than the other London newspapers, and John Walter defended the practice reasonably November 24, 1792:

. . . The Times, we are well assured, is higher in number than any other Morning Print, and that there are not above three others which sell near half and not many one-third of the number. We know that some agents[3] will resort to Papers low in sale, to get them inserted cheaper, but their Principals will best judge whether their interests are best consulted, as the more their intentions are circulated, the better their end is obtained.

Advertising poured into the *Times* in such volume that it was forced to publish supplements to carry them all. The first of these appeared May 23, 1818, with a statement which pointed out complacently that the *Times* more than deserved the patronage of its clamoring advertisers and that the sup-

[2] *Ibid.* p. 303.

[3] Note that advertisements reached the *Times* through the advertising agents already operating in London.

plement was issued as a free newspaper though it cost the publisher money.

> We know now how much we owe to our advertising friends; but they will have the kindness to recollect that the preference which they show to this journal results from its more diffuse circulation and greater sale; and that our preeminence in these respects can spring only from, or be maintained by superior talent in the political and literary departments. But in our zeal for supplying this, we have unavoidably fallen into arrears with our advertising friends . . . whose favours in consequence crowd our bureaux to such an excess that we have been obliged to adopt the novel, and to us very expensive expedient of publishing two sheets in one day; paying, as we find we are obliged to do, the stamp duty upon both, and presenting one of them gratuitously to the public.

The supplement was soon being published regularly twice a week.

Despite this, the *Times* fought repeal of the newspaper tax for fear that repeal would work to the advantage of rival newspapers and encourage more cheap newspapers to spring up. In Parliament, Bulwer-Lytton pointed out, June 14, 1832, that if a twenty-line advertisement were published in a London newspaper every day for a year, the total cost, because of the advertising tax, would be £202-16s. The same advertisement could be run in a New York newspaper for a year and cost only £6-15s.-6d. The tax restricted advertising, restricted sales, and restricted the number of people who could afford to buy a newspaper.

Brougham was for repeal of the newspaper taxes, as a political measure. Gladstone wanted to reduce the advertising tax; Disraeli to abolish it. Even after the advertising tax was killed, August 4, 1853, the *Times* fought to retain the tax on newspapers themselves. It warned, March 20, 1855,

> What the London papers have to expect is that in the manufacturing districts, there will be published early in the day and circulated by private hands, a cheap class of papers giving all the news which we believe our principal attraction, and to obtain which we spend immense sums of money. We can easily conceive that it will answer the purpose of enterprising gentlemen to republish our news by 10

o'clock for the metropolitan circulation and two and four o'clock for the provincial districts.[4]

When the last of the taxes on knowledge, the tax on paper itself, was finally abolished, the *Times* noted the fact wryly in a leading article, May 28, 1861: "We are sick of the controversy. We hope and trust that this will be the very last day of this Paper War, and that from this day forward every Englishman will not only have in his house a cheap Bible, but also a penny newspaper, a Cocker's Arithmetic, a Miscellany, a novel in weekly parts, and a bandbox duty free." The *Times* reduced its price to 3d.

This gradual economic freeing of the press and advertising resulted not only in cheaper subscription and per copy prices to the public, but also in larger circulations, in the establishment of more daily newspapers, and the appearance of more advertising in all of them. The *Times* had about a hundred advertisements a day in 1800, but four times that many in 1840. The total circulation of England's newspapers rose from 24 million in 1820 to 122 million in 1840. When, first, the tax on advertisements was abolished, then the tax on the newspapers and on paper, the field was free.

Meanwhile, in an effort to avoid the taxes, other forms of advertising had developed. Sampson describes colorfully the profusion of signs, billboards, sandwich men, sidewalk advertisements, and advertising processions of London in the first half of the nineteenth century. It was an anarchical melée. Maurauding bill posters, "external paper hangers," descended nightly on the city, plastering their signs on every available surface, whether the wall, the sidewalk, or the door of a householder. They vied with each other in happy desecration, racing for the best spots, defacing the work of their rivals, overplastering what they could not tear down.

A law was passed in 1839 making it an offense to paste bills on property without permission of the owner. The law could

---

[4] The *Times'* fears were not unfounded. The *Daily Telegraph*, which became its principal rival, was established as soon as the tax was abolished in June, 1855. The *Telegraph* sold at 2d., dropped its price to 1d. the next year.

not be enforced. The external paper hangers, paste buckets full and long brushes ready dipped, were having too good a time. The undertakers devised a manoeuvre which was much admired. They pasted their smaller bills on likely spots in other postbills.

Dynamic signs came with the static. The sandwich man was invented, a man walking with placards attached front and back. This led to processions of sandwich men, each carrying part of the message, like a row of Burma-Shave advertisements going by a stationery motorist in the twentieth-century United States. Floats of a kind were devised, huge mockups of articles for sale paraded through the streets. Inspired advertisers hired troops of derelicts, dressed them in uniforms, and marched a seedy burlesque of the Guards or a company of foot through the streets as an advertising scheme, until a law was passed forbidding such unseemly conduct.

Earnest S. Turner in his determined exposé of the wickedness of advertising, quotes no less a critic than Thomas Carlyle on the evils of these displays.[5] Carlyle's characteristic distaste was exhibited in *Past and Present*, 1843.

> The Hatter in the Strand of London, instead of making better felt-hats than another, mounts a huge lath-and-plaster Hat, seven feet high, upon wheels; sends a man to drive it through the streets; hoping to be saved *thereby*. He has not attempted to make better hats, as he was appointed by the Universe to do, and as with this ingenuity of his he could very probably have done, but his whole industry is turned to *persuade* us that he has made such! He too knows that the Quack has become God.[6]

An astounded French observer in 1850, three years before the newspaper advertising tax was lifted, looked in amazement on the streets of London.

> In Piccadilly, St. James's Street, everywhere in fact where the crowd was densest, one met men transformed into walking advertisements. One wore a scarlet boot as a headdress, was wrapped in a

[5] *The Shocking History of Advertising* (New York: E. P. Dutton, 1953), p. 72.

[6] Carlyle missed the point. The man wanted to *sell* the hats so he could keep on doing what the universe appointed him to do.

garment entirely composed of cardboard, and carried a flag bearing
a bootmaker's name and address. There were others in all sorts of
groteque accoutrements. When the goods advertised need long explanation, the man is concealed in a closed-up sentry-box. They wall
him in between four boards, clap a little roof on top, and he rotates
slowly to allow the passer-by to read what is written on the placards.
This pitiable tortoise, victim of commercial enterprise, moves slowly
in his unwieldly shell with hesitating, uncertain movements.

Publicity invades even the asphalt pavement. It relies on the frequent rain and the habit people have over here of looking down as
they walk. When the weather is fine, dust dulls the surface and
nothing much is visible. But as soon as a shower has washed it clean
the characters appear, letters blossom under your feet, and you find
yourself walking on gigantic posters. In this way the stone flags of
London are made as productive as a field of wheat.[7]

In time, when repeal of the tax on advertisements led to a
greater rush for newspaper space, outdoor advertising stations were set up and bill posting and paint fell under regulations which must have made street life seem somewhat dull
to the Londoners of the day.

London newspaper advertising was rampant now. The
magazines of the day, as they did not yet carry advertising
except for themselves or for books their owners published,
could be very moral about it and sometimes greatly shocked.[8]
What is surprising is that more often the best of them were
warmly interested in advertising, which they saw as an accurate running comment on the age, and temperate in their
appraisals. The *London Magazine* waxed mildly ironic, February, 1825, when it mocked advertisers' claims for the merit
of their wares and their reiterated warnings against substitutes
and "counterfeits," but the more thoughtful magazines and
reviews treated the subject seriously and with considerable
respect.

It was not advertising but faked literary publicity that
aroused the ready ire of *Fraser's Magazine* in the 1830's. The
newspapers bulged with the advertisements of fiercely com-

[7] Francis Wey, *Les Anglais Chez Eux*. Quoted by G. H. Saxon Mills,
There Is a Tide. . . (London: William Heinemann, Ltd., 1954), pp. 15-16.
[8] Today it is the periodicals which publish little or no advertising that
are most often dismayed by its wickedness.

Tobacco & Snuff of the best quality & flavor,
At the Manufactory, No. 4, Chatham street, near the Gaol
By Peter and George Lorillard,
Where may be had as follows :

Cut tobacco,	Prig or carrot do.
Common kitefoot do.	Maccuba snuff,
Common smoaking do.	Rappee do.
Segars do.	Strasburgh do.
Ladies twist do.	Common rappee do.
Pigtail do. in small rolls,	Scented rappee do. of dif-
Plug do.	ferent kinds,
Hogtail do.	Scotch do.

The above Tobacco and Snuff will be sold reasonable, and warranted as good as any on the continent. If not found to prove good, any part of it may be returned, if not damaged.

N. B. Proper allowance will be made to those that purchase a quantity.　　　　　May 27—tm.

The pipe-smoking Indian leaning on a hogshead of tobacco was a Lorillard trademark in 1760. This first Lorillard advertisement dates from May, 1789.

Parading in truncated pyramids, these red-nosed advertising men were the envy of small boys in the London streets of 1850. (Bettman Archive)

peting booksellers and publishers whose presses were turning out trash by the ton. Each new volume was hailed as a masterpiece. Book advertising, which had filled columns, spilled over into larger space. The first full-page advertisement in the *Times* was for a book in 1829. At least, this was advertising, paid commercial announcements which pretended to be nothing else. It was unpaid advertising which masqueraded as criticism which *Fraser's* attacked again and again.

Blurbs for new books were written by the author's friends or by paid hacks, then passed off in the magazines as reviews. Publishers, who knew then as now that favorable reviews sell more copies of a book than any advertising, forced authors to write reviews of their own books, then planted these as unbiased critical opinion in magazines they owned or controlled. Authors rolled logs for each other, and editors connived at the deception.

Under its colorful, dissolute, fierily articulate little Irish editor, William Maginn, with Thackerary and Carlyle as its sharp-penned staff critics, *Fraser's* slashed hotly. Joyously, it ridiculed its many enemies and sometimes lampooned even its friends. The magazine was unbridled in its derision of the authors, politicians, and economists it disliked. Thackeray advised Bulwer-Lytton to stop using scent and hair oil and limit himself to three clean shirts a week. Maginn, who had got his Grub Street training on a dozen London journals, screamed abuse at Disraeli, most women novelists, Thomas Moore, all imitators of Byron—and sold out entire issues of *Fraser's* by his antics. His scurrility grew so extravagant that an infuriated author attacked and nearly killed the publisher James Fraser with a loaded riding crop and later fought a ludicrous duel with the befuddled editor.

Maginn reserved some of his finest abuse for all rival editors and publishers, especially for Colburn and Bentley, who owned the *New Monthly Magazine*, the *United Service Journal*, the *Court Journal*, the *Sunday Times*, and enjoyed part ownership and control of the influential *Literary Gazette*. He accused Colburn and Bentley of "puffs, point-blank, oblique, inferential." He named and numbered books published by the house which were lauded in their magazines. In 1830, the first year of its existence, *Fraser's* condemned the practice of puffery and these particular practitioners with this diatribe:

> The secret of success is involved in the right use of one grand, cabalistic word—PUFF; ay—PUFF—PUFF—PUFF. And as Gnatho gave his name to one sect and Tartuff to another; as pickpockets are known after their *maximus Alcides* Barrington[9] and philosophising jack-asses and howling materialists after their molten moon-calf of worship, old Jerry Bentham; so literary puffers and trumpeting booksellers should form themselves into a special guild, and choose Henry Colburn for their head.

In another issue of *Fraser's*, Maginn pictured Bentley as a clown herding the public into a circus menagerie to show off the tigers, baboons, and mocking birds who were Colburn and Bentley's authors.[10]

A generation later when *Fraser's* was owned by the book-publishing house of Longmans and edited by James Anthony Froude, historian and disciple of Carlyle, the magazine found itself awed by the power of advertising. In March, 1869, before the full force of modern advertising had begun to make itself felt, *Fraser's* said:

> It is stated that Archimedes asked to be accommodated with a sufficient lever base and declared that if he had it he could lift the earth. . . . Here in our most enlightened age, we have discovered a force far more potent than any Archimedes could imagine, and can stir the world as easily as any push-pin . . . My force is the advertisement . . . "The Advertisement," beats all your nostrums into miserable pretences and shams and is too omnipotent for even imagination to grasp at its illimitable powers.

The men who founded the forthright *Edinburgh Review* in 1802 had made their advertising debut by trying to steal an apothecary's head of Galen. They pursued the subject with determination and in far greater detail some years later.

---

[9] George Barrington, real name Waldron, was eventually transported for his skill. While a convict at Botany Bay he is supposed to have written the famous lines:

> True patriots we, for be it understood,
> We left our country for our country's good.

[10] Miriam M. H. Thrall, *Rebellious Fraser's* (New York: Columbia University Press, 1934), p. 83.

Sydney Smith, annoyed at his failure to obtain early pre-
ferment in the church, and little Francis Jeffrey, who had
failed at law in Scotland and journalism in London, took
an almost pathological pleasure in polite destruction. To them
literary criticism often meant demolition. The *Edinburgh
Review*, which Jeffrey edited for twenty-six years with
Smith as principal contributor, attacked with malevolent
intent. Having set themselves up as arbiters of taste, and
practically invented the modern book review which still
shows their influence, they found little to their liking. Jeffrey
was essentially narrow-minded. Smith, clever and egotistical
exhibitionist, was more interested in the display of his mor-
dant wit than in a balanced appraisal of a book or idea. They
made the *Review*, which had the then large circulation of
twelve thousand, a feared and fearful engine.

The *Review* announced that Wordsworth would never
do. It heaped scorn on Shelley, contempt on Keats, turned
even on Scott, who, in defense against his erstwhile friends,
urged on John Murray the establishment of the *Quarterly
Review* in 1809.[11] It unwisely castigated Byron for *Hours of
Idleness*, his first book of poems, bringing down on it the
scathing satire of the poet in "English Bards and Scotch
Reviewers."

The *Edinburgh Review's* first essay into comment on advertising was light and frolicsome in October, 1805. Delighted, it quoted amusing specimens. This, identified only
as being from an Irish newspaper, was the happiest.

> Lost, on Saturday night, but the owner does not
> know where, an empty sack with a cheese in it. On
> the sack the letters P.G. are marked, but so com-
> pletely worn out as to be illegible.

[11] Henry Brougham and Francis Jeffrey collaborated on an article which
attacked the English upper classes and demanded reform of the English
constitution. Scott wrote John Murray, who became editor of the
Quarterly, "The last No. of the Edin. Review has given disgust beyond
measure owing to the tone of the article on Cevallo." David Stewart
Erskine, Earl of Buchan, was so infuriated he kicked the issue from his
Edinburgh house into the street "to be trodden under foot by man and
beast."

Surprisingly, Jeffrey—insofar as his temperament would allow—defended some advertising, and American advertising at that, in another early volume of the *Edinburgh Review*. Reviewed in the issue for April, 1807, was *The Stranger in America* by Charles W. Janson, a lawyer who had returned to England after some years residence in Rhode Island. Janson had filled one chapter of his book with advertisements collected from the American press.

In none of these [announced the *Review*] is there anything striking; and they furnish not the slightest color for an opinion prejudicial to the taste of the country. The London newspapers of a single week, and the provincial papers of England any one day, would supply a much longer chapter of "eccentric advertisements" (as our author calls them) and furnish better reasons for doubting the good sense or correct taste of this country. . . . It is scarcely necessary to add, that we urge this only against an inference from the American advertisements, and by no means as a denial that taste, in the United States, must necessarily be at a low ebb.

The *Edinburgh Review* unsheathed its sharp pen against advertising in February, 1843. "The Advertising System" is in typical *Edinburgh* vein, caustic, ironic, knowledgeable, assured. Its anonymous author had Smith's style and a destructive blade. Yet, and to his apparent surprise, he was unable to run advertising through the body. Advertising proved too formidable an opponent. The reviewer could do little more than pink. He began with a question which, in the end, he was forced to leave unanswered.

Here within the compass of a single newspaper [the *Times*] are above five hundred announcements of wants or superfluities—remedies for all sorts of ailments—candidates for all sorts of situations—conveyances for those who wish to travel, establishments for those who wish to stay at home—investments for him who has made his fortune, and modes of growing rich for him who has that pleasure yet to come—elixirs to make us beautiful, and balsams to preserve us from decay—new theatres for the idle, new chapels for the serious, new cemeteries in pleasant situations for the dead;—carriages, horses, dogs, men-servants and maid-servants, East India Directors and Governesses—how is all this to be disregarded without wilfully shutting our eyes to the progress of society?

The essay went on for forty pages of quotation and illustration without the author's attempting a conclusion. As so many have done before and since, he ridiculed patent medicine advertising. One, Cockle's Antibilious Pills, he found, was recommended by ten Dukes, five Marquises, seventeen Earls, eight Viscounts, sixteen Lords, one Archbishop (Armagh), fifteen Bishops, the Adjutant General, the present Attorney-General, the late Attorney-General, the Advocate-General, Sir Francis Burdett, Sir Andrew Agnew, Alderman Ward, and Mr. Sergeant Talfourd. "The list may give rise to curious speculation as to the comparative biliousness of the higher classes."

The best puff for Macassar Oil, he decided, was an experiment staged by Joseph Grimaldi. With one bottle of the oil, the magician turned a deal box into a hair trunk. A vendor of Bear's Grease cautioned users to wash their hands in warm water after using his product lest they turn into a bear's hairy paws. The *Edinburgh* ridiculed most book advertising. It would be as easy and as justifiable to deride publishers' blurbs today. A little enviously, the writer considered some of the advertising for Tanner's Pens.

> Richard Tanner's celebrated, resplendent, unparagoned Caligraph, incomparable, preeminently approved, graphometrical, prophylactic, paralleled, trichotomical, coadjurant, pliancy unparalled, self-renovating, ever-pointed, emendated, denticuled, spheroidical . . .

Anyone, the reviewer complained, could write out a string of hard words at random, but he put them all down with evident relish.

The *Edinburgh Review* had an old score to settle with Byron. The article attacked him for weeping crocodile tears in sympathy with press and public. It attacked him a few pages later for living for days together on biscuit and soda water, sometimes even potatoes and vinegar, "to escape the disgrace of obesity." It attacked him for his extracurricular advertising interests. Warren's Shoe Blacking was England's first "national advertiser." Its advertising had made its name

a household word, and its famous product was used in castle
and cottage. George Cruikshank had drawn its trademark,
a cat with arched back spitting at its reflection in a highly
polished Hessian boot. Warren's advertising copy was done
in verse which was read throughout England. Said the *Edinburgh:* "When 'Childe Harold' was accused of receiving six
hundred a year for his services as Poet-Laureate to Mrs. Warren,—of being, in short, the actual personage alluded to in
her famous boast, 'We keeps a poet,'–he showed no anxiety
to repudiate the charge."[12]

Several times again the writer slipped into obvious enjoyment of the life and color in advertising and quoted absurdities at length and with pleasure. He jerked himself erect and
made one more try to be his properly censorious *Edinburgh*
self. "There is no disguising it, the grand principle of modern existence is notoriety. Hardly a second rate Dandy can
start for the moors or a retired Slopseller leave London for
Margate without announcing the 'fashionable movement' in
the morning papers." But this was mere boasting. It was
journalism, publicity. It was not advertising at all, and the
Edinburgh writer knew it. There is a reluctant fairness and a
repetition of the basic question on his last page.

The best things are often the most liable to be perverted to the
worst purposes; and constant exposure to the assaults of charlatanry is
probably a part of the price we must be content to pay for the blessings of education and the freedom of the press. But then comes the
question how, or where is all this to end? Are we to sink back into
stolid indifference with each his bushel over his light, or to rush
madly through the streets announcing our merits and pretensions—
as Boswell ran about at the Shakspeare festival with "Corsican Boswell" inscribed upon his hat?

Two years later another Scots periodical first turned its
attention to advertising. This was a very different magazine

---

[12] Later articles on advertising—*The Quarterly Review*, June, 1855;
Harper's Monthly Magazine, November, 1866,—say it was the proprietor
of Packwood's razor strops, an advertiser since Addison's day, who proudly
explained, "La, Sir, we keeps a poet" in answer to an inquiry about his
advertising and indicated that the poet was Byron. Possibly Byron was
copywriter on both accounts.

from the *Edinburgh Review*, published and written by men of different ilk from Sydney Smith and Francis Jeffrey. It was less pretentious, more warmly human, but no less shrewd in its appraisal of advertising.

Williams Chambers, bookseller, printer, later lord provost of the city, and his younger brother, Robert, established *Chambers's Edinburgh Journal*, which became simply *Chambers's Journal*, in Edinburgh in 1832. Their avowed purpose was "to take advantage of the universal appetite which now exists" for periodical reading and "to supply that appetite with food of the best kind." Over a long period, *Chambers's* showed a lively and friendly interest in advertising. The editors delighted in the color, energy, and humor they found in newspaper advertisements and collected the specimens that pleased them most.

At various times *Chambers's* carried pieces on the advertising in the *Times*, in the penny weeklies of London, and in the United States. *Chambers's* noted Sampson's work approvingly when it was published, mentioned the famous article on the history of advertising in the *Quarterly Review* of June, 1855, and delved into the newspapers of the English past for additional matter, publishing charming little collections of quaint seventeenth- and eighteenth-century advertisements.

Robert Chambers, for the articles bear the mark of his antiquarian interests and pleasant style, was not uncritical. "The advertisements of swindlers and quacks," he wrote in 1878, "have upon more than one occasion been noticed in these pages," but it was the reflection of past and contemporary life in the advertisements, particularly those in the agony column of the *Times*, the theatrical notices in the weeklies, the jobs wanted pleas in many newspapers, the puffery of auctioneers, and the effusions of indisputable characters that pleased him most. He traced down earlier advertisements than others had found in the English press and built plots of whole novels, complete with characters, scenes, and incidents, about advertisements culled from contemporary journals.

"In the whole range of periodical literature there is no greater curiosity," *Chambers's* said, Saturday, March 29, 1845, "than the columns daily devoted to advertisements in the Times newspaper." The front page of the *Times* was filled with jobs wanted advertisements by governesses, tutors, tailors, gardeners, and shopmen. These advertisements spilled over with the romance and pathos of life—love, ambition, thievery, conceit. A novelist of merely "ordinary tact," *Chambers's* thought could construct a whole plot out of this *Times* front-page advertisement.

> To Charles.—Be at the pastry-cook's at the corner of S—— Street at two. Jemina is well.—Alice.

This one told a different story. Admiration and indignation both show, and what the advertiser asks is completely reasonable.

> If the clever artists, male and female, who combined to relieve an elderly gentleman of his letter-case and purse on Friday evening last will return the former with the papers it contained, they will oblige. The case and papers are of no use to them.

Job supplicants, *Chambers's* noticed, always spoke well of themselves. Invariably they were honest, industrious, and talented. Some were exceptional. This advertiser in the *Times* for February 22, 1845, considered himself, in a mellow philosophical way, at least that. Obviously he did not lack experience, self-knowledge, or a kind of gentle aplomb.

> A CHARACTER—The noblemen and gentlemen of England are respectfully informed that the advertiser is a self-taught man, a "genius." He has travelled (chiefly on foot) through the United Kingdom of Great Britain and Ireland, in Holland, Germany, Switzerland, France, Italy. He has conducted a popular periodical, written a work of fiction in three volumes, published a system of theology, composed a drama, studied Hamlet, been a political lecturer, a preacher, a village schoolmaster, a pawnbroker, a general shopkeeper, has been acquainted with more than one founder of a sect, and is now (he thanks Providence) in good health, spirits,

and character, out of debt, and living in charity with all mankind. During the remainder of his life he thinks he would feel quite at home as secretary, amanuensis, or companion to any nobleman or gentlemen who would engage a once erratic but now sedate being, whose chief delight consists in seeing and making those around him cheerful and happy. Address, A.Z., at Mr. P——'s.

Advertisers often offered rewards, a sweetener, a "douceur," to anyone who would help them obtain posts they sought. Sweeteners ranged from five to five thousand pounds, depending on the value of the job or sinecure obtained. One gentleman did not want a post. He wanted money, lots of it and right now. The reward he offered in January, 1844, when this advertisement appeared in the *Times*, was unusual, and it is doubtful that his advertisement attracted many offers.

A MAN OF RANK, holding a distinguished public office, moving in the highest society, and with brilliant prospects, has been suddenly called upon to pay some thousands of pounds, owing to the default of a friend for whom he went guarantee. As his present means are unequal to meet the demand, and he can offer no adequate security for a loan, the consequences must be ruin to himself and his family, unless some individual of wealth and munificence will step forward to avert this calamity by applying 4,000 pounds to his rescue. For this, he frankly avows, that he can, in his present circumstances, offer no other return than his gratitude.

A different class of advertisers peddled their wares and urged their arguments in the English penny weeklies. These were people who had little money, who scrambled to live, and whose desperation or determination showed in their advertisements. The want-ads in these papers were not for fortunes or sinecures, nor even for post as high up the scale as governess, parlor-maid, or tutor. They were for hair-dressers' assistants, fortune tellers, portrait engravings, free-beer houses, and female drapers' assistants. *Chambers's* wrote of them in "An Undiscovered World," Saturday, April 7, 1866. Shopkeepers, sounding like those in H. G. Wells' *History of Mr.*

Polly a half-century later, advertised to free themselves of profitless and burdensome enterprises.

> Pork-Butcher's — Marylebone — Trade 60 pounds Weekly—Hammer and Down want the right man for this,—Bustling Locality—Every Convenience— Rent low.

Entertainers inserted *Variety*-type advertisements of their wants or availability.

> Wanted, a Serio-Comic Lady. No Stamps. Three days' silence a Negative. Miss Adelina Perkins may write; address Theatre Royal, Bricksville. Wanted to learn. Step-dancing and Hornpipe. State lowest terms and Particulars. H.B., Royal Exchange.

Chambers's wrote more than once of advertising in the United States. The periodical's attitude was usually one of mingled admiration and awe. October 4, 1879, it said:

> Our friends across the water conduct their advertisements in their usual go-ahead style. Not content with posters and newspaper publicity, for miles along the country roads the fences are painted over with names of quack medicines, and the rocks give their testimony in a clear and unmistakeable way . . . The vein of drollery with which the Americans are so richly endowed never gives its owner more satisfaction than when managing at one and the same time to puff his own goods and hint a flaw in those of his neighbor. For instance, the road between Troy and Albany were painted over every few yeards with the name C——.[13] . . . varied by "C—— is Nice" and "C—— would cure a mad buffalo.

A far-seeing firm in the "statuary line" seized the golden opportunity and added, "When it Kills, buy your monuments at Bacon's." "In no manner," commented *Chambers's* "can we so well obtain, at a rapid glance, a view of the salient points of generations that have passed as by considering those small voices that have cried from age to age from the pages of the press, declaring the wants, the losses, the amusements, the money-making eagerness of the people."

---

[13] C——, named in the *Chambers's* text, is a patent cathartic, a great national advertiser in the United States in the late nineteenth and early twentieth centuries. It is still widely advertised and sold.

English advertisers could be almost as alert. August 24, 1878, *Chambers's* quoted a choice bit to prove it. In England, home of the detective story, an enterprising editor advertised in a newspaper, "Sensational, distressing details of revolting murders and shocking suicides respectfully solicited."

In June, 1855, the periodical which Sir Walter Scott had urged John Murray to found as a Tory organ in opposition to the Whig *Edinburgh Review*, published a long, historical article which has become an advertising classic. Scholarly, comprehensive, modestly written, "Advertisements" is the original source of many of the facts concerning the first advertising in English newspapers and the authority for the text of many of the original advertisements reprinted in subsequent books and articles.

The author of the article in the *Quarterly Review* wrote with serious intent. "It is our purpose to draw out, as a thread might be drawn out from some woven fabric, a continuous line of advertisements from the newspaper press of this country since its establishment to the present time, and, by so doing, to show how distinctly from its dye, the pattern of the age through which it ran is represented." The author was well aware that a country's advertising offers a fairly complete, if richly complex, picture of its social and political life.

The writer delighted, as *Chambers's* and even, to some extent and seemingly against its will, the *Edinburgh Review* had done, in the color and quaintness of the older advertising. He was sensitively moved, as were the others, by the appeals in the top of the second column of the front page of the *Times*. He was astounded at the number and variety of contemporary advertisements and at the vast sums of money being expended in advertising.

In 1851, there had been 2,334,593 separate advertisements in the papers of Great Britain and Ireland, and the number had largely increased after repeal of the tax on advertising in 1853. May 24, 1855 a single issue of *The Times*, which was then a newspaper of sixteen pages, contained 2,575 ad-tisements.[14] Packwood and Warren's had led in advertising volume in the 1820's. The great advertisers then were Holloway's Pills, which was spending £30,000 annually; Moses and Sons, pills, who spent £10,000; Rowland and Co., Macassar Oil, etc., £10,000; Dr. De Jongh, cod-liver oil, £10,000; Heal and Sons, bedsteads and bedding, £6,000; and the tailor, Nicholls, £4,500.[15]

"The variety is perhaps as astonishing as the number of advertisements in the Times. Like the trunk of an elephant, no matter seems too minute or too gigantic, too ludicrous or too sad, to be lifted into notoriety by the giant of Printing-house Square," commented the *Quarterly* reviewer.

The agony column of the *Times* is still in place on the front page. In 1843 the *Edinburgh Review* had quoted amusing extracts.

> F——y and M——e are implored to return home.
>
> To R.E.L.—You have only a week more. Repent and reform within this time, or we cast you off forever.[16]
>
> If William will return to his affection parents, he shall not be snubbed by his sister, and be allowed to sweeten his own tea.
>
> To M.N.—If you don't choose to come back, please return the key of the tea-caddy.

The *Quarterly* author quoted other pieces which he found less humorous, from the *Times* agony column in 1850. It was strange, he said, how the heart was touched.

> The one-winged Dove must die unless the Crane returns to be a shield against her enemies.
>
> B.J.C. How more than cruel not to write. Take pity on such patient silence.

[14] *The Times* in 1958 is seldom larger, sometimes smaller, and contains far fewer advertisements.

[15] It must be remembered that London newspapers circulate nationally. From the viewpoint of circulation, advertising in them is comparable to advertising in nationally circulated magazines in the United States. This was true in 1855 and, comparatively, still true.

[16] Sydney Smith hated Methodism and seldom lost a chance to ridicule it. This would have appealed to his sense of humor.

Sometime insertions in the column were in cipher. Sometimes there appeared alarmed warnings to write no more because enemies had decoded the messages. One man victimized a series of poor governesses through seductive advertisements in the columns of the *Times*. The *Quarterly* writer rejoiced that he had been discovered and punished. He quoted the pleasantly ridiculous and the mysterious and macabre. In 1841 an advertisement in the *Times* front-page personal column was this:

Postage Stamps—A young lady, being desirous of covering her dressing-room with cancelled Postage Stamps, has been so far encouraged in her wish by private friends as to have succeeded in collecting 16,000! these, however, being insufficient, she will be greatly obliged if any good natured persons who may have these (otherwise useless) little articles at their disposal would assist in her whimsical project. Address E.D., Mr. Butt's, glover, Leadenhall Street, or Mr. Marshall's, jeweller, Hackney.

A *Times* personal in 1845 did not sound quite as innocent:

To the Party Who Posts His Letters in Prince's Street, Leceister Square.—Your family is now in a state of excitement unbearable. Your attention is called to an advertisement in Wednesday's Morning Advertiser, headed "a body found drowned at Deptford." After your avowal to your friend as to what you might do, he has been to see the decomposed remains, accompanied by others. The features are gone; but there are marks on the arm; so that, unless they hear from you today, it will satisfy them that the remains are those of their misguided relative, and steps will be directly taken to place them in the family-vault, as they cannot bear the idea of a pauper's funeral.

Though the *Times* led the other London newspapers in circulation, 60,000 daily, and in advertising volume, it had no monopoly on English advertising at the mid-century. The *Morning Post* was the favorite medium for fashion and high life. The *Morning Advertiser* bulged with the copy of the licensed victuallers. *Bell's Life* carried most of the sporting advertising; the *Era*, the theatrical; the *Athenaeum*, the book advertising. As the leading weekly, the *Illustrated News* carried advertising of many different kinds.

Other media had their share too. It was costing Madame Tussaud £90 a month to advertise in the horse-drawn London omnibuses.

8

Origins of the Advertising Agent

THE UNITED STATES owes still one more advertising innovation to England, though English writers are quick to blame
it on the French. The idea is attributed to no less an intelligence than Montaigne's. Montaigne, writing in No. XXIV
of the first book of his Essays, published in 1580, credited his
father with the notion. The short essay, "On a Defect in our
Policies," opens with this sentence:

> My whilome-father, a man who had no help but from experience
> and his owne nature, yet of an unspotted judgement, hath heretofore
> told me that he much desired to bring in this custome, which is, that
> in all cities, there should be a certain appointed place, to which,
> whoever should have need of any thing, might come and cause his
> business to be registered by some officer appointed for that pur-
> pose; . . .

Thus, the older Montaigne argued, anyone who had pearls
to sell or wanted a servant or company on a trip to Paris, or
who wanted a master or food, books, payments, gifts, or to
tell of bargains and sales, could make his wants known to
someone who would relate his needs to those who could satisfy them. The "officer appointed" became, in effect, the
advertising agent.

It took some time, a half century, but Montaigne's proposal became fact in France when in 1630 a Paris physician,
Theophraste Renaudot, opened an office where advertisements could be posted for three sous each.

In England, March 5, 1610, James I by Letters Patent appointed two gentlemen of his privy chambers, Sir Arthur Gorges and Sir Walter Cope, advertising agents for the kingdom. The king's grant observed that all commerce consisted,

> . . . eyther in buying or selling or borrowing and lending. And for that a great defect is daily found in the policie of our State for want of some good trusty and ready means of intelligence and intercourse between our said subjects in that behalf. By means whereof, many men oftentimes upon occasion of necessity and sudden accident, are inforced to put away and sell landes, leases, or other goods and chattels, to great losse and disadvantage for want of good and ready means to give generall notice and publique intelligence of such their intentions to many that would (if they knew whereof) as willingly buy as the others would gladly sell.[1]

Under the Letters Patent, Gorges and Cope were empowered to open an office anywhere they wished and to keep registers or calendars of such commercial advice as they saw fit. They set up their agency in Britaines Burse, an exchange on the Strand. The condition had been set that no man was to pay more for the service than pleased him. It was unlikely anyone wanted to pay more than the terms demanded, so probable that the office went out of business for lack of profit.

At any rate, Letters Patent were granted by Charles I, December 13, 1637, to Captain Robert Innes to set up a similar office. Innes was to institute an office "wither masters or others having lost goods, women for satisfaction whether their husbands be living or dead, parents for lost children, or any others for discovering murders or robberies and for all bargains and intelligences might resort as they pleased."[2] Recompense again was to be voluntary.

The two knights and the captain had been court favorites

---

[1] Quoted by J. B. Williams, *A History of English Journalism to the Foundation of the Gazette* (London: Longmans, Green and Co., 1908), p. 159. Williams gave as his source *A True Transcript and Publication of his Majestie's Letters Pattent for an Office to be Erected and called the Publicke Register for Generall Commerce, etc, John Budge, 1611.*

[2] *Ibid.*, p. 161.

appointed to what they undoubtedly hoped would be lucrative posts. Now came the first agency entrepeneur. In 1649 one Henry Walker set up in business.

There is [he announced] an Office of Entries to be erected on Monday next for great profit and ease of the City's of London and Westminster and parts adjacent, as it is in France and other parts, where the people find great benefit by it. And for 4d. any person may both search and record his entry and have notice of a Chapman or what is desired. 1. Whether he be to sell, let, mortgage, Lands, houses, leases, plate, jewels, chattells, goods, printed tickets for public debts, and merchandise of all sorts whatsoever, or such as will disburse money on securities. 2. To be entertained as Gentlemen's Chaplaines, Secretaries, Stuards, etc. and also Gentlewomen nurses, servants, etc. 3. To make known the time of their setting forth of any ships for what part they are bound and where passengers etc. may repaire to the merchants or owners for commerce and contract. And so coaches etc. 4. In sum, whatsoever is made known to the publique by expensive way of Bills posted or otherwise may be speedily known for the said 4d. only and no more charges. The office is to be opened on Munday morning next, at the Fountain in Kings Street and so continually day after day, where the clerks are to be at all times ready to make searches and entries.[3]

A competitor set up an opposition office and tried to draw off some of Walker's accounts. A year later Adolphys Speed opened an office, "Generall Accomodations by Addresse." He would perform the same services as Walker but charge differently. The poor would receive his services free; others would be charged sixpence.

Like the modern advertising agencies, these offices accepted advertising. Unlike agencies today, they did not place the copy in external media, but in one medium, their own, and charged consumers and potential customers a fee to use it. They profited both from their clients and the public, in fact, made clients of the public. They offered no services other than acceptance of the copy and exhibition of it to the interested. Not for some time were other agency concepts thought up and offered for profit. It was in 1710 that Addi-

[3] *Ibid.*, pp. 162-63.

son, after appearance of his *Tatler* paper on advertising, was
approached by an ambitious and far-sighted applicant who
suggested that he prepare the advertiser's copy for him, that
he be accorded the exclusive right to do this, and that he place
all the advertising he wrote in one medium.

The proposal was made in a letter which Addison promptly
published in the *Tatler*, No. 228, Saturday September 23,
1710.

Mr. BICKERSTAFF,

I AM going to set up for a scrivener, and have thought of a
project which may turns both to your account and mine.
It came into my head, upon reading that learned and useful
paper of yours concerning advertisements. You must understand, I have made myself master in the whole art of advertising, both as to the style and the letter. Now if you and
I could so manage it that no body should write advertisements besides myself, or print them any where but in your
paper, we might both of us get estates in a little time. For
this end, I would likewise propose, that you should enlarge
the design of advertisements; and have sent you two or three
samples of my work in this kind, which I have made for
particular friends, and intend to open shop with. The first
is for a gentleman, who would willingly marry, if he could
find a wife to his liking; the second is for a poor whig,
who is lately turned out of his post; and the third for a person of a contrary party, who is willing to get into one.

Despite the pictures printed of him, his setting, and his
activities in some contemporary American fiction, and the
sharply adverse opinions expressed by some authors of critical
articles in segments of the periodical press, the modern advertising agency man can claim honorable lineage. His is
legitimate professional descendant of the wit and sceptic,
Montaigne, and of mid-seventeenth-century English nobility
and gentry.

The first advertising agent in the United States went mad.
After operating in Boston, New York, and Philadelphia
through the middle years of the nineteenth century, Volney

B. Palmer grew violently insane, and Horace Greeley hired a man to look after him.[4]

Palmer first solicited advertising for the Mt. Holly, New Jersey, *Mirror*, which his father edited, later for the *Miner's Journal* of Pottsville, Pennsylvania. He is supposed to have set himself up as an agent in Philadelphia in 1841, drumming up trade for country newspapers and selling wood, coal, and real estate on the side, resembling the London shopkeepers whom the *Times* and the other British papers appointed to accept their advertising for them. In 1845 Palmer set up a branch office in Boston and soon afterward another in New York.

Volney B. Palmer was plump, pompous, wore brass buttons on his blue coat, gold-rimmed spectacles, and carried a gold-headed stick. "He was . . . of good address, genial, and pleasant in manner, and had a good command of language. . . . He had more self-possession and assurance than any man I ever knew." So wrote another early agent, S. M. Pettingill, who worked as clerk and canvasser for Palmer in Boston from January, 1848, to January, 1849, and then, establishing precedent for today's practice, started a rival agency of his own. In *Reminiscences of the Advertising Business*, Pettingill continued his description of Palmer.

At 10 o'clock he would sally out, calling on the most important advertisers first. He would walk into the counting-room of merchants, calling for the principal and announce himself and hand his card with a pleasing address, and with as much assurance as if he were a customer who was about to purchase a large bill of goods. . . .

If he found the party he was calling on willing to listen . . . he would make a well-considered statement of the benefits of advertising in general, and to the party he was addressing in particular. He would mention parties who had made fortunes by the use of judicious advertising. He would show how he (the merchant) could easily double his business and profits by a like course. He would point out the places where he should advertise and how he should do it; he would generally enforce his words by some well-told stories, and

---

[4] John Manning in *Fame*, an advertising paper edited by Artemus Ward, cited by Earnest Elmo Calkins and Ralph Holden, *Modern Advertising* (New York: D. Appleton & Co., 1905), p. 18.

get all parties into good humor and laughing heartily. He would
end up by asking if he might be permitted to make out an estimate
for the merchant's advertisement. He would say he would charge
nothing for his estimate or setting up of his advertisement. The
advertiser would be under no obligation to give him an order if he
did not like it, etc.[5]

The next day Palmer would return with the estimate and
the list of newspapers he advised. He usually walked out
with a contract. As advertising agencies do now, Palmer
considered the media his principals. His position was that
he acted on behalf of the newspapers, and it was from them
he abstracted his commissions. Palmer charged only a modest
25 per cent, but he also billed the newspapers for postage and
his commissions on uncollected bills and on space for which
the advertiser neglected to pay at all.

Palmer must have suffered inwardly from the charm and
bluff good humor he forced himself to assume as a supplicant
for advertising. The inner conflict thus induced may have
contributed to his ultimate insanity. When he could be so
with safety, he was obnoxious. Frederic Hudson, writing in
1873, spoke of "Those mild, persuasive, industrious agents of
the old school, Hooper, Palmer, Pettingill, Oatmen," but
Hudson was a generation removed from them and perhaps
had no direct knowledge of their characters and activities.[6]
Their own words and the judgments of their contemporaries
tell a different tale. Palmer not only demanded his 25 per
cent commission on advertising he obtained, but also insisted
he was entitled to the same commission on any advertising
sent direct to newspapers he represented. When Samuel
Bowles of the *Springfield Republican* reasonably objected,
Palmer exploded furiously. He told Bowles that he could
explain the principles of business to him but was unable to
furnish him with the brains necessary to understand the
explanations.

On Palmer's death his Philadelphia office was taken over

[5] Quoted by Calkins and Holden, *op. cit.*, pp. 17-18.
[6] *Journalism in the United States from 1690 to 1872* (New York: Harper
& Bros., 1873), p. 737.

by Joy, Coe & Company. This became Coe, Wetherill and Company which was absorbed by N. W. Ayer & Son in 1877. In this way, Palmer was the progenitor of one of the world's largest advertising agencies.

When S. M. Pettingill, having followed Palmer from office to office and learned how it was done, set up his rival agency, Palmer was just as indignant as is the modern agency when absconding account executives walk off with a lucrative account, or two or three or a half dozen, and found their own advertising agency. Palmer claimed the exclusive right to represent every important newspaper. He wrote them all, warning them against Pettingill as a dangerous imposter. The newspapers, anxious to get all the advertising they could and hoping to get more from two agents than from one, ignored his claims and encouraged Pettingill.

Pettingill outstripped Palmer in more than one respect. He began to prepare copy for some of his advertisers. One of these was George W. Simmons, owner of a clothing emporium on North Street, which was called Oak Hall. Simmons was wealthy, socially accepted even in Brahmin Boston, and the name of his store was famous. "Oak Hall" was plastered everywhere on fences, walls, rocks, buildings, and in the newspapers. A climber of the period hauled and grunted his way up to the Old Man of the Mountains on Franconia Notch in the White Mountains. When the intrepid adventurer reached the top he found VISIT OAK HALL, BOSTON painted on the rock.

Simmons contracted with Pettingill to write a fresh Oak Hall advertisement every day to appear in all of Boston's ten or twelve newspapers. Easy enough at first, the chore became difficult. Pettingill turned to rhyme for variation. With typical effrontery, he signed some of this doggerel "Prof. Littlefellow" and some of it "Prof. Shortfellow." In error, or perhaps deliberately, the *Boston Post* signed one of the advertisements "Prof. Longfellow." Longfellow, at the height of his fame as a poet and teaching in Harvard, just across the Charles from Boston, was not amused. He demanded an end

to the unsanctioned use of either his name or any of Pettingill's fanciful variants for the benefit of Oak Hall.

In 1852 Pettingill went to New York, where he opened as
S. M. Pettingill & Co., and continued his profitable mimicry
of Volney B. Palmer. As so many advertising men of his
generation did, perhaps because they recognized a kindred
spirit in the pulpit orator, he joined the congregation of
Henry Ward Beecher's Plymouth Church in Brooklyn, even
finding a boarding house nearby so as to be near his hero.
According to his own suspect account, he got a valuable
client when Robert Bonner came to him with advertisements
already in type for the extravagantly advertised *New York
Ledger*. During the Civil War, Pettingill got lucrative contracts for the placement of railroad advertising. Pettingill
evidently did very well for himself from his Park Row office,
well enough to arouse the dislike and suspicion of his fellows,
who liked him no better than he had liked his first employer,
Palmer.

"Mr. Pettingill," wrote John Manning, "was vain as a
peacock, and easily flattered, entirely destitute of imagination,
and had no real perception of the meaning of the Sermon on
the Mount, and the writings of St. Paul were as much out of
his reach as if they had never been translated."[7] Manning
credited the success of S. M. Pettingill & Co. to the abilities
of Pettingill's partner, James H. Bates, "Mr. Bates being a
gentleman of education, of wide reading, and a man fully
capable of taking a large view of matters and methodizing
and perfecting a business system for any line of commercial
work."

By this time the man destined to become the most important and typical nineteenth-century advertising agent of
them all was at work. This was George P. Rowell, a farm
boy from New Hampshire who descended on Boston in 1858
as a canvasser and bill collector for the *Post* at $8 a week. He
canvassed and collected so efficiently that his pay in time was
raised to $18 a week, but Rowell had other ideas. In New

[7] Quoted by Calkins and Holden, *op. cit.*, p. 26.

York he had seen advertising on theatre programs. He introduced the idea in Boston and made over $600—plus a case of California wine, a sole-leather trunk, and a pair of pantaloons paid him in lieu of cash. This opened Rowell's eyes. In 1865 he set himself up as an advertising agent in Boston, but on a completely new plan.

Instead of merely levying a commission on the newspapers, Rowell bought up advertising space from the country weeklies in large quantities and doled it out in small "squares" to advertisers at retail. He bought as cheaply as he could and sold as dearly. His profits were prodigious. He taxed the newspapers for his commissions as well, taking an additional heavy discount for cash payment.

New York lured as a richer field for his talents, and Rowell took them there. His plan worked so well that by July 4, 1871, when he was thirty-three years old, the penniless farm boy had amassed a modest fortune. He had a bad cough, a flushed face, he couldn't sleep—but he had $100,000. At that point he decided to take four months vacation every year and did. When he was forty-two, he took seven years off to play at farming. Rowell could do about as he wished, for his agency profits kept rolling in, and his advertising accounts mounted as the owners of patent medicines sought his useful services and Rowell sought for patent medicines of his own to advertise into added fortune.

In Rowell, business acumen, humor, and sentiment were all nicely balanced on a basis of sound New England materialism. He liked money and admired rich men. His highest praise was to say that some concocter of nostrums had got or almost got or left millions of dollars when he died. Yet Rowell did more for advertising than merely make money out of it. He had early a shrewd idea of what advertising was, and he found out through long and varied experience what it could and could not do.

"Advertising," he wrote, "is publicity, a means of causing it to be known what service you or I can render, what wants we can satisfy; and the reasons why that service should be sought at our hands."[8] When advertising worked, it wrought miracles; but it did not always work, it did not always pay.

As a general thing the advertiser cannot tell whether a particular advertisement pays him or not. The most he knows, as a rule, is that when he advertises most he does most business, and makes most money; and when he saves on his advertising his profits at the end of the year are less than they were in the other years when he thought perhaps he was wasting money in advertising.[9]

Rowell, in furthering his own business, did what he could to give the advertiser at least some idea of what he was spending his money for. In 1869 appeared the first issue of *Rowell's American Newspaper Directory*. Patterned after *Mitchell's Directory of the Newspapers of Great Britain*, the volume was the first attempt to list all the newspapers of the United States and to give an accurate estimate of the circulation of each. Most newspaper publishers had evaded announcement of actual circulation counts. When they did publish a figure, it was almost always exaggerated. Rowell did his best to give advertisers the facts. Publishers claimed bitterly that he understated their circulations. Libel suits were threatened about once a week. None were actually prosecuted, and new editions of the directory appeared regularly.

Rowell did advertising a service—and, as usual, profited vastly. The directory was a very profitable venture. Though there was no actual connection, Rowell admits that many newspaper publishers thought that the circulation figures given for their papers depended on whether or not they advertised in the *Directory*. It seemed wiser to advertise in it. Rowell's charge for advertising in the volume was $75 a page, though broken up and sold in smaller units, a page often brought in twice that amount. By 1901 *Rowell's American Newspaper Directory* carried 1,221 solid pages of advertising. The work, without advertising, is now published annually as *N. W. Ayer & Son's Directory of Newspapers*

[8] George P. Rowell, *Forty Years An Advertising Agent* (New York: Franklin Printing Co., 1906), p. 31.
[9] *Ibid.*, p. 332. This is still about all the advertiser can know.

and Periodicals, and is a standard reference work in advertising and publishing.

Rowell's most profitable accounts were patent medicines. For years, P. H. Drake of Plantation Bitters was his largest customer. The pages of Rowell's autobiography glow with stories of Drake, of Joseph Burnett (flavoring extracts, cocaine, and Dr. Jonas Whitcomb's asthma remedy) who married his son to James Russell Lowell's daughter; of Dr. J. C. Ayer, owner of a dozen trademarks, who finally went insane; of the Nova Scotian who owned and advertised Fellow's Hypophosphites; of Dr. J. H. Schenck and his Mandrake Pills; of Dr. H. T. Helmbold of Buchu, who went insane too; of Col. Hostetter, of Hostetter's Bitters, who left $18 million when he died. Moved to emulate the accomplishments of these men, Rowell gained control of several remedies, even advertising at one time for a suitable trademark that he could advertise into riches. Rowell did not do too well with Grace's Salve and Upham's Freckle, Tan, and Pimple Banisher, but he did much better later on with Ripans Tabules.

Most of the advertising agents were enthralled by the patent medicine profits. Pettingill owned several in time. Lord & Thomas in Chicago owned and advertised them. N. W. Ayer & Son acquired an interest in several in lieu of cash on unpaid bills. Patent medicine and advertising were almost synonymous in Rowell's mind. The value of a patent medicine trademark, he realized, was the amount of money spent in advertising it. The product had no value in itself. Some nostrums, Rowell ruefully discovered, refused to sell despite the good dollars spent in exploitation. When one did catch the public's eye and stomach, it would continue to sell and bring in money years after all advertising was stopped.

In 1888, Rowell, who had always wanted a publication of his own and felt that advertising should have its own voice, founded *Printers' Ink,* naming the trade magazine after one of his profitable sidelines. Ever since that time *Printers' Ink* has been the standard and respected advertising trade medium.

George P. Rowell took advertising seriously. He advised young men who thought of entering the agency business

about their morals, manners, and dress. He was no enemy
of marrying the boss's daughter, at any rate, some young
woman of good social position and adequate income. He
told the young advertising hopeful to be good, to be healthy,
to be direct, to seem a humble and earnest devotee of his employers' interests—but not to be afraid and not to make a
nuisance of himself. He was to be considerate, civil, respect-
ful, and to use a deprecating smile when it seemed useful.
Rowell did not "think it advisable to be too well attired.
That the clothing appeared to be well brushed, well cared for
but inconspicuous, is better, I think, than to have it of a quality that is noticeably fine." There should be no unusual
"style" affected.[10]

Rowell dominated, but he did not have the advertising
agency scene to himself. Agents multiplied and were drawn
to the profit centers of commerce like flies to a honey pot.
John Hooper, originally a canvasser for Greeley's *New York
Tribune*, was considered the first advertising agent in New
York. Slow, methodical, he had no office but carried his
bills, blanks, and contracts about with him. Pettingill, who
was Rowell's friend and had his offices near him on Park
Row, throve. L. F. Shattuck, operating as Peaslee & Co.,
scored a coup during the Civil War. Through political con-
nections, he got all the advertising of Jay Cooke & Co., appointed to market government bonds. Working for Carlton
& Smith at $15 a week was a clerk named J. Walter Thomp-
son. The agency specialized in religious papers, but Thompson became interested in the monthly magazines as a possible
new advertising medium. To this time, most of the literary
monthlies had refused to sell space. Induced by Thompson's
arguments, a number of them agreed to try it and let Carlton
& Smith add them to their list.

When Carlton turned back to publishing and selling
books, his real interest, Thompson bought him out and in
1864 founded the J. Walter Thompson Company which long
has been the world's largest advertising agency.

At this time, A. L. Thomas was still learning his trade
10 *Ibid.*, p. 325.

under Evans and Lincoln in Boston, an agency which solicited
for the *Youth's Companion* and other religious papers. Thomas
went on to far greater things as a founder of Lord & Thomas
in Chicago, the advertising agency which later in the century
produced A. D. Lasker.

New York, rather than Boston or Philadelphia where
many of them had started, had already become the center of
activity for these early advertising agents, but agents and
agencies were beginning to appear in news and commercial
centers across the country. Their furious machinations struck
awe into the beholder. One Boston agency advertised that
it would place advertisements in a list of twenty-two papers
in suburban towns at a rate defying competition. It would
do more than that. It would also write the advertising. It
would not only write the advertising, it would do what every
advertiser always wants, it would guarantee editorial mention
of advertised products and services.

The Great Western Improved Newspaper Advertising
Company in St. Louis proclaimed facilities for inserting advertisements on a new plan at a low rate in over two hundred
Western and Southern newspapers "belonging to them by
contract."

This effort paled by comparison with that of The Milwaukee Wisconsin Northern List of Newspapers. Its scheme,
which it proudly described as "Our Plan of Advertising,"
was nothing less than syndication.

> At the breaking of the war [the agency advertised], when printers
> had largely gone to the front, we devised the plan of printing one
> side of the country newspapers and using a certain space for adver-
> tising purposes to pay us for the type-setting and press work. . . .
> We have increased our advertising to such an extent that the price
> to the country newspapers for printed paper is considerably less than
> the cost of white paper at the mills.
> Now if an advertisement should be sent direct to 200 newspapers,
> four squares in length, the publishers would set the type 200 times. . . .
> This at fifty cents per thousands ems of type-setting, the usual rate,
> would amount to $100. Our price for such an advertisement is only
> $50, or one-half the cost of type-setting, counting nothing for the
> insertion in the papers themselves.

There followed a list of over 200 newspapers in Wisconsin, Illinois, Michigan, Indiana, Iowa, and Ohio, with a total circulation of 250,000 a week. Then came the offer:

AN ADVERTISEMENT

insert in

ALL THE NEWSPAPERS

printed at the office of the

Evening Wisconsin

will reach

250,000 SUBSCRIBERS per Week

The *New York Tribune* claims to print 300,000 papers per week. *The Tribune's* charge—and a very reasonable one too—is $25 for ten lines, one week in this circulation; that is for $25 they print ten lines 300,000 times, and send it through the mails to subscribers.

For $12.50—just half the sum—the *Evening Wisconsin* prints an advertisement of ten lines and sends it to 250,000 subscribers in a week.

"This remunerative branch of journalism," exclaimed Hudson, watching the manoeuvres of the agents, "is now arranged on the most expansive scale by the different advertising agents all over the country. It is wonderful to see the perfect system of their arrangements."[11]

These early advertising agents were ambitious, shrewd, determined, impervious to rebuff. They had pushed themselves into an unprotected niche in the commercial structure and, tenaciously, they stayed there, dickering as best they could with the powerful city newspapers, dictating to the weaker country papers, urging timid businessmen to advertise, encouraging advertisers to advertise more, buying, selling, and promoting patent medicines. The more advertising,

[11] *Op. cit.*, p. 735.

the richer their commissions and all the profusion of per-
quisites and pickings to be had by those nimble enough to
scramble for them in the post-Civil-War welter of commercial
and industrial expansion. Glib, facile, industrious, fiercely
competitive, they depended on their wits and their agility,
yet they acknowledged a hero. S. M. Pettingill had expressed
their awe in 1856. "Mr. P. T. Barnum understands the true
philosophy and art of advertising as well as any living man."[12]

[12] Calkins and Holden, *op. cit.*, p. 25.

9

Phineas Taylor Barnum:
"I Thoroughly Understood
the Art of Advertising . . ."

PHINEAS TAYLOR BARNUM disliked work. He shuddered at it early in the flamboyant career which began with his birth on a farm near Bethel, Connecticut, in 1810, and did not close until the proprietor of The Greatest Show on Earth, "The Prince of Humbug," the impresario who invented freaks, baby, and beauty shows, discovered Tom Thumb, introduced both Jenny Lind and Jumbo to the American public, and was himself a greater attraction than them all, died in 1891. He entertained a century with gusto, ingenuity, and spectacular success. He could do it, as he admitted in more than one of the many editions of his *Autobiography*, because, "I thoroughly understood the art of advertising, not merely by means of printer's ink, which I have always used freely, and to which I confess myself much indebted for my success, but by turning every possible circumstance to my account."[1]

Barnum escaped the parental farm as soon as he could. He went to clerk in his grandfather's village store. In this he reveled. The store was a place of barter. Cute Yankees tried to outsmart a cuter Yankee storekeeper. You traded with the expectation of cheating or getting cheated. No

---

[1] Waldo R. Browne, *Barnum's Own Story*, the Autobiography of P. T. Barnum combined and condensed from the various editions published during his lifetime (New York: The Viking Press, 1927), p. 102.

quarter was given. All admiration was for smartness; there was only contempt for the one who let himself be outwitted.

Barnum sold sugar, salt, and molasses, but soon he learned a trick worth, conservatively, two of that. He sold lottery tickets to the hired men, the villagers, and to millhands from nearby Danbury; tickets worth up to two thousand dollars for each drawing. In 1829 he took his lottery gains and founded the *Herald of Freedom*, an abolitionist newspaper. Journalism was not Barnum's metier. Facts were too confining. Barnum went to New York. Nothing offered exactly the opportunity he sought until, July 15, 1835, he read an advertisement in the Philadelphia *Inquirer*. The advertisement described a showing of Joice Heth, who was being exhibited in Philadelphia as the 161-year-old nurse of George Washington. With the aged negress were papers purporting to prove both her antiquity and authenticity. One was a bill of sale from Washington's father, Augustine Washington, dated February 5, 1757. In it Joice Heth was described as being then 54 years old.

Joice Heth was totally blind and had no teeth. Her left arm was clenched immovably across her chest. The fingers of her left hand were drawn nearly into a fist, finger nails four inches long extending above her wrist. Her big toe nails were a quarter inch thick. She had been coached to remember all the details of George Washington's childhood, including the cherry-tree story and kept repeating, "I raised him. I raised him." Barnum was convinced, if not of the genuineness of Joice Heth, at least of her possibilities as an exhibit. The Philadelphia showman was not doing too well. Barnum raised a thousand dollars, bought the right to Joice Heth, and took her to Niblo's Gardens in New York where he opened in August of 1835.

Barnum flooded the press with stories about this childhood nurse of George Washington. He had the story of her life put out in pamphlet form. He had a crude picture of Joice Heth printed on handbills and plastered the New York streets with posters. "She has been a member of the Baptist Church for upwards of a hundred years," Barnum wrote piously in his advertising, "and seems to take great satisfaction in the conversation of ministers who visit her." If the ministers went, it was certainly all right for papa and mamma to take Sally and little Johnny. The newly started *New York Herald*, eager for bright news, gave Joice Heth great space. The other newspapers followed suit. Piety and patriotism made curiosity a virtue. Mobs descended on Niblo's and paid their admission. Barnum made fifteen hundred dollars a week.

He pushed his receipts higher by attacking the whole thing as a fraud and a hoax. "The fact is," he wrote to the newspapers, who indignantly printed his letters, "Joice Heth is not a human being . . . simply a curiously constructed automaton, made up of whalebone, india-rubber, and numerous springs ingeniously put together and made to move at the slightest touch, according to the will of the operator. The operator is a ventriloquist."

At the height of her popularity, Joice Heth died. The publicity did not. An autopsy showed the deceased negress to have been about 80 years old. Barnum had Joice Heth buried in his family plot and ran a new series of articles exposing the imposture and proclaiming his own good faith. The *Herald* ran his stories all through September of 1837, and the public knew that P. T. Barnum was a good and trusting man who had been taken in even as it was. There was pleasure in that.

This success turned Barnum definitely to show business. He bought Scudder's Museum of Natural Curiosities and its Rival, Peale's Museum, combined them and in 1842 opened what was to be a New York landmark for generations. Barnum's American Museum on lower Broadway was illuminated with roof lights. A noisy band played on the gallery. Handbills fell like rain. Sandwich men paraded around it. Signs were emblazoned on its walls, and huge banners were strung across the street before it. Studiously, a man laid a brick on the sidewalk, regarded it thoughtfully, laid another a few feet farther on, then another. Mystified strangers followed him until he led them through the doors of the American Museum.

"It was the world's way then, as it is now, to excite the community with flaming posters, promising almost everything for next to nothing," wrote Barnum. He was too modest. He had made it the world's way.

I confess that I took no pains to set my enterprising fellow-citizens a better example. I fell in with the world's way; and if my "puffing" was more persistent, my advertising more audacious, my posters more glaring, my pictures more exaggerated, my flags more patriotic and my transparencies more brilliant than they would have been under the management of my neighbors, it was not because I had less scruple than they, but more energy, far more ingenuity, and a better foundation for such promises.[2]

For two hundred dollars Barnum bought a model of Niagara Falls. He advertised it in gigantic posters which proclaimed that real water ran over the falls. Visitors to the Museum were surprised to find that Niagara Falls was just eighteen inches high and that the cataract dashing from such splendid heights in the posters was pumped and repumped out of one barrel of water.

From Moses Kimball, proprietor of a Boston museum, Barnum purchased a mermaid which had been exhibited in England twenty years earlier. He had reports written and printed in out of town newspapers and sent to New York papers from Montgomery, Alabama; Charleston, South Carolina; then from Washington and Philadelphia. The reports stated that a Dr. Griffith, acting as agent for the Lyceum of Natural History in London, had purchased the mermaid in the Orient and was on his way back to England with the treasure. When "Dr. Griffith," actually a Barnum assistant named Lyman, reached New York, Barnum had the sea marvel exhibited to a special gathering of naturalists and scientists invited to the Concert Hall. Purchase of the "Fifi Mermaid" by Barnum was announced only after all this advance publicity and an advertisement which stated that "hundreds of naturalists and other scientific gentlemen had beheld it with wonder and amusement." Undoubtedly they had experienced both emotions and several more. A huge

[2] *Ibid.,* p. 104.

painting outside the American Museum showed a beautiful mermaid about eight feet long. Illustrated handbills showed capture of the mermaid in the island of the Pacific. The mermaid was actually the preserved head of a monkey attached to the dried body of a fish.

> The public appeared to be satisfied, but as some persons always *will* take things literally, and make no allowance for poetic license even in mermaids, an occasional visitor, after having seen the large transparency in front of the hall, representing a beautiful creature, half woman and half fish . . . would be slightly surprised to find that the reality was a black-looking specimen of dried monkey and fish that a boy a few years old could easily run away with under his arm.[3]

The public loved it, both the show and the being bilked. They loved Barnum, a practising psychologist before the term was invented, for duping them.

Barnum had more than paid for the American Museum out of his first year's intake. He had only one worry. Money poured in on him so fast that he was actually embarrassed, he said, to carry out his original plan of laying out the entire profits of his first year in advertising.

He engaged bands of Indians to dance and whoop. He staged baby shows. He heard about a herd of tired buffalo brought to Hoboken from the West and advertised a free buffalo hunt. It was free, but Barnum had bought all ferry receipts across the Hudson to New Jersey and made three thousand dollars as his day's profit. Then he shipped the surviving buffalo to Camden and staged the same show with equal profits across the Delaware from Philadelphia.

He had Arctic whales pulled out of the St. Lawrence and exhibited them alive in tanks in the Museum. They kept dying. He kept sending for more whales.

Then in Bridgeport, Barnum found Charles S. Stratton. The five-year old boy was less than two feet high and weighed only sixteen pounds. Barnum obtained permission of the child's parents and opened with him Thanksgiving Day, 1842, as General Tom Thumb, aged eleven.

[3] *Ibid.*, p. 116.

Tom Thumb was one of Barnum's greatest successes. More than 100,000 people paid to see him the first year. Songs and toys were named after him. Barnum had a miniature coach built, and the coach, drawn by four Shetland ponies, liveried coachmen resplendent on the box, flourished through the New York streets every day that General Tom Thumb was on stage.

Equipped with letters from the incorruptible Horace Greeley and from the irreproachable Edward Everett, once editor of the *North American Review* and president of Harvard, then ambassador to England, Barnum took Tom Thumb to Europe. He dressed him as Napoleon, Frederick the Great, and other historical figures. The Duke of Wellington was fascinated. Queen Victoria was so pleased at their first meeting that she had them twice again at the palace. The general sang "Yankee Doodle" for her, and she presented him with a full court costume. The English and French nobility vied in their admiration of the dwarf. He became the rage. Barnum bestowed a favor when he allowed the General's coach to be seen in the royal enclosure at Longchamps. Five million people saw Barnum and General Tom Thumb on a three-year tour of Europe. Their fame was world-wide when they returned to New York.

It was in 1850 that Barnum brought Jenny Lind, the Swedish singer who for moral reasons—which Barnum highlighted in his advertising—had quit the opera for the concert stage. This effort eclipsed everything that Barnum had done to this time, and the advertising and publicity he arranged in advance were the most elaborate he had attempted. For weeks before her arrival, he plied the newspapers daily with stories about Jenny Lind, her voice, her appearance, her purity. He capitalized on the fact that she would get one thousand dollars for each concert and would give all her fees to charity.

"A choice bouquet carefully stuck in the bosom of his white vest," as a contemporary newsman reported, Barnum climbed aboard Jenny Lind's ship at quarantine. A crowd of thirty thousand was waiting at the pier as the ship docked.

A torchlight procession of volunteer firemen escorted her through the streets. Tickets for the first Castle Garden concert were auctioned off. On Barnum's advice that the publicity would be well worth it to him—and it was—Genin, the hatter, bid in the first for $250. Ten thousand people got into the Garden that night. Thousands more stood outside straining to hear. Receipts from the first six concerts were eighty-seven thousand dollars. Daily the newspapers announced which charities had shared in Jenny Lind's bounty.

After the first New York series, Barnum and Jenny Lind made a triumphal tour of the country. The singer emerged a rich woman, and the showman more famous and prosperous than ever. By 1858, he was back in England again, this time lecturing in London, in the provincial cities, even at the ancient universities on "The Science of Money-Making and the Philosophy of Humbug." Dr. Barnum knew what he was talking about on both counts.

On his return from England this time, Barnum built for himself at Bridgeport a replica of the pavilion of King George IV at Brighton. The intricately designed Indian palace, with its complexity of columns and arches, he named Iristan. It was further advertising for the world's foremost showman. To complete the illusion of exotic orientalism, Barnum kept an elephant and had it set plowing across the same field near his home every time a New York, New Haven and Hartford train passed.

At the Museum, General Tom Thumb posed as Frederic and Napoleon. He posed as a Greek statue, sang, danced the Highland Fling in complete clan regalia, strutted in his Citizen's Dress of France. The General, still a child, personable, intelligent, must have had a wonderful time. Advertising of the Museum's attractions never slowed—for General Tom Thumb, for other dwarfs, for giants, boa-constrictors, "industrious fleas," jugglers, ventriloquists, educated dogs, models of Dublin, Paris, and Jerusalem. There were Grand Festival Performances for every holiday, shows nearly every hour of every day and evening. For thirty cents (fifteen for children under ten) the visitor could see thoroughbred horses,

a trick pony, and "a galaxy of equestrian stars in new and
dashing acts of horsemanship." In time there was Major
Colvin, aged eleven, nineteen inches high, and weighing only
fifteen pounds—"the smallest dwarf ever exhibited"—and
"the beautiful miniature lady, Miss Lizzie Read." There was
John Battersby, the living skeleton, and Hannah Battersby,
his wife, who weighed 720 pounds. One show boasted in
addition "Bohemian Glass—Blowers, two glass steam engines
in motion, a three-horned bull, an albino boy, and a fat
woman snake charmer."

Barnum told how he did it as he went along. The first of
his autobiographies was published in 1855 as the *Life of
P. T. Barnum, Written by Himself*. Once on a tour with
Tom Thumb he had found a freak horse in Cincinnati. The
beast had a naked rat's tail, but hair curled tightly over the
rest of his hide. After hiding it in his Bridgeport barn until
his advertising could take effect, he exhibited the animal as
having been captured by Col. John Charles Fremont and his
brave men in the Rockies. The "nondescript," as Barnum
named it, was, he said, "made up of the Elephant, Deer,
Horse, Buffalo, Camel, and Sheep." Barnum produced it at a
time when the public was panting for news of the Fremont
expedition. "The community was absolutely famishing.
They were ravenous. They could have swallowed anything
and, like a good genius, I threw them not a 'bone,' but a
regular tid-bit, a bon-bon—and they swallowed it at a single
gulp."[4]

It was but a short jump from all this to the circus. Bored
with a term in the Connecticut legislature, defeated for Congress, Barnum took a private car full of guests over the Union
Pacific, then started to organize "The Greatest Show on
Earth." With three rings under the main top, he opened in
Brooklyn in April, 1871. The next year, as for how many
years after, he opened the season at Madison Square Garden.

Barnum imported freaks, monstrosities, birds, spectacles,
and other beasts for Barnum & Bailey's, but greatest of them

4 *Ibid.,* p. 250.

all was Jumbo. Barnum bought the gentle, huge African elephant from the Royal Zoological Society in London at a time when the Society was low in funds. No sooner was this treachery discovered than the British press rose in mighty wrath and denounced him for stealing the famous elephant from helpless English children, who for years had been allowed to ride Jumbo on visits to the zoo. Barnum could not have planned it better. He did all he could to arouse further indignation in the English newspapers and welcoming fanfare in the American. He made his importation of "The Only Mastadon on Earth," "The Gentle and Historic Lord of Beasts," as noteworthy an international event as Napoleon's escape from Elba. It was Jumbo people stormed the circus to see. Jumbo feeding out of third-story windows as he scuffed along was the crowd-catching spectacle of every Barnum & Bailey parade.

The American Museum caught fire and burned down. It did it again. The winter quarters of the circus at Bridgeport burned, many of the animals perishing in the flames. Iristan itself was demolished by fire. Barnum hastened to publicize his fiery misfortunes, assuring the newspapers that insurance never covered more than a fraction of his losses. The newspapers thought and hinted differently. "I don't care much what the papers say about me, provided they will say something," was Barnum's retort in 1877. When Jumbo was killed in a railroad accident, sacrificing himself, Barnum quickly informed the papers, to save a baby elephant, he imported Alice from the Zoological Gardens, billed her as Jumbo's widow, and posed her next to the stuffed body of her lord. He took his entire circus to England in 1889. No feature drew more thunderous applause than the opening with Barnum circling the arena in an open carriage.

P. T. Barnum made himself a compelling figure. He made showmanship, with advertising as part of it, big business. He opened the eyes of the public not only to his exhibitions and entertainments, but also to what advertising and publicity could accomplish. He made American folk figures of Jenny Lind, Tom Thumb, and Jumbo. He made an even more heroic figure of himself as the most typical of all typical

American go-getters. Some of the European idea of the
American, and some of the American's idea of himself reflect
the character, deeds, and writings of P. T. Barnum. If Americans will good naturedly tolerate shams, applaud the swindler, and admire the duplicity of public figures, provided
they are successful at it, it is in large part because Barnum
taught them the entertainment value in such things; and
taught them, too, that their own credulity and acceptance
were amusing and somehow admirable. He defrauded them
again and again and let them share in his enjoyment of the
joke.

Tell them it's Santa Anna's wooden leg. They know its
not, but they'll believe it anyway. Call the Lancashire Bell
Ringers the Swiss Bell Ringers, and they'll be Swiss from now
on. Show them how the dried monkey's head is fastened to
the dead carp, and they'll insist it's a mermaid anyway.
Knock a half dozen years off Charlie Stratton's age, and
they'll love him whether he's five, eleven, or a hundred.

The air around Barnum might be redolent of roast elephant and scorched horse, but it was invigorating too with
the good smells of coins newly minted and dollar bills freshly
printed or impregnated with sweat from greasy hands. Everybody who went to New York headed for the American
Museum, as later they pressed in under the big top to see
the wonders and be able to tell the folks back home they had
seen Tom Thumb or Jumbo, or possibly glimpsed Barnum
himself. They loved him for his bald and boundless effrontery, for his instinctive knowledge of their gullibility, and
they pressed their money on him in homage.

Of his early career Barnum wrote, "I bought Americans
with brass, for gold and silver I had none." He bought them
with printers' ink too, and the bill poster's brush and paste
pot. Advertise, Barnum warned, or the chances are the
sheriff will do it for you. "I knew that every dollar sown
in advertising would return in tens, and perhaps in hundreds,
in a future harvest."

You might not be able to fool all of the people all of
the time, but you could delude enough of them most of the
time to make the attempt delightfully profitable.

10

Mid-Nineteenth-Century
and Civil War Advertising

ADVERTISERS LIKE BARNUM, agents like Rowell and his contemporaries, patent medicine manufacturers like the English
Holloway who was opening the United States as a market
for his Carter's Little Liver Pills, and Dr. J. C. Ayer, whose
Cherry Pectoral, sarsaparilla, and many other remedies brought
him millions and the distinction of having a Massachusetts
town named in his honor, had advertising vigorous and
thriving by the mid-nineteenth-century mark.

In England dogs walked the sidewalks of London with
part of an advertising message fastened to their collars and
the rest of the message dangling from their tails. Sandwich
men carried the teaser on a board in front and the clincher
on a board at the back, and the *Times* was swollen with
advertising. June 21, 1851, it reported: "Our impression of
this day will be found to consist of twenty-four pages, the
extraordinary pressure of advertisements having compelled
us to add an extra sheet to our already ample dimensions . . .
today no less than four thousand advertisements will make
known the wants of the community throughout the length
and breadth of the empire." In England the *Times* was and
remained the great advertising medium. Even when the
Telegraph outstripped it in circulation and was distributing
almost three times as many copies. The *Times* retained its
advertising patronage. It was read by the people of money
and influence that advertisers wanted to reach.

In the United States it was the *New York Herald* that seized and, for fifty years after its founding, retained the lead in advertising volume. James Gordon Bennett set and adhered to strong advertising policies. He made the rules, enforced them, and the *Herald* dominated the scene. The Scots-born Bennett, who had starved for two days before he found a shilling on the Boston pavement, then served his time as a reporter in New York, Charleston, Washington, and Philadelphia, knew his trade thoroughly. When he started the *Herald* in 1835, with five hundred dollars, in a cellar with a plank across two barrels for office and desk, he did almost everything himself. Rising at five, he wrote his editorials and squibs before breakfast. He read, clipped and pasted the exchange and wrote his news columns during the morning, covered Wall Street and wrote his financial news—a Bennett innovation—took in the advertisements and the cash in the afternoon. He wrote the book reviews, the sketches, and as many of the advertisements as he could.

The *Herald* gave all the news Bennett could gather, gave it colorfully and often sensationally. Bennett played up fires and murders, exposed what he considered financial frauds, got himself beaten up more than once, and reported the attacks in full. Within a year his circulation climbed to thirty thousand and sometimes to forty thousand daily. Rival editors attacked him. Bennett gave them his answer in the *Herald* for October 29, 1836: "I am building up a newspaper establishment that will take the lead of all others that ever appeared in the world in virtue, in morals, in science, in knowledge, in industry, in taste, in power, in influence." Certainly he built up, and deliberately, New York's strongest advertising medium.

Bennett did not do this by chance. Though, as indicated earlier, he later renounced the connection and denounced his benefactor, he signed a profitable contract with Dr. Benjamin Brandeth in 1836. He had already instituted other advertising innovations. Bennett realized clearly what it took many of his competitors far longer to discover, that advertising is news. People wanted to read it just as much as they wanted

to read the reports of the day's happenings. He cut all illustrations out of advertising in the *Herald* so that no one advertiser would have the advantage of that attraction over the
others. All advertising he ran in clean, solid columns, every
advertisement typographically like those around it except for
the two-line initial capital letter with which it began. No
advertisement was allowed to break the column rule. As
soon as he could afford the luxury and make his demand
stick, he announced that he would take no advertisement for
more than two weeks' insertion. He wanted fresh advertising as well as fresh news.

That was early in 1847. At the end of the year, Bennett
announced that beginning with the first of January, 1848, the
Herald would accept no advertisement for more than one
day's insertion. He would extend no credit. Payment for
the advertisement would have to be made at the same time
that the copy was delivered over the counter. At the same
time Bennett announced that he would give no free publicity. There would be no editorial notice taken of any
advertising.

Advertisers did not accept Bennett's dictates without protest. Many wanted to use type larger than that used in the
body of the paper. This was not permitted. They wanted
larger display. Bennett would not permit that either. Undoubtedly there were complaints about the cash payment he
demanded. Bennett was on safe grounds. His circulation
was such, and the reputation of the *Herald* with its readers
was so strong, that advertisers who wanted returns for their
investments were compelled to use the paper. At one point
Bennett refused to accept the advertisements of Barnum's
American Museum and of the Maretzek Opera. Affronted,
the New York theatrical managers met and issued an ulti-
matum. The *Herald* would print Barnum's and the Opera's
advertising or none of them would advertise in the *Herald*.
Bennett decided he would take none of their advertising.
The managers then boycotted the *Herald*. They went further. In their advertising in the other New York newspapers
they inserted a line reading: "This establishment does not

advertise in the New York Herald." The attack, of course, backfired, and the *Herald* throve on the free publicity. In less than a year Bennett had all the theatrical advertising back.

One advertiser, as sensational in his own way as Barnum in his and as shrewdly profligate of advertising expenditure, managed to circumvent the Bennett rules that he was unable to break. This was another publisher, the famous Robert Bonner of the *New York Ledger*. Bonner, who had been a printer on the *Hartford Courant* and a proofreader on the *New York Evening Mirror*, started a small print shop in New York. One of his jobs was to print the *Merchant's Ledger* which had been founded in 1847 as a journal for the dry goods trade. Bonner purchased it in 1851, changed its name to the *New York Ledger*, dropped the business and financial matter and substituted fiction, essays, biographies, and verse with family appeal. Using many of the methods of the mass magazine of today, he soon had the most spectacular period-ical of the century.

He sought out and bought the big-name writers of the time, paying them top prices for their output and advertising both the sums he paid them and the *Ledger's* exclusive right to their output. In 1853 he hired the prolific Lydia Sigourney, pious poetess of Connecticut. In 1855 he contracted with the equally prolific Fanny Fern (Mrs. Charles Parton, wife of the popular biographer) for stories at a hundred dollars a column—an unheard of price which Bonner widely adver-tised. As George Horace Lorimer did for *The Saturday Evening Post* a half-century later, he built up a stable of popular and sensational writers: George D. Prentice, John G. Saxe, Col. W. B. Dunlap, Mrs. Southworth, Alice Cary, Augusta Moore, Emerson Bennett, T. S. Arthur. He ran one after another the melodramatic serials of Sylvanus Cobb, Jr., published Emma Southworth's *The Hidden Hand*, Arthur's *The Little Foxes*, Dr. Henry W. Wadsworth's *Raphael; or, The Fugitives of Paris*. This was typical *Ledger* fare, senti-mental, pious, melodramatic. Bonner did even better than that.

He scored a tremendous coup when in 1859—less than five

years after he had established the new *Ledger,* by which time he already had the incredible circulation of 400,000 in a country whose total population was only thirty-one million— he got Edward Everett's "Mount Vernon Papers," a speech on Washington which the scholar-orator-politician had been delivering for the benefit of the Ladies' Mount Vernon Society. Everett, who wrote for the *Ledger* for the remainder of his career, was won by ten thousand dollars which Bonner contributed to the Mount Vernon fund. It took twice that amount to get Henry Ward Beecher. Bonner paid him twenty thousand dollars for his novel, *Norwood.* In another master stroke Bonner got James Gordon Bennett, Horace Greeley, and Henry J. Raymond of the *New York Times,* all as contributors to the same issue of the *Ledger.* He advertised that the *Ledger* would publish a story by Charles Dickens telegraphed from England. The attempt failed, but Bonner got a new Dickens short story anyway, paying five thousand dollars for it. By paying them liberally, Bonner got work from Bryant, Longfellow, Harriet Beecher Stowe, and all the college presidents he could find. He had a penchant for college presidents.

Not a line of advertising appeared in the *New York Ledger.* Bonner would not have it. His was a literary paper for family consumption. He made enormous profits on his circulation alone, something which few periodicals have ever been able to do. There was no advertising in the *Ledger,* but there was *Ledger* advertising in every newspaper of any size across the country.

When Bennett would not allow him display, Bonner outwitted him by the simplest possible device, repetition. He took squares, then columns, finally pages of the *New York Herald* to say:

        THE NEW YORK LEDGER
        THE NEW YORK LEDGER
        THE NEW YORK LEDGER
        THE NEW YORK LEDGER
        THE NEW YORK LEDGER

until the space he had bought was filled. Or he varied the pattern by writing:

THE NEW YORK LEDGER
THE NEW YORK LEDGER
THE NEW YORK LEDGER
    WILL BE FOR SALE
    WILL BE FOR SALE
    WILL BE FOR SALE
TOMORROW MORNING
TOMORROW MORNING
TOMORROW MORNING
    THROUGHOUT THE UNITED STATES
    THROUGHOUT THE UNITED STATES
    THROUGHOUT THE UNITED STATES
AND NEW JERSEY
AND NEW JERSEY
AND NEW JERSEY

There are two stories of how Robert Bonner developed his sensational advertising. One is that he contrived, despite the *Herald's* restrictions, to get more display into several modest advertisements than Bennett approved. Bennett asked Bonner to mend his ways. Bonner thereupon ordered one sentence run over and over again, run in without blank lines in a single paragraph until a column had been filled.

"How do you like that?" he asked Bennett the next day.

According to this version, Bennett laughed and admitted, "I guess we had better let you have your own way hereafter."

The other version of the Bonner story, long current about New York, is that it was all the result of a mistake. Bonner, struggling with his new property, decided to risk a small advertisement for the *Ledger*. He wrote, "Read Mrs. Southworth's New Story in the Ledger," and sent a boy over to the *Herald* office with it. Bonner had marked the copy for "one line," but his handwriting was so bad the *Herald* typesetter read his notation as "one page."

Bonner was aghast when the paper came out. He had no money to pay for such an advertising outlay. He got it when, as a result of the unique advertisement, a complete edition of that issue of the *Ledger* was exhausted and he was forced to reprint. It was this incident, if this version is accepted, that converted Robert Bonner into the most spectacular and successful advertiser of his time.

Bonner used teaser copy. He would print part of a Cobb serial in a *Herald* advertisement, refer readers to the next issue of the *Ledger* for the rest of the tale. When the *Ledger* plant was destroyed by fire in 1860, Bonner distributed its printing among other New York shops and advertised in newspapers throughout the country: "Unless we are burned out more than once a week, *The New York Ledger* will be ready Monday morning on all news-stands of the United States, the Sandwich Islands and New Jersey."

Bonner spent as much as twenty-seven thousand dollars in one week to advertise the *Ledger*. He invested a hundred and fifty thousand in a single year. He took what was probably the largest amount of space ever purchased by one advertiser in a single issue of a newspaper when he paid Bennett two thousand dollars for one advertisement of the *Ledger* in the *New York Herald* of May 6, 1858. The advertisement was of seven pages, and Bennett was compelled to double the size of the issue from eight to sixteen pages. The advertisement so worried some of Bonner's friends that his minister called on him to remonstrate with the madman about his extravagance. The clergyman tried to reason with Bonner. Would not a single ten-line advertisement, costing about four dollars, have served the same purpose? Bonner asked whether he would have noticed it. The perturbed minister admitted that it was possible he might not have seen it. "Then," exulted Bonner, "you have demonstrated the correctness of my policy. Every reader of the *Herald* is as astonished as you are. This is the secret of advertising. Eureka!"

Whatever he spent in advertising, Bonner said, was always back at his office and more money with it before he could return from placing his copy. "COBB AND THE LEDGER," "FANNY FERN AND THE LEDGER," "LEDGER-OUT!, LEDGER-OUT!, LEDGER-OUT." The advertisements kept running in the *Herald*, the message repeated till columns were filled. He planted his profits in more advertising and reaped more profits. "More money is spent upon the *Ledger* to make it a good paper," he wrote in a *Ledger* editorial, "than is spent upon any other paper in the world. . . . It has the largest number of great and distinguished writers. . . . The principal Bishops, Doctors of Divinity, and Clergymen write for it. . . . Distinguished public men, including Foreign Ministers, Members of the Cabinet, and Senators in Congress write for the Ledger. . . ."

Bonner became a millionaire. The *Ledger* was issued from its own marble palace in downtown New York. Bonner bought fast horses, which he loved to drive. He would not permit them to race for money, possibly because he felt his readers would not approve such gambling, but ran match races with Commodore Vanderbilt and others of his friends over country roads north of the city. The Commodore admired the *Ledger* as much as any other reader. Bonner spent a half-million dollars on his stables. He could afford to, and he could afford to become as dictatorial in his own way as Bennett. He warned his readers against fake subscription agents, evidently abroad then as now. "We employ no traveling agents. If any party pretends to act as such, you can put him down as a swindler." He was always glad to get letters from readers, he added, but he had no time to answer them. "Don't expect it of us; and don't send us any manuscripts."

Bonner ran one newspaper advertisement, at least, that was not for the *New York Ledger*. His strenuous exertions had injured his health. He bought a place in the country to recuperate. A few seasons in it were all he could stand.

A COUNTRY SEAT FOR SALE WHERE THERE IS FEVER AND AGUE

I hereby offer for sale my country residence at West Morrisania, near Melrose Station, where I have lived for the past three summers, but do not think I could live much longer. . . . Any doctor, with a large family, who has a specific for fever and ague, would find this a most eligible situation. The neighborhood is full of the disease, and if he could keep it out of his own family, it would give him a reputation which would insure his fortune. . . . The mosquitoes thus far have not been so much affected by the fever and ague as to prevent their biting—in fact, it is a good place for mosquitoes. I bought it to please my wife, and shall leave it to please my whole family. Terms, cash. . . . Those wishing to purchase it will apply immediately. I want to get away from it as fast as Dexter can carry me.

Robert Bonner

Ledger Office, No. 90 Beekman Street, September 18, 1867.

P.S.—The town authorities have begun to make alterations in the street adjoining, and if they drain the place as well as they do the pockets of the landholders, it may become healthy.

The Dexter mentioned in the advertisement was Bonner's most famous trotter. Asked whether he had purchased the horse for advertising purposes, Bonner denied it. His attitude was different from that of Barnum who used everything he did, saw, thought, or could appropriate, as advertisement. "Some people," Bonner said, "are silly enough to think I bought Dexter as an advertisement. I bought him because I wanted to beat Commodore Vanderbilt and have the fastest horse in the world. . . . I never engaged a writer, or bought anything, or did anything as an advertisement. . . . When I want advertisements, I pay for them as advertisements."[1]

S. M. Pettingill was moved to awe at the accomplishments of the advertiser he claimed as his client, though the evidence is that Bonner placed most of his advertising direct. Pettingill exclaimed piously that Mr. Bonner was a remarkable instance of what a poor boy of his own unaided efforts and indomitable will, but guided by strict moral principles, could accomplish in this country.

Bonner's advertising influenced that of other advertisers in the *New York Herald*. A typical issue of the *Herald* in 1860 carried thousands of small-space advertisements. The front page, which bore no editorial matter, covered Shipping, The Turf, Amusements (Niblo's Gardens, Wallach's, George

[1] Hudson, *op. cit.*, p. 654.

Christy's Minstrels, the Winter Garden, the American Museum), and New Publications. The back page was all Auction Sales, Real Estate, and Newspapers. One paper, the *New York Weekly*, advertised a "Literary Gem of Purest Ray Serene." The gem was *Mildred; or, The Child of Adoption*. The body of the advertisement read down the column:

> *MILDRED* is well worth reading.
> *MILDRED* is charming.
> *MILDRED* is splendid.
> *MILDRED* is interesting.
> *MILDRED* touches the Human Heart.
> *MILDRED* will make you laugh.
> *MILDRED* will make you cry.
> *MILDRED* will instruct you.
> *MILDRED* will teach you.
> *MILDRED* will learn you.
> *MILDRED* will be read by gentlemen.
> *MILDRED* will be read by ladies.
> *MILDRED* will be read by boys.
> *MILDRED* will be read by girls.
> *MILDRED* will be read by everybody.

Rooms to Let, Boardings and Lodgings, and Dry Goods advertising occupied all of one page except part of a column, headed Astrology, which listed the claims of a dozen fortune tellers. Page 9 consisted entirely of hundreds of small-space advertisements under two polarized heads: Situations Wanted and Help Wanted—both Female. Most of the jobs offered or solicited were in domestic service.

Chickering & Sons, who had been "awarded thirty-eight prize medals for the superiority of their manufacture over the past thirty-five years," offered Mason & Hamlin Melodrones and Harmoniums besides their own pianos. I. E. Singer & Company offered a brand new style of sewing machine "designed for all manufacturing purposes, noiseless in operation, very rapid, capable of every kind of work. Price only $110." A domestic model was available for seventy-five dollars. August Belmont & Company expressed their willingness to issue letters of credit for travellers. There were still no illustrations in any of this advertising. No advertisement was allowed to break the column rules. No display type was used. The best ambitious advertisers could do in order to achieve some slight prominence was to imitate the devices established by Robert Bonner.

One theatrical advertisement was printed repetitively in this pattern:

LAURA KEENE	AGNES ROBERTSON
LAURA KEENE	AGNES ROBERTSON
LAURA KEENE	AGNES ROBERTSON
AS	AS
AS	AS
AS	AS
COLLEEN RUACH	COLLEEN RAWN
COLLEEN RUACH	COLLEEN RAWN
COLLEEN RUACH	COLLEEN RAWN

The Franklin Museum in Grand Street used a variant of the Laura Keene arrangement.

MODEL ARTISTS		MODEL ARTISTS
MODEL ARTISTS		MODEL ARTISTS
MODEL ARTISTS	CAN BE SEEN	MODEL ARTISTS
MODEL ARTISTS		MODEL ARTISTS
MODEL ARTISTS		MODEL ARTISTS
MODEL ARTISTS		MODEL ARTISTS

Henry Mailliard abandoned vertical balance for diagonal appeal.

MAILLARD'S CHOCOLATE
Chocolate de Sante
Chocolate a Families
Chocolate de la Vanilla
Chocolate double Vanilla
Chocolate par Excellence
Chocolate Ferugineux
Chocolate Homeopathis
Chocolate Creams
Chocolate Caramels
All of the above of the best quality, and equal to any imported chocolate and does not cost half the price.

That advertising in the *Herald* produced results is clear not only from the volume which appeared daily in its pages, but from at least one statement made by the paper itself. It carried a news item in September, 1869, saying that its office boys had demanded a raise in wages because of the increase in their work load. An investigation was launched to see if there really was increased work sufficient to warrant the raise. The increase was granted when the volume of mail pouring into the *Herald* in response to its advertising was discovered. In a single noon mail of one day, the *Herald* reported that there were, in addition to the great bulk of other mail, 628 letters in response to advertising that had been printed the day before.

The *New York Herald* was famous, infamous according to some, and later notorious, for its Personals. Included in this issue were these:

> OSCAR.—I Answered Your Letter and Received None. Note at the Herald Office Box for you. I.R.

> WILL MRS. H——F, who formerly resided at N—— Ave., and recently at 112 —— St., please send present address to Astor House, A.B.X., Herald office.

> A family living in Brooklyn having lost an only daughter wishes to adopt as their own an interesting girl from six to ten years old. An orphan from American parentage preferred. Address adoption, Herald Office.[2]

By its issue of April 13, 1869, the *New York Herald* ran to eight columns of editorial comment, thirty-eight columns of news, and fifty columns of advertising. The journalistic historian, Frederic Hudson, found in all these advertisements, "the hopes, the thoughts, the joys, the plans, the shames, the losses, the mishaps, the fortunes, the pleasures, the misery, the

---

[2] Had the proper agencies been established, an international agreement might have been effected. The *Springfield Republican*, May 9, 1863, quoted an English newspaper: "A clergyman wishes to exchange two little girls, aged 9 and 7, either together or separately for two boys."

politics of the people." *Herald* personals improved or degenerated, depending upon the critic, as they went on.

> And Thine Eyes Are Not Hidden. Yes!
> Vis-A-Vis

> MAUD—WILL NOT BE PRUDENT FOR ME TO WRITE. I want to see you so much. LITTLE FRIEND.
> VENUS—FRIDAY, AT 3: SATURDAY, AT 11 and 3.
> JUPITER

> WILL THE LADY IN THE BROWN DRESS THAT LEFT Stage at Canal Street about 6 p.m. on Wednesday, and went to Brandeth House, and afterwards noticed gentleman passing through the halls and downstairs, please send address, in strict confidence, to S.T.H., Herald office.

> I "LIKE BIRDIE."

> Wanted—A situation as son-in-law in a respectable family. Blood and breeding no object, being already supplied; capital essential. No objection to going a short distance into the country.[3]

> A young gentleman on the point of getting married is desirous of meeting a man of experience who will dissuade him from taking such a step.

> GILFILLAN—"IF EVER I CEASE TO LOVE."—I SUPPOSE you are still living as I have not seen any obituary notice; I have neither seen, heard of, or from you since I saw you two weeks ago; it is very unkind not to communicate when it can so easily be done . . . C.

> DEAR CHARLES—SHOULD SUCH A TRIFLE AS A HANDY hat-brush sever love? Come to your ruffled LU-LU.

---

[3] The unblushing directness of this contrasts with the indirectness and modesty of a comparable advertisement in the *Times* (London) in 1841. "To Girls of Fortune—Matrimony. A bachelor, young, amiable, handsome and of good family and accustomed to live in the highest sphere of society, is embarrassed in his circumstances. Marriage is his only hope of extrication. This advertisement is inserted by one of his friends. Ingratitude was never one of his faults, and he will study for the remainder of his life to prove his estimation of the confidence placed in him.—Address, post paid, L.L.H.L., 47 King Street, Soho.—N.B. The witticisms of cockney scribblers deprecated."

ABSOLUTE DIVORCES LEGALLY OBTAINED FROM DIF-
ferent states; desertions, etc. sufficient cause; no
publicity; no charge until divorce granted; advice
free.—Attorney, 180 Broadway.

ARE YOU HAPPY IN MAKING ME MISERABLE? WHY
do you continue to avoid me? Have you forgotten
your solemn promise made me? T.H.E.

James Gordon Bennett and Horace Greeley, with Henry
J. Raymond and Charles A. Dana, both Greeley graduates,
running a poor third, dominated the New York, thus the
American journalistic and advertising, scene throughout most
of the nineteenth century. Greeley, though his *Tribune* did
very well, never became the force in advertising that Bennett
was, but on this as on most subjects that attracted his attention, he expressed his opinions forcefully and rendered advertising unique service both in this country and in England.
Quixotic, shrill, emotional, generous, vituperative, sympathetic to all kinds of radical causes ranging from Fourierism
to Transcendentalism and back to women's suffrage, Greeley
seldom if ever made a moderate statement. He was not
moderate in his opinions about advertisings. Not to advertise, he cried, was "to close one's eyes to the light and insist
upon living in perpetual darkness." Like Bennett, he refused
to run free publicity for anyone. The daily *Tribune* was
second only to the *Herald* in New York, and the very influential weekly *Tribune,* with a circulation of 200,000, had a
page of advertisements for which Greeley received from two
to five dollars a line.

As Benjamin Franklin had done nearly a hundred years
before, gaining an important concession for the American
colonies, Horace Greeley testified against the British stamp
taxes in London. On a visit to Europe in 1851, he was called
before a Parliamentary committee on which Richard Cobden
and Milner Gibson sat, to give his opinions regarding the
stamp tax on newspapers and the tax on advertising. Greeley
gave them with firmness in the high-pitched tones and characteristic manner that seem to make themselves heard and

felt in the verbatim report that the *Tribune* printed in September, 1851.

All the profits from a newspaper, he instructed the Parliamentary committee, were from advertising; from circulation there were none. The English duties on advertising were prohibitive and destructive. In the United States many people read newspapers principally for their advertising. "Now the advertisements are one main source of the value of daily newspapers, and thousands of business men take them in mainly for those advertisements." They would not buy the papers if the advertisements were not in them, and the advertisements would not be in them in New York if there were a tax comparable to that levied in England. The circulation of the *Times* was such that "everything is advertised there." The tax worked to the advantage of the *Times* and against the other English newspapers. With its space in demand, the *Times* could absorb the tax, charge high advertising rates, and still make a profit. "If we had a duty on advertisements now, I will say not only that it would be impossible to build a new concern up in New York against the competition of the older ones, but it would be impossible to preserve the weaker papers from being swallowed up by the stronger ones."

Greeley's opinions about his contemporaries were as strong and as strongly uttered as his opinions about advertising. He quarreled with Charles A. Dana, when Dana left him to buy and edit the *Sun*. He dubbed Henry J. Raymond, a newsman as politically ambitious as Greeley himself, the "little villain," and the name stuck. Samuel Bowles II and the *Springfield Republican* Greeley admired. The *Tribune* called the *Republican* "the best and ablest country journal ever published on this continent."

A cleanly laid out and printed, handsome paper, the *Republican* was independent, forthright, well written. Bowles' editorials were pithy and pungent. At one time an antiabolitionist sheet, the *Republican* became as strongly antislavery. It came out vigorously for Abraham Lincoln. It was a paper of influence with a wide circulation throughout the free territories. Though the paper was dignified and adopted a high moral tone, Bowles struck at what he saw as evil, attacked Jim Fisk, Jay Gould, and Boss Tweed so strongly that on a visit to New York he was seized and jailed by city officials in the pay of the Ring and the Erie looters with which the Ring worked.

The *Republican* under Samuel Bowles II was a force in American journalism and in advertising. Circulating five thousand copies of its daily and ten thousand copies of its weekly edition, there was truth in its standing advertisement: "Business men of all classes are reminded of the advantages of advertising in The Springfield Weekly *Republican*, whose circulation is alike extensive in all interior New England and and among New England people of the West.

"No country paper in America, and very few city journals, have so large a circulation.

"Price of advertising—Eight Cents a line each insertions."

The pages of the *Republican* accurately reflect the advertising of the Civil War period in papers outside New York and the other metropolitan centers of the East. Echoes of the troubled times, even before the conflict broke out, appeared in some of the commercial notices in the *Republican*. March 23, 1861, a nurseryman advertising trees and shrubs for sale, began, "President Lincoln Inaugurated, and the Good Times Are Coming as We Hope . . ." April 22, 1861, another advertiser had "Remedies for our National Troubles. The great body of the people of this nation are looking with intense anxiety for the development of some policy which the present administration may see fit to adopt for adjustment of our national troubles . . ." Meanwhile the public could assuage its anxiety by purchase of the advertiser's silks, shawls, etc. "As Civil War stares us in the face, we must have more money and less goods," stated an advertiser of clothing, reasonably enough.

April 30, 1861, after Fort Sumter had been fired upon, the tone of the advertisements changed. "Wanted Immediately —25 men to work on Harness and Military Work, W. H. Wilkinson, Main Street, Springfield, Mass." The great armory and arsenal, established under George Washington, made Springfield a center in the manufacture of war material. By the end of May, 1861, there were advertisements in the *Republican* for military equipment: "Military Accoutrements— H. G. Batty, Springfield, Mass., is prepared to manufacture, at very short notice, all kinds of Military Accoutrements, such as Belt Plates, Buckles, Badges, Rifle Powder Flasks, Cap Carriers, Cartridge Boxes, Scabbards, Etc." Other advertisements were headed, "Volunteers, Attention!" There were paid advertisements for volunteeers themselves.

Patriots of Springfield
Arouse to the call of your country—fill up the ranks at once and finish up the work.
200 Able Bodied Men Wanted
at the
City Recruiting Office,
Cabin in Court Square.
Highest Bounties Paid with Choice Regiment
$627 to New Recruits $727 to Veterans
And State Aid to Families
$400 cash down as soon as mustered into service
Office open every day

The *Republican* carried not only these appeals for recruits for the army and the navy, but also for bids in the manufacture of armament and ammunition, and for every commodity, including the newspaper itself, whose advertisers saw a chance to turn the wartime situation into profit. Advertisements for volunteers, for coffee, fireworks, offers to handle pensions or to send our brave boys the newspapers at half price, used the same patriotic slogans and were couched in the same patriotic terms. There were secessions on prices in lamps, low prices and no compromise, everything for the sake of the Union in selling domestic fabrics.

Just before Christmas of 1861 the Springfield Amateur Musical Club was holding a Benefit Concert for Our Noble Volunteers. Six months later an advertisement cried, "The Union Must Be Saved!" It was to be saved by shooting off firecrackers purchased from the advertiser. "Much complaint has been made," another advertisement began, "that letters sent to Soldiers at the Seat of the War by home friends, fail to reach their destination." Some of these failures were caused by faulty addresses, but most of them by use of the wrong kind of envelope. The advertiser was in a position to supply the right kind. "Truth Will Prevail," another advertisement announced. The truth was that Old African Coffee was the best.

Just as American periodicals made generous terms for servicemen in World War II, the *Springfield Republican* advertised: "There is a great demand from the soldiers for fresh and interesting reading, particularly for newspapers. In answer to suggestions from the Army and from friends of the soldiers at home . . . we will send the *Republican* for the soldiers, at half the usual rates. . . . Let us have a generous response from the friends of the soldiers!"

The government needed war matériel as well as men. The *Republican* carried government advertising for the opening of bids from the factories of the North for all kinds of equipment. Typical was:

Ordnance Office   War Department
Washington, February 23, 1864

Proposals will be received by the War Department until Tuesday, March 8, at 4 o'clock p.m., for the delivery at the Springfield Armory, Mass., of 6,000 single sets of wrought iron work for United States Artillery Harness . . .

Detailed specifications followed. Proposals were to be addressed to George D. Ramsay, Brigadier General, Chief of Ordnance, who signed the advertisement. Proposals for the Navy were advertised by the Bureau of Steam Engineering of the Navy Department for the Navy yards at Kittery, Charlestown, Brooklyn, Philadelphia, and Washington.

Besides men and matériel, the government, like every government at war, wanted money. Again and again government bonds were offered for sale.

There was no romantic appeal to patriotism in this bond advertising, no suggestion that the government was trying to control possible inflation. The bonds were offered as a business proposition, and the interest rates were better than those the United States offered during World Wars I and II.

> Ten—Forty Loan
>> First National Bank of Springfield, Designated Depository of the United States, Springfield, March 29, 1864.
>
> By authority of the Secretary of the Treasury this Bank will receive subscriptions on account of
>
>> UNITED STATES BONDS
>
> authorized by the Act of March 3, 1864, bearing date March 1, 1864, redeemable at the pleasure of the Government after ten years and payable from date, bearing interest at five per cent a year, payable on Bonds not over one hundred dollars annually, and on all other Bonds semi-annually in coin.
>
> Subscribers will receive either Registered or Cupon Bonds, and the interest may commence with the day of subscription, or on the first day of March, as they prefer. . . .

An advertisement, July 6, 1864, listed further inducements to the purchasers of

>> The Government Loan
>> of
>> $200,000,000
>
> This loan is authorized by Act of Congress of March 8, 1864, which provides for its redemption in Coin, at any period not less than ten or more than forty years from its date, at the pleasure of the Government.
>
> Until its Redemption, five per cent interest is to be paid semi-annually in Coin. Its Exemption from State or Local Taxation adds from one to three per cent per annum to its value.
>
> The rate of Interest on the loan, although but five per cent in coin, is as much greater in currency as the difference between the market value of currency and gold. As a rule, the five per cent securities of all solvent governments are always par or above, and currency new funded in the National Loan will be worth its face in gold, besides paying a regular and liberal percentage to the holder.
>
> No securities offer so great inducements, it is believed, as the various descriptions of U.S. Bonds. In all other forms of indebtedness, the faith or ability of private parties or stock companies or separate communities only is pledged for payment, while for the debts of the United States the whole

property of the country is holden to secure the payment of both principal and interest in coin. . . .
Subscriptions will be received in currency by
First National Bank of Springfield, Mass.
Second National Bank of Springfield, Mass.
Third National Bank of Springfield, Mass.
And by all National Banks which are depositories of Public money, and all

Respectable Banks and Bankers

throughout the country (acting as agents of the National Depository Banks) will furnish further information on application and
Afford Every Facility to Subscribers

The South was advertising too, urgently, emotionally, for men, horses, recruiting sergeants, money. Tailors offered to visit any county in the State of Georgia and cut uniforms for whole companies. There were advertisements warning against goods of northern manufacture.

VOLUNTEER
NOW or NEVER

THE LAST CHANCE

The Gallant sons of Georgia and Alabama are rushing to the rescue! They will not suffer themselves to be dragged in by conscription but willingly and patriotically are rallying to their country's defense!

The undersigned have authority to raise a Company, and when seventy-eight men are mustered in, will receive marching orders.

Those who wish to join will do well to call soon, as our Company is nearly complete.

All cannot get in, but those who come first will be received.

Bounty money will be paid and extra inducements to every man as soon as he is mustered in.

Geo Walton Knight
Anderson G. Jones
G. E. Thomas
Samuel McClary

The same April 29, 1862 issue of the *Columbus Enquirer* advertised for mounted men as well as for foot soldiers.

CAPTAIN O. S. RAGLAND'S CAVALRY!

Fifty Dollars
Bounty
Twenty-five Dollars
Clothing Money

A few more men wanted to run the Company up to 100 men. All who wish to go into

A FINE COMPANY OF DRAGOONS

will do well to call immediately and enroll their names at the *Enquirer* office, where a list will be kept open.

Recollect, our country is invaded; we must whip the fight or be forever disgraced. Recruits will furnish themselves with horses.

O. S. Ragland, Captain

All Confederate recruits were unable to bring their own mounts, and the artillery as well as the cavalry needed them.

ARTILLERY HORSES WANTED

The Quartermaster General of the Confederate States Army has authorized me to purchase the horses for my Battery. Mr. William Ingram, a member of my Company, has been appointed to buy them. I appeal to my patriotic fellow-citizens of Russell County. Bring your good horses (none other will answer) and dedicate them *without any extortiou* [sic] to the service of your country. And if you do it at all, do it at once. Mr. Ingram is at Columbus, and prepared to buy and pay for horses.

J. F. Waddell
Capt. C. S. Artillery

In the *Southern Federal Union*, October 8, 1861 appeared one of the South's typical advertisements for funds to prosecute the war.

CONFEDERATE STATES
LOAN!

The undersigned, Commissioners of the Confederate States Loan, in and for the State of Georgia, announce to the public that the books for the subscriptions to the Loan are re-opened at the following points, namely: Savannah, Augusta, Macon, Columbus, Milledgeville, Rome, Atlanta, Athens, Washington, and Albany. We will send books &c. to the other points if requested to do so, and if it be deemed expedient by us.

Five millions only of the fifteen million loan have been called for, and eleven millions have been responded to—no subscriptions being at a less rate than par, and some as high as ten percent. premium. The present exigencies of our national crisis call for the balance of this Loan and we have no doubt that our fellow-citizens will cheerfully respond to that call. Let it be remembered that, in what they call this advance, they are making an investment at 8 per cent per annum (which investment is secured by a special sinking fund.) and that subscriptions may be made in any sum from fifty dollars upwards. . . .

An abounding patriotism has carried, and is carrying, our brave brothers and sons in sufficient numbers to the field, and we doubt not that the same fervid feeling will support them there, by rapidly filling the remainder of this Loan.

E. Starnes

J. Milligan   Commissioners

Wm. B. Johnston

As in the North, and as in other wars in other times and other places, some advertisers saw the chance for a bonanza. One patent medicine advertiser went into a frenzy of patriotism in the *Columbus Enquirer*, March 9, 1861.

WAR! WAR! WAR!

Is Declared Against Pains of Any Kind by
    Dr. A. W. Allen's

SOUTHERN LINIMENT

And every Southerner will be satisfied by using one dollar's worth that they have no further use for Northern Liniments. For family and Plantation use it has no equal. It cures Rheumatism, Neuralgia, Strains, Bruises, Burns, Fresh Cuts, Pains in the Back or Limbs, Cholic in Man or Beast, and is

the only certain Remedy known for Blind Staggers in
Horses; and every one will find it a savings of time and
money by keeping a supply on hand.

Caution to everybody.—Don't use any more Northern
Liniment until you have given the Southern Liniment a fair
trial.

Samuel Bowles II and the Springfield *Republican* were
concerned with patent medicines too, but not with virtues
added by geographical distinction. In the midst of its Civil
War news and advertising, the *Republican*, January 3, 1864,
ran a long editorial: "Quackery and Vice; Advertisements
that Encourage Crime." The editorial was directed at the
advertisements for aphrodisiacs and cures for venereal disease to be found in most British and American periodicals.

. . . There is something marvelous in the spread and dominion of
quack medicines, and the never-failing appetite of people for them.
And if they were only quack medicines and killed people off gently
and quietly, there might not be so much harm done. To be sure, it
was rather hard when a nurse not long since gave a dose of that
"harmless" soothing syrup to a precious first-born son, on whom
many hopes rested, and laid him down in the sleep of death. But that
was not a calamity beyond a narrow circle.

But the nostrums are not mere quack medicines; they are many
of them made for specific and guilty purposes, which they state
more or less clearly, according to the degree of decency of the paper
in which they appear, always making it a rule to go as far as they
dare by direct statement and declaration. Advertisements cost money,
and it is painful to imagine the extent of mischief which can sustain
all this outlay and make it pay! . . .

Is it possible to any way waken the attention of the good and the
right-minded to the mischiefs of quackery in general, and of this
particular form of quackery, whose object is the encouragement of
vice and immorality? What matters it that they do not perform
what they promise? Their deluded victims are none the less led on
to their destruction, the unwary lured, the vicious encouraged, the
innocent ruined.

Bowles could suggest only the arousing of public sentiment
as a means of combating the evil, but public sentiment was a
"capricious, intangible thing, so hard to reach, so hard to
manage when it is reached." He knew another truth. "Men

love quackery, and after it they will go, while the more arrant the pretension, the better they like it. It is perfectly marvelous to see what an enormous and palpable bait they will swallow." He knew, as he had said earlier and his father before him, that the press depended on the patent medicine advertiser. Bowles tried to close optimistically, but he was unconvincing. "It is money against money, and if the papers have no conscience, virtue must bid higher than vice and keep the channel pure."

Samuel Bowles returned to the attack later at the end of the year. December 21, 1864, the *Republican* lead editorial was on "Indecent Advertisements in Religious Papers." After a long, nineteenth-century introduction, Bowles wrote:

> The notoriety which some eminent professed religious papers, such as the Independent and New York Observer, have obtained for printing harmful, indecent and sometimes quack medicines—making up their pages something like the mixed cargo of missionaries and rum that Sandwich Island vessels used to carry out,—we see is enjoying the benefit of English observation for the strange anomaly it presents.

An English army surgeon, Dr. Henry King, who was in the United States to inspect medical institutions in New York, professed himself shocked at the number and constant iteration of such advertisements and said he understood the religious papers were the worst offenders. "Nor is this the worst evil. The indecency and suggestiveness of some of them are abominable. . . ."

It was the newspapers of weak circulation and uncertain finances that needed advertising of this kind. The powerful journals could dispense with it. In 1865 the *New York Herald* announced: "All objectionable medical advertisements will be rigorously excluded from this paper as soon as existing contracts have expired."

11

John Wanamaker:
"Advertising ... Exerts
an Irresistible Power."

A YEAR AFTER the close of the Civil War a writer in *Harper's
New Monthly Magazine* concluded an article on advertising
with this advice:

    I. To Merchants—(1) Advertise. (2) Advertise liberally.
         (3) Advertise conspicuously.
    II. To the People at Large—(1) Read the Advertisements.
         (2) Study them, and verily they shall be for your profit.[1]

The writer was preaching to zealots who had already been
converted. Every rock with surface broad enough, and facing in a direction from which it could be seen, and every
cliff which some adventurous painter had been able to climb
was daubed over with signs. Every fence, every unoccupied
building, the boardings around every large construction site,
even the New York curbstones, shouted advertising messages.
Fences along the highways and railroad rights of way wore
advertising in letters from six inches to two feet high. Bridges,
especially covered bridges, bore huge advertising signs. The
"Medicine Bridge" at Lexington, Virginia, had painted over
its whole length, "Wicoma—The Perfect Cure." The covered bridge over East Creek in Rutland, Vermont, cried
"Just Suits Tobacco, Cut Plug."

[1] "Newspaper Advertisements," *Harper's New Monthly Magazine*, November, 1866, p. 789.

P. T. BARNUM'S
New and Only Greatest Show on Earth.

IN WATER-PROOF TENTS, COVERING SEVERAL ACRES. $1,000,000 INVESTED.
A GREAT AND AMUSING ACADEMY OF OBJECT TEACHING.

Museum, Menagerie, Circus, and Hippodrome.

Will travel by rail, on 100 Steel Cars of its own, passing through New York, the Canadas, Michigan, Illinois, Minnesota, Wisconsin, Indiana, Iowa, Missouri, and Texas. The Museum contains 100,000 rare and startling curiosities, including the most remarkable Captain COSTENTENUS, a Greek nobleman, who was

TATTOED FROM HEAD TO FOOT

in Chinese Tartary, as punishment for engaging in rebellion against the King.

The **MENAGERIE** consists of by far the largest collection of living wild animals that ever travelled, among which are the $25,000 Hippopotamus from the river Nile, Sea Lions from Alaska, Giraffes, the African Llioness and her little royal Cubs, no larger than cats, a picture of which occupies a full page in HARPER'S WEEKLY of April 28th. The six beautiful jet-black $30,000 Trakene Stallions, from Paris, present amazing and ENTIRELY NOVEL performances, which have been witnessed with delight by over 200,000 ladies, gentlemen, and children this spring at Barnum's great Hippodrome Building in New York. This picture shows them

An elephant, a mermaid, a Duryea Buggyaut, or naughtiness in Tartary—it was all fascinating and edifying to Barnum and customers. (Bettman Archive)

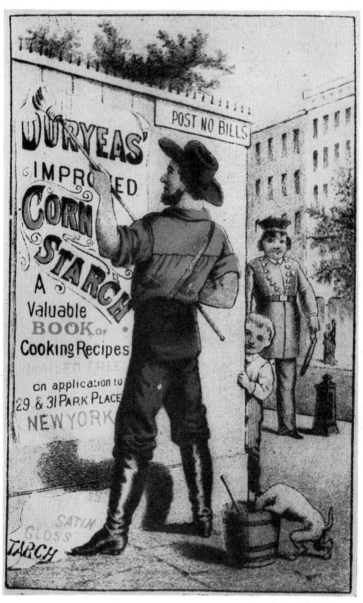

A dog that is going to be ill, an early Keystone cop, and an advertising man diligent at his trade on the sidewalks of New York. (Bettman Archive)

A familiar sight along country roads was the brightly painted wagon with its shining team of fine horses in brass-bespangled harness standing nearby while the paint or paste artist put up his signs for pain killers, hair restorers, ready reliefs, or adjurations to patronize the peerless, nonpareil bargain emporium in the nearest town. Voting notices, theatrical advertisements, screaming patent medicine claims, over-sized railway and steamship timetables were tacked or pasted on fences about New York's City Hall, and strangely costumed men bore banners with strange advertising devices through the city's streets. Elaborately decorated wagons carted signs extolling the virtues of Gosling's shoe blacking through these same New York streets.

In 1869 the fences around the new post office being built on lower Broadway advertised advertising, at least advertising as it was practiced by George P. Rowell. The contractor had rented the space to an unsuccessful entrepreneur (Rowell described him as "a rank outsider") who got discouraged after sticking up a few miscellaneous bills. The dexterous Rowell seized his chance. He had the entire fence surrounding the partially completed structure on Mail Street, Broadway, and Park Row plastered with large posters stating that all the U.S. newspapers could be seen at the advertising agency of George P. Rowell & Co., No. 41 Park Row. The right of the building contractor to sell the space was disputed and the signs came down, but not before Rowell's advertising had been up for several days. The world had seen it. It was, Rowell said, the best advertising he ever did.

The occupants of slow-moving wagons, buckboards, buggies, and surreys saw advertising all along their country routes. Six-inch boards nailed to fence posts proclaimed the virtues of nostrums, clocks, underwear, or asked, a little later, "Do You Wear Pants?" If you did, it was suggested, Plymouth Rock Pants were the best. Travelers could read at their leisure, chuckle, remember. Other fence post signs, perhaps meant to attract the attention of the horse itself, advocated the nourishing qualities and taste delights of various brands of feed.

Some signs moved with the traffic. The wagons, and in winter the sleighs, of drovers were covered with advertisements for headache remedies, bitters, or stock company performances. Brightly covered umbrellas on farm wagons or on horse-drawn rakes and mowing machines had on them advertisements for feeds, farm supplies, and implements.

The walls and roofs of barns along the way already bore the work of the advertisers. It was all the paint some of them wore. Farmers or farmer's wives often spent the rental pittance for the chance to read more advertising in the newspapers and periodicals. In the 1860's one New England spinster had rented out the sides and roof of her barn. A gale blew off the roof and damaged the walls. The advertiser refused to pay. The spinster was indignant when she wrote to a magazine editor to explain why she had not the money to renew her subscription. As only some of the letters in the barn advertisements were missing and only parts of others gone, she felt the advertisement was more interesting than it had been and that she should be paid accordingly.

In Philadelphia a merchant was rapidly becoming as indefatigable and as conspicuous an advertiser as anyone could wish. His signs were everywhere, on fences, on handbills, in the newspapers.

Wanamaker and Brown's
popular

OAK HALL

S. E. Corner
Sixth and Market
W. & B.[2]

John Wanamaker, destined to become one of the country's merchant princes and a voluble and spectacular advertiser well into the next century, was born the son of a Philadelphia

---

[2] Wanamaker evidently adopted the name of the earlier Boston store. Until 1955 when one entire block of buildings was torn down to enlarge the park about Independence Hall, the words "Oak Hall" were still visible in bronze letters sunk into the pavement at the southeast corner of Sixth and Market Streets.

bricklayer. At fourteen he was an errand boy for a book-
store at $1.25 a week. He shifted to a men's clothing store,
gave that up to travel in the West for his health, and at the age
of nineteen, became the first paid secretary of the Y.M.C.A.
at a thousand dollars a year. In 1861, when he was twenty-
two, he and his brother-in-law, Nathan Brown, opened Oak
Hall with a capital of $3,900.

Wanamaker did not open quietly. He took into the clothing business all the evangelical fervor of his church and
Y.M.C.A. associations and all the showmanship of P. T.
Barnum. Before the store actually opened, he littered Philadelphia with small handbills which read simply, "W. & B."
A second bill announced the opening of Wanamaker and
Brown's new store. It was announced and planned as a made-
to-measure business, but Wanamaker was able to buy the
stock of a bankrupt ready-to-wear maker of men's suits. He
bought cheap and he sold cheap. Receipts from the first day's
business at Oak Hall were $20.67. Wanamaker spent twenty
dollars of the amount in the *Public Ledger* to advertise a sale
of complete men's suits for a total price of three dollars. He
went on from there.

A large part of Oak Hall's business during its first years
was in Civil War officers' uniforms, but Wanamaker pushed
his whole line with flamboyant advertising and publicity,
pushed it with such success that within ten years Oak Hall
was the largest men's retail clothing store in the United
States. He had signs one hundred feet long built along the
Pennsylvania Railroad tracks into Philadelphia. He loosed
huge balloons and gave free suits to anyone who captured one
after it had come down. He marshaled parades of men wearing wire frames twisted into the shape of yachts with Oak
Hall pennants flying from their masts. He dressed employees
in costume and sent them out to blow hunting horns from
tallyho coaches drawn by six horses. Sometimes the coaches
were on the highways and byways for a week at a time.
Wanamaker continued to ply the newspapers with his advertising, spending with deliberate profligacy.

Nathan Brown died in 1868, but Oak Hall continued as
Wanamaker and Brown. In 1869 Wanamaker opened another store, a more fashionable shop, on Chestnut Street. In
1876, with characteristic fanfare, he plunged into the great
Wanamaker department store enterprise.

The department store idea was not new. The first department store in the United States is supposed to have been
established in Duxbury, Massachusetts, in 1826 by James,
Nathaniel, and Peleg Ford. James T. Ford & Company sold
logwood, plows, aloes, hay cutters, Epsom salts, whale oil,
night caps, powder, shot, pills, nails, tents, wigs, meat, candy,
and other sundries, running their business up to $150,000 an-
nually. It was spectacular at the time, but the Ford's venture
paled beside a comparison with that of the Irish immigrant,
A. T. Stewart, who opened a small dry goods store in New
York in the late summer of 1823.

Stewart devised and offered the then novel policy of "One
price for all and no haggling." He bought and sold with
great shrewdness, took on a larger store. During the depression of 1837 he bought at auction goods of merchants who
failed, got himself a still larger store in 1838, and then in
1846 built his "Marble Palace" at Broadway and Chambers
Street. He drew the fashionable trade of the time, made
Stewart's known for its integrity and the good taste of its
merchandise. In 1862 he built a building eight stories high
that covered the entire block between Ninth and Tenth
Streets and Broadway and Fourth Avenue, a site not abandoned by Wanamaker, who took over Stewart's late in the
century, until 1955. In 1862 it was the largest retail store in
the world.

Stewart was awarded large army and navy contracts during the Civil War. These with his retail civilian trade brought
him an average yearly income of nearly two million dollars.
He paid low wages, exacted strict obedience from his help,
advertised little, became one of the acknowledged business
leaders of the day and a financier of such repute that Grant
offered him the Secretaryship of the Treasury. Stewart noted
Wanamaker approvingly, and Wanamaker imitated Stewart's

policies—the one price, exchanges, refunds, courtesy to the customer—with the one great difference that Wanamaker advertised blatantly where Stewart confined himself to modest newspaper announcements. Stewart, many times a millionaire, died the same year that Wanamaker opened his big Philadelphia store.[3]

Wanamaker picked a huge, outmoded freight depot of the Pennsylvania Railroad at 13th and Market Streets, where the Wanamaker store still stands, for his 1876 venture. He opened what was at first a combined dry goods and men's clothing store with tremendous advance publicity and a stock worth a half million dollars; opened to a crowd of nearly 70,000 curious customers. It was the year of the Centennial Exhibition, and Wanamaker did well, travelers from all over the country being drawn by its advertising-established fame to visit Wanamaker's "Grand Depot." After the Fair closed, Wanamaker tried to interest other Philadelphia merchants in renting space in his vast acreage. Failing in this, he inaugurated the collection of specialty shops under one roof which became the modern department store. The Wanamaker advertising grew in volume and developed characteristics that made it a model for other advertisers, but this was in the later decades of the nineteenth century and in the early twentieth century.

The retail merchant was merely the first to express in local advertising the upsurge of renewed business energy that came with the end of the Civil War. The immediate postwar period was one of explosive commercial and industrial expansion. Railroads had speeded their development for war purposes. The factories of the North had been geared for

[3] Stewart's great wealth led to a sensational sale, about which there was the kind of bargaining he eschewed, after his death. His body was stolen from the churchyard of St. Mark's in the Bouwerie, and offered the family, after a few months, for $200,000, the body snatchers communicating with the executor of the estate through the personal column of the *New York Herald*. The parties haggled over the price. More than a year later on a Westchester road at night, a Stewart relative met a mounted man who led him to the casket which was in a wagon on a side lane. The final price was $20,000 in gold. The body was reburied in a Stewart real estate development near Garden City, Long Island.

The printer used every type face he could find for an advertisement of the new Wanamaker emporium in the first issue of *Farm Journal*.

production of war matériel. More tracks were laid as the war-interrupted migrations to the West began again. New mines were discovered and put into operation. Industry began to spread from the East across the Appalachians. Western towns boomed as commercial and industrial centers. The volume of manufacturing grew and with it the competition for new markets. A nation released from bitter and costly sectional conflict began to go about its business, and business was its business—manufacturing, selling, developing new lands, building new towns, populating new territories. It was these forces which led to the release of a veritable flood of advertising in the 1880's and 1890's, national advertising this time by manufacturers as well as by retailers, and in new national media, media made possible by methods of transportation developed during the war.

Many forces contributed to the development. There was, as there seems always to be, the impatient desire of the individual which, through contagion, becomes the desire of the community, to make up for time lost in war. The Industrial Revolution, diverted, swung back on course. The country was rapidly changing from an agricultural to an industrial economy. Soldiers had traveled and were restless. In their campaigning they had discovered new products that they liked in parts of the country they had not known. They wanted them again. Immigrants from the East wanted in the West the familiar objects they had known at home.

People who had been in a hurry before the war were impelled to new haste. They had no time to grow their own food, card and spin the wool from their own sheep, and make their own clothes. They were mining, lumbering, building new settlements. They grew and made less for themselves and their families, bought more, and wanted some assurance of the quality of what they bought.

Up to the time of the Civil War the largest advertising expenditure ever made is said to have been three thousand dollars spent for a Fairbanks scales advertisement in the *New York Tribune* and other papers. This was a manufacturer advertising a product he had made for sale wherever it could be shipped. This and a few other articles such as Singer Sewing machines were exceptions. Most products were made locally to be sold by local dealers for local consumption. Occasionally some manufacturer broke through the restrictions imposed by distributive facilities and consumer habit, but then only by dint of application aided by good fortune.

Samuel Colt was a young man in Hartford when he invented his pistol with the revolving cylinder. His idea was to sell them in quantity at a substantial profit. He finally managed the finances to begin turning them out in a factory in Paterson in 1837. The government from whom he solicited orders was unimpressed. Colt failed in 1843. Colt, still trying to promote his product, gave one to an army officer he met in Washington. With the Colt this officer shot his way out of ambush during the Mexican War. General Taylor was impressed and had a thousand ordered. Colt capitalized on the incident and attendant publicity, set up a crude assembly line such as Eli Whitney was using to manufacture rifles and was established.

Western settlers knew the Colt name well enough, but it was one of the few they knew. When they went to the general store to buy axes, knives, crackers, flour, molasses, or clothes, people asked for no particular brands. The storekeeper sold the article he had. He filled his customers' molasses jugs out of one barrel, weighed their crackers out of a bin, scooped tea or coffee out of the barrel. Manufacturers seldom bothered to affix their names to axes, shovels, or suits. As long as their drummers brought in the orders, they were content. It was the buyers themselves who began to differtiate between the goods of one manufacturer and those of another. Often the makers' names were stamped, or literally branded with a hot iron, on cases of tools, guns, axes, knives, or on crates of other merchandise. Men and women became familiar with the names and marks and began to ask for those they preferred.

The concept of branded merchandise, basic in national advertising, thus stemmed in part from stated consumer preferences. It resulted also from competition and changes in the system of retail distribution. As long as there was a pent-up demand for merchandise of all kinds resulting from the Civil War and the subsequent population, economic, industrial, and commercial growth, the distinguishing of one maker's goods from another's was unimportant. People would buy anything and everything offered. Especially in the newer communities, they needed staples of all kinds, and they wanted luxuries. When increased production facilities and improved means of transport began to catch up with the demand, competition, as always under such circumstances, became marked.

The Stewart–Wanamaker development of the one-price department stores forced the general stores and the specialty shops in cities to enticement of customers by offering greater variety, improved goods, and better display. Other retailing developments forced the value of some means of identifying goods of claimed superiority. In New York George Hartford was managing what became the first of the red-fronted stores of The Great Atlantic & Pacific Tea Company. The chain store had become a reality. In Watertown, New York, Frank W. Woolworth was clerking in a store in 1870 and experimenting with the idea that led to the opening of his first five-and-ten cent variety store a few years later. The first of the large mail order houses, Montgomery Ward, was founded in 1870. Sears Roebuck followed, and the mail order houses began to make serious inroads on the retail merchant's business.

In 1870 the U.S. Patent Office had only a handful of trademarks registered. There were 121 in 1871. Trademarks and brand names poured in as manufacturers hastened to record some that had been in use for a half century and new ones seized on to differentiate their products from those of competitors. By 1875, 1,138 marks had been registered. These names and marks were the essential facts in the deluge of national advertising that was to come. There were 10,568 of them by 1906; nearly 69,000 twenty years later.

None of this happened all at once. It did not happen by plan or by date. There was no single leap from quaintness to spirited appeals, sometimes humorless stridency, in advertising. Swelling population, population movements, increased industrial production, changes in wholesale and retail selling methods, all had something to do with it. Mechanical inventions, the contagious belief in material progress, the liberalization of newspaper advertising regulations, the scurryings of advertising agents in their attempts to foment business, changing styles in women's dress and in men's opinions, all contributed to the mounting wave of advertising in the last decade of the nineteenth century. Inspiration helped. Boredom, restlessness, and the thirst for excitement helped more. The bustle and the bicycle craze contributed as much as the profundities of the economist.

The atmosphere, the spirit of the times, the prevailing winds, were all favorable. With the active support of evangelical piety, financial success was the goal if not the obligation of the individual. Failure, if not sinful of itself, at least proved the lack of industry, application, and godliness. Poverty was unclean, and probably the result of drink. The bitterly fought Civil War had freed the American spirit for the pursuit of profit with an intensity and singleness of purpose that had not previously been possible. The opportunist was free to exploit people and other natural resources in the savage battle for fortunes that were piled atop fortunes. There was a lot of prosperity lying around, and it was meant for the enjoyment of those strong enough to seize it.

Horatio Alger had written the American story. From rags to riches, from the log cabin to the White House was the way it was supposed to be; and the riches was a social compulsion as strong as the rags and cabin were admirable. Fierce aggressiveness, sanctioned by indestructible Victorian materialism, drove men and business into uncontrolled competition, and advertising was a way to compete.

12

The Magazines
Succumb to Advertising

THE EMERGENCE OF the magazine as an important advertising medium made possible the upsurge of advertising in the post-Civil War years of the nineteenth century. To the beginning of this period, the newspaper had been the primary medium, with most of the magazines, like Bonner's *New York Ledger,* carrying no advertising at all, advertising only for the books published by the house owning the periodical, or at most, a few mild announcements. Before 1900 the magazine had become the medium par excellence for the newer kind of advertising in which manufacturers of branded merchandise sought wide national markets for their products.

The older magazines were literary monthlies or quarterlies patterned after conservative English models. They were accustomed to looking solely to their subscription lists, and what subsidies they could get, for their rather lean support. In some instances, apart from the literary and intellectual pretensions on which the magazines laid claim to public support, their proprietors looked upon them chiefly as a means of disseminating publicity for their other publishing ventures.

The American literary magazines took themselves seriously, and advertising was not part of their intent. Typical of their attitude and appearance was the *Southern Literary Messenger,* which Edgar Allan Poe edited from 1835 to 1837. Its issue of July, 1844, carried one notice carefully labeled "Advertisement" in capital letters on its inside front cover. It was a dignified notice of "Lieut. Maury's Paper on the Gulf Stream and Currents of the Sea," which was respectfully

dedicated to "The Navy and Commercial Marine of the
United States." The only other matter in the entire issue
which approximated advertising was the brave but rather
wistful description of itself as "The Literary Organ of the
South and West" on the magazine's dun brown back cover.
The leading principle of the *Messenger* was "In the promotion
of a pure NATIVE LITERATURE, and of a devoted NATIONAL
SPIRIT." The *Messenger*, the editor said,

> Has now been established TEN YEARS, during which it has over-
> come MANY AND GREAT OBSTACLES—[One was Poe's persistent drink-
> ing for which he was finally discharged] and attained a wide circula-
> tion and very high character. The efforts of the present Editor will
> be strenuously devoted, not only to the PRESERVATION OF ITS ANCIENT
> FAME, but also its CONSTANT IMPROVEMENT. In this, the flattering
> testimonials he has received during the last twelve months lead him
> to believe that he has already succeeded.

The sea change which the literary periodicals underwent
showed even in the oldest, most conservative, and most intellectual of them all. *The North American Review*, founded
in Boston in 1815, completely disdained advertising for many
years. Edited first by William Tudor, later by such dignitaries as Edward Everett, Jared Sparks, J. G. Palfrey,
Charles Eliot Norton, James Russell Lowell, Henry Adams,
and Adams' student, the historian turned politician, Henry
Cabot Lodge, the *North American* took itself seriously as a
vehicle for the dissemination of Boston culture to denizens
of less favored parts of the United States. Advertising was
incompatible with its close Harvard affiliations and its historical and belletristic approach to life. By the close of the
nineteenth century the *North American* was competing commercially and successfully both with its patrician peers and
the vulgar newcomers among the periodicals. Its once innocent pages were wide open to advertisers, and it was running
to fifty profitable pages of assorted advertising every issue.

Harper's New Monthly Magazine was founded in 1850 to
present selections from other periodicals, mostly English, to
American readers. Such material cost little or nothing. It
promised to "transfer to its pages as rapidly as they may be

issued all the continuous tales of Dickens, Bulwer, Croly, Warren, etc.," and it did. The monthly magazine of 144 pages was an immediate financial success and useful to the Harpers, who reserved it as a private preserve for advertising the books they published. The monthly circulation of fifty thousand which the magazine soon achieved made it ideal for the purpose. Other advertisers tried to get into its pages. *Harper's* refused them admittance. In the early 1870's Fletcher Harper summarily refused an offer of eighteen thousand dollars a year for the last page for advertising the Howe Sewing Machine. *Harper's* spurned all but its own advertising until 1882. By the 1890's *Harper's Magazine* led all others in advertising volume.

When the *Atlantic Monthly* was founded by the literary elite of Boston, Cambridge, and Concord in 1859, with Lowell as editor and Oliver Wendell Holmes as chief contributor, it did not consider advertising respectable and admitted none to its pages. Like the *New York Ledger*, the *Atlantic* advertised, but did not sully its pages with the advertising of others. A typical *Atlantic* newspaper advertisement in its early years, impressive now for the names it listed, was this one.

The
Atlantic Monthly
For
October, 1863,
Is Ready Today,
Containing an Important Article Entitled
Our Domestic Relations; or, How to Treat
The Rebel States
By Hon. Chas. Sumner
Together with contributions from:

John G. Whittier
Ralph Waldo Emerson
J. T. Trowbridge
Rev. D. A. Wasson
Mrs. A. D. T. Whitner

Henry D. Thoreau
J. P. Quincy
Rev. F. H. Bedge, D.D.
Mrs. Hopkinson
G. B. Prescott
C. C. Hazewell
and other popular writers

By this time Ticknor and Fields had taken over the financially insecure Phillips, Sampson & Company and James T. Fields had made himself editor, largely to save the salary of $2,500 annually which had been paid Lowell. Needing the revenue, Ticknor & Fields also began to accept advertising. They not only accepted it, but also made what must then have been spectacular attempts at display.

The May, 1866, issue of the *Atlantic Monthly* had its entire back cover given over to the advertising of photographic materials, albums, stereoscopes and stereoscopic views, photographic cards, and a "Complete Photographic History of the Great Union Contest" with pictures of all the principal battles. The inside front cover was split horizontally by advertisements for the Florence Lock-Stitch Sewing Machine (Best in the World! Great Simplicity! Great Capacity!) and Steinway & Son's Grand, Square, and Upright Pianofortes. Miscellaneous smaller advertisements of clothing, books, steel pens, Dr. J. W. Poland's White Pine Compound, La Forme's Patent Nursing Bottle, shoe dressings, carpet sweepers, window shades, restaurants, life insurance, took up most of the back pages of the issue. There were larger advertisements for the banking house of Jay Cooke & Co. at the corner of Wall and Nassau Streets in New York, which offered government securities of all issues, and for Depew and Potter, which offered more of the same plus other services. Potter just had his name printed at the bottom of the advertisement, but Chauncey M. Depew was already "Late Secretary of the State of New York." Milton Bradley of Springfield, Mass., had a large display advertise-

ment for Bradley's Patent Croquetries backed against the
advertisement of a competitor for "American Croquet Games
. . . Boxwood Sets, which for Superior Strength and
Beauty of Finish are Unsurpassed."

The most surprising display of the *Atlantic's* early advertising ingenuity was a four-page pink section inset after the
front cover. This was premium position stuff with magnificent jumbles of display types and even an etching illustration of Elias Howe in a large advertisement for "The
Oldest Machine in the World," the Howe Sewing Machine.
Other advertisements in the section were for wagons and
carriages, bronze goods, carpetings, and for books. One
brand-new book was already in its thirteenth thousand. This
was *Snow-Bound*, "A Winter Idyl by John G. Whittier,
with Fine New Portrait and Two Illustrations." It was, of
course, a Ticknor & Fields imprint. Another new book, this
published by Carleton in New York—for whom J. Walter
Thompson worked—was *Josh Billings—His Book.*

Two years later, the *Atlantic* having definitely succumbed
to the postwar commercialism which had gathered full force
by 1868, the January issue carried much more advertising
and much more of it for patent medicines and cosmetics.
Book publishers, Tiffany and Company, Clark's Cotton, the
Gorham Manufacturing Company (which warned sternly
against all inferior British and American imitations of its
Electro-plate flatware), The Great American Tea Company,
and Steinway and Florence again, were represented with substantial space; but the more noticeable advertisements were
for hair dressings and cures. Turner's Tic Doulereux or
Universal Neuralgia Pill, "the Undoubted Cure for All Ex-
cruciating Ills Known as Neuralgia or Nervous Ache," had
half the back cover. Its effects were magical. On an inside
page Dr. Babcock's Hair Dressing, its purity guaranteed by
S. Dana Hayes, State Assayer for Massachusetts, was announced as "Scientific, Rational, Safe." Russian Salve was
"a pure vegetable ointment," and Dr. J. W. Poland's Humor
Doctor was "An Invaluable Medicine for Purefying the
Blood." No curative claims were made for the New Grecian

Style Billiard Tables, a gaming device it seems even stranger to find advertised in the proper *Atlantic*.

The issue carried what must have been another noteworthy advertising innovation at the time. Between pages 32 and 33 of the editorial matter was bound a green "Atlantic Monthly Advertising Slip." As magazines now, the 1868 *Atlantic* did not use salable space for blowing its own brassy fanfare. The slip that month advertised "*The Atlantic Almanac*, unique in American Literature," edited by Oliver Wendell Holmes and Donald G. Mitchell (Ik Marvel). It also promoted *Atlantic* gift books and authors, Dickens, Emerson, Curtis, Hawthorne, Lowell, Whittier, Alice Cary, Owen Meredith, Harriet Beecher Stowe, Grace Greenwood.

Roswell Smith was the son of one Asher Smith who wrote a book entitled *How to Get Rich*, published in 1856. The son took his father's advice, made himself rich early through real estate and the law, traveled abroad and in Geneva met J. G. Holland of the *Springfield Republican*. The magazine which the writer and the businessman planned became literary *Scribner's Monthly* in 1870. It took some advertising from the start, but it was not until 1881 when Smith broke from Charles Scribner, bought out Holland, and changed the magazine's name to the *Century Illustrated Monthly Magazine*, that it became a formidable advertising medium. The energetic Smith began the outright solicitation of advertising for the magazine edited by Holland's erstwhile assistant, Richard Watson Gilder.[1] Smith pushed advertising so successfully that the *Century* was soon the leader in advertising volume among the established illustrated monthly magazines.

The *Century* did not hold this position long. Once convinced and encouraged, or perhaps dismayed, by the success of its rival, *Harper's* discarded the remnants of its reluctance in 1882 and began a comparable drive. By 1890 it had outstripped the *Century*, and it maintained the advantage, estab-

[1] Smith paid Hay and Nicolay $50,000 to write their life of Lincoln for the *Century*. He conceived the idea of the *Century* dictionary, and at one point had paid out $600,000 for production with no returns yet in. It was Smith who proposed and began publication of *St. Nicholas* in 1873.

lishing itself as a powerful medium with a large and valuable circulation all through the 1890's.

By September, 1893, the ancient and honorable, but irretrievably converted *North American Review* had quartered its fourth cover for Royal Baking Powder (Absolutely Pure); W. & J. Sloane (Axminsters, Wiltons, Velvets, Moquettes, Brussels); W. Baker & Co.'s Breakfast Cocoa, which had got itself a Gold Medal at Paris in 1878; and Waterbury Watches, whose advertisement savored of the stud farm and the track— "Well-bred watches *result from noble ancestry*, early association, discipline, and natural selection."

There were forty-two other pages of advertising. These were for furniture, food, clothing, medicine, resorts, schools and colleges, bicycles, lecturers, pianos, baby foods, soap, cement, and shirts. One for a new product was illustrated with a chef and a badly tilted balance. In the best modern, scientific style, the text read:

> Lard has been weighed and found wanting: Wanting in the first essentials, purity and healthfulness. COTTOLENE . . tested by eminent physicians and cooking experts, found to be more healthful, more economical, and more durable than lard for every culinary use.

Advertising now had got far beyond the comparatively simple and neighborly approach to a local audience that it had used in the newspapers for more than a century. In this issue of the *North American*, investment advisers plugged for real estate, in Chicago, Florida, and even in Palestine (Texas), which was issuing ten, fifteen, and twenty year 6-per-cent debenture bonds. Millais' famous "Bubbles" took up a whole page for Pears' Soap. The Baltimore Hernia Institute offered a certain and painless cure for hernia and rupture. Cuticura, Pond's Extract, Syrup of Figs, and Londonderry Lithia Spring Water would accomplish almost everything anybody needed, but what they failed to cure, Brigg's Respirator would surely mend. Many of these concoctions and contrivances were advertised in full pages, but one advertiser evidently felt that three tight lines of copy would reach all his prospects among the discriminating readers of *The North American Review.*

OPIUM
Morphine Habit Cured in 10 to 20 days. No pay till cured, Dr. J. Stephens, Lebanon, Ohio

How far *Harper's* outstripped its rivals at this point can be seen by a glance at the November, 1899, issue of the magazine which, so its cover announced in large red type, was "Reduced in Price, Enriched in Quality." It was a heavy issue containing short stories, serials, a profusion of the fine black and white illustrations for which *Harper's* was famous, brightly written articles on Boston at the Century's End, on India, Siberia, Cuba, and "America in the Pacific and Far East." Among the contributors were William Dean Howells, Frederic Remington, and John Kendrick Bangs.

This fat and profitable issue of *Harper's* carried a full 135 pages of advertising to 163 pages of editorial. All of the major book publishers ran page advertisements. There was a three-page advertisement, in editorial style, under the reproduced logotype of the *Times*, London, for the *Encyclopædia Britannica*, which the *Times* was willing to sacrifice at half price. Many of the other well-know magazines found it worth advertising in generous space in *Harper's: Scribner's*, the *Youth's Companion*, which took a double-spread, the *Century*, *St. Nicholas*, and the *Independent*.

This was the end of the century. Advertisers were announcing their plans for the opening of the heralded twentieth century. Food, beverages, insurance, cosmetics, patent medicines by the dozen, beer, stoves, mattresses, cigars, whiskey, typewriters, cameras, shingles, pens, sleighs, carriages, gloves, suits, underwear were all going to be bigger and better. There would be hooks and eyes ("See that Hump?") in 1900, as there had been for years. There would also be "spun-glass linings," garters, stoves, phonographs and gramophones, sewing machines, and even an automobile. Under a spread eagle atop a globe of the world, fluted and garlanded Grecian pillars with the Muses at their bases bordering the text of the advertisement, a picture of the shining vehicle at the bottom, appeared in reverse-lettered flowing script:

"Locomobile"

The Latest and Best

HORSELESS CARRIAGE

Combines all requirements for an ideal and practical pleasure or business vehicle. No better will be made. Time cannot improve it.

$600

Delivery in Sixty Days

Harper's had a select and moneyed clientele. There were excursions to California and to the Mediterranean advertised, to Denver, and Jamaica. Bonds, boats, glassware, electrical novelties, binoculars, revolvers, beef extract were offered for their delectation. Altman's had everything your heart could desire. So did John Wanamaker's.

This was the richness of living as the nineteenth century closed. Here in the *Harper's* advertising was all the food and drink, tobacco, silver, travel, recreation, the fine liquor, and the plenitude of good books that the carriage trade could ask. One advertisement was for the carriage itself. A graceful model displayed by the French Carriage Company of Boston, showed that "ripeness in design which at once distinguishes them." Significantly, the Locomobile advertisement was a full page, while that of the French company was a quarter-page announcement. This may or may not be read as indicative of the changes that were taking place in the world and the way in which these are reflected in advertising, but the whole of this *Harper's* issue showed both the full change that had swept over the United States in thirty years' time, and the way in which eager advertisers worked to reach a lucrative market through the pages of what was perhaps the leading literary and cultural monthly.

There was definite significance in the *Harper's* drop in price to twenty-five cents a copy or three dollars a year an-

nounced on the cover. The literary and literate monthly
magazines were choice and powerful advertising media at the
turn of the century. Their circulations and advertising rev-
enues were at peaks from which those of these class monthlies
which survive have since so markedly declined. Their position,
which they did not relinquish through choice, had already
been threatened. They were soon toppled from their influence and prosperity by cheaper magazines, addressed to a
far wider reading public. In the 1890's these magazines, made
financially possible through the Postal Act of 1879, which
granted favorable mailing privileges to magazines because of
the educational nature of their contents, were already climbing to the positions of journalistic and commercial influence,
and to the profits which magazines of this type still enjoy.

These were magazines which did not originate as literary
periodicals, but were founded deliberately as business ventures. Their intent was not to serve as organs of expression
for a group of authors and as vehicles for the dissemination of
culture, the founding purposes of such magazines as the
North American, the *Atlantic*, and to some extent of *Harper's*,
Scribner's, and the *Century*, but to make money. They were
directed not at the educated few but at the newly literate
many; not at the wealthy, but at the prospering middle
classes untouched by, untroubled by, and uninterested in the
literary monthlies. They set out to achieve large circulations,
but not to depend at all on circulation for revenue. They
were founded, in reality, as advertising media.

The most important of them at this time, in the order of
their appearance, were *Ladies' Home Journal*, 1883; *Cosmopolitan*, 1886; *Munsey's*, 1889; *McClure's*, 1893. Two men,
both from Maine, but distinct and distinctly different, were
the innovators and pioneers in major magazine publishing of
this kind. One of them, Cyrus H. K. Curtis, was recognized
in his own time not only as one of the leading magazine publishers of the day, but also as one of the most important figures
in the new advertising. Social historians since that time have
verified the judgment.

The Gibson girl appeared with her male counterpart in the parlor and on the links in advertising for *Life* in *Harper's Magazine*, Nov. 1899.

The other figure was Frank A. Munsey, and it was he who
definitely challenged the position of the established monthlies
and defeated them in commercial competition. Born the son
of a Maine farmer, Munsey had little formal schooling. The
ambitious boy went to work at the age of fifteen. In the best
Alger tradition, he became a Western Union telegraph operator, went into magazine publishing, operated a profitable
grocery chain, speculated successfully in Wall Street, and
died worth millions of dollars. In the process he made himself undoubtedly the most-hated magazine and newspaper
publisher in New York. Besides buying and killing two
famous Philadelphia women's magazines, *Godey's Lady Book*
and *Peterson's Magazine*, together with a half dozen lesser-
known periodicals, Munsey merged or destroyed the *New
York Morning Sun*, the *New York Press*, the *Globe*, the *Mail
and Express* and finally Bennett's *New York Herald*, which
he sold to the *New York Tribune* when he failed in his efforts
to buy Greeley's old paper from the Reid family.

Frank Munsey deserted his telegraph key in Portland to
found his first magazine in 1882.[2] This was the *Golden
Argosy*, a periodical for juvenile readers which he patterned
after *Golden Days*, a Philadelphia magazine which had Oliver
Optic, Horatio Alger, James Otis, and Harry Castleman as
contributors. He had difficulties with his venture, but there
was no questioning Munsey's ambition, hard work, courage,
or determination. Munsey was his own editor, clerk, advertising solicitor, bookkeeper, and sometimes contributor, during the years of his early struggles. His magazine suffered
various changes, emerged in 1889 as *Munsey's Weekly*, then
in 1891 as *Munsey's*, a monthly magazine of the same size and
format as *Harper's*, *McClure's*, and *Cosmopolitan*, its chief
rivals.

Munsey's did not succeed immediately. The bitterly determined, dictatorial Munsey had several years more of strug-

[2] Edward Bok, who was to become editor of *Ladies' Home Journal* in
1889, quit his job as a Western Union operator in the same year to work
for Charles Scribner and as a sideline started the *Brooklyn Magazine* for
the young people of Henry Ward Beecher's Plymouth Church in Brooklyn.

gle, but he knew what he was trying to do. As Curtis was doing with his women's magazine in Philadelphia, Munsey was trying, with a general monthly, to reach the mass, untapped audience who had not been reached by the better magazines and advertisers who recognized the wealth to be extracted from such a market. In his efforts to do this, Munsey risked a dangerous and decisive move in 1893.

McClure's Magazine had appeared in May, 1893, at fifteen cents a copy. John Brisben Walker cut the price of *Cosmopolitan* to twelve and a half cents in July. In September Munsey announced: "There are times when it is well to get down to bed rock—to get away down to the very substratum of things. At ten cents per copy and a dollar a year for subscriptions in advance. *Munsey's* will have reached that point, a point below which no good magazine will ever go, but to which all magazines of large circulation in America must eventually come."

Munsey's move created a sensation. The powerful American News Company refused to distribute the cheap magazine. Munsey fought the company and won. Less than five years later, Munsey could claim "the biggest circulation of any magazine in the world." By 1901 he claimed double the combined circulation of *Harper's*, *Scribner's*, and the *Century*. Munsey drove now for advertising. With the circulation, the appeal of his ten-cent price, the popular but respectable editorial material (including O. Henry) he offered his readers, he had little trouble getting it.

Munsey did more than that. He set his advertising rate at a dollar per page per thousand—that is, one dollar for every thousand of circulation. By this time he was making about a million dollars a year, which was what he wanted to do. He sold something to people who had not known before that they wanted it, made money for himself, and incidentally contributed to the rise of advertising volume. *Munsey's* became so powerful that in 1898 Frank Munsey took another and even more daring move. At a meeting of the Sphinx Club, the advertising men's own association, in October, 1898, he flung his gauntlet. Advertising agents, Munsey felt, made too much money. Their commisions still ran as high as they could manage, from a low of 10 to a high of about 40 per cent. It was money out of his pocket. "A commission," he told them, "is paid for a purpose, and that purpose is nothing more or less in very truth, than bribery . . . a bribe to influence the advertiser's trusted agent to place advertising with the publisher."[3] Munsey announced he would no longer pay. Angered agency men accepted the Munsey challenge. They saw to it that he would have no commissions to pay. *Munsey's* began to lose advertising. Munsey very quickly went back to the old system.

Munsey's great competitors were *McClure's* and *Cosmopolitan*. The rivalry between *Munsey's* and *McClure's* was sharp. Samuel Sidney McClure, Irish immigrant and graduate of Knox College in Illinois, where he had met John S. Phillips, started the country's first newspaper syndicate in 1884, peddling the work of Kipling, Howells, Stevenson, and other popular writers of the time to newspapers across the country. It was to further this business venture that he founded *McClure's Magazine* in 1893. Not yet started on the muckraking activities which were to make it famous, *McClure's* in the 1890's was bringing delighted readers the work of the English writers McClure's syndicate handled and with it the writing of such American story tellers as Joel Chandler Harris, F. Marion Crawford, and George W. Cable. It was *McClure's*, with *Munsey's* and *Cosmopolitan*, which marked the shift in magazine content from poetry, literary criticism, and the formal essay to light fiction and journalistic reporting of contemporary events.

McClure was a brilliant editor. *McClure's* did well editorially, especially with Conan Doyle in its stable. It did even better in advertising. In July, 1894, *McClure's*, only a year old, was running Bret Harte, Robert Louis Stevenson, and an early piece by Ida M. Tarbell on "A Chemical Detective Bureau," the municipal laboratory in Paris. It had an

[3] George Britt, *Forty Years—Forty Millions, The Career of Frank A. Munsey* (New York: Farrar & Rinehart, Inc., 1933), p. 101.

article on Alphonse Daudet and a good photographic section, "Human Documents."

The same issue had eight pages of advertising preceding the editorial matter and twenty following, exclusive of covers. The inside front cover was all Buffalo Lithia Water; the inside back cover was Roger & Bros. "Most Artistic and Serviceable Electro Silver-Plated Flatware." The back cover was quartered by Ivory Soap (it still floated), Ferris Brand hams and bacon; Cosmo Buttermilk Soap; and G. & J. Pneumatic Bicycle Tires (used on all Ramblers). On the inside pages were, among others, Primley's California Fruit Chewing Gum, the Densmore, Remington, Williams, and Calligraph Typewriters, Murray & Lanman's Florida Water, various corsets, tonics, watches, Niagara Falls, anti-fat pills, railroads, resorts, Hire's, deLong's, bicycles, cocoa, scientific suspenders, Ed Pinaud's, life insurance, and a list of advertised schools, including R. G. Williams Select Family School in Amherst, Massachusetts, and Mt. Holyoke College in South Hadley, opening for its fifty-eighth year.

By the turn of the century, actually June, 1901, a typical issue, *McClure's* advertising volume has shot up from 28 to 102 pages. *McClure's* was helping to establish the name and fame of Sapolio, Ivory Soap, Lea & Perrin's Sauce, Welch's Grape Juice, Van Camp's Soups, Cream O'Wheat, Knox Gelatine, Hire's Root Beer, American Radiator, 1847 Rogers Bros., Cable Pianos, Smith & Wesson Revolvers, Wheatena, Hart, Schaffner & Marx, Stein-Bloch, Corticelli Thread, Johnson's Wax, Kodak, the National Biscuit Company, Gem Safety Razor, Woodbury's Soap, Boston Garters, President Suspenders, Ostermoor Mattresses, B. T. Babbitt, Elgin Watches, Regal Shoes, O'Sullivan's Heels, Pearline, Rubifoam—in short, most of the national advertisers of the day.

The pages of *McClure's* were crammed with the claims of soaps, corsets, bicycles, most of the larger railroads, scores of resorts, and six times as much advertising for schools and colleges as the magazine had had in 1894. There was profuse use of illustration, even in the school advertising. A naked dress sword slashed through the advertising of Montclair

Military Academy which announced, "Manliness, obedience, and punctuality are developed by a military system which does not tolerate a suggestion of hazing." The National Biscuit page, a heavy stock inset, was lithographed in color, its blonde Dutch girl holding a package of Uneeda Biscuit in her chubby hands on one side of the page while Ramona and Athena Sugar Wafers tumbled out of delicately tinted jars and lay strewn on dainty napkins on the other.

By 1900, *Cosmopolitan*, which had begun publication in New York in 1887 after a year in Rochester, had 107 pages of editorial matter and almost as many of advertising. Its contributors included Mark Twain, Henry James, William Dean Howells, Conan Doyle, Kipling, H. G. Wells, and Grant Allen; as formidable an array of writers as any magazine could boast. There was sex appeal in pictures of Maxine Elliott, Sarah Bernhardt, Mary Anderson, and Julia Marlowe, selected to illustrate an article on feminine beauty by Columbia's colorful and finally tragic Prof. Harry Thurston Peck. The *Cosmopolitan*, under Walker, remained a vital and lively, entertaining magazine. A few years later its writers included, in one issue, W. W. Jacobs, Booth Tarkington, Ambrose Bierce, and Edwin Lefevre. The beauties this time were Rose Farquhar, Lillie Langtry, Clarita Vidal, Lucille St. Clair, and Marie Doro. There was an article on "The Real John Weaver," Philadelphia's reform mayor, and another on the bison of the Western plains by Major Gordon W. Lillie, "Pawnee Bill," himself. Feature of the issue was the lurid confessions of a New York detective, an ex-captain of police, whose saga of vice and crime was illustrated by pictures of helmeted members of the force drawing their trusty Colts on Bowery malefactors.

Every page in the fat advertising section carried the legend at the bottom, "When you write please mention the Cosmopolitan." Every big advertiser was in the profusely illustrated magazine, but prize of them all was the full page for the Evans Vacuum Cup, a Scientific Method of Growing Hair. Depicted was a fat man wearing a double-decker helmet with various tubes and wires attached. This fearsome device, "based on logical and scientific principles," carried a money-back guarantee and was fully described in a sixteen-page booklet offered free by the advertiser. Pears' Soap appealed to even higher authority. Its advertisement quoted Bacon: "Cleanliness of body was ever esteemed to proceed from a due reverence to God, to society, and to ourselves."

These were the older magazines, refurbished and revitalized, and, with one notable exception, the new popular monthlies which were the means of conveying the new, modern advertising to the public. The exception was not a general monthly of standard size published in New York, but a larger magazine published in Philadelphia, for a flattered, eager, and multiplying group of women readers.

13

Cyrus H. K. Curtis:
"Advertising is the Essence
of Public Contact."

Cyrus H. K. Curtis, like Frank Munsey, was born in Portland, Maine. Like Munsey, he went into periodical publication as a money-making business. Both were conservative Republicans. Both grew wealthy. There the resemblance ceases. Curtis built where Munsey destroyed. It was Curtis who made both the modern magazine and modern advertising big business. Most of the periodicals Munsey founded have vanished, often killed by Munsey himself. Curtis' publications remain possibly the most representative and certainly among the most durable American magazines.

Early in the 1880's, reversing the approach of most earlier magazine publishers and realizing the power of the new force developing in advertising, Curtis conceived the idea of magazines of vast circulation made possible and profitable through national advertising. This advertising support would enable the magazines to pay high prices for the best writing and art obtainable, draw more readers, result in still greater advertising volume. In a sense, Curtis saw the editorial contents of his magazines as incidental to advertising. This was the approach to which he adhered.

It was advertising Curtis knew, understood, used, and over which he ruled in an even larger world than that of the publishing empire he founded. It was primarily as an advertising man that he was known to his contemporaries. In 1915 Calkins dedicated *The Business of Advertising*, "To Cyrus H. K. Curtis, the Man Who Has Done Most to Put the Modern Conduct of Advertising on the Right Basis." He used a photographic portrait of Curtis as frontispiece. Under a copy of the same official portrait, which he used as illustration in *The History and Development of Advertising*, 1929, Frank Presbrey wrote simply: "The chief figure in modern advertising."

"Do you know why we publish the *Ladies' Home Journal?*" Curtis asked an audience of advertisers at one point early in his career. "The editor thinks it is for the benefit of American women. That is an illusion, but a very proper one for him to have. But I will tell you; the real reason, the publisher's reason, is to give you people who manufacture things that American women want and buy a chance to tell them about your products."

Curtis began early in both periodical publishing and advertising. As a thirteen-year-old schoolboy, using an old hand press for which he had paid two dollars and a half, he began publication of *Young America*, a weekly which he wrote, solicited advertising for, printed, and sold for two cents a copy. After a brief period as a dry goods clerk in Portland, Curtis went to Boston as a newspaper advertising solicitor. In Boston in 1872 he and a partner began publication of the *People's Ledger*. It did not prosper. In 1879, Curtis moved to Philadelphia and began publication of the *Tribune and Farmer*, a four-page agricultural weekly with a subscription price of fifty cents a year.

In the *Tribune and Farmer*, Louisa Knapp Curtis ran a department devoted to women's interests. Noting its popularity, Curtis decided to issue it as a monthly supplement. The first issue of *Ladies' Home Journal* appeared in December, 1883. It was of eight pages, containing fashion notes, advice on child care, an illustrated serial, articles on cooking, needlework, and handicrafts—and advertising. Success of the venture was immediate, so much so that Curtis soon abandoned the *Tribune and Farmer* to concentrate on his new magazine, which had a circulation of twenty-five thousand by the end of the first year.

Curtis sought out big-name writers, starting with Louisa M. Alcott, then at the height of her fame. Borrowing the money, he advertised, advertised, and advertised. Within another six months, he had doubled his circulation. He doubled it again six months later, reaching one hundred thousand. Curtis raised advertising rates, increased the size of his magazine, advertised, and drove circulation to seven hundred thousand. In the first five years of the existence of the *Ladies' Home Journal*, Curtis spent more than a half-million dollars, mostly borrowed, in advertising. In 1889, the *Journal* then six years old, he advertised to the full his hiring of Edward Bok away from Scribner's to be editor of *Ladies' Home Journal*. Bok would be the youngest, highest-paid magazine editor in the country. He would be the only man to edit a woman's magazine. The *Journal's* subscription price was doubled, from fifty cents to one dollar a year.

Curtis testified to his faith in his own medium by advertising in the *Journal* in January, 1889, offering substantial cash prizes to those sending in large numbers of subscriptions. The first prize was five hundred dollars. His was not the only advertising in the sixteen-page issue. The *Journal* was already a department store where women across the country could shop for hair curlers, self-wringing mops, jewelry, hairpins, plain or ornamented, a dozen varieties of corsets, parlor organs, toothpaste, beauty soap, laundry soap, soap that was just soap, books, dolls, tools, toys, kitchen helps. . . . They could read in the advertisements that "1000 Gentlemen Want You—to take an interest in their well-fare and comfort. You cannot commence better than by urging them to shampoo regularly with Packer's Tar Soap, a remarkable remedy for, and preventive of, Dandruff and Baldness."

Farm women in Indiana, Fifth Avenue matrons in New York, debutantes in Wellesley, and sub-debutantes in Nashville were lured with this one:

Braided Wire Bustles Have Come to Stay

For Women Understand They Cannot Afford to

Let Them Go

If a woman has too large hips, the Bustle relieves them of their protuberance; if she have no hips at all, apparently the Bustle supplies the lack; if she have too large an abdomen, the Bustle gives her symmetry; if she be too tall and thin, the Bustle helps her, if she be too short and broad, the Bustle helps her none the less. Of course, there is only one in a thousand so perfectly proportioned, and the other nine hundred and ninety-nine will still avail themselves of its usefulness.

By 1893 the *Ladies' Home Journal* had thirty-four pages, a different, color-illustrated cover each month, and pages of finely reproduced illustrations inside the issues. It had such contributors as William Dean Howells, Mamie Dickens, who wrote of her father, Charles Dickens, Ella Wheeler Wilcox, Hamlin Garland, Mrs. Lyman Abbott, and everywhere Edward Bok, either as himself or as "Ruth Ashmore." There were pages of waltzes by Reginald de Koven and marches by John Philip Sousa. Five years later, the fifteen-year-old magazine had forty-eight instead of the original eight pages. It was printed on slick stock, heavily illustrated, and its circulation was an unbelievable 850,000. Advertising had done it. Edward Bok shared the sentiments of his employer who was now also his father-in-law. In a 1898 editorial he wrote that wherever the mail went, the *Journal* went. It circulated to fifty-nine of the globe's sixty-five civilized nations. He and Curtis both knew what made this possible.

The fact must never be forgotten that no magazine published in the United States could give what it is giving to the reader each month if it were not for the revenue which the advertiser brings the magazine. It is the growth of advertising in this country which, more than any other single element, has brought the American magazine to its present enviable position in points of literary, illustrative, and mechanical excellence. The American advertiser has made the superior American magazine of today possible.

By 1900 the *Ladies' Home Journal,* "monthly Bible of the American home," as it came to be called by admirers and envious detractors, had soared past all competition to the mystical mark no other magazine had ever achieved. Its circulation was one million.

By this time Curtis was spending hundreds of thousands of dollars of the profits of *Ladies' Home Journal* to advertise a new property, a magazine whose name was destined to become virtually a synonym for national advertising. In 1897, after an appeal to his sentiment and not as a deliberate investment, Cyrus Curtis had paid one thousand dollars for a wagonload of old type and the name and title to a decayed and practically defunct Philadelphia weekly called *The Saturday Evening Post.* For a year he let the ancient periodical creak along as it had done. Its two thousand subscribers got the same tired old short stories and serials, which was about all the *Post* had been running for years under the editorship of a Philadelphia newspaper reporter who got ten dollars a week for clipping and pasting it up in his spare time.

Then Curtis decided to revitalize the *Post* and do much the same thing with it in the general weekly field as a magazine for men as he had done with *Ladies' Home Journal* as a woman's monthly. It would be a weekly magazine of fiction and light articles directed to the American businessman, just as the *Journal* was directed to his wife. It would be sold at just half the ten-cent price of the established weeklies, *Harper's Weekly, Frank Leslie's,* and *Collier's.*

Curtis looked around for an editor and decided on Arthur Hardy, a former *Cosmopolitan* editor. Hardy was in Persia as U.S. Minister. Curtis arranged to meet him in Paris and left *The Saturday Evening Post* in charge of George Horace Lorimer, a thirty-one year old reporter from the *Boston Post,* son of a Baptist evangelist, who seemed to want the job. Curtis missed connection with Hardy, returned from abroad, found Lorimer carrying out his plans so well for the *Post* as a magazine of business success stories that he made his appointment permanent, and George Horace Lorimer became to *The Saturday Evening Post* what Edward Bok was to *Ladies' Home Journal.*

The *Post* grew slowly. Had not Curtis poured money into advertising and promotion, it might not have gone at all. The deficit reached $800,000, then $1,000,000, then $1,250,-000, but *Ladies' Home Journal* was good for it. Circulation for the five-cent magazine was driven up from 2,231 in 1897 to 33,000 in 1898, to 97,000 in 1899, to 182,515 in 1900. Advertising moved more slowly. *Post* advertising revenue, despite Curtis' heavy promotion, showed a gain of less than $2,000 in 1898 over 1897, and it took tremendous effort to push it to $59,388 the next year. Then came the first big jump, to $159,572 in 1900. Growth from that point on was fantastic—to $1,058,934 by 1905, three times as much by 1909, over $5,000,000 by 1910. After that for many years advertising in *The Saturday Evening Post* grew by at least a million dollars, usually by three or four or five millions, each year. Circulation passed the million mark in 1909.

One of the first large-space advertisers in *The Saturday Evening Post* was the Prudential Insurance Company of America, which took 112 lines, February 25, 1899. Quaker Oats took the first two-color advertisement, the back cover for September 30 of the same year. The first automobile advertisement in a magazine that was to become famous for its automotive advertisements, was in the issue of March 31, 1900. It was a one-inch single-column advertisement placed by W. E. Roach, who described himself as successor to Roach & Barnes, 821 Arch Street, Philadelphia. Roach's car was advertised as "The automobile that gives satisfaction; highest award at the National Export Exposition in Philadelphia, Pa., in 1899. Prompt delivery, catalog for 2-cent stamp."

Now advertisers tumbled into the *Post.* The venture for which the publishing trade had almost universally prophesied only complete and early failure was a fantastic success. Lorimer was shaping the magazine. Curtis was selling it. When it was obvious that nothing was going to stop the forward impetus of the magazine, Curtis and his wife went off for an Italian tour, and were led the usual rounds of Naples, Venice,

Florence, Rome. Curtis, a small man physically, smoked huge black cigars. He had difficulty obtaining them. A sympathetic observer, who knew him and was traveling the same circuit, found Curtis one night in his suite at the Hotel Danielli at Venice, the table literally covered with boxes of cigars. They were all the hotel had in stock. None was the kind he smoked. Curtis waved at them unhappily. The cigars were bad, and he was excessively bored with Italy's churches, painting, statuary, and ruins. His interest was in business, in the economic life of his time, not in relics of the past.

Curtis was restless away from the advertising he had helped create, knew, and so thoroughly understood. The one bright spot in the week for the unwilling traveler was the regular cable from George Horace Lorimer telling him how many lines of advertising the current issue of *The Saturday Evening Post* had closed with.[1]

---

[1] Earnest Elmo Calkins, *"and hearing not . . ."* (New York: Charles Scribner's Sons, 1946), p. 212.

14

Bacon, Tea, and Soap
—Thomas Lipton and Thomas Barratt

PART OF THE IMPULSE and impetus behind the force which burst into the eruption of advertising in the United States in the 1890's sprang from England. It sprang from the untrammeled energies and uninhibited advertising of two men. One of them sold soap. The other, Thomas Lipton, sold ham, butter, bacon, and tea.

Thomas Lipton was born in 1850 in Glasgow of Irish parents, a circumstance which enabled him to claim in later life that he was Scottish or that he was Irish, as the occasion seemed to demand. His parents, importing their stock from Ireland, ran a small butter and ham shop in one of the poorer sections of Glasgow. Lipton began to help in the shop as a small boy, and he was a salesman from the start. He soon suggested that his mother sell all the eggs. They would look larger in her small hands. He began to imitate the dialects of their Scotch and Irish customers, so that he could reply in the accents of a buyer's own village, immediately establishing a friendly relationship. It was a trick he used for years. "I am not exaggerating when I say that in this way I made thousands of customers. Each thought Thomas Lipton came from his or her own home town and spread the news among friends."[1]

[1] Sir Thomas Lipton, *Leaves from the Lipton Logs* (London: Hutchinson & Co., Ltd., 1931), p. 25.

As soon as he left school, Lipton looked around for larger
worlds to conquer. The largest accessible seemed to be the
United States. He made his way to America and spent the
next five years working as a grocer's clerk in New York, as a
field hand on rice plantations in the South, as a streetcar con-
ductor, and at anything else that offered. America was the
advertised land of opportunity. Lipton, by his own admiring
admission, was pushful, self-reliant, and ambitious. Yet, somehow, fortunately for him, he did not prosper as an immigrant
in the United States, though he did find one treasure. In New
York he saw and remembered this advertising couplet:

> The man who on his trade relies
> Must either bust or advertise

Lipton went back to Glasgow. On his twenty-first birth-
day, with a total capital of one hundred pounds, he opened
his first store on Stobcross Street. He spent half his savings
on furnishings and inventory, kept the rest for contingencies
that never came. It is easy to see why. Lipton opened early,
closed late. He kept his store brightly shining. He wore
white overalls and an apron. When there were no customers
in the shop, he went outside and polished the window so he
could salute passers-by with a cheery greeting. He also undercut the prices of all his competitors in the crowded, dense-
ly populated central district of the busy manufacturing city.

He worked hard, he said, but ". . . that would have counted
for little if, even at this very early stage of my career, I had
not been quick to grasp how great can be the Power of Advertising."[2]

Lipton's first advertising venture was a handbill urging
housewives to patronize his market. Next he had a poster
prepared emphasizing his low prices. Then he took a small
newspaper advertisement to push his extra-fine bacon. He
had a large wooden ham painted and hung before the shop.
The sun melted the paint, and people came to laugh at Lipton's greasy ham. If humor was what they liked, Lipton
would give it to them.

[2] *Ibid.*, p. 95.

He bought two pigs, had them scrubbed clean, had pink and blue ribbons tied around their necks, and had them driven through the Glasgow streets under a banner reading, "Lipton's Orphans." Mummy and daddy were ham and bacon in the Lipton market. He bought more pigs. The pigs, with crowds following them and an Irish countryman in knee-breeches and billycock hat driving them along with his shillelagh, were driven finally to the shop itself. Their sides painted, "I'm going to Lipton's. The best shop in town for Irish bacon," they tied up Glasgow's horse-drawn traffic, causing great excitement. Lipton hired a cartoonist to do drawings of them with gag lines that directed always to his shop.

He bought cheap and direct from producers, sold direct to the public, and he used every advertising device he could think of. He thought of many, for he thought of little else. For a period of at least twenty years, he says, all of his spare time went to dreaming up new advertising schemes.

By the end of three years, Lipton was able to open a branch shop in Glasgow. Six months later he opened another. He opened one in Dundee. He kept on opening shop after shop everywhere he could in the United Kingdom. Always he waited on the first customer himself. Always he arranged loud advance publicity.

He issued thousands of Lipton one-pound notes. They were facsimiles of those issued by Scottish banks but read across the face: ". . . promise to pay on demand at any establishment for 15 shillings, ham, butter, and eggs as offered elsewhere for One Pound Sterling." The notes were at least a sensation. Many were redeemed at Lipton shops. More got into general circulation and were used as currency, to pay debts, or thriftily deposited in collection plates at church.

Lipton fitted concave and convex mirrors in each of his shops. The one marked "Going to Lipton's" showed people elongated and miserable; the other, marked, "Coming from Lipton's," showed them fat and happy. He hired balloons to drop advertising telegrams. He recruited an army of two hundred men, dressed them as Chinese, marched them be-

tween sandwich boards extolling his tea. Like Barnum, he
imported his own Jumbo. This Jumbo was a huge cheese he
had made and shipped from Whiteborough, New York. For
weeks in advance, Lipton advertised that it was being made,
that it had been shipped, that it was on the high seas, that it
had taken all the milk of eight hundred cows for six days to
make it. Crowds greeted Jumbo at the docks. Lipton had it
hauled by steam engine to the window of one of his stores.
Gold sovereigns were hidden in the cheese. Police were
called out to protect the huge crowds that swarmed on Chris-
mas eve when the cheese was to be cut. Lipton imported
larger three-ton cheeses, had them dragged to the stores by
circus elephants, hired a hundred Edinburgh University students to cut one, advertised, as a police warning, that people
ran the risk of being choked on the gold sovereigns. Droves
came begging to be choked.

As Lipton's business expanded, his advertising swelled.
Ireland proved an inadequate source for his markets. Lipton
began to buy dairy products in Switzerland and Denmark.
His second invasion of the United States was far different
from his first. He opened his own Chicago pork slaughter-
house where he killed three to four hundred pigs a day, moved
it later to South Omaha and raised his daily slaughter rate to
from two to four thousand. When he went into the tea
market, Lipton defied the established interests and began to
raise his own tea on his own Ceylon estates, package it, and
sell it direct to the consumer. He moved his huge business,
for Lipton had ten thousand employees now in his factories,
plantations, warehouses, and stores, from Glasgow to London.

All of this was accompanied by the loudest possible fanfare. Lipton started his own printing plant to do advertising designs and posters in twenty different languages, and
he sent his multilingual advertising all over the world. He
covered the United States with his advertising, spending vast
sums on campaigns for Lipton's Tea. "Lipton" was painted
in huge letters on the fleet of refrigerator cars that moved his
pork products across the continent. In England and in the
United States his newspaper advertising never stopped. Lip-

ton entertained royalty aboard his yacht, the *Erin,* and American celebrities—Mark Twain, Edison, Henry Ford—as well.
That was advertising too. Four times his various *Shamrocks*
raced for the America's Cup. Four times Lipton failed, but
the advertising was invaluable. Lipton was admiral of a fleet
of thirty-three craft, including launches and tenders, which
were manned by a complement of 198 captains, pilots, naval
architects, engineers, firemen, cooks, messengers, and secretaries. Advertising had paid him well.

The man who sold soap was Thomas A. Barratt. Once
upon a time, so the story goes, a Cornish hairdresser with his
scents and pomades made his way to London. In 1790 he set
up in London's Soho and soon attracted distinguished patrons,
some of them French nobility who had fled to England.
Andrew Pears compounded his own beauty preparations,
rouges, creams, powders, and dentifrices, and soon a fine soap.
It was mild, fragrant, and beautifully translucent. He continued to cut, singe, and curl hair, but he also began to sell
the soap. He alone knew its secret ingredients but, as always,
rivals began to counterfeit his discovery. They could not get
the translucency, but they could sell their harsher soap in a
similar package. To put a stop to this, Pears began to sign
his name to every packet of his own soap.

The business prospered. In 1835 Pears brought in a grandson, Francis, as partner and opened a larger shop to make his
soap. Greatly daring, he canvassed, a little timidly, for new
customers and began to spend about eighty pounds a year in
advertising. He took a great-grandson of the founder, another Andrew Pears, into the prospering business and in 1865
admitted Thomas Barratt as part owner. Barratt put up seven
thousand pounds.

Barratt was joint proprietor, bookkeeper, salesman, and
commercial traveler. Over the futile protest of the Pears
family, he became advertising director as well. Barratt en-
visoned advertising on a scale not yet attempted by any other
manufacturer. He began to spend vast sums wildly, frightening Francis Pears out of the business. He plastered posters
everywhere. Pears' Soap, he proclaimed to the world, was

pure, healthy, and made you beautiful. Barratt backed his claims with proof and testimony.

He got doctors and chemists to guarantee his product. The President of the Royal College of Surgeons and Dr. Redwood, Ph.D., F.C.S., F.I.C., professor of chemistry and pharmacy at the Pharmaceutical Society of Great Britain, swore Barratt told the truth. Barratt announced everywhere that authorities found Pears' Soap had "the properties of an efficient yet mild detergent without any of the objectionable properties of ordinary soaps."[3]

So much for the purity. Now for the beauty. Barratt persuaded Lillie Langtry, famous actress, to agree that "Since using Pears' Soap, I have discarded all others." Barratt exploited this testimonial all over England. It became so famous that *Punch,* choosy in such matters, did it the honor of parody. April 26, 1882, it published a pen and ink drawing of an unkempt tramp, obviously dirty, obviously smelly, bent laboriously over a table and writing carefully, "Two years ago I used your soap, since when I have used no other." Barratt had thousands of copies of the cartoon reproduced and distributed it everywhere. He used it in newspaper and magazine advertising, and Pears' waxed larger and more profitable than ever. Barratt used the same tramp in later advertisements. One showed him, dirtier than ever, rushing, distraught, for a Royal Humane Society life belt on the Thames embankment. A sign over the life belt read, "Whilst There's Life, There's Soap." A cake of Pears' lay at his feet.

In 1886 Sir John Millais painted his grandson blowing bubbles. The curly headed child, in velvet suit and ruffled lace collar, bowl in lap and clay pipe in hand, was looking upward at a floating, iridescent bubble. The *Illustrated London News* purchased the oil painting and used it as a colored supplement. Barratt paid the magazine £2,500 for the painting. Millais, though others attacked him for his commercialism, offered no objection when Barratt told him of his plan to use it in advertising Pears' soap. Obviously the

---

[3] Edward Ellison, "The Story of Pears," *Progress,* Summer, 1950.

Punch presented this hirsute derelict to Pears', who happily exploited his beautifully unwashed state in a series of humorous advertisements.

iridescent bubble could have been made by no less delicate
a soap.

This move by Barratt caused a new sensation, and led to
other advertisers' seeking out and buying other art works and
using them for advertising purposes, an outcome which Millais
may have foreseen and certainly approved. Barratt used other
pictures in later advertising. One of the best known was that
of an infant struggling to get out of his tin bath on a bright
oriental rug to reach a cake of Pears' Soap which had fallen
on the floor beyond his reach. Captioned "He won't be happy
till he gets it!" this advertisement, too, struck the public fancy.

When Barratt decided to invade the American market, he
knew exactly how to go about it. Americans were always
awed by authority, and one authority outweighed all the rest.
He went to Brooklyn, pushed his way through a snowstorm,
and arrived in the midst of a reception at the home of Henry
Ward Beecher. After the guests had left, he told Beecher
who he was and what he wanted. Beecher laughed, sat down,
and wrote the desired testimonial. Accounts of the incident
do not mention the price paid.

Barratt hurried back to New York and bought the whole
front page of the *New York Herald*. He reprinted it in hun-
dreds of other newspapers and magazines, and in leaflets.
Beecher's testimonial first appeared on the back cover of
Ladies' Home Journal, in May, 1889. Under the heading
PEARS' SOAP in large black capitals, a bust portrait of Henry
Ward Beecher with his flowing locks and noble brow in the
upper left-hand corner of the advertisement, the text read:

> If CLEANLINESS is next to GODLINESS, soap must be considered
> as a means of GRACE and a clergyman who recommends
> MORAL things, should be willing to recommend soap. I am
> told that my commendation of PEAR's Soap has opened for it
> a large market in the UNITED STATES. I am willing to stand by
> every word in favor of it I ever uttered.
>
> A man must be fastidious indeed who is not satisfied with it.

Pears' with a large factory in England and luxurious London offices was now an internationally known product, and

Thomas A. Barratt famous on two continents for his advertising. It never relaxed while Barratt was in charge.

He was determined to make soap and Pears' synonomous. "How do you spell soap?" one of his advertisements asked. "Why P-E-A-R-S', of course!" He asked an even more famous question. "Good Morning! Have you used Pears' Soap?" Greeting and answer became popular repartee. Some men and women were afraid to greet each other before noon for fear of the inevitable response. Children taunted each other with the words. It was impossible to open an American magazine without seeing the face of a pleasant gentleman looking over his newspaper to greet the reader with "Good Morning! Have you used Pears' Soap?" Impish elders taught babies just learning to talk the proper reply should some stranger happen to bid them good morning. In 1890 in the *North American Review* the heading of a full-page advertisement was in script, "Good morning! Have you used Pears' Soap?" The rest of the page in bold face was used to say simply:

Paris Exhibition, 1899

PEARS obtained the only gold medal awarded solely
for toilet SOAP in competition with ALL THE WORLD.

Highest possible distinction.

Barratt had brought science, the stage, the church, high art, and a commonplace greeting to the uses of advertising. This was no mean feat, for most of what he accomplished had not been done before he did it. He has a right to his position in the advertising story. He was shrewd enough to use sentiment, too, particularly with his American readers, and sentiment went with poetry, at least with verse, in his day.

The back cover of *Ladies' Home Journal*, December, 1896, showed a lady and a gentleman, in discreet negligee in the privacy of their living room. They faced a framed picture of "Bubbles" on the wall of their warm and happy home. The word "Pears'" appeared in the body of the advertisement only on the deep frame of the picture. Hovering wispily in the

Pears' Soap won an advertising triumph with this cheery greeting. It harassed the family at breakfast and bedeviled the populace all day.

background were the bewigged ghosts of eighteenth-century gentlemen and their ladies. The verse imprinted on the scene was this:

> Thrice blessed be "the tie that binds
> The fellowship of kindred minds."
> The past and present join to praise
> The soap that's brightened both their days.
> Pears' binds the men and maids today
> With those a hundred years away.
> Gallants and dames and maids and men
> Find Pears' perfection—now and then.

Another advertisement in the *Ladies' Home Journal* series showed a sweet young girl, face transfigured with devotion, in the choir loft of her church, "Singing the praises of Pears' Soap."

In 1897, at a time of minor international crises, Barratt, the international advertising man, attracted great notice with an advertisement which emphatically declared: "Pears' Soap and an Anglo-American alliance would improve the complexion of the universe."

In 1899 a full page in *Harper's* was given to reproduction of a painting. Its subject was a gentle, white-haired lady in mobcap, fascinator about her shapely shoulders, holding a very recognizable cake of soap. The legend beneath was simply, in flowing script, "Old Friends." A line beneath the border framing the picture read: "The purity and refreshing qualities of Pears' Soap give it a charm over all others." Nostalgia, even then, was good for sales.

So was the hard manliness of war on the African veldt, sun, khaki, sand, the British Empire, and one of the world's romantic soldiers of fortune. A page in *McClure's* in 1901 showed a torn newspaper clipping, beneath it a cake of Pears' Soap. The clipping read that Winston Churchill, "the English war correspondent," had come to the conclusion that "the distinguishing characteristic of the English-speaking people as compared with the other white races is that they wash and wash at regular intervals." Churchill had decided in 1901 that England and the United States were bound by a common tie. He wrote: "England and America are divided by an ocean of salt water, but they are united by a bath tub of fresh water and soap." And, of course, said the advertisement in its own person, "it's—" the sentence was completed by the wording on the cake of soap displayed:

MADE BY

PEARS

IN GREAT BRITAIN

In 1901 Pears took the entire back cover of *Ladies' Home Journal* in color to announce that it had just won another prize, this one at the Paris Exhibition. It was Pears' twenty-first international award.

Barratt knew what he was about. He also knew his own place in the scheme of things. "Any fool," he said, "can make soap. It takes a clever man to sell it."

15

Impresarios, Agents, and Scribes

THE DELUGE OF ADVERTISING in the 1890's was brought about largely through the ambition and industry of the advertising agents. They were gadflies stinging the timid or torpid businessman into advertising, opportunists whipping up competition everywhere, order chasers who gave each other no quarter. Most of them were buyers, sellers, and procurers of newspaper, magazine, and poster space, and most of them pretended to offer no other service. Their concern was not the advertiser or the medium but themselves. They placed advertising where it would do them the most good, in space they controlled or could buy cheap, or in periodicals from which they could wrest the largest commissions, up to 50 per cent—a percentage they could often increase by devious means to considerably more. Unfettered by ethics, willing devotees of the flexible commercial morality of the hotly competitive day, they were traders who assumed no responsibility beyond that of making as much money as they could.

Despite the dignity of their beards, their stand-up collars, and their broadcloth coats, they were a raffish lot in the eyes of many of their contemporaries, who considered advertising as something between a bastard form of journalism and an illegitimate offspring of business. Most of the agents were colorful individualists. For a time the group included even "Petroleum V. Nasby" (John R. Locke), owner of the *Toledo Blade*, in which he ran the humorous letters which so delighted

229

Abraham Lincoln. Locke was for a time a partner of James H. Bates, who had been earlier with Pettingill. He was a poseur who dressed like the backwoods Kentuckian he had invented, drank much, talked about drinking more than he drank, owned with Bates the forerunner of the Remington typewriter. Locke-Nasby quit advertising finally to lecture on temperance.

Most of the agents had been in patent medicine advertising. Patent medicines remained their largest accounts. They dabbled in patent medicines continually, buying and selling trademarks, swapping space for pills and liquors they could sell for money or merchandise. Some of them returned to the patent medicine field after trying others. The stuff was valueless if not pernicious. Advertising alone gave it value. It was patent medicine advertising tested a man's mettle. Patent medicine could give an advertising man a sense of accomplishment. They had few illusions about what they did or about each other.

J. Walter Thompson had persuaded the established magazines to accept advertising. As soon as he could, he went further than that. He bought up all the space in the magazines which consented to run advertising, then peddled it to other agents as well as to advertisers, pulling down two fat commissions. The magazines had to pay a commission to the agent placing the copy and another to Thompson.[1]

A. D. Lasker explained how the system worked in 1898. J. Walter Thompson by this time controlled all the space in most of the women's magazines as well as in the general monthlies: ". . . if we placed an advertisement in the *Delineator* we got at that time 25% commission. If I remember, the rate was $2. We paid $1.50 and then Thompson got 25¢ on everything we or any other agent placed, and Thompson got 75¢ on everything they placed."[2]

---

[1] Earnest Elmo Calkins, "Fifty Years of Advertising," *Printers' Ink*, September 19, 1947, p. 43.
[2] A. D. Lasker, *The Lasker Story . . . As He Told It* (Chicago: Advertising Publications, Inc., 1953), p. 2.

The Thompson monopoly forced the *Century, Scribner's,* and *Harper's* into setting up advertising departments and managers of their own, but J. Walter Thompson could still boast to Calkins, "No one will ever make as much money out of advertising as I have!"

Thompson was not alone in such agency practice. N. W. Ayer, as Lasker points out, controlled the agricultural papers in much the same way that Thompson controlled the general and women's magazines; Lord & Thomas controlled the religious periodicals. "The trick," Lasker explained, "was to twist the list around and get the most you could on it." Few frowned on this profitable legerdemain. It was what advertising agents did and were expected to do. If there were moralists in the 1890's who did not share the general admiration for such twisting and turning, they must still have found the pecadilloes of the advertising agents insignificant compared to the magnificent piracies of the real manipulators of finance and industry.

These agents merely placed advertising. They did not prepare it. Preparation of copy was the work, at this time, of an entirely different group of men, of advertising writers. Some of these were in the employ of merchants or manufacturers. More of them were independent writers who sold their work to advertisers. Some even set themselves up as ad-writing bureaux. They were "literary men," in the parlance of the era, not businessmen, as the agents considered themselves.

One of the successful and admired writers of advertising was John E. Powers. Powers, who had been a subscription agent for the *Nation*, went to England as a salesman of sewing machines, and he conquered the country for Willcox and Gibbs. Sewing machines turned up in advertisements disguised as news. They came in prose, and they came in rhyme. Powers even got actors dressed in traditional costumes to demonstrate the machines in Christmas pantomime at Drury Lane. Britain laid low, Powers steamed back to the United States. He went to work for Lord & Taylor. It was for the New York department store that he developed his characteristic short, pithy style of newspaper advertising. He did it so effectively that John Wanamaker hired him away and took him to Philadelphia.

Powers studied Wanamaker's products, talked to people trying to find out what consumers wanted, brought product and want together in brief, lively advertisements. He wrote simply, saying, "The commonplace is the proper level for writing in business, where the first virtue is plainness, 'fine writing' is not only intellectual, it is offensive."

Wanamaker exulted in the money Powers' advertisements brought in. He reiterated his faith in advertising. "Every cent I have spent in advertising has created tangible assets that could be converted into cash." The largest local advertiser of his time, and the most successful, Wanamaker could afford to pontificate about it. "Advertising," he said at another time, "is no game for the quitter. Advertising does not jerk—it pulls. If stuck to, it will exert an irresistible force." Wanamaker had other theories about advertising: "When times are hard and people are not buying, that is the very time advertising should be the heaviest. To get people to buy, you must advertise. I believe in advertising all the time. I never stop advertising."

In Wanamaker, Powers had an employer after his own heart, but Powers had one habit which, even when it worked, was bound to irritate an advertiser-employer. He insisted on telling the literal truth in his advertisements. One day as Powers was going through the Wanamaker store the manager of the rubber department told him they had a lot of rotten gossamers (light waterproofs) they wanted to get rid of. Powers wrote in his next day's advertisement: "We have a lot of rotten gossamers and things we want to get rid of." The raincoats were sold out that morning.

In another advertisement he offered neckties reduced from a dollar. "They're not as good as they look, but they're good enough—25¢."

Wanamaker bought the output of a hat factory, 600 hats, 300 with English labels, 300 with American. Powers wrote: "You can take your choice and have an English label or an American label in your 'iron hat.' " As a sales device, Wanamaker decided to put English labels in all the hats. Powers

then told the public in Wanamaker advertising that the hats
were half American, half English, but that there were English
labels in all of them. This was a little too much frankness.
Wanamaker had the labels replaced as they had been. Powers
wrote a final advertisement which somehow got printed without Wanamaker's seeing it. This advertisement read:
"We've changed back to the original labeling. Now you
can have an American hat with an American label." Wanamaker fired Powers.

Powers now entered the lists as a free lance, battling for
Scott's Emulsion and Beecham's Pills; Beecham's and Carter's
Little Liver Pills, having conquered hither, were reaching for
outer Gaul. Besides jousting for the high-paying patent medicines—Scott's is said to have paid Powers a hundred dollars a
day—Powers plied his talent for Macbeth Lamp Chimneys and
Murphy's Varnish. What became known as the "Powers'
style" in advertising was better exemplified in his work for
some of these than in his earlier Wanamaker copy. Terse and
evocative statements were the Powers' hallmark.

> I don't make all the lamp chimneys; no trouble with mine.
>
> Macbeth

> Nobody else apparently dares put his name on his lamp chimneys.
>
> Macbeth

Powers could wax literary and eloquent when he wished, yet
make his points in simple, authoritative statements:

"The Excellent in the Permanent"

So says Tennyson, and so says Nature. The finest things are
the things that abide. Iron rusts out; stone crumbles to dust;
gold remains untarnished for ages. "Fine" does not always
mean "frail." Among the things of its class, the finest is
always the firmest, or solidest, or strongest, and the most
durable. Diamond is harder than glass, because it is finer. A
persian rug wears longer than a common carpet, because it is
finer. Mahogany outlasts hemlock because it is finer. It is
exactly so with varnish; a cheaper grade, composed of poorer
materials, is like basswood or shoddy cloth. Only fine varnish
can be strong and firm and durable. It costs a little more, and
it is worth a great deal more.

At Wanamaker's Powers was succeeded by another advertising writer whose name has become legendary. This was
Manly M. Gillam. Gillam was managing editor of the *Philadelphia Record*, a newsman who had paid little attention to
advertising until the *Record's* publisher asked him to write
some sort of advertisement to sell the butter from his herd of
Holsteins. Gillam imitated the Wanamaker style of advertising so successfully that the butter was quickly sold, and John
Wanamaker himself came to the *Record* office to find out
who had written the advertising. He hired Gillam in 1886,
and Gillam began to fill anything from a half column to two
or three newspaper pages daily—for Wanamaker was spending between $300,000 and $400,000 a year—with what he
described as "common-sense," straightforward, newsworthy
advertising.

Enoch Morgan's Sons Company had no less an advertising
writer when they started extensive advertising of Sapolio in
the 1870's than Bret Harte. The Sapolio advertising was done
through cartoons and humorous illustrations. Harte wrote
the first series of accompanying verses, helping to start the
jingle craze that swept over advertising a few years later.

Nath'l C. Fowler, Jr., was coming along now. In the
late 1880's, though he had begun with corsets, he became
noted for his advertisements for Columbia bicycles. By 1891
he was an advertising agent in Boston, but he gave this up to
devote all his time to writing advertising. Fowler's was a
practical, no-nonsense approach. Advertising was to sell
goods, not to be humorous, whimsical, or entertaining. "All
this poppycock advertising may look well," he said, "and like
the sensational preacher create a tremendous stir, but the question is: 'Does it sell goods!' "[3] Fowler believed in concen-
trating on a central sales point and in hammering at it.

He was far removed in temperament and practice from
another writer of advertising who quit the Larkin Soap Company in Buffalo in 1893 to found the Roycroft Shop and write
advertising for Wrigley, Elgin, Heinz, Knox Hats, Gillette

[3] Quoted in *Printers' Ink*, Fifty Years, 1888-1938, July 28, 1938.

Razors, and Steinway Pianos. Hubbard, who became most widely known for his "Message to Garcia" in 1899 and for ornate and precious "Little journeys"—"Little Business Journeys," "Little Journey to the Home of Steinway Pianos," "Little Journey on Stetson Hats"—proudly signed his work, "An Advertisement by Elbert Hubbard." Hubbard drowned on the *Lusitania* in 1915.

Most advertising writers were then, as now, anonymous. A whole tribe of mute, inglorious Miltons—more inglorious than mute—none of whom achieved the fame of Powers, Gillam, Harte, Charles Austin Bates, Fowler, or Hubbard, wrote the rhymes, slogans, and sentiments for the advertising cards of the 1870's and 1880's. A horde of unknown artists did their atrocious best for the humorous and sentimental pictures on the cards.

The cards, most of them cardboards of about three to five inches were printed and distributed by the hundreds, the thousands, the tens of thousands, and probably by the millions. They were sold to retailers, department stores, manufacturers, and everybody who could be persuaded to have his name imprinted on a gross or a ton or two. Children collected them. Small boys swapped them. Adults pasted them in albums. There are still private collections of thousands of them which are exhibited in museums from time to time, and even shelved in public libraries. Bustles, corsets, shoe polish, magazines, all kinds of patent medicines, hammocks, soap, sewing machine, spool cotton, stoves—virtually everything was advertised on these cards. Dry goods stores, dentists, shirt manufacturers, used them with indiscriminate abandon.

One Lydia Pinkham card showed two small girls dressed in the height of the day's fashion, their arms about each other. The sentiment was conveyed by the single word, "Grandchildren." One asked a group of pictured men, obviously a tramp, a workman, a dude, a banker, and a businessman, "Is Marriage a Failure?" The answer was, "Not if your wife uses SAPOLIO." A Florence oil stove card in two panels showed a worn-out housewife collapsed with a palm leaf fan in her hand before a red hot coal stove; then a happy young

housewife and her gleeful children dancing before a cool
Florence stove.

One card, showing an irate older man dousing a younger
man with a hose, advised suitors that they need not worry
when a father turned cold water on them, not if they were
wearing the recommended brand of celluloid collar and cuffs.
One side of a Wanamaker card, meant evidently for rural distribution, read: "When you want samples of dry goods from
the city and wish to be sure of latest styles, lowest prices, and
quick reply, address: John Wanamaker, Grand Depot, Philadelphia." The reverse side showed two lovebirds billing and
cooing in a wreath of flowers and advised, "Take from my
mouth the wish of happy years."

Crude humor and cloying sentiment were the rule on the
advertising cards, most of them lithographed in violent colors.
Wild West scenes, bustled beauties, comic Negroes, dilapidated tramps, flowers, childhood scenes, they were the valen-
tines of trade and industry to people who treasured them as
art and wit or poetry. One beauty showed a young woman
at her sewing machine, a vase of flowers nearby, her cat sitting
on the Brussels carpet, her canary hanging from the ceiling.
On the wall a sampler said:

> J. & P. Coats'
> Best Six Cord
> SPOOL COTTON

On the white cloth in the machine was spelled out, "For hand
and machine, white, black, and colors." Leaning negligently
on the sill of the open window, visible through the folds of
the curtains held back with loops of blue ribbon, was a straw-
hatted gentleman fingering his luxuriant moustache. The
hero was whispering to the shy seamstress:

> Strong and reliable my love shall be
> As that thread ever is to thee.

It would take a strong-willed consumer of the 1880's to with-
stand an advertising appeal like this.

Mothers fondled their darlings, tramps leered, white hunters chased buffalo, ships bounded through storms, fat men beamed and thin men scowled on the advertising cards. Workmen struggled to get into boots not properly softened with the proper harness oil, popular actresses smirked, and great athletes showed their muscles. There was something for everybody on the advertising cards, and a livelihood for advertising writers and artists.

Some cards came in series. They were given away as purchase premiums and a come-on device. The customer who had got one with her starch would certainly send her little boy back to buy some bluing so they could get the next installment of the story. One set showed the horrible results which would accrue if people turned to other beverages than the Great Atlantic & Pacific Tea Company's tea and coffee. The first card showed a silk-hatted gentleman drinking a gin cocktail in a vile saloon. The next card showed him drinking a whiskey straight, then "A Claret Punch" showed him giving a bloody nose to the bartender. "A Brandy Smash" was a real brawl. On the last card the disheveled, dilapidated, and dejected gentleman was sobering up in jail. The card's title was "Bread and Water."

Acme, "The Best Bar Soap," saved a child's life in another series. Clutching a bar of Acme in his chubby little fist, the child fell into a well. It was dark and cold in there and he was almost sure to drown. Instead, he rose to safety on a well-full of suds. Admiring spectators exclaimed, "Why the foam is bringing him up!"

Some of the cards were very elaborate. An English soap-maker used a foldover. A gilt-framed picture hung against a papered interior wall on the front of the fold. In the picture a frantic housewife, perspiration falling like rain from her reddened face, scrubbed away at her washing. This was labeled, "The old way." When a tab was pulled at the bottom of this cruel scene, everything changed. The pretty housewife sat peacefully reading. The hands of a clock behind her easy chair pointed to five minutes to one. Her work was done. The wash flapped briskly in the breeze outside an open window. The advertising message on the back clinched the story.

Woman stood for hours over the steaming odours of poisonous materials and inhaled bad health.

SUNLIGHT
SOAP

Altered all that.
It did away with the toil which *SHATTERED THE LIFE OF THE HOUSEWIFE.*
Its use entails no boiling, no toiling. Rub it well on the clothes, let them soak a while, rinse in clean water, and the washing is done.

1,000 pounds
for any impurity in
SUNLIGHT SOAP

Other than the patent medicine manufacturers and vendors, large local advertisers like John Wanamaker, and a handful of manufacturers like Fairbanks, Royal Baking Powder, Singer, Steinway, and Sapolio, there were few general and regular large advertisers in the 1870's and 1880's. Many business men and many companies thought advertising undignified, worse than that, disreputable, and, worse even than that, an unnecessary expense. They manufactured to sell to jobbers. It was up to the jobber and then the retailer to move the stock. The idea of pre-selling the consumer on products and brands and of reaching dealers by inciting consumer demand was not yet fixed. Many manufacturers felt no need of boasting of their wares to the public. The competition might interpret their advertising as a confession of weakness as well as evidence of bad taste. Advertising was unethical: it "wasn't done." In some quarters, this prejudice continued for a long time. A. D. Lasker said that as late as 1898, when he joined Lord & Thomas in Chicago, most legitimate manufacturers had to hide their advertising plans or the advertising itself, if that were possible, from their bankers. Most bankers felt that a manufacturer who advertised was unreliable. He put himself in the patent medicine class.[4]

Evolution came with the speed of revolution in the 1890's. As one manufacturer ventured timidly into advertising, then, gaining courage as he saw sales mount, dashed into more advertising and larger space, his alarmed competitors followed. Advertising struck and spread swiftly through contagion. Two or three or a half dozen brands of a product were advertised when none or one had been advertised before. Advertisers began to use larger space in magazines and newspapers and to compete for favorable position. Innocence vanished before skill as advertisers sought professional help to make their advertising more noticeable and more effective than the advertising of their business rivals.

It was in the late 1890's that the professional copywriters and the art man appeared in the larger advertising agencies. With them came pictures, puns, jingles, slogans, alliterative copy. Advertisers struck for attention through cleverness in their copy, phrases that people would note and remember. The new copywriters were to become celebrated in the trade. Men like Nathaniel Fowler, Charles Austin Bates, Artemus Ward, John Kennedy, Claude Hopkins, Earnest Elmo Calkins. Some of them became advertising agents themselves or advertising agency executives, but it was as copywriters they did their work in the 1890's and into the 1900's, leaving their mark on much of the advertising of the time.

Artemas Ward was an advertiser, an advertising writer, and an agent. An outspoken character, he directed the advertising of Sapolio for more than thirty years, writing much of it, assigning more of it. As Ward & Gow, he controlled streetcar space in New York and other cities, and cornered all the advertising on the New York Elevated. Charles Austin Bates, who had been manager of a department store in Indianapolis, came to New York in 1893 to write advertising, opened an office, wrote voluminously about advertising, and had the good sense to hire Earnest Elmo Calkins. Calkins

[4] *Ibid.,* p. 9.

was an advertising writer whose work lent warmth and color to some of the best and most characteristic advertising of the time. In Chicago, John Kennedy and Claude Hopkins, both fabulously successful copywriters, came out of patent medicines and in outlook and attack never strayed far from the patent medicine methods. Both were compulsive salesmen.

The forces were gathering in advertising, the agents, the writers, and the advertising managers and space salesmen of the media. One of the most colorful of the last group was Thomas Balmer. Balmer, who had been a tobacco salesman, went to work at the age of forty-five for Cyrus H. K. Curtis, who put him in charge of the western office of *Ladies' Home Journal*. Balmer seems to have been one of the original go-getting salesmen. *Printers' Ink* called him one of the greatest advertising salesmen who ever lived. Calkins described him as rushing wildly about the country, his white whiskers flying in the wind, as he berated advertisers and blew up volume.

Despite all this, Balmer believed in fact. He wanted to know why some advertisers who were in *Ladies' Home Journal* one year were out the next. To find out he studied six hundred cases of advertising failure and decided that the three chief causes were insufficient size of space, single insertions, lack of continuity and checking on advertising results. With these conclusions, Balmer attacked his customers and prospects, demanding large orders and frequent orders. If an advertiser handed him one that he thought too small, he would offer to put the money in a hat and shake for it. He refused to let a man start advertising if he thought his business was not ready for it or if he thought the advertiser did not plan to repeat until there was some chance of the advertisements' paying.

Balmer was the "dynamic," fast-talking, hypnotic, high-pressure salesman a quarter century ahead of his time. "If it wasn't for these white whiskers of mine," he told Calkins, "I'd have had my face slapped many a time." Balmer is credited with having helped incite the large-scale advertising of men's clothes, paints, spices, carpets, cereals, and several other products.

Through the energies of these impresarios, scribes, and agents, advertising techniques were being fashioned, and some of the small change of advertising wisdom was being accumulated. Well in advance of his time, an English agent formulated and presented with whimsical illustrations the modern advertising doctrine of "frequency and continuity." He gave sound reasons for its necessity:

The first time a man looks at an advertisement, he does not see it.
The second time he does not notice it.
The third time he is conscious of its existence.
The fourth time he faintly remembers having seen it before.
The fifth time he reads it.
The sixth time he turns up his nose at it.
The seventh time he reads it through and says, "Oh, bother!"
The eighth time he says, "Here's that confounded thing again!"
The ninth time he wonders if it amounts to anything.
The tenth time he thinks he will ask his neighbor if he has tried it.
The eleventh time he wonders how the advertiser makes it pay.
The twelfth time he thinks perhaps it may be worth something.
The thirteenth time he thinks it must be a good thing.
The fourteenth time he remembers that he has wanted such a thing for a long time.
The fifteenth time he thinks he will buy it some day.
The sixteenth time he makes a memorandum of it.
The seventeenth time he is tantalized because he cannot afford to buy it.
The eighteenth time he swears at his poverty.
The nineteenth time he counts his money carefully.
The twentieth time he sees it, he buys the article, or instructs his wife to do so.[5]

The advertising forces were not only gathering, they were beginning to merge their efforts. The advertising agent was beginning to develop into the advertising agency and to pull together the work of the space broker, the copywriter, and

[5] Thomas Smith, *Hints to Intending Advertisers* (1885). This portion of his promotional piece for Smith's United Advertising Agency of London was reproduced with its amusing illustrations by Bob Wettstein and Associates, Los Angeles, in an advertisement in *Western Advertising,* February, 1957.

the space salesman. The color-lithographed back cover of
Ladies' Home Journal, January, 1897, bore a large picture of
two brawny village blacksmiths, sledges poised over a piece
of red hot iron just lifted from the glowing coals.

STRIKE NOW!

It's the business of the blacksmith to know when to strike. . . .
This is also true of the business man. Business is striking; the
best business is striking at the right time and in the right way.

1897 finds a multitude of men with business to be shaped.
Conditions are what they work on. The conditions today
seem more favorable than for years. Will they strike now?
Will you?

The second part of right striking depends on what you strike
with. Our hammer is newspaper advertising. It renders almost every form of business enterprise more feasible and
more profitable. For proof of this look around you.

In twenty-eight years we have paid more than TWENTY
MILLION DOLLARS for newspaper advertising. At no time
have our convictions of its utility been so strong, or our
facilities for doing it well so great as today. . . .

N. W. Ayer & Son
Newspaper Advertising Agents   Philadelphia.[6]

N. W. Ayer & Son, which could lay some claim to being
the oldest and was soon to become and remain for years the
largest firm of advertising agents, was really the creation of
the son, F. Wayland Ayer. The father had been a none too
prosperous schoolteacher, proprietor finally of a female semi-
nary in Philadelphia. The son tried teaching first, quickly
gave it up in 1868 to solicit advertising for the *National Baptist.* Both father and son were puritanically religious. A year
later, F. Wayland Ayer, with a capital of $250, decided to
become an independent advertising agent and persuaded his
father to join him. The two started out with a list of eleven
religious papers, extending their services to Presbyterians,

---

[6] Choice of a woman's magazine for this advertisement appears strange,
but F. Wayland Ayer had extended Cyrus Curtis large advertising credit
with which to establish *Ladies' Home Journal.* Evidently Curtis was paying
back part of the debt in space.

Catholics, Lutherans, and Methodists, instead of confining them to the Baptists.[7]

Ayer throve. Like most other agents then, he throve on patent medicine business, handling the advertising for cures of cancer, consumption, fits, stuttering, for "Compound Oxygen" which cured every illness, for Kennedy's Ivory Tooth Cement, which made "Everyone his own dentist," for nostrums, aphrodisiacs, hair restorers, and for Rock & Rye which, at $4 a gallon, was a "Sure Cure for Lung Diseases." Success enabled him to buy out Coe, Wetherill & Co., successor, once removed, to Volney B. Palmer, the first U.S. advertising agent. Through pedigree thus purchased, Ayer could trace his agency back to 1841. By 1876, the Centennial year, N. W. Ayer & Son had twenty employees, was doing an annual business of $132,000, and claimed it could insert advertising in any United States or Canadian newspaper.

The agency grew with the times. Ayer took on the accounts of John Wanamaker, Jay Cooke & Co., Montgomery Ward, Ferry Seeds, the Singer Sewing Machine, and Mason & Hamlin's Organs. It handled the advertising for many schools and colleges, with Harvard heading the list. N. W. Ayer's dignity was affronted when in 1874 or 1875 an older man whose opinion he valued told him that he respected him as an individual, but could not respect the business in which he was engaged. Advertising agents, he said with some contempt, were merely drummers. He offered to get Ayer a respectable job in some decent enterprise.

Instead of accepting the offer, the bruised and injured Ayer determined that he would attempt to bring some order, possibly some ethics, into the advertising agency jungle of trickery, manipulation, and connivance. A specific result of this decision was his announcement in 1875 of what he called the Ayer open contract. To this time, trade practice had been for the agent to make the best space-buying and commission deal he could with publications which did not an-

[7] Ralph M. Hower, D.C.S., *The History of an Advertising Agency* (Revised ed.; Cambridge, Massachusetts: Harvard University Press, 1949), p. 29.

nounce their advertising rates. N. W. Ayer & Son now proposed to advertisers that it assume the responsibility for their advertising, the selection of media, and charge only a specified commission on the actual cost of space. The plan, modified as it was put into use, was adopted. F. Wayland Ayer was able to get a little further away from the "drummer" epithet at which he had winced.[8]

In continual and sharp competition with other advertising agencies, Ayer began to offer services which would encourage prospects to become customers. Primitive marketing advice was one of these. In 1879, fighting with George P. Rowell & Company for the advertising of a manufacturer of threshing machines, N. W. Ayer hastily and laboriously concocted what is claimed to be the first crude marketing survey. This research showed the manufacturer by states and counties where the best markets lay for his machines. The advertiser was delighted and offered to buy the survey results. Ayer told him it was not for sale. It was his without charge if the agency got the placement of his advertising. Rowell lost the account he had had the year before.[9]

Ayer got other accounts during those boom years of advertising: Procter & Gamble, Burpee Seeds, Timken Machinery, Fairy Soap, Cottolene, Gold Dust. It found other ways of making money. It acquired space cheaply in outside publications by trading it for space in two publications it started, the *Advertiser's Guide* and the *Ayer & Son's Manual for Advertisers*. In imitation of George Rowell's *American Newspaper Directory*, it started an *American Newspaper Annual* in 1880. It not only sold the volume and the circulation information it contained to advertisers but also, again in imitation of Rowell, sold advertising in the book. Ayer persuaded publishers to advertise in the *American Newspaper Annual* in exchange for space in their newspapers, hardly a practice which would lead to impartiality in the selection of media. The *Annual*, which absorbed Rowell's *Directory* along the line, and is now *N. W. Ayer & Son's Directory of Newspapers and Periodicals*, took advertising until 1914.[10]

Despite all these increased and widening activities, Ayer

8 *Ibid.*, pp. 50-71.   9 *Ibid.*, pp. 71-4.   10 *Ibid.*, pp. 82-3.

did not hire a full-time copywriter until 1892, nor an art man until 1898. The agents looked upon copywriters as an expensive nuisance and art men as an inexcusable luxury.

Ayer was solely a newspaper agency. It signed itself in its *Ladies' Home Journal* advertisement in 1897 only as "Newspaper Advertising Agents." It remained so until J. Walter Thompson announced he was adding newspapers to his list of magazines. Ayer immediately added magazines as a defensive move. Competition and the beckoning profits of the magazines, burgeoning now with national advertising, caused the change.

A full-page Ayer advertisement in *Harper's,* November, 1899, was chaste, dignified, and solemn. It was unillustrated. Only a border ornament surrounded the generously spaced message. Magazines were mentioned in the signature, but the body of the advertisements still emphasized the paramount importance of the newspapers in the Ayer scheme of things.

Where
the Battle
is really Won

The author of "With Kitchener to Khartum" points out that the wonderful battle of the Atbara was really won in in the workshops of the Sudan Military Railway. The difference between Wolseley's failure and Kitchener's success was a difference in preparation—not courage.

We see the same difference in Newspaper Advertisers. Out of ten men who have the pluck to spend, there's not more than one with the patience to plan.

Our interest in a Newspaper Advertising Campaign centers in the workshop stage. If you are of the one-in-ten kind, with a serious problem and a serious purpose, let's confer— but before the battle.

N. W. AYER & SON
Philadelphia

NEWSPAPER ADVERTISING
MAGAZINE ADVERTISING

Ayer, which had likewise frowned upon outdoor advertising, was forced to comply with the wishes of an advertiser

in 1898 and entered then into paste and paint. In 1899 it
announced formation of a new outdoor advertising department. The agency was now active in what were then the
three largest fields of advertising.

It used them all that same year to inaugurate what was up
to that time its largest account and campaign. The campaign
was perhaps the most ambitious the country had seen. It was
the joint effort of Ayer and the newly formed National Biscuit Company and one of the first to advertise an entirely
new product and new product idea. Ayer devised a name for
it, "Uneeda Biscuit." It coordinated its advertising with the
sales efforts of the company in presenting the public with a
new trade-marked product in a distinctive container which
was made airtight to protect its contents.

Uneeda Biscuit was one of the first packaged foods, one
which led in the trend away from the bulk foods offered the
American family to the packaged products bought and consumed today. It led in a movement for sanitary packaging
which has had a strong and probably beneficial influence on
American dietary habits and health, on the distribution of
foods, even on the development of supermarkets and self-
service in grocery chains, and thus on the way in which
ordinary modern life is lived.

N. W. Ayer & Son, in presenting and carrying through a
complete advertising plan which utilized newspapers, magazines, and outdoor in presenting Uneeda Biscuit, provided
perhaps the first example of the full-fledged modern advertising agency at work. It acted not merely as publicity agent for
the National Biscuit Company but worked with the client in
the details of a complex merchandising operation. Ayer was
a recognized pioneer in this instance. Such agency operation
was not to become standard for some years.

F. Wayland Ayer was the first advertising agent to collar
a million dollar account. "With the probable exceptions of
John Hooper and L. F. Shattuck," George Rowell remarked
wistfully in 1905, "Mr. F. W. Ayer is now, and long has
been, the richest man in the business."[11]

[11] Rowell, *op. cit.,* p. 443.

Intrepid advertising men on more than usually slippery ground struggle to erect a sign on the rapids below Niagara Falls in 1881. (Bettman Archive)

A beautiful new plow calls for white tie, tails, and monocle. Holsum bread out-tastes a wedding cake. Advertising cards of the 1880's. (Bettman Archive)

16

Rhymes and Rhymesters

THERE WERE THOSE in business in the 1890's who disdained advertising as not quite respectable, yet some of it—always a happy circumstance when it can be achieved—was beginning to delight the public. People might cavil at the advertising which stained the white cliffs of Dover and insist it be scrubbed away. They might rise up and pass laws when "St. Jacob's Oil" was smeared in large letters on the rocks at Niagara, but they quoted Sapolio proverbs with gusto, reveled with the happy folk of Spotless Town, breathlessly followed the adventures of Phoebe Snow, as later they followed the Perils of Pauline, and were to fall in love with a small boy yawning his way to bed with a lighted candle and a Fisk tire over his shoulder. With an innocence, a gaiety and a gusto that have long since vanished from advertising, the copywriters shared their fun with the workaday world.

Sapolio began its advertising in the early 1870's. Its first newspaper advertisement was just a smudged picture of a man's head. A frying pan was added to the advertisement. Then came pictures showing the man's head reflected in the scoured pan as if in a shining mirror. Then came the magic word, "Sapolio."

Enoch Morgan used cartoons and jingles from the first. One of its advertisements in 1877 showed a dejected, blackened, paste-pot artist looking hopelessly at a long board fence which, though it bore the regular "Post No Bills" warning, was covered with advertisements for Bixby's blacking and for all kinds of soaps. There was no place for the bill poster to

paste up the Sapolio advertisement he held in his hand. The
verse, said to be by Bret Harte, under the cartoon read:

> His brow was sad but underneath
> White with "Odonto" shone his teeth
> And through them hissed the words, "Well blow
> Me tight if here is ary show "Sapolio"

This was amazing in its time but thin and meager stuff in
contrast to the Sapolio advertising that was to come when
Artemus Ward was made Sapolio's advertising manager.
Ward began to spend money at a rate which soon made
Sapolio one of the biggest advertisers of the time.[1]

Ward made Sapolio advertising bright, alert, amusing,
quotable. He published it in newspapers and placed it in
magazines, but depended most on advertising on car cards and
on El station platforms. The population of the United States
was nearing sixty-three million, but 12 per cent of the population was illiterate. Everybody could not afford magazines;
many did not bother with the newspapers. Most city people
went to work, and they went on the surface cars or the El
trains. If they could not read, there was certain to be someone amused enough to read the Sapolio advertisements aloud.
They were worth reading; and it was the streetcar and El
riders who lived in such a way they needed a cleaner like
Sapolio around the house. Sapolio they could afford. Ward
saw to it that they saw, read, or heard "Sapolio" wherever
they went.

> A clean nation has ever been a strong nation
> Fortify with Sapolio
>
> If we could teach the Indian to use Sapolio
> It would quickly civilize them

---

[1] Something of Ward's casual advertising philosophy and ideals may be
seen in this remark of 1890, "When an advertising writer has truth enough
to be generally trusted, tact enough to be generally depended upon, force
enough to be wholesomely respected, and business experience enough not
to jump through his collar—then this happy combination of talents may
insure him salary enough to drink Bass at his lunch." Quoted in *Printers'
Ink, Fifty Years*, p. 27.

> A Bright Home makes a Merry Heart
> Joy travels with Sapolio

The maid and scrubwoman on their way to work were faced with this:

> Two servants in two neighboring houses dwelt
> But differently their daily labor felt
> Jaded and weary of her life was one
> Always at work and yet 'twas never done
> The *other* walked out nightly with her beau—
> But then she cleaned with Sapolio.

When the Spanish-American war came along, no one and no other thing was as patriotic as Sapolio. "Dewey and We Cleaned up with Sapolio!" a sailor shouted, waving a cake of Sapolio out of the advertisement. Another sailor and his cannon stood stoutly beside a housewife washing paint. "The man of war and the woman of work both appreciate Sapolio." Ward had a run on sailors while "Remember the Maine!" was America's war cry.

> A sailor's wife, a sailor's joy should be
> Yo-ho! Yo-ho!
> But when he does his work at sea
> His aid, like hers, is seen to be
> Sap-O, lio!

U. S. came to mean not the United States but "Use Sapolio." Oxen hauled a covered wagon across the prairies, outriders looking like Buffalo Bill galloping alongside. U. S. (Use Sapolio) was painted on the canvas of the wagon. "The advance of civilization," said the advertisement, "is marked by the sale of Sapolio."

As the war died out of the news, Artemus Ward turned to the arts. An advertisement in *Ladies' Home Journal* for October, 1897, was elaborately devised. The initial letters of each line of the jingle were surrounded by circles. Matching circles at the end of each line showed pictures of the entertainers the verses praised.

Monday
   S is for Sarah [Bernhardt] so slight but so grand
Tuesday
   A is for Ada [Rehan], first star in our land
Wednesday
   P is for Paderewski plays pianos for gold
Thursday
   O for Ocero the dancer so bold
Friday
   L stands for Lillian [Russell] America's pride
Saturday
   I stands for Irving [Sir Henry] who walks with a stride
Sunday
   O stands for others who sing as they go

      Because they earned rest with SAPOLIO

In 1900 Ward launched his first series of Spotless Town pictures and verses. Though, according to Calkins, Ward did not acknowledge the debt for some years, both drawings and verses were done by Kenneth James Fraser. Spotless Town was a scoured village, evidently Dutch, with odd houses and cobbled streets, where scrubbed characters danced and sang the praises of Sapolio. Children learned to read from the Spotless Town jingles. They learned them as if they were nursery rhymes. They sang them at play instead of Ring-Around-the-Rosey or Pepsi-Cola Hits the Spot!

There was the policeman, the mayor, the doctor, the butcher, baker, and Maid of Spotless Town. They all danced and they all talked in rhyme.

      This is the maid of fair renown
      Who scrubs the floors of Spotless Town,
      To find a spec when she is through
      Would take a pair of specs or two
      And her employment isn't slow
      For she employs SAPOLIO

      I am the mayor of Spotless Town
      The brightest man for miles around
      The shining light of wisdom can
      Reflect from such a polished man

And so I say to high and low;
The brightest use SAPOLIO.

This is the butcher of Spotless Town,
His tools are bright as his renown
To leave them stained were indiscreet,
For folks would then abstain from meat.
And so he brightens his trade, you know,
By polishing with
SAPOLIO

Fraser's fondness for puns is obvious. Once in a while he lost his inspiration and once, anyway, his patience. He came out from behind the scenes to confess his frustrations. With a picture which showed all of the characters dancing in chorus-line fashion he wrote:

We dance because of the great renown that greets the folks
  of Spotless Town
Our jests have won a wondrous name, our gestures too are
  known to fame
But we're averse to verse, you see; it hampers versatility,
And as we've shown how jingle goes
We'll now descend to simple prose—USE SAPOLIO.

Sapolio did not jingle alone. Other cleansers, some for things, some for people, sang their own praises. To the rhythm of Baby Bunting, Procter & Gamble sang:

Dainty clothes and tender skin
Need pure soap to wash them in.
Nurse and mother must be sure
Baby's bath is sweet and pure.
Ivory Soap

N. K. Fairbanks sang a different song in *Ladies' Home Journal*, January, 1892

A man works from
Sun to Sun
But a woman's work
Was never done

Until Gold Dust
Came to her ken. And now
She's through *before*
The men.

The claims of other soap makers were too serious for such
light treatment. Woodbury's Facial Soap was sold to men
through *Journal* pages in the 1890's by the pen and ink outline of a man's moustached face with the soap maker's claims
stamped across his face. He looked as if he had smallpox.
Pyle's Pearline used the sentimental approach. A full-page
picture entitled "My Busy Day" showed a small girl laden
with dust pan, scrubbing brush, wooden pail and mop, a ker-
chief wrapped about her head. The text said only: "Millions
Use Pearline! Beware of imitations."

It took full pages of extravagantly worded copy every
month in 1891 for Cuticura Soap to do justice to its virtues:
"The only really successful preventive and cure of pimples,
blotches, blackheads, red, rough, and oily skin and most com-
plexional disfigurations is the greatest of all Skin Purifiers and
Beautifiers, the celebrated CUTICURA SOAP."

Earnest Elmo Calkins, who, twenty-two years apart, wrote
two pleasant autobiographical reminiscenses of his life in advertising, was born, grew up, and went to school in a mid-
western village.[2] At Knox College he edited the undergradu-
ate paper which had been founded there by S. S. McClure.
He struck out for New York and a writer's career in New
York. For a year he worked as a printer on the staff of *The
Butcher's Gazette and Sausage Journal* run by one Hermann
Klotz. The names of both periodical and employer sound
improbable, but they were only too real to young Calkins.

A year of Klotz-administered fear and starvation was all
he could stand. He fled back to the Middle West and a job in
a department store in Peoria. Department store advertising
proved to have its drawbacks. Calkins got together a sheaf
of his writing and sent it to Charles Austin Bates in New

---

[2] *Louder, Please!* (Boston: The Atlantic Monthly Press, 1924); *"and
hearing not . . ."* (New York: Charles Scribner's Sons, 1946).

York. Bates hired him as a copywriter at $15 a week. Calkins stayed three years writing for Bates, his salary creeping up to $35. Then Ralph Holden, who had worked in the freight department of the Baltimore & Ohio in Philadelphia, got a job with Bates. Holden was bright, aggressive—and his wife had worked on the *Ladies' Home Journal* so he knew Edward Bok. This was an asset. Holden persuaded Calkins, and they opened their own advertising writing shop.

Cyrus Curtis liked some of Calkin's copy and came with an offer to buy. He wanted some of the same kind done for The Curtis Publishing Company. He would pay them a fee equivalent to what they would have got had they had the placing of the copy in one of his magazines. A little later on Calkins & Holden got an order for a series of advertisements for horsefeed. They struck it rich on that one. The manufacturer, Edward Ellsworth, also put out two grain foods for human consumption, H-O and Force.

It was for Force that Ernest Elmo Calkins developed Sunny Jim. Ellsworth's advertising manager had already bought from two young girls a cartoon picture and a rhyme. The picture showed a crabbed old gentleman in top hat, spectacles, and for some reason a pigtail, at the left of the panel, poking miserably along with his stick. The same old gentleman, smiling and twirling his stick, strode into the panel from the right. Between the before and after pictures was lettered:

> Jim Dumps was a most unfriendly man
> Who lived his life on a hermit plan.
> He'd never stop for a friendly smile
> But trudged along in his moody style—
> Till "FORCE FOOD"
> Once was served to him
> Since then they call him "Sunny Jim."

Ellsworth's advertising manager ordered a series of such jingles and pictures. Calkins and Holden went to work. Minnie Hanff had written the original jingles. Calkins wrote many more. Popular versifiers like Oliver Herford, Caroline Wells, and Madison Cawein, poet laureate of Kentucky, were called on when Calkins ran dry. Sewell Collins, a theatrical poster artist, roughed out drawings, and Earl Horter inked them in. The Sunny Jim advertisements were run in 45,000 streetcars and in 12,500 newspapers in the United States. They appeared in paint and on posters. Sunny Jim became an international character. Ministers preached sermons about him; judges pointed morals from the bench by reference to his sterling qualities. Sunny Jim became the name for the favorite child in a family, the synonymn for sweetness and light in human behavior. He got into the dialogue of popular plays, was a central character in a musical comedy and the subject of innumerable cartoons.

An early jingle gave the sad reason for Jim Dumps original gloom:

> Jim Dumps for months had not been strong
> And that was why he trudged along
> As dumpish as a rainy day,
> Nor had he one kind word to say
> Till one bright day—what joy for him,
> FORCE changed him to Sunny Jim.

He had his little difficulties, one that all his readers shared.

> Jim Dumps would fume at cars so slow
> When from his work at night he'd go;
> When heavy dames stood on his corn,
> He'd curse the day that he was born,
> But now there's FORCE at home for him
> No crowded cars daunt Sunny Jim.

Like so many of his admirers, Sunny Jim had a family, and he felt the same anxiety about his offspring that other parents felt.

> Jim Dumps a little girl possessed
> Whom loss of appetite distressed.
> "I des' tant eat," the child would scream
> Jim fixed a dish of FORCE and cream,
> She tasted it—then joy for him,
> She begged for more from Sunny Jim

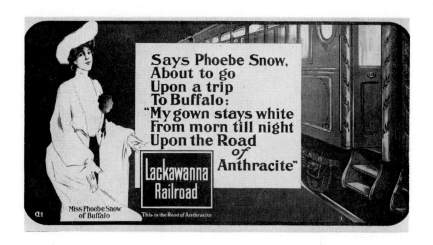

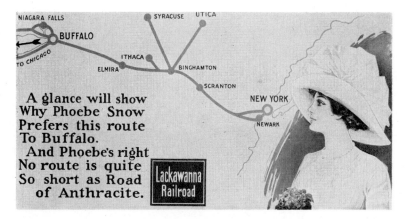

The same generation which thrilled to the Perils of Pauline followed the travel tales of spotless Phoebe Snow (of Buffalo) on changing car cards.

This very proper maid seems attempting to heed a contemporary shoe polish advertisement on New York El platforms: "Brighten Up Your Understanding."

As his fame grew and Sunny Jim became an international symbol of the cheerful outlook on life, he began to talk directly to the world, advising health, optimism, sunniness, and the cause of it all—Force. In signed advice in advertising in the women's magazines he urged, "The best food is the best doctor—the doctor himself will tell you so." He told mothers that "Force makes the youngsters grow strong *all over*—body, bone and brain." In another of Sunny Jim's chats with mothers he confided, "Force is peculiarly adapted to the growing boy and his lusty appetite."

As a result of Sunny Jim, Force was outselling all its rivals. As Sunny Jim said, it was being eaten for breakfast in thirteen languages. It was selling so well that envious competitors had circulated a rumor that Force contained some harmful ingredient. Sunny Jim tried righteously to ignore the slander, but finally was forced to acknowledge it. The company spent $50,000 combating the rumor in its advertising and posted a reward of $5,000 to anyone, professional chemists included, who could prove that Force contained anything but wheat, barley-malt, and salt. Sunny Jim abandoned the distasteful subject and went on with his column on "Be Sunny." At the end of it he offered the Force recipe book. It was entitled *The Gentle Art of Using "Force."*

Calkins turned his facile pen to the writing of another famous series of advertising jingles. The advertising manager of the Lackawanna Railroad, not long out of Yale, decided that railroad advertising should be something more than time-tables reproduced in newspaper space. To differentiate the Lackawanna from competing roads, he decided that it was "the Road of Anthracite." To dramatize the cleanliness of the Lackawanna in a day when most passengers expected to end a train journey sooty and cinder-dusted from the soft coal smoke pouring from the engine, he devised the character of a young girl dressed in white who would still be dressed in white after a Lackawanna trip. He tried to get the idea into verse but could not find a rhyme for Lackawanna. His first advertisement in newspapers and on car cards were simply about "a maiden all in lawn who boarded the train

early one morn" that ran on the Road of Anthracite. He
turned to Calkins for help and Calkins gave the young girl
her name and wrote the first rhyme. It was this:

> Said Phoebe Snow
> About to go
>   Upon a trip to Buffalo:
> My gown keeps white
> Both day and night
>   Upon the Road of Anthracite

Phoebe went on to a series of romantic (and spotless) adventures. The Lackawanna gave her not only pure passage,
but comfort, courtesy, sound sleep, and high romance. Upon
the Road of Anthracite she met a man, also in white, and,
finally, they were married by a bishop traveling, of course,
on the same train. The bishop, evidently something of a non-
conformist, was clad in white too.

The original Phoebe Snow was a well-known model of the
day. She and later other models were posed and painted in
oils for the streetcar cards and posters that were used first.
Soon Phoebe was on billboards, painted signs, in the newspapers and magazines. She was even cut into hundreds of
pieces for jigsaw puzzles. Phoebe Snow, who became almost
as well known as Uncle Sam and much more alluring, never
got enough of riding on the Lackawanna. She sat drowsily
across the aisle while a beaming porter made up her berth for
the night.

> The evening flies
> Till Phoebe's eyes
> Grow sleepy under
> Mountain skies
> Sweet dreams all night
> Are hers, till light
> Dawns on the Road
>   of Anthracite

When Phoebe awoke in the morning, there was little for
her to do.

> When nearly there
> Her only care
> Is but to smooth
> Her auburn hair.
> Her face is bright,
> Her frock still white
> Upon the Road
>   of Anthracite

Phoebe was pictured with the white-moustached engineer in his striped cap and smock jacket which was almost as clean as her own dazzling raiment.

> Miss Snow draws near
> The cab to cheer
> The level-headed
> Engineer
> Whose watchful sight
> Makes safe her flight
> Upon the Road
>   of Anthracite

Phoebe's admiration was extended to all the train crew, even the flagman. There was a reason.

> Miss Snow you see
> Was sure to be
> The object of
> Much courtesy.
> For day or night
> They're all polite
> Upon the Road
>   of Anthracite

So popular were the Mother-Goose kind of rhymes and rhythms in advertising that they earned both the flattery of imitation and the serious criticism of the envious. Ward & Gow and the streetcars had all the best of it. The magazines, comparatively neglected by the jingle writers, did not mind pointing out the flaws in this competitive advertising. *Munsey's Magazine*, July, 1900, charged that the advertising poet

did not seem to take his high calling seriously enough. "Why
is it that the rhymed advertisements which assault our eyes
in the surface and elevated cars are generally so atrocious and
so pointless? . . . If a thing is worth rhyming at all, it's worth
rhyming well. So come, ye dealers in dress goods, ye soap
sellers and pickle purveyors, and employ our rising young
Longfellows and Lowells and Alfred Austins, and the course
of trade and literature will alike be benefited." Better literature in the streetcars "would be true philanthropy as well as
true art, for it is in the car panels that the majority of citizens
take their daily reading."[3]

Scribner's was indignant and even more outspoken. "If
defective versification be a real foundation of enduring poetry, beyond doubt the rhymes that set forth the virtues of
all sorts of things on street-car panels are likely to become
immortal. It may not be going too far to say that these
couplets and quatrains are worse in quality than are some of
the various things they apostrophize."[4] The Scribner's writer
admitted the streetcar laureates suffered under one handicap.
The trademark was sacred. The poet could not turn
"Magee's Dog Soap" into "Magee's Soap for Dogs" just for
the sake of the feet in his line. Yet the poet owed it to the
public to do better. "It must ever be a shame that the verses
in these flying cars are not on an artistic level with the illustrations which, whether mediaevally grotesque or soulfully
impressionistic, are always interesting examples of the schools
they represent, and never fail to appeal pleasantly to the
people who are jarred by the lines that accompany them.
Such a combination . . . is enough to make people of ordinary
intelligence shun poetry."

Calkins himself had a different complaint. He was, after
all, an advertising man first, a poet second. In 1905 he was
talking not so much of the verse published in the jingle advertisements but of the ones submitted and rejected, for cause,

---

[3] *Munsey's Magazine*, July, 1900, p. 566.
[4] "A Plea for Better Street Car Poetry," *Scribner's Magazine*, March,
1902.

by the advertiser. "It would seem that the would-be author, after ignoring every rule of rhythm, rhyme, grammar, and construction, would certainly be able to make at least a straightforward statement about his goods, but he fails even to do that."[5]

5 Earnest Elmo Calkins and Ralph Holden, *op. cit.*, p. 326.

17

Folk Characters
and Slogans

ADVERTISING DOGGEREL LARGELY disappeared even before the streetcars which made them familiar to men, women, and children vanished from the streets of most American cities. Two other allied innovations which came with the rich and richly varied advertising of the 1890's have lasted far longer. Jim Dumps and Phoebe Snow were only two of the galaxy of advertising characters, birds, beasts, children, and lovable comics presented to the world and taken to the bosom of the public. The "Best by Test" of Pyle's Pearline and the Prudential's "The Rock of Gibralter" were but two of the slogans made so familiar through advertising repetition that the many knew them as well as their own names.

Everyone knew the herd of buffalo drinking undisturbed at the life-giving spring of Buffalo Lithia Water, "Nature's Great Remedy for Bright's Disease of the Kidneys, the Gouty Diathesis, Stone of the Bladder, etc." There could have been few who did not know the cowled and bearded monk, staff in hand, resting wearily at the foot of a tree and reverently examining the bottle of St. Jacob's Oil in his hand. St. Jacob's Oil, which cured "Rheumatism, Bruises, Headaches, Stiffness, Neuralgia, Burns, Chest Cold, Soreness, Sore Throat," was selling at the rate of twenty million bottles every year.

The very first trademark registered by the U.S. Patent Office, October 25, 1870, was the eagle, granted the Averill Chemical Paint Company of New York. The trademark was

Faithful Nipper

The Big Stick

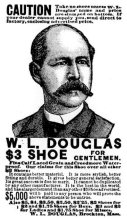

The $3.00 Shoe Man

The Yawning Fisk Boy

La Belle Chocolatiere

ARROW
COLLARS and SHIRTS

MEDORA is a lower Belmont, the best liked collar style ever introduced. There is now a Belmont for every man—

GLASGOW	BELMONT
2⅝ inch	2⅜ inch
MEDORA	CHESTER
2⅛ inch	2 inch

2 for 25 cents

AN ordinary shirt may be right when you buy it, but an Arrow Shirt will be right when you wear it.

$1.50 and more

Send for Booklets
CLUETT, PEABODY & COMPANY
461 River Street, Troy, N. Y.

© 1912, BY C. P. & CO., N.Y.

For long years the famous Arrow Collar man was advertising's beau ideal of masculine beauty, sartorial resplendence, and clean-cut Americanism.

described in the application of Seth M. Cady, president of the company:

> In the foreground, on a rock, with the word chemistry upon it is an eagle holding in his mouth a paint-pot or canister, with a brush, and a ribbon or streamer, on which are the words, Economical, Durable, Beautiful. Below the feet of the bird is represented water, upon which is a steamer and other vessels. In the background is a bridge or viaduct, with a train of railroad cars upon it. Further in the background are seen buildings and manufactories.

The patriotic motif flared in many of the earlier picture marks, but it was not these which caught the public mind and heart. It was the animals and people given character, warmth, and friendliness by imaginative advertising treatment. Some of them have endured for well over a century.

"La Belle Chocolatiere," a buxom German chambermaid carrying a glass of water and a cup of chocolate on a breakfast tray, was painted by Jean-Etienne Liotard in Geneva and purchased in 1743 for 120 sequins by Count Algarotti for Augustus of Saxony, King of Poland. It has hung in the royal collection at Dresden since then. The German maid is known to millions, for she has been appearing since 1825 in the advertising of Walter Baker & Company, one of the earliest consistent American advertisers.

In London in the 1890's an artist, Francis Barraud, inherited a fox terrier on the death of his brother. One night he noticed the interest the dog, Nipper, displayed in listening to a wax cylinder record on his small phonograph. Barraud painted his interpretation of the scene. The original picture showed his brother's coffin and his own phonograph. He called the picture "His Master's Voice." Barraud sold the picture—coffin painted out—to the Gramophone Company, Ltd., in London. Nipper came to the United States when the Victor Talking Machine Company was founded in 1901 and acquired rights to the picture which since 1928 have belonged to RCA.

When the National Biscuit Company was starting its campaign for Uneeda Biscuit in 1898, Joseph G. Geisinger, one of the advertising group working on the project, dressed his nephew Gordon Stiles in black boots, yellow slicker, and sou'wester hat and had him photographed. From the photo- graph was done the color reproduction which became the Uneeda Biscuit boy.

His advertising counterpart was not adopted until 1913. Deciding to advertise, the Morton Salt Company acquired an advertising agency which did not, at first, pay much attention to the small account. It finally produced some drawings and slogan suggestions. The agency had already discarded one drawing which showed a small girl under a big umbrella, a cylinder of Morton Salt under her arm, and the salt escaping through its spout. It was this drawing the company chose. The matter of a slogan was debated at length. Finally some- one thought of "It never rains but it pours." This was twisted to, "When it rains, it pours," and a new character, the Morton Salt girl, was born.

The playful kittens entangled in Corticelli silk were al- ready known, and were to be known by the millions who saw not only the company's magazine advertising but what was long one of the most pleasing and spectacular electric signs of Broadway at night. The Gold Dust Twins and Aunt Jemima were still to come. William and Andrew Smith had inherited the family restaurant in Poughkeepsie and with it one item sold at its confectionary counter. They realized the value of the cough drops and began to exploit them in open bowls given dealers for display. On these bowls first appeared their pictures, long known as "Trade" and "Mark," which came eventually to be used on their pocket packages and in the advertising of Smith Brothers Cough Drops.

The famous Campbell Soup Kids, first used on car cards, as were most of these figures, seem to have had no human originals. The pair of roly-poly red-cheeked twins were painted by Grayce Gebbie Drayton in 1904, possibly as whimsical symbols of childhood, and have been used in Campbell advertising ever since.

In the home of an executive of the Cudahy Packing Com- pany in the late 1890's was a picture of a Dutch boy and girl. In a corner of the picture another girl was chasing a goose with an upraised stick. This picture provided both product name and character when Cudahy began to manufacture and sell Old Dutch Cleanser. The original Dutch Cleanser picture was of a stocky Dutch woman, her face hidden by her big bonnet, chasing dirt with a big stick. She became so well known that she was used to lampoon the "Big-Stick," trust-busting activities of President Theodore Roosevelt and later to sell war bonds, driving away enemies as Dutch Cleanser drove away dirt. In recent years the stocky Dutch woman has been rejuvenated and appears now as a slender and smiling blonde girl.

The Dutch Boy used for a half century to advertise the National Lead Company's paint was Irish. O. C. Harn, then the company's advertising manager, devised the idea and took it to the agent, George Batten. Batten had some sketches made by an artist. Working from the artist's sketches, Lawrence Carmichael Earle did the original painting, using a boy named Michael Brady for a model.

The benign looking old Quaker with his broad-brimmed black hat, shoulder-length white curls, and eighteenth-century coat and neckerchief must have occurred naturally to someone once the name Quaker Oats had been decided upon. His mild and wise countenance must have inspired confidence, and in the 1890's he was solemnly advising people to eat less meat.

> Most people eat too much, and many of the most painful and dangerous diseases are the result. Those who eat Quaker Oats have less desire for meat, and they will always tell you that they feel better.

"If too much animal food be eaten," warned the advertisement in quoted italics directly under the idyllic portrait, as if the words of wisdom were those of the good Friend, "we are liable to produce gout and disorder of the liver, not to speak of indigestion.—*Practical Dietetics*."[1]

[1] Grape-Nuts, at about this same time, was being sold as a beautifier. A warning finger pointed to the spot on the face of a pictured beauty of the Lillian Russell era. The blemish was "The Old-Fashioned Beauty Spot." But, "There are no blotches on the face of Beauty when fed on Grape-Nuts. The true pink- and white complexion is made on the *inside* of the body. Change your diet and use some of the delicious dishes from the free recipe book found in each package of GRAPE-NUTS. The food is a straight road to health and comfort. There's a reason."

The smiling Negro waiter of Cream of Wheat advertising
had his origin in an actual waiter who once served Colonel
Emory Mapes, head of the Cream of Wheat Company, in a
restaurant. Chef's cap on his head, long-handled ladle over
his right shoulder, a bowl of Cream of Wheat on a tray in
his left hand, the waiter and his happy smile were seen everywhere in the advertising pages of the 1890's, usually with the
warning, "Be Sure That Above Trade Mark is on Every
Package."

One of the most famous of all the famous advertising
characters and one of the best loved was not born until 1907.
The Fisk Tire Company was founded in Chicopee, Massachusetts, in 1898, succeeding Spaulding & Pepper, a company
which had been making bicycle tires. Fisk added pneumatic
automobile tires in 1899 and soon began to advertise. One
night in 1907 a New York commercial artist, Burr E. Griffin,
struggled unsuccessfully to seize on a new idea for the Fisk
advertising. About three in the morning he gave up, deciding
it was long past time to retire. There it was! Instead of
going to sleep the artist went back to his drawing board and
sketched out the small boy in sleeper suit, yawning sleepily
as he started for bed with his lighted candle in one hand and
a Fisk tire slung over his shoulder. Fisk immediately adopted
the "Time to Re-Tire" picture and slogan, though they were
not copyrighted until 1910 and did not appear in the company's national advertising until 1914, when the Fisk "Time
to Retire" boy made his debut in *The Saturday Evening Post*
of March 7th. There was no original subject for Griffin's
sketch, only his sleepiness and his imagination.

Fisk, a division of the United States Rubber Company
since 1939, has used the appealing small boy and the phrase
ever since. He appears on every Fisk car and truck tire, in all
local and national advertising, on posters, in booklets, calendars, outdoor displays, even in six-foot plaster statues exhibited by dealers who sell Fisk products. Small boys have
dressed as the Fisk tire boy to win prizes at costume parties,
innumerable political and satirical cartoons have used the
figure, and his appearance is almost standard at ceremonies

where an aging clerk or executive, clutching his gold watch, pin, or scroll, listens embarrassed and bewildered, to the laudations brought on by his retirement from some company.

With the rhymes and the advertising characters—or without them—went the slogan. The slogan was the *sine qua non* of advertising in the 1890's. The advertised product without a slogan cringed naked in public.

Some slogans had been well known for years. Ivory Soap had been 99 and 44/100ths per cent pure since 1882 when Harley Procter, sales manager of the Cincinnati soap-making firm his father had founded, named the new white soap they were beginning to make, decided on the mathematical limitations of its purity, and that the most newsworthy item about it was that "It Floats." The story is told that Procter was inspired one Sunday at church when he heard a passage from the Psalms which read: "All thy garments smell of myrhh, and aloes, and cassia out of the ivory palaces whereby they have made thee glad." Procter seized on the word "ivory" as the name for the product and proceeded with his determination to make it a household word. "It Floats" and "99 and 44/100ths per cent pure" have been noised about consistently ever since. It is virtually impossible to see a cake of Ivory without thinking of the phrases or to read or hear the phrases without thinking of the soap.

The goodness and purity of Ivory got into doggerel in a humorously illustrated advertisement of February, 1885:

> "For years I've lived around the house,"
> Said Mrs. Rat to Mrs. Mouse,
> "I still remember well the day
> We entered here, the first of May,
> While coming up the water-spout
> We met a party moving out.
> Said they, 'What e'er you chance to steal
> In searching round to find a meal,
> Of this you may be always sure—
> The Ivory Soap is good and pure.'
> Since then I've proved it thro' and thro',
> By outward use and inward too,

And found it free from every ill
As water from a mountain rill.
It comes from oils that never sink
And answers both for meat and drink.
'Tis harmless as a piece of cheese
And with the old and young agrees.
No other home I'll ever choose
While Ivory Soap these people use."

In 1888 George Eastman invented both a portable camera and a name for it, Kodak. He deliberately coined the distinctive name for what was then a novel product and set out both to educate the public as to what it was and what it could do. The Kodak was loaded with film at the factory and had to be returned to the factory for developing. It was as simple as that, and it was this simplicity in operation Eastman had to impress on people who had known only the large and mysterious gadgets of the professional photographers for whom they sat to get their "likenesses taken." Eastman spent $25,000 in advertising the first year, and the slogan he used and kept on using was "You Press the Button—We Do the Rest." So successful was Eastman's camera and his advertising that he very nearly overshot his mark in making "Kodak" and "camera" synonymous. The public by this time had been so well educated that they were apt to call any camera a Kodak. Eastman changed his slogan to, "If It Isn't an Eastman, It Isn't a Kodak."

"See that Hump?" was a familiar question in newspapers and magazines in 1891 and throughout the decade. It was the slogan for what was then a very necessary item of women's dress. The slogan became one of the most familiar of them all. Often there was very little to its owner's advertising than the slogan and an explanation. Quarter-page advertisements in the magazines read:

On the face
and back of every
card of genuine
De Long Patent

Hooks and Eyes will
be found the words:

See that
hump?

Richard & De Long Bros.,
Philadelphia

Soon the battle cries of commerce—for "slogan" was originally "sluagh-ghairm," a Gaelic rallying cry—were echoing in advertising for products of many kinds. Plymouth Rock still asked anxiously, "Do you Wear Pants?" One bicycle maker declared that "Victor Sets the Pace." "Whose Picture is This?" asked Woodbury's Soap. "Pill After Pie" was suggested by Ayer's Pills. "Cascarets Work While You Sleep." "It Beats—As It Sweeps—As It Cleans" was for a carpet sweeper. "Hammer the Hammer" emphasized the safety of the Iver Johnson revolver. "Ask Dad—He Knows." What Dad knew was the quality of Sweet Caporal cigarettes.

The story is that the founder of the Packard Motor Car Company was asked about the performance of his car. He could think of no good answer on the spot and suggested the inquirer "Ask the man who owns one." "He Won't Be Happy Till He Gets It," "His Master's Voice," "Chases Dirt" were other early slogans, and they were followed by hundreds, some of them still in use.

Postum used "There's A Reason," as did Grape-Nuts. Diamond Dyes punned, "It's Easy to Dye"; Carnation Condensed Milk came "From Contented Cows"; Ingersoll was "The Watch that Made the Dollar Famous." In England Beecham's Pills were "Worth a Guinea a Box," and Punch was "The Paper that IS England." "Have you a little fairy in your home?" asked Fairy Soap.

The fashion that began in the 1880's and 1890's continued long into the twentieth century with: "Say It With Flowers," "Hasn't Scratched Yet" (Bon Ami), "Covers the Earth," (Sherwin-Williams paint), "No Metal Can Touch You" (Paris Garters), "Eventually—Why Not Now" (Pillsbury's

Flour), "You Just Know She Wears Them" (McCallum Silk
Hosiery), "Not a Cough in a Carload," (Old Gold Cigarettes), "The Beer that Made Milwaukee Famous" (Schlitz),
"Aged in the Wood," (Velvet Tobacco), "Barrelled Sunlight" (U.S. Gutta Percha Paint Company), and a host of
others. "The Flavor Lasts" came early for Wrigley's Chewing Gum; "The Instrument of the Immortals" did not come
until 1921 when Raymond Rubicam wrote it for Steinway
Pianos which already had been advertising for the greater part
of a century. "The Skin You Love to Touch" came when
sex appeal was injected into toilet soap advertising; "Blow
Some My Way" when the drive was on to make cigarette
smoking by women socially acceptable.

Some slogans were the happy inspiration of manufacturers
or advertising men. Some were deliberately sought for and
found. "Say It With Flowers" was manufactured by P. F.
O'Keefe on the order of the American Florists Association,
but "I'd Walk a Mile for a Camel," was originally a stranger's
chance remark to a bill poster. The camel on the Camel
cigarette package and in all Camel advertising got there
simply because R. J. Reynolds saw and admired a fine old
camel in a circus which was playing Winston-Salem. Reynolds and a photographer had a hard time taking the animal's
picture, as he was interested and wanted to see what was
going on. A keeper had to keep pulling his head upright.
The annoyed animal jerked his head high, shut his eyes,
stiffened his tail and in that position has come down to pos-
terity and probably will go on to immortality.

In the early 1930's a Viennese artist saw and sketched a
napping gray cat and sold the picture to an American gallery.
It was reproduced as "The Sleepy Cat" in the pictorial section of a New York Sunday newspaper. C. L. Probert, a vice-
president of the Chesapeake & Ohio Railroad, an animal
fancier who had pets of all kinds on his farm, saw the picture
and rushed to the office of the advertising director with whom
he had been seeking a way to dramatize a new C. & O. train,
the air-conditioned George Washington. They devised the
slogan "Sleep Like a Kitten," attached this to the picture of

the cat, and Chessie made her first appearance in *Fortune*, September, 1933. The public took to Chessie as an early generation had taken to Jim Dumps and Phoebe Snow. People wrote asking for copies of the original advertisement. Chessie calendars were distributed by the million. Chessie, who later had twin kittens for advertising purposes, became another popular advertising character and another identifying slogan was established.

Advertising slogans and characters are in reality an extension of the trademark. In many cases they actually are the trademark; in others they serve to emphasize and extend the identification which the trademark gives an advertised product. The trademark, as such, has a very old history. It was originally imposed on the craft guilds of the Middle Ages to fix responsibility on the maker for the worth and value of his product. The trademark thus came to be seen as a guarantee of excellence, an assumption of responsibility by the manufacturer, and a protection to the public, but it has served its greatest use in advertising. The trademark may be a symbol, a picture, a name distinctively reproduced over a long period, or a conventionalized monogram, like that of the Great Atlantic & Pacific Tea Company or the General Electric Company. Trademarks are usually chosen with care to be easy to pronounce, simple in design, attractive in appearance, affixable to the product, and susceptible of graphic or printed reproduction.

It is impossible to say what the first trademark in actual use, as distinguished from the first of the more than 650,000 now registered under United States law, actually was. It is safe to say that one of the earliest used in this country was the four hands clasped in a square of The Philadelphia Contributorship for the Insurance of Houses from Loss by Fire, an organization founded in 1752. Another early mark was the circled B, arrows, and Maltese cross of Wade & Butcher, cutlery manufacturers. Wade & Butcher obtained permission to use the mark from the Sheffield steel craftsmen and have used it since early in the eighteenth century.

Sometimes an advertiser is fortunate enough to find a useful trademark in his own name. This is not always deliberate. Gladstone lent his name to a piece of luggage, recognized now by many who never heard of the prime minister. Lord Lister, the father of antiseptic surgery, has been immortalized as the first two syllables of a mouth wash. The first Lord Brougham, the same who helped or hindered Sydney Smith in stealing an advertising sign in Edinburgh in the eighteenth century, was long remembered for the type of light enclosed carriage he preferred and which came to be named after him. Victoria's Prince Consort, Albert, survived for a time as the name of a man's coat, then of a well advertised tobacco. Samuel Colt played on his own name when in 1865 he adopted a rampant colt as trademark for his revolvers.

Modern times have seen purposeful use of names for brand identification. Two cars were named after R. E. Olds, the Oldsmobile, and the Reo. The initials B.V.D., virtually synonymous for men's underwear in the 1920's, were the initials of three men, Bradley, Voorhis, and Day. Clarence Birdseye, though he broke it in half, gave his own name to Birds Eye Frosted Foods.[2]

Other advertisers have had to seek out the symbols, characters, brands, and slogans with which they identify and advertise their products. Many, as most of those discussed, were chosen through happy inspiration or some relationship which pleased the originator. The Greyhound bus got its name when a tavern keeper looked out at the battleship gray bus stopping before his inn and decided it looked like a greyhound. Leo, the Lion, long the trademark of Metro-Goldwyn-Mayer, was chosen simply because Howard Dietz, then advertising director of the film company, had gone to Columbia College whose football song is "Roar, Lion, Roar."

Elsie, the Borden Company's cow, was for a few years just

[2] Clarence Birdseye liked to tell the story of the origin of his name. An ancestor had been page-in-waiting to an English queen and attended her on hunting trips. When a hawk circled and dived toward the queen, the page shot him through the eye with an arrow and was dubbed Birdseye by the relieved queen.

a cartoon advertising character. The public insisted she was real. At the World's Fair in 1939 visitor's kept asking where Elsie was. Borden took a cow named "You'll Do Lobelia" from its exhibit, ensconsed her in a boudoir, and she was Elsie. Since then various Elsies of the Borden Company have gone on nation-wide tour. A newspaper report in 1955 said Elsie had been seen by fourteen million people at the fair, and by many more millions on tour. Elsie's head, backed by a yellow daisy, was painted on all company trucks. She appears in magazine and television advertising. Her likeness has gone out on billions of packages of Borden's products. Piggly-Wiggly grocery stores got their names because the chain founder's mother had improved on the usual nursery-version and counted her baby's toes with, "This little piggly-wiggly went to market, this little piggly-wiggly . . ."

Such inspirational haphazardness in the selection of brand names, characters, symbols, and slogans is considered nothing less than horrendous by some of the scientists of modern advertising. The hit-or-miss methods employed by the originators and exploiters of most of the famous names and slogans are judged deplorable. Psychologists, sociologists, and electronic computers have proved that only those should be chosen which arouse pleasant associations and connotations of hidden delights. Brand names must be pat, easy to remember, short, pithy, designate the product. Psychological tests are used to reveal consumer revulsions and abhorrences, perhaps unconscious, toward certain names and symbols. The outgoing receptivity of others are tested by equally exhaustive research techniques. After, and only after, all this has been done will a respectable consultant nominate a dozen or a thousand names, symbols, or slogans for the panting advertiser. One agency is said to have proposed five thousand names for a new lipstick before one could be found which did not arouse rhythmic pulsations of forgotten hatreds and suggested only properly sensual and sentimental delights. Once two young girls could bring forth Sunny Jim, and Earnest Elmo Calkins could pick Phoebe Snow simply because the name fitted the rhythm of his line. Once a rapid-fire writer named G. Herb Palin roved the land dashing off slogans for advertisers at 10 for $100. Now motivational research and mechanical brains combine to click out pre-tested, pre-digested, and usually rather dull names and phrases.

When a pharmaceutical house was having trouble devising more names that sounded authentically medical, scientific, frightening, but not too frightening, the proper emetics were fed the proper electronic mechanism, and it disgorged 42,000 potential trademarks for revolutionary new drugs. This is not only a little frightening in itself, but it seems unfair to Sunny Jim, Phoebe Snow, The Ham What Am, That Schoolgirl Complexion, and to the helpless public, most of whom own neither a social scientist nor even a small electronic computer with which to fight back.

18

Bonebreakers to Safeties
—Bicycle Advertising

AN ENGLISH INVENTION of 1876, successfully marketed for the first time in 1885, wrought a small industrial and social and a large advertising revolution when it was introduced into the United States. There had been bicycles in France, England, and Scotland long before—celeripedes, Draisienes, high-wheelers, boneshakers, and ordinaries—but it was not until J. K. Starley of Coventry perfected the safety bicycle which he sold as the Rover that cycling became a craze in the United States.

Colonel Albert A. Pope of Boston had seen and been fascinated by the high-wheelers on display at the Centennial Exhibition in Philadelphia in 1876. He went to England the next year and brought back several models. He had a few American counterparts built, but they were unsatisfactory and cost too much to manufacture. He returned to England, studied English manufacturing processes further, and began to manufacture Columbia bicycles at the Weed Sewing Machine Company factory in Hartford. Pope experimented further, improving his machines as improvements were made in England and in the Hartford factory.

The sportsmen speeders on high-wheelers and ordinaries were the first American enthusiasts. They formed themselves into clubs which amalgamated into the League of American Wheelman. By 1881 the League had twenty-five thousand members. The appearance of the safety bicycle sent its membership soaring, as the development of the Rover and the Columbia transformed what had been a dangerous sport for hardy males, inured to falls from the dizzy heights of their metal mounts, into a safe but thrilling pastime for both men and women. When in Belfast, John Boyd Dunlop invented the pneumatic rubber tire, the bicycle swept everything before it.

The bicycle seized the imagination of Americans and changed their mode of life and dress as nothing had done before. Between 1890 and 1896 they spent $100 million for bicycles.[1] The bicycle offered speed, fun, freedom, adventure, and a chance to look around. It was the first device that enabled people to go from here to there and back under their own power. The church inveighed against the bicycle as sinful; obviously it gave too much pleasure to be moral. Manufacturers of jewelry, clothing, and cigars screamed in agony that people were spending all their money on the diabolical contraptions and had none left to invest in their wares. The theater cried out against the unfair competition which was leaving them with empty houses. Even the barbers complained. Men would not take the time to shave before they were off for a spin, and the worst of them were tending their new handlebar moustaches at home.

IT WAS WORTH WAITING FOR!

WHAT?

WHY, THE WARWICK PERFECTION

BICYCLE.

It has more Genuine Improvements than any Wheel on the American or European Markets.

Agents and Wheelmen, keep a Lookout for it!

Warwick Cycle Mfg. Co.

SPRINGFIELD, MASS.

A high-wheeler in the United States, a penny-farthing in England, a bonebreaker everywhere, this was the 1870's forerunner of the safety bicycle.

[1] Coons, Hannibal, "Bicycles Built for All," *Holiday*, July, 1948, p. 83.

Ecstatic men and women paid no attention. Though the moralist railed, women discarded cumbersome bustles and restricting corsets for more comfortable clothes in which they could cycle. The manufacturers developed special models for them and devices to prevent their flowing skirts from catching in the wheels. The League of American Wheelman and the dominant Pope Manufacturing Company demanded improved roads everywhere, signs showing directions and distances to towns and villages, cycle paths apart from the roads choked with the horse-drawn traffic of cities. They got almost everything they demanded, for the cycling vote got too large for politicians to ignore. There were cycling parties, cycling picnics, cycling parades. Champion bike riders were pitted against each other in heroic tests of speed and endurance. Sweating century riders tortured their thighs and almost burst their calves to cover a hundred miles in twelve hours. Those who succeeded got gold badges, with an added bar for every extra hundred miles ticked off.

Men and women gloated over their shining bicycles. They spent hours polishing and oiling them—occasionally lost a finger twirling the chain of an upturned machine. They argued bitterly over the comparative merits of the Columbia, the Rover, the Rambler, the Victor, the Humber, the Mitchell, the Monarch, the Stanley, the Acme, and all the others. They saved dollars, dimes, and nickels to get the hundred to a hundred and fifty dollars which most bicycles cost, perspired as they patched punctures, sang, "Daisy, Daisy, Give me your answer, do!" as they coasted gaily downhill to struggle panting up again. They rubbed liniment into their screaming muscles, stood up when they were too saddle-sore to sit down, matched their endurance against their eagerness and, according to temperament and etiquette, scorched or pedalled sedately off again.

There were one hundred manufacturers of bicycles competing with Columbia by 1896, hundreds of thousands of bicycles on American streets and roads and the new cinder paths. The makers of parts and accessories were working overtime to keep up with the orders of the manufacturers and the demands of the bicycle shops which were in every neighborhood. There was even by the mid-1890's an eager market in England for American machines, for the craze had crossed the Atlantic, and the English manufacturers were not able to keep up with the demand.

Bicycle advertising was pumping just as hard as the bicycle factories and the bicycle riders themselves. This was a new kind of advertising. It was noticeably different in many ways from other advertising. Many of the large regular advertisers had the field to themselves. It was Pears' and Ivory soap, James Pyle's Pearline, and Sapolio. Their advertising was not competitive. Each had built and was maintaining its own market; each had a virtual monopoly. In contrast, bicycle advertising was strongly competitive. It was not for a low-priced article which cost little to make and was quickly consumed, making for constant repeat purchases. It was for an item of comparatively complex manufacture, expensive, and durable. The advertising was competitive. It was for a completely new product, it was based on new appeals, and offered new enticements. Over a million bicycles were in use by 1893.

The leading bicycle advertiser was the pioneer Columbia. Colonel Pope had started advertising even before he had the safety to sell. Nathaniel Fowler had written advertisements for Columbia high-wheelers in 1883. One of them showed a man on a high-wheeler and a woman on a tricycle touring down a country road.

By 1894 Columbia was advertising "A Wheel designed for the special use of lady riders only." It was the Model 35 at $125. A year later Columbia advertised: "1896 Machines in 1895." The advertisement continued: "—advertising has for months been conspicuous by its absence. 1895 Columbias at $100—finest, easiest-running bicycles ever produced at any price—have been doing their own advertising. You see them everywhere." Pope hired artists to paint pleasant posters of cycling scenes. The entire back page of *Ladies' Home Journal* for one issue of 1896 was a poster advertisement in Maxfield

Columbia was the leading manufacturer and advertiser, with the loquacious, corset-trained Nath'l. C. Fowler doing most of the copy.

Parrish blue showing a group of graceful young men and women on the stone bridge of an English-looking village.

The advertising of the Columbia's competitors was more insistent and less colorful. It lacked the sureness of the Columbia displays. The Lady Sterling was "built like a watch." It was: "A *beautiful* wheel for the ladies who appreciate the beautiful, a *strong* wheel for ladies who don't want to bother their brothers, nor go to the repair shop themselves." The Napoleon advertised that it held the world's record for ten miles; the Jenkins Cycle Company made a companion, Josephine," for women. It was the "Easy-Riding Gendron" and the "Smooth-Riding Crescent." Crescents were "Sky High," and the Monarch's cry was, "Leads the World!" The Sylph sold "Wheeling Companionship" down romantic country roads. The Overman Wheel Company's Victorian was "Queen of the Safeties—a Fit Mount for American Women." The Monarch was "The Apex of Bicycle Perfection." The Mead Cycle Company of Chicago was a persistent advertiser of "Bicycles Below Cost," last year's models and, always, "Agents Wanted."

Morrow and New Departure Coaster Brakes, C. & J., Hartford, Lattina, and Palmer tires and Delaware Special Puncture-Proofs, Christy Saddles, New Departure Bells— such accessories were as vigorously advertised as the bicycles themselves. The bicycle got an entire industry advertising in mass and against each other for public favor, consumer preference, and purchase.

Before the bicycle bonanza was over, the established manufacturers were faced with terrifying competition from a formidable adversary. A supersalesman, feared by manufacturers and retailers alike, who had already made devastating inroads in other lines of merchandise, declared a bicycle price war.

Richard W. Sears, born in Stewartville, Minnesota, had, in the Munsey-Bok tradition, first become a telegraph operator. As a railroad station agent in Redwood, he began to sell gold-filled watches for a Chicago company. In six months he made five thousand dollars, a fortune that enabled him to found R. W. Sears Watch Company in Minneapolis in 1886. The next year he moved to Chicago, began to advertise, and hired a young watchmaker from Lafayette, Indiana, named Alvah Curtis Roebuck. Sears bought discontinued works from makers, stuffed them into cases, and peddled them through express agents. He sold on the installment plan, on the club plan, advertised continually in the rural press, and did so well that at twenty-five he retired and returned to Minneapolis.

His retirement did not last long. In Minneapolis he founded, with Roebuck, the Warren Company, broadening his watch and jewelry line to include sewing machines. In 1891, after another quick success, he retired again and sold the business to Roebuck. This retirement lasted a week. Sears bought back a half interest and issued the first Sears' catalogue featuring watches, jewelry, shoes, and baby carriages. He advertised heavily, directing his advertising to the farmer and the farmer's family, the workman, and the mechanic.

The hostility of local merchants closed many newspapers to Sears. He concentrated on the farm papers which welcomed mail-order advertising. He used them and the religious magazines to push his merchandise at prices that looked like less than cost. Sears' one appeal was price, and the purpose of all his advertising was simply to list, describe, and emphasize the price advantages he offered against all competition.

The early Sears advertisement was meant to attract attention, to establish his mail-order business in a hurry. It was the price list of a supply house with no pretense at literary or artistic niceties—high-pressure selling, description, exhortation, and promise, with *caveat emptor* understood and sometimes necessary.

In 1889 Sears headed one advertisement which he ran in a number of country papers: "An Astonishing Offer!" It was. The illustration showed a sofa and two chairs. The text declared that, "as an advertisement only," this beautiful set of furniture would be sent during the next sixty days to everyone who would send ninety-five cents "to pay expenses

of boxing, packaging, advertising, etc." The furniture itself
was described as made of "fine, lustrous metal frames, beautifully finished and decorated, and upholstered in the finest
manner with beautiful plush." Those who risked sending the
ninety-five cents, received a set of doll's furniture. The word
"miniature" had appeared in very small type in the first line
of the advertisement.[2]

All Sears newspaper and magazine advertising was an in-
ducement to examine his catalogue. Advertisements in *Comfort, Fireside Visitor, Good Stories, Happy Hours,* and the
like, as later in the big magazines, were crammed with prints
display, prices, and a catalogue offer. The back cover of
Vickery's *Fireside Visitor,* April 1, 1894, was typical. Sears'
Minneapolis and Chicago offices were spotted on a page-size
globe of the world. The globe was encircled with, "CHEAP-
EST SUPPLY HOUSE ON EARTH—Our trade reaches around the
world." The advertisement offered: "the big catalogue of
3,000 engravings which we send free to anyone on application . . . The Grandest Book of Information to BUYERS ever
printed. IT COSTS NOTHING!"[3]

Sometimes the catalogue was known as "The Great Wish
Book"; sometimes Sears' advertising in *Hearth and Home* and
the other rural papers called it "The Consumers' Guide."
Every year it got fatter with new offers. In 1895, describing
itself as "the largest handlers of Clothing in America," Sears,
Roebuck offered men's suits at $4.98 and sold them by the
carload. Another year Sears waged an all-out campaign for
its cream separators, underselling the regular manufacturers
by about half. Sears followed this with a drive on sewing
machines, using sixteen monthly magazines and forty weeklies
and semiweeklies as well as his catalogue.

Sears was becoming an important advertiser. In 1898 he
spent $392,775 on his purely utilitarian type of advertising.
This was 13 per cent of his sales for the year and almost half

[2] Boris Emmet and John E. Jeuck, *Catalogues and Counters, A History
of Sears, Roebuck and Company* (Chicago: University of Chicago Press,
1950), p. 44.
    [3] *Ibid.,* p. 62.

his total operating expense. In 1900, he spent $606,786; by 1907 he was spending more than $5 million a year.[4]

It was in 1898 that Sears, Roebuck began to wage war on the bicycle industry. In the *American Woman*, April, 1898, Sears offered a bicycle for $13.95 which could be obtained for a down payment of $5.00. The language of the advertisement was obscure and misleading, according to the company's historians, but there is no doubt that Sears deliberately undertook to undercut the entire market in a vast promotion based on price. Sears issued thousands of circulars illustrated by a proof of the catalogue advertising of his bicycles. He sent these to names on his address lists with a note saying that for two dollars he would send another thousand circulars and a stamp for pressing the addressee's name on them. When ten of the circular-order blanks bearing the name were sent in, the contractor would receive a free bicycle.

Sears contracted through an agent with two thousand newspapers. Each would give him a stipulated amount of advertising space during the year in exchange for a Sears bicycle. Sears was busily concocting new schemes to sell his cure-all electric belt—particularly recommended for sick headaches, nervous diseases, and backaches, for weakness, and discouragement. He was dreaming of selling 1,000 cream separators a day as easily as he had sold 250. He was convinced that Sears, Roebuck would drift into installment selling on what he called *Big Things*, by which he meant buggies, sewing machines, organs, pianos, and furniture, but not on little things. Soon he was crying in all his advertising, "Send No Money!" He was wondering whether they had not been wrong in assuming that cities were not their market and insisting it was their duty to prove the assumption true. The super-salesman had others things to think about, but he kept his presses busy turning out his bicycle circulars and catalogues during 1898, kept his advertising and publicity shrill

[4] *Ibid.*, p. 83. In all forms of advertising, including salaries of its own advertising staff, Sears, Roebuck spent $58½ million in 1955, according to *Advertising Age*, September 10, 1956.

in the religious and farm magazines. In one year he sold 100,000.

Sears won no complete victory in the bicycle war. His were not precision machines to delight the expert nor built to arouse aesthetic appreciation. They lacked the prestige of the Columbia, the Overman, or the Stanley. He neither cornered the market with his utilitarian machines nor buried the bicycle industry under the avalanche of his promotion. A late opportunist in a field where others had pioneered, engineered, and developed, he skimmed but a comparatively small and not very rich portion of the cream. The market built by the bicycle manufacturers had been established when Sears attacked. Actually, the market had begun to subside by 1898. The class market was about saturated, and it had been the market which responded to the advertising of the manufacturers and made the bicycle fashionable and popular. The bicycle was descending the social scale when Sears opened his appeal to the mass market on a price rather than a quality appeal.

The bicycle craze wore itself out, partly through over-enthusiasm, partly because the bicycle was gradually replaced in the United States by the newly developing automobile. The bicycle as a means of locomotion for American adults began to die out before 1900, but it did not diminish to the stature of a steed for schoolboys before it had changed women's dress and manners, brought better roads, made people conscious of a landscape larger than that visible from their own streets or farmyards, and had, quite literally, paved the way for the automobile.

Bicycle advertising instilled the idea of spending a considerable sum of money for a pleasure vehicle. Installment payments and trade-in were established as sales policies for durable merchandise. The agency-distribution scheme, which the automobile manufacturers adopted, was tried and tested. As the bicycle dwindled, many of its manufacturers turned to making automobiles, as did the Pope Company itself. The Stanley was a bicycle before it became a steam automobile.

Many of the first cars, among them the Ford, ran on bicycle wheels.

The advertising of bicycles stimulated all advertising in the 1890's. It led to more advertising of other things, and to greater clamor in the advertising of them all. Advertising was a good thing. Magazine advertising was even better. It did not much matter which magazine paid the agents their commissions or helped bring in the widening markets manufacturers had to have.

The *Smart Set* was founded in 1890 as a journal for society. It became, rather like the *Yellow Book* in London, a magazine for and by the aesthete as well as the socially élite. In no way a natural commercial medium, the "little magazine" waxed fat on the enthusiasm of advertisers and agents. The rich pages of advertising in the *Smart Set* for October, 1902, bore no indication that they were addressed only to the rich and well-born sophisticates who would appreciate "A Magazine of Cleverness," as the *Smart Set* always described itself on the cover.

The smart set evidently ate Ralston Purina Foods, drank Red Top Rye Whiskey, had constipation, consumption, obesity, torpid livers, shaved, wore collars and underclothes, suffered bunions, guzzled beer, and wanted to go to California just like the readers of less pretentious periodicals, but they did not bike in 1902. One testimonial advertisement outdid all other testimonials. A four-page advertisement for the Pianola of the Aeolian Company carried praise for the instrument by Paderewski, Hofmann, Rosenthal, Bauer, Sauer, von Dohnanyi, Moszkowski, Bloomfield-Ziegler, Silvinski, and de Pachmann. There was still room for big-muscled men and large-busted women to advertise health courses and, under a large advertisement for Pabst beer and over a smaller one for Mrs. Winslow's Soothing Syrup, was one for a guaranteed and painless cure—and a free trial treatment—for the MOR-PHINE habit. The St. Paul Association of Chicago admitted their cure, "on a Vital Principle heretofore unknown and lacking in all others" would also "restore the nervous and physical systems and remove the cause" in cases of addiction to opium, laudanum, cocaine, and other drugs.

There were pages of steamship and railroad advertising, but not a single bicycle advertisement. It was all over except for the effects of bicycle advertising manifest on almost every page of the magazine. There were, though, two advertisements for an automobile. Pictured as something like a cutter on bicycle wheels, priced at $650 at the factory, one car had just won new recognition.

> TWO of the nine Blue Ribbons (100 per cent) for completing a strenuous 100 miles run without stop, at Chicago, August 2, 1902, were awarded

THE OLDSMOBILE

> The judges could not be shaken from their conviction that THE OLDSMOBILE IS THE BEST THING ON WHEELS, for there is nothing to watch but the Road, and all roads are alike to the Oldsmobile, which is built to run *and does it.*

The other automobile advertisement was for "the most practical automobile in the world." The illustrations showed two stylishly dressed women in large hats sitting gingerly upright on the back seat, the proud owner in front with a chauffeur in a visored cap holding tightly to the tiller.

> THE ONLY automobile that has won EVERY Endurance Contest held in America is the

HAYNES-APPERSON

Runabout,	6 horse-power,	2 passengers,	$1,200
Phaeton,	9 " "	2 "	1,500
Surrey,	9 " "	4 "	1,800

19

The Chicago Discipline

THE NEXT SIGNIFICANT change in the advertising and the advertising approach came not in New York, where most of the country's twenty to twenty-five loosely organized agencies were situated, but out of Chicago. It was propelled by one man in one agency, but the man was Albert D. Lasker. It was accomplished by Lasker with the help of two advertising copywriters, but the copywriters were John E. Kennedy and Claude C. Hopkins.

They helped make copywriting a central function of the advertising agency. They brought new ideas, new concepts, new practices, a new attitude, and a new morality into advertising. They did on a large scale things that had never been done at all. They used advertising as if it were magic to create industries and fortunes, change human habits, and transform valueless properties into million-dollar estates. They did it for money—lots of it—but seemingly, as much for love of the power they could exercise. These men became the experts, the almost fanatical mercenaries, of a new, bolder, and almost terrifying kind of advertising.

A. D. Lasker, a Texan who had worked briefly as a sports writer on the New Orleans *Times Democrat,* joined Lord & Thomas in 1898, just six years after the agency had been founded in Chicago. His starting salary was ten dollars a week. By 1904, when he had obtained a quarter interest in the business, he was making fifty-two thousand dollars a year. Before he died in 1952, Lasker said he had made $40 or $60 million out of advertising. He was not quite sure which.[1]

[1] *Printers' Ink,* June 6, 1952.

Lasker was a driving enthusiast, an inspired salesman, a mesmerist, egotistical, daring, confident, and triumphant. He despised research. He was seldom impeded by facts.[2] He converted by contagion of his own fervor. "So far as I know," Claude Hopkins marveled in 1927, "no ordinary human being has ever resisted Albert Lasker. He has commanded what he would in this world. . . . Nothing he desired has ever been forbidden him."[3]

One day in 1899, as Lasker tells the story, he was seated talking with A. L. Thomas when a card was sent up from the saloon downstairs. Somebody whose name was John E. Kennedy said he knew Lasker did not know what advertising really was. If Lasker would come down to the bar, he would tell him. Thomas did not know who Kennedy was, neither did Lasker, but he thought he might as well go down. He descended to the intellectual discovery of his life. John E. Kennedy, who had resigned from the Canadian Northwest Mounted Police to become a salesman and highly paid advertising writer for Dr. Shoop's Restorative, was tall and handsome with a handlebar moustache. Advertising, Kennedy solemnly told Lasker, was "Salesmanship in Print."

It was a revelation. Lasker was transported.

Immediately he hired Kennedy at a widely advertised twenty-eight thousand dollars a year and all expenses, which made him the most highly paid advertising writer in the world. Together they started out to teach everybody that

[2] James Webb Young in *The Diary of an Ad Man* (Chicago: Advertising Publications, Inc., 1944) reported that in later years a Lord & Thomas man tried to persuade Lasker to set up a market research department. "What good would it do?" Lasker wanted to know. "A stack of figures a foot high wouldn't change my mind if I didn't agree with them." Young, a famous copywriter and J. Walter Thompson executive, used the story to show the reliance most skilled advertising men place on their own intuition.

[3] Both Lasker and Hopkins left full accounts of their activities. *The Lasker Story . . . As He Told It* is the stenographic report of an informal talk Lasker gave Lord & Thomas executives in April, 1925. It appeared in installments in *Advertising Age* in 1952 and 1953 and was later reprinted in booklet form by Advertising Publications, Inc., Chicago. Claude Hopkins' *My Life in Advertising*, originally in *Advertising & Selling*, was published by Harper's as a book in 1927, then reprinted serially in *Advertising & Selling*, February-July, 1946.

advertising was salesmanship in print. They talked to people about it. They issued booklets about it. With evangelical zeal, they spread the new gospel. They declared that the day of the slogan in advertising was over. The day of long, convincing copy, of salesmanship at its most persuasive, had come. Kennedy began to write his patent-medicine spiels, filled with conviction, promises, underlinings, packed copy in small print, for Lord & Thomas accounts. "Salesmanship in Print!" Lord & Thomas had something to sell, something that had never been heard of before, a truth which had never been recognized. They were not selling space. They were not peddling slogans. They were selling salesmanship in print, and salesmanship in print sold everything. Lord & Thomas billings skyrocketed. A mere $900,000 when Lasker joined the agency, they mounted to nearly $2 million by 1902, to nearly $2.5 million in 1903, and that was only the beginning. Kennedy left Lord & Thomas in 1906, but the miracle had been accomplished.

Lasker still had a half dozen copywriters, the largest stable kept by any agency at the time, but no one of Kennedy's stature and magnetism, and he could not find a peer. Then he met Cyrus H. K. Curtis on a train. Curtis was smoking one of his exaggerated black cigars and reading a copy of *Life*, the humor magazine. He put it down and told Lasker he was about to order a bottle of beer. An advertisement he had just read had made him thirsty. Lasker, he suggested, had better find out who wrote that convincing advertisement and hire him. Lasker did. The man was Claude C. Hopkins.

Hopkins, born in 1866, was already an experienced and dedicated advertising copywriter, a man as shrewd, astute, and possessed as Lasker himself. He had started out in Michigan with the idea that he wanted to be a minister and had even been a boy preacher, but soon perceived the economic emptiness of such pursuit. He then went to a business college in Grand Rapids where the instruction was so poor, he said later in a revealing remark, that he might as well have spent the time at a university studying dead languages. He

became a bookkeeper, then began to sell Bissell Carpet
Sweepers. This was the real beginning.

Bissell had paid the great John E. Powers for a piece of
advertising copy. Hopkins, still a youth, showed Bissell the
copy was all wrong, wrote his own, and it was accepted.
Powers sued and collected his fee, but it was Hopkins' copy
that was used and sold sweepers. Now, as Lipton dreamed
of ways to sell pork, ham, and tea, Hopkins dreamed inces-
santly of ways to sell carpet sweepers. He had already discovered two secrets, both of which he remembered and
applied throughout his career. To get ahead, you had to
please people. He strove to please. To make people buy,
you had to give them reasons—good, sound, selfish reasons
why they should. He gave them reasons endlessly.

Hopkins wrote his sweeper copy to women. He offered
them the privileges of vacuum cleaner ownership. He offered sweepers in different kinds of woods—mahogany, maple,
walnut, birch. The wood did not help or hinder the operation of the sweeper, but it pleased women. He filled his
direct-mail letters with reasons why women would benefit
from owning Bissells. His letters, he says proudly, sold more
carpet sweepers than the combined efforts of fourteen salesmen on the road.

Convinced now that he could sell anything, including himself, Hopkins answered a Swift & Company advertisement
for an advertising manager. He had everyone he knew write
Swift letters praising his character and abilities. He got the
job and took on the Swift product they were finding most
difficult to sell. "Cotosuet" differed not at all from competitive shortenings, but Hopkins moved it in mass, sold it in
carloads. He had studied the sales methods of canvassers and
fakers. He was convinced they were the best in the world.
One thing those patter artists did was demonstrate. Hopkins
had a huge cake baked with Cotosuet instead of lard and put
it on display in the window of a large Chicago store. The
police had to be called to hold back the crowds. It was as
spectacular a success as Thomas Lipton's Jumbo cheese.
Hopkins built more and larger cakes and displayed them in

other cities, getting finally to New York with the largest cake of all and the most spectacular success. Hopkins knew that if you wanted to sell—and he wanted to sell more than anything in the world—you had to cater to the millions. That was what he did.

Spurred on by his successes, Hopkins went into patent medicines. Medicines, he knew, were worthless merchandise until a demand was created. The nostrums offered a real test to a man whose only determination was to sell and to sell at a profit. Like Kennedy before him, he went to Dr. Shoop's Restorative in Racine, Wisconsin. There he devised the scheme of selling six bottles for the price of five and having a local druggist provide a warrant of money back if the medicine did not work. It always worked, as Hopkins knew any patent medicine would. The patent medicines made people think they felt better. The effect was psychological.

It was then Hopkins went to Schlitz Beer. He went through the Schlitz plant and saw the bottles being cleaned with steam. It was a process every brewery used. Hopkins seized on it. The reason why Schlitz beer was pure was because Schlitz cleaned their bottles with steam. He did not say Schlitz alone did this, but he made it look as if Schlitz alone took this wonderful and costly precaution for the benefit of its drinkers' health. Once the advertising had appeared, other brewers hesitated to claim they did the same thing. It would look as if they were imitating Schlitz. Again and again Hopkins, by his own boast, used this device of singling out a process common to competitive advertisers and playing it up as the original and sole possession of his client.

At the same time Hopkins was doing the advertising for Liquozone, a patent medicine that he was convinced had saved the life of his young daughter. He sold it in the same way and with the same guarantee he had used with Dr. Shoop's Restorative. The product had been failing. Hopkins drove it up to a net profit of $1,800,000 in his first year. He opened his druggist-warranty campaign in city after city. He invaded Europe. Liquozone set up an office in London, where it employed three hundred people, a factory in France,

another elaborate office in Paris. Within two years he had
Liquozone advertising being printed in seventeen languages
and the medicine selling all over the civilized world. Hopkins' recital of the triumph of Liquozone sounds like H. G.
Wells' recital of the progress of *Tono-Bungay*; it was just
such a product and such advertising methods that Wells
burlesqued in his full-length satire of 1909.

In Paris, Hopkins, driven beyond his strength by his compulsion to sell, broke down. He was sent home to rest. Lasker,
who was to break down himself a few years later and from
the same cause, sent for him, and Hopkins, after three months
of rest and drinking milk, was soon back at it harder than
ever.

Hopkins was a man after Lasker's own heart. Lasker
exulted when he found him. Hopkins was even further advanced in the mysteries of advertising than Kennedy had
been. Hopkins, too, had a magic formula. It was "Reason
Why." Advertising had to give people reasons why—beautiful reasons why they would benefit by purchase of whatever it was. The two went to work. Armed with the later
revelation, they went at it with almost delirious enthusiasm.
Again Lasker had a doctrine to spread. Hopkins broadcast
by precept and example. The first major test came by way
of a brand of canned pork and beans.

Hopkins sent out door-to-door scouts. They found most
households baked their own beans. Immediately Lord &
Thomas started a campaign against home baking of beans.
Hopkins gave the reasons why beans baked at home could
never be digestible. Hopkins told how the company used
only especially selected beans and soft water; how they were
baked for hours at tremendous heat in steam ovens. He also,
for he knew the supreme sales value of something for nothing,
gave away free samples. When a luncheon was held at the
factory, no one could tell whether he was eating his own or
a competitive brand, so Hopkins simply advertised to women
that restaurants served the brand and many men ate them for
lunch. As he reiterates, the brand had no unique properties.
A bean was a bean was a canned bean; but Hopkins told the

story first and gave the customers the reasons why his bean was best.

Levitated by his triumph, Lasker and Hopkins sailed on into soaps and cereals, as later they went into automobiles, tires, automobile accessories, and the application of their kinds of advertising methods to politics and government.

Breakfast foods already had a substantial advertising history. The American Cereal Company had put Quaker Oats on the market in 1878 and begun to advertise immediately. Pettijohn's, Mother's Oats, Hornby's Oats (H.O.), Grape-Nuts, and Shredded Wheat had come along in the 1890's. There were stories behind many of them.

Once a lawyer named Henry D. Perky, who suffered from dyspepsia, had noticed a man in a Nebraska town, where he was trying a case, eating for breakfast what appeared to be grains of wheat. Accosted, the stranger confessed it was boiled whole wheat. Perky tried some with milk and cream, liked it, found he could eat it without disastrous results, and decided he had a commercially valuable idea. He began to make Shredded Wheat Biscuits on the second floor of a Denver grocery. He peddled the biscuits from house to house. In 1895 he opened a shop in Worcester, Massachusetts, and began to sell the biscuits for use in puddings, muffins, and fruit combinations. He got an advertising agent, and they cooked up a long list of menus, even founded an institute of domestic science where young women were trained to demonstrate Shredded Wheat. Then the advertising man realized that Shredded Wheat Biscuits were not for puddings at all. They were a breakfast food. In 1900, a genius in sales strategy, Perky built his model factory, a "Palace of Light," at Niagara Falls, and Shredded Wheat became a part of the romantic scene and firmly fixed as a leading cereal.

Grape-Nuts and Post Toasties had their colorful history too. C. W. Post, then forty, went to a sanatorium in Battle Creek, Michigan, with a nervous breakdown. He was a salesman and an inventor who had worked with bicycles, plows, and mechanical pianos. In Battle Creek his interest, quite naturally, was transferred to health and health foods.

He emerged improved in health and, like Perky, with a profitable idea. Soon Post had a line of cereals, a Battle Creek Sanatorium of his own, and much, much money.

Other cereals had more prosaic origins, some of them descending straight from horse feeds. All were pushed by advertising of patent-medicine abandon. In fact, the cereals were often advertised for their medicinal properties. Quaker Oats advertised against meat. Shredded Wheat denounced too much meat and railed against white flour. Egg-O-See said, "Take that meat away." Cereals described themselves as brain and nerve food as well as bone and muscle builders. Grape-Nuts once claimed that by discontinuing all other foods and washing out the intestines, appendicitis could be avoided.[6] Samples of cereals of many kinds were strewn about the entry ways of people's houses, premiums came with, or for, the packages bought. Cereal markets were opened by all the methods by which they are still sustained.

Quaker Oats was among the leaders. Its old Quaker trademark was well known. Its slogan was, "The Smile That Won't Come Off." The smile came on when you ate the Quaker Oats. Like so many others, the slogan had been jingled in the 1890's:

> "What! Quaker Oats!" exclaimed the kid.
> "I think I'll eat some"—and he did.
> When o'er his youthful features slid
> The smile that won't come off.

Quaker Oats was firmly established, but two other cereals belonging to the same company were languishing. Wheat Berries and Puff Berries were, in fact, collapsing. The owners of the breakfast foods had sought advice in vain from nineteen agencies before they came to Lord & Thomas. In ten minutes, Lasker reports, he and Claude Hopkins solved it all. They told the Quaker Oats Company to stop showing pictures of Japanese and Chinese eating rice in their advertisements. Americans did not want to be turned into Asiatics.

    [4] Gerald H. Carson, "Early Days in the Breakfast Food Industry," *Advertising & Selling*, October, 1945.

They told them to use one name for both cereals. The cereals became Puffed Wheat and Puffed Rice. They told them to charge more. If people would pay ten cents for three and a half ounces, they would not care how much more they paid. The company raised its prices. Hopkins put his "Reason Why" to work now. He looked over the manufacturing process and soon discovered that the reason why Puffed Wheat and Puffed Rice were appetizing and healthful breakfast foods was that they were "Shot from Guns."

The purity, edibility, wholesomeness, and high romance of the puffed cereals were dramatized in this one phrase. The swollen grains were shown cascading from the very cannon's mouth in advertising illustrations, and even in mobile displays.

The Lord & Thomas team of Lasker, Hopkins, Salesmanship in Print, and Reason Why went on and did for soap, automobiles, toothpaste, shaving cream, national politics, tires, and a few other commodities what they had done for patent medicines, cereals, and beers. But most of these triumphs came later in the seventeen-year Lasker-Hopkins alliance. By 1912 Lasker, worn out by the very intensity of his enthusiasm, his love of advertising, and his inspired application of the advertising dogma he believed, preached, and practiced, broke down. His wife took him to Europe. He could not, he said, talk for five minutes without weeping. He spent months in a sanatorium, returned to Chicago, found he still could not work, and went to Mexico to recuperate further.

By this time Lord & Thomas was billing about $8 million of advertising a year. Lasker rejoined his company as World War I started in Europe, but was soon absent looking after his growing investments in the companies of his clients, then as a propagandist for the Republican Party. Lasker's greatest advertising triumphs were to come with Lucky Strike in the 1930's; yet he and John E. Kennedy and Claude Hopkins had already affected the course and character of advertising.

They made copy the important ingredient in advertising, and they made the preparation of convincing copy the chief service provided by the advertising agency. They sold the idea of "the hard sell" in strong, all-out campaigns for quick results. They discovered that advertising worked best for low-priced, quickly consumed articles where the advertising itself was the chief production cost and one of the product's most valuable assets. Hopkins, in particular, made a business of finding out what consumers wanted ("research") and then claiming that what he was advertising offered exactly those qualities.

Almost always his Reason Why was an appeal to the emotions; and always, as he reiterated, he appealed to the selfish interests of consumers. He did not ask them to buy anything or to do something. He offered them something, whatever he thought it was they wanted most. He did not claim a dentifrice was pure, but that it made you beautiful. He did not say one car was better than the others, but that the man who made it was an expert and a hero.

Hopkins and Lasker both thoroughly understood that to sell and to sell profitably, you had to talk to and convince the masses. They learned that nothing convinced like arousing a strong demand through hard advertising pressure. Once the demand was created, all the rest followed. People, sheeplike, follow the crowd. They do not judge values. They do not think. They want what they have been made to believe everyone wants and is buying. Hopkins called this "trend of the crowd" the most effective device he had ever found in advertising. Like Lasker, he made millions from the discovery.

The most significant Lasker-Kennedy-Hopkins accomplishment was to fasten down more firmly the change that was already taking place in advertising when they started their ministry. Advertising was no longer a matter of an individual's seeking the attention and favor of other individuals or of a small retailer currying the patronage of the community. It was the full-scale drive of large manufacturers of branded merchandise for national and international markets. The message was not, come to me or my store and buy, but go to any shop anywhere and buy. Lord & Thomas drove the nail in deeper by advertising always to the consumer, bypassing the wholesalers and retailers who might be the direct customers of the manufacturer. The jobber would buy and the retailer would stock what the consumer demanded —if the consumer was subjected to enough salesmanship in print and confused by enough reasons why he should do as he was told.

Lasker himself said in a conversation with James Webb Young, probably in the 1930's, that only three things of major importance had ever happened in the history of the advertising agency business: the original Ayer contract, his hiring of John Kennedy and dramatizing copy as the most important advertising element in an agency, and the injection of sex into advertising when J. Walter Thompson dreamed up "The Skin You Love to Touch" for Woodbury's Soap.[5]

---

[5] Young, *op. cit.*, p. 101.

20

Duryea to Model T—Early Automobile Advertising

THE FORWARD THRUST OF advertising, as the tempo of American life itself, was immeasurably accelerated and intensified by two young men who in 1892 were completely innocent of any such intent. All that Charles E. Duryea, who had been making bicycles, and his brother, J. Frank Duryea, a mechanic and toolmaker at the Ames Manufacturing Company in Chicopee, Massachusetts, wanted to do was design and build a vehicle which would actually move under its own propulsion.

They borrowed a thousand dollars from Erwin F. Markham of nearby Springfield. For seventy dollars Charles Duryea purchased a second-hand phaeton. Charles returned from Chicopee to his bicycle making, in Peoria, Illinois, and J. Frank and Erwin Markham went to work on the project in the machine shop of W. J. Taylor & Sons in Springfield. They built a one-cylinder gasoline engine, devising their own ignition system and improvising a spray carburetor out of a perfume atomizer and an alcohol burner. They improvised, puttered, and tinkered for more than a year.

Saturday, September 16, 1893, the *Springfield Evening Union* reported:

A new motor carriage which, if the preliminary tests prove successful is expected will revolutionize the mode of travel on highways and do away with the horse as a means of transportation, is being made in this city. It is quite probable that within a short time one may be able to see an ordinary carriage in almost every respect run-

ning along the streets or climbing country hills without visible means
of propulsion. This carriage is being built by J. F. Duryea, the designer, and E. F. Markham, who have been at work on it for over a
year. The vehicle was designed by C. E. Duryea, a bicycle manufacturer of Peoria, Ill., and he communicated the scheme to his
brother. . . .

After dark, five days later, J. Frank Duryea and Markham
took a harnessed horse to the shop on Taylor Street and
hauled the completed vehicle to the home of Markham's son-
in-law on Spruce Street. The next morning they made their
first trial run on Spruce and Florence Streets in Springfield.[1]
The motor wagon coughed, chugged, and spluttered, then
took hold. It worked! "The first tests of the motor carriage
built by J. F. Duryea and E. F. Markham," the *Union* reported that evening, September 22, "have been made, and
although the carriage runs very well, it does not give perfect
satisfaction to its inventors and some changes will be made
in the mode of transmitting the power from the gasoline
motor to the main driving shafts."

The changes were made, and the first American gasoline
automobile—though no one yet knew "automobile" was to be
its name—was taken for another half-mile test November 9.
Duryea made more changes in his clutch and transmission,
and in January, 1894, the Duryea horseless carriage ran perfectly for five miles.

In 1894 the Duryea brothers formed the Duryea Motor
Wagon Company in Springfield, and J. Frank built a two-
cylinder Duryea, dubbed the Buggyaut, to enter a race in
Chicago sponsored by the *Times-Herald*. Twice postponed,
the first automobile race in the United States was held on
Thanksgiving Day, November 26, 1895. Nearly a hundred
vehicles had been entered, but only six—two electrics, three
European-made Benz cars, and the Duryea—managed to reach
the starting line. It was cold and blustery, snow from an
early blizzard still on the ground, when they started from
Chicago at 9 o'clock in the morning to race to Evanston and

[1] J. Frank Duryea, *America's First Automobile* (Springfield, Mass.:
Donald M. Macaulay, 1942), p. 16.

back, a distance of 54 miles. An umpire rode with each of the tense drivers. J. Frank Duryea drove the car he had built. Charles came up from Peoria to witness the race.

Crowds had braved the weather to gather at every vantage point along the early part of the route. Nothing like this had ever happened before. They marveled as the vehicles got under way, struggled to a start, then settled down to a steady pace. Those who had come to scoff were soon rewarded. The French De La Vergne, winner of a Paris-Bordeaux race, was forced out on the Midway when its solid rubber tires spun in the snow. The two electrics negotiated Michigan Avenue and the run up Lake Shore Drive, but the exertion exhausted their batteries. The R. H. Macy Benz entry provided greater excitement. It collided with a horse-car before its engine sputtered out. One driver of a Mueller-Benz, after enduring all he could, was too chilled and numbed by the cold to continue. His frozen replacement lost consciousness at 55th and Halstead, and the umpire had to grasp the controls and bring the car wobbling across the finish line. It was the only other car to complete the race.

Despite one stop of 55 minutes to repair the steering apparatus and another of nearly an hour when an astounded tinsmith was awakened from an after-Thanksgiving dinner nap to help mend the sparker, the Duryea won, completing the 54-mile course in 7 hours and 53 minutes. It was a complete triumph for the only American-made gasoline car in the race.[2]

With a newly won reputation and two thousand dollars in prize money, the Duryea Company immediately began manufacture of more of their motor wagons. John Brisbane Walker of *Cosmopolitan* announced an automobile race for Memorial Day, 1861, from New York's City Hall up the Hudson to Irvington and back. The Duryea entered four of their motor wagons against a field of foreign and American-made cars and won every prize for a total of three thousand

[2] *Ibid.*, p. 20-23; also Major Lenox R. Lohr, "Fifty Years of Motor Cars, 1895-1945," Newcomen Society of England, American Branch, New York, 1946.

dollars more. The prize money enabled them to make more cars, a total of twelve in 1896. Two of these were sent to England where they performed even greater feats than those they had demonstrated in Chicago and New York. November 14, 1896, some forty automobiles, steam cars, gasoline cars, and electrics, raced from London to Brighton. J. Frank Duryea, who started among the last, quickly took the lead and drove his Buggyaut into Brighton almost an hour before the car which was placed second.

Duryea Motor Wagon Company,

SPRINGFIELD, MASS.

MANUFACTURERS OF

Motor Wagons, Motors, ...

Automobile Vehicles of all kinds.

Duryea's first illustrated advertisement for the first American automobile showed the manufacturers already appealing to women.

The advertising which these racing victories brought the Duryeas was tremendous, but they gained even more effective advertising from another of the cars they made in 1896. Barnum & Bailey opened The Greatest Show on Earth at Madison Square Garden in 1896 with a Duryea Motor Wagon as the show's featured exhibit. Posters billed the marvel as:

> The famous Duryea Motor Wagon, or Motorcycle, the identical HORSELESS CARRIAGE that won the great race in Chicago last November.

Barnum & Bailey used the Motor Wagon in place of Jumbo in their street parades everywhere the circus traveled. The Duryea twisted and turned down the street among the elephants, steam calliopes, clowns, and caged lions. It was a

greater marvel than them all. Millions of people saw an automobile for the first time in the circus parades or in the
menagerie tent where the car was put through its paces.

The Duryea Motor Wagon was advertised in the first
issue of the *Horseless Age*, November, 1895. This was the
first advertisement for a complete automobile. In March,
1896, the Duryeas ran what is described as the first illustrated
automobile advertisement. In 1896 an advertisement of "The
Duryea Motor Wagon Company, Springfield, Mass., Motor
Wagons, Motors—Automobile Vehicles of All Kinds" showed
a fashionably dressed woman driving one of their Motor
Wagons, a woman companion, also gowned and hatted in the
mode, riding with her—the first appeal to women in automotive advertising.

There had been steam-propelled vehicles in both Europe
and the United States before the Duryeas made their first car.
Daimler and Benz had produced and driven a four-wheeled
motor carriage in Germany in 1886. Panhard et Lavassor had
concocted a horseless carriage in Paris in 1892, and there had
even been a Paris-Rouen automobile race in 1894. Others,
basing their pretensions on various claims, notably George
Selden, have asserted precedence in idea or partial construction of a complete automobile in the United States, but the
1893 Duryea stands in the Smithsonian Institution as "the first
marketable automobile in America." Charles and J. Frank
Duryea were the first to manufacture cars for sale, the first
to publicize them, to advertise them, and, as almost all later
manufacturers did, to prove their cars in racing and winning.
This was the beginning of the astounding new era in American life and in American advertising.

J. Frank Duryea joined forces with the Stevens Arms
Company of Chicopee to produce one of the finest of early
American cars, the famous Stevens-Duryea. Colonel Pope
of Columbia Bicycle in Hartford approached Charles Duryea
with an offer to build the Duryea Motor Wagon in his Hartford factory and pay the inventor a royalty of five dollars
on each one turned out. Duryea asked fifty dollars and the
venture stopped there. Charles Duryea went on to manu-

facture a new car with two rear wheels and only one in front. It proved impractical, and the Duryea Power Company in Reading, Pennsylvania, returned to making the conventional four-wheeled car. By 1907 Charles was offering for $1,500 a Duryea Phaeton, a runabout that could be changed into a touring car by lifting an extra rear seat into place. In Hartford, Colonel Pope and his associates went on to manufacture a long line of cars, the Columbia, the Pope-Hartford, the Pope-Tribune, the Pope-Toledo, and the electric Pope-Waverly.

Other inventors and makers quickly followed the Duryeas, often working alone and in complete ignorance of what others were accomplishing elsewhere. Elwood Haynes designed and drove his first car July 4, 1894. It was made by Edgar and Elmer Apperson in Kokomo, Indiana. Henry Ford produced his first gasoline-driven automobile in 1896. In Cleveland, Alexander Winton built his first one-cylinder car in the same year. Charles Brady King was already driving the first automobile in Detroit, a high delivery wagon powered by a gasoline engine. Ransom E. Olds made and drove his first gasoline automobile in 1897.[3]

Machinists, bicycle makers and repairmen, manufacturers of motors, motor parts, wagon builders, and workmen of inventive skill and ingenuity in many places began to tinker feverishly and to plan and somehow produce electric, steam, or gasoline-driven vehicles that somehow could be coaxed into motion. Small boys raced shouting alongside. Frightened horses reared, and their angry owners shouted curses as the oil-smeared inventors and adventurers tried out their noisy, smoking chariots.

As soon as a new vehicle proved itself, their inventors scrabbled for funds, begging and borrowing small sums wherever they could, and began to make more cars for sale. F. O. and F. E. Stanley founded the Stanley Steam Car Com-

---

[3] "A Chronology of the Automotive Industry," *The New York Times*, March 9, 1952; C. G. Glasscock, *The Gasoline Age* (Indianapolis: Bobbs-Merrill, 1937), p. 20. Merrill Denison, *The Power to Go* (Garden City, N. Y.: Doubleday & Co., Inc., 1956.

pany in Newton, Massachusetts, in 1897. R. E. Olds founded
the Olds Motor Vehicle Company in Detroit in 1899 and
began to make the first mass-produced car. By 1899 eighty
companies were making or preparing to make automobiles of
one kind and another.[4] By 1902 the Autocar, Winton, Locomobile, Austin, Elmore, Packard, Peerless, Gaeth, Pierce-
Arrow, Pullman, Rambler, White, Cadillac, Franklin, Marmon, and Studebaker had all come along. By 1904, 121 companies were making or assembling automobiles.[5]

Frock-coated, silk-hatted Samuel Bowles II refused to ride
in an early Duryea. His excuse was that it would look undignified. Automobiles were for young mechanical enthusiasts
with grease on their hands and hope in their eyes. Farmers and city folk alike railed against the dangerous contrap-
tions that frightened horses into running away and, if they
were not legislated out of existence, would soon ruin everything in sight. *The New York Times*, in 1897, feared that
the automobile had come to stay, but it was sorry. "Man
loves the horse, and he is not ever likely to love the automobile . . . nor will he ever get quite used, in this generation,
to speeding along the road behind nothing."[6] A motor ambu-
lance rushed President William McKinley to the hospital
when he was shot and fatally wounded at the Pan-American
Exposition in Buffalo, September 6, 1901, but the adventurous
Theodore Roosevelt, when he first risked stepping into a car
in 1902, had it followed by a horse and carriage in case it
broke down.

It was for reasons like these that, as soon as manufacturers
began to make automobiles and offer them for sale, they began to advertise. They had to convince people that the automobile was not a passing fad, that cars would actually go, that

    [4] Glasscock, *op. cit.*, p. 38.
    [5] C. J. Perrier, "An Abstract of Automotive History," *Dun & Brad-
street's Monthly Review*, December, 1935. Since the beginning, according
to "Roll Calls" of private passenger cars and commercial vehicles compiled by the Promotion Department of the *Saturday Evening Post* in 1952,
there have been 2,726 different makes of automobiles sold in the United
States and 1,801 makes of trucks and busses.
    [6] David L. Cohn, *op. cit.*, p. 151.

they would not explode, that they were not mechanical dragons which would devour men, women, children, and horses. People and horses were fascinated but afraid. Farmers and villagers, officials and police all along the thousand-mile jungle route from New York to Bretton Woods, New Hampshire, harried the stout souls who entered thirty-three cars in the first Glidden Tour in 1905. The adventurers were beset and bedeviled by freshly dug mud holes, brand new ordinances, speed traps, ropes strung across the road—by any device that would hinder, hamper, or, preferably, annihilate the smoking monsters and the rich demons who drove them.

The car makers had to demonstrate both the speed and durability of their products. They had to break down the prejudice and envy shrill in the derisive taunt of "Get a horse!" They had to prove that the automobile was not the expensive toy of the idle rich whose imported cars were the playthings of Newport and New York, that, instead, it was safe, practical, pleasurable.

It was to advertise his car that Alexander Winton drove from Cleveland to New York in 1897, an almost impossible journey through mud and dust over almost impassable roads (where there were roads at all). It took him ten days. The first automobile show was held in Madison Square Garden in New York in 1900 with sixty-six companies exhibiting at a time when there were only eight thousand cars in the United States, many of them imported, and just 144 miles of paved highway. In 1901 Roy D. Chapin drove one of the first curved-dash Oldsmobiles from Detroit to New York in seven and a half days, achieving an almost incredible average speed of ten miles an hour. Given the road condition and the time consumed by necessary repairs when spare parts and road service were unavailable, it was a magnificent record.

In 1901 Henry Ford challenged Winton to a ten-mile race on the Grosse Pointe track outside Detroit. Ford won with a time of 13 minutes, 23 4/5 seconds for the ten miles, but Winton made a mile in 1 minute, 14 2/5 seconds, an incredible speed and a record. Racing and cross-country trips advertised the new automobiles, automobile shows gave them further publicity, but newspaper and magazine advertising brought the automobile to the public at large.

All the makers advertised, and it was necessary for one more very practical reason. Most of the companies manufacturing or assembling automobiles were very shakily financed. Often they needed the cash from the sale of one car in order to build the next. There could be no installment selling of automobiles yet. The money had to come in, and advertising was the way to get it. Large space was the rule. Where other industries had usually started with advertisements of a few inches, the automobile manufacturers were in a hurry. Quarter pages, half pages, and full pages displayed their claims.

The first automobile advertisements in *The Saturday Evening Post*, which quickly became the leading national advertising medium for the automobile, was March 31, 1900, for: "Automobiles that Give Satisfaction—Highest Award at the National Export Exposition in Phila., Pa. 1899. Prompt Delivery—Catalogue for 2 cent Stamp." The advertiser was W. E. Roach (Successor to Roach & Barnes) 821 Arch St., Phila., Pa. The car shown in the illustration was a horseless buggy with a single headlamp attached to the dash board and what looked like slightly over-sized bicycle wheels wearing thin, pneumatic tires.

In 1902 the Oldsmobile was in the *Post* boasting that it was "just as useful in winter as in summer." It guaranteed a speed of forty miles an hour without tonneau, forty-five with it on, and claimed it could carry 1,500 pounds easily and safely. Cadillac, Packard, Peerless, Ford, Winton, Overland, and Franklin were all advertising in *The Saturday Evening Post* in 1903. Reo was there by January, 1905, Studebaker by March, 1907.

Every maker had his specific claims, and few of them were modest. In 1900 the Porter Company of Boston was advertising its Porter Stanhope steamer as "The Only Perfect Automobile." Adjuring the public to order now to ensure early delivery, the manufacturer said simply:

The Porter Stanhope is the Perfect Automobile. It is handsome and elegant in its lines and conforms in its design to the modern horse carriages. Safe, simple and durable. Boiler is absolutely non-explosive and water-feed automatic. It is free from all complications in its mechanism, so that an engineer is not necessary to its use. Fuel is cheap and obtainable everywhere. It is noiseless and free from all odor and vibration. The Burner (or engine fire) is of low draft and so protected from the air as to be unquenchable in all weathers. It is controlled by one lever only, as in times of danger several levers are confusing . . . WRITE NOW.[7]

Price was $750.

The steamer was still, as it remained for some years, a formidable competitor of the gasoline-driven automobile. The White and the Stanley were famous early. A Stanley established a world speed record of 127 miles an hour at Ormond Beach, Florida, in 1906. A White steamer led Theodore Roosevelt's inaugural parade in 1905, and Taft had a White while he was President.

Every advertiser of every make and kind of car had his slogan. The first Model A Ford in 1903 was the "Boss of the Road." The Haynes-Apperson was "The Only One that Always Won." In 1903 it had "Won every endurance contest held in America, every contest or race ever entered, more records than any other make in the United States, and was the only gasoline car that ran the contest from New York to Boston and back without repairs or adjustments OF ANY KIND." The Packard in 1903 was already advising people to "Ask The Man Who Owns One."

In *The Saturday Evening Post* in 1905 the air-cooled Franklin was the "Speed Merchant." The Winton was exclaiming over its twin springs. The Autocar boasted "Finger-Reach Control." Columbia Gasolene Cars, made by Pope in Hartford, were "Built of the best materials in the world under methods and processes more advanced than those employed in any automobile factory other than our own." In the *Post* of 1906, Cadillac was "The Car That Achieves"; Franklin urged, "Buy with your mind as well as your eyes"; Reo was

[7] Floyd Clymer, *Early American Automobiles* (New York: McGraw-Hill Book Co., Inc., 1950).

"The Positive Car"; Oldsmobile, the cut showing a man and woman motoring gaily down a pretty rural road, was "Your Best Entertainer." The Mitchell was "The Car You Want."

Ramblers were heavily advertised in 1906 and 1907, often in full pages of *The Saturday Evening Post*. Of its Model 24 at $2,250 the Jeffrey Company said, "In this car is embodied every modern feature that has withstood the severe test of practical service, and each has been refined and developed to the highest degree of mechanical perfection." Studebaker presented "Simplicity versus Multiplicity" in chassis design and construction. The Single-Cylinder Cadillac at about $800 for the Model K Runabout was "Supreme Among Small Cars." A Reo was shown straddling a sharp peak. "A Mountain of Evidence," the copy read, proved "The Clean-cut greatness of REO Performance." Most of the automobiles claimed mechanical excellence, speed, durability, performance, but there were other appeals. One manufacturer of a $600 car proclaimed: "For His Majesty, the Average Man; for his family and for professional purposes, THE JEWEL is easily the most attractive proposition in all the land."

Automobile advertising poured into *Post* pages during the next few years; pages, double spreads, and cover advertisements for scores of makes—the Kissell Kar, Chalmers, Owen, Abbott-Detroit, Haynes, Elmore, Speedwell, Apperson, Oakland, Mitchell, Marmon, Stearns-Knight, Buick, Willys-Overland, Peerless, Paige, Hupmobile, the Excelsior, Auto Cycle, the Harley-Davidson and Indian Motorcycles, and even the Motorette, a tiny three-wheeled car on a motorcycle body selling for $325, and the Cygnet Rear Car, a motorcycle with a tublike body behind the rider for his family. The Hupmobile had been "built for the express purpose of battering down the defenses of the man who hesitates about buying a car." Chalmers had six models for the buyer to choose from, even a closed car, a coupe at $2,400 and a limousine at $3,000.

The Black began in 1904 to promote itself with "For Ease of Riding Without a Peer." Aerocar was "The Car of Today, Tomorrow and for Years to Come."

The advertising agencies and the copywriters swarmed to promote the new product which was multiplying advertising billings and fast racing to the front of nationally advertised products—a big, durable machine with infinite sales possibilities, a product costing hundreds of dollars, the most expensive and breathtaking device offered the public thus far. The first cars had hardly been built and driven when presto! a giant industry sprang up. Advertising could hardly keep pace.

The automobile became the bulwark of all national advertising. By 1911 production had reached a value of $160 million and automobiles were taking up an estimated one-eighth of all advertising space in nationally circulated magazines— more than the combined linage used in advertising all food products.[8]

Critics exclaimed that magazine fiction had degenerated into a dream world in which the hero's progress was marked by a trail of gasoline smells and that readers were encouraged to believe that no one was socially desirable unless he owned and drove or rode in an automobile. Woodrow Wilson, politically ambitious president of Princeton, declared in 1908 that nothing had made for undemocratic class distinction like the motor car.

A. D. Lasker claimed that Lord & Thomas handled the first automobile advertising, giving *The Saturday Evening Post* the first order it ever had for a double spread in other than the center position in the magazine. This was for John Willys. Lasker even advanced the money for the expenditure to prove the efficacy of his advertising. With the Reo account, Lasker said, he started all big modern automotive advertising.[9] The problem, as Lasker saw it, in the early days was to give people confidence in the automobile, and he and Claude Hopkins decided that the way to do it was to establish public confidence in the man who made the cars so that customers would accept the product. Hopkins told just how they went about it.

  [8] Kathleen Ann Smallzried and Dorothy James Roberts, *More Than You Promise* (New York: Harper and Bros., 1942), p. 195.
  [9] Lasker, *op. cit.*, p. 25.

Hopkins' first automobile advertising was done for Chalmers. He featured the company's chief engineer so successfully that the man was made head of the U. S. Aircraft Board during World War I. Hopkins then took on Hudson—which broke away from Chalmers because Chalmers had too large a selling organization—and, by stressing its engineering perfection, built up the Hudson. Hopkins claimed another great success with Willys, an Elmira storekeeper and Overland agent who took over the automobile company simply by paying a back payroll of $450. In the advertising he wrote for Willys, Hopkins explained that insistent public demand from Overland users had virtually forced Willys to undertake to supply the new Willys-Overland.

When the Reo got into financial difficulties, Hopkins told R. E. Olds that he would take on the advertising account on three conditions. They were these: the new car had to be called "Reo the Fifth," Olds would have to sign the advertisements so as to give them the full benefit of his great name and reputation, and Olds would have to call Reo the Fifth "My Farewell Car." When Olds demurred that he had no intention of retiring, Hopkins pointed to the example of Sarah Bernhardt, who had made seven farewell tours of the stage, and told Olds that every farewell was subject to reconsideration. Olds agreed, and Hopkins says this led to yet one more automobile advertising success which he designed and engineered. Hopkins then took on tires and built up a tremendous demand for Goodyear.

The Buffalo-born city editor of a newspaper in Toledo forsook journalism to become a writer of automotive advertising copy and the most famous and successful of them all. Theodore Francis McManus, who formed his own Detroit agency, McManus, Inc., handled the advertising for the Pope-Toledo, Pope-Hartford, Pope-Waverly, American Underslung, Detroit Electric, Speedwell, Apperson, Elmore, Cadillac, Willys-Overland, Hupmobile, Dodge, and later the Chrysler. McManus was the copywriter who built up the Packard reputation, made the Dodge name synonymous with stability and honest workmanship; and did reputation-building copy for the Hupp-Yeats Electric, American Simplex, Jackson, Everitt, Premier, Stearns-Knight, Scripps-Booth, Liberty, and others.

McManus, who never learned to drive an automobile, made millions of dollars out of automobile advertising. He was shrewdly conscious of what he was doing. He said that long-continued advertising of a given make of automobile put something into the car that was not installed at the factory—its reputation. This became as much a part of the car as its name or one of its component parts, and it affected not only the buying public but also the manufacturer himself. "The big point is that the root idea or principle expressed in the advertising not only influences and guides the public but actually becomes the all-controlling policy of the advertiser and his organization."[10]

One day while riding a train in 1915, McManus wrote on the back of an envelope an advertisement for Cadillac which became probably the best known automobile advertisement that has been written in the United States. The advertisement, which appeared in *The Saturday Evening Post*, January 2, 1915, has long been acclaimed as one of the finest ever written for any product. The name "Cadillac" appeared in trademark form in the severe ornamental border outlining the unillustrated black and white page advertisement. It did not appear at all in the body of the copy which was headed "THE PENALTY OF LEADERSHIP." The single column of wide-bordered type began: "In every field of human endeavor, he that is first must perpetually live in the white light of publicity. Whether the leadership be vested in a man or in a manufactured product, emulation and envy are ever at work. . . ." Great achievement of any kind, McManus pointed out, brings both great rewards and fierce detraction. He ended: "That which deserves to live—lives." Millions of copies of this advertisement have been reproduced and distributed. "The Penalty of Leadership" appears regularly on every list compiled of great advertisements.

[10] "Auto Pioneer," *Tide*, October 1, 1940; *Advertising & Selling*, October, 1940.

ℭhe
PENALTY OF
LEADERSHIP

IN every field of human endeavor, he that is first must perpetually live
in the white light of publicity. ¶Whether the leadership be vested
in a man or in a manufactured product, emulation and envy are ever at
work. ¶In art, in literature, in music, in industry, the reward and the
punishment are always the same. ¶The reward is widespread recognition; the punishment, fierce denial and detraction. ¶When a man's
work becomes a standard for the whole world, it also becomes a target
for the shafts of the envious few. ¶If his work be merely mediocre, he
will be left severely alone—if he achieve a masterpiece, it will set a million
tongues a-wagging. ¶Jealousy does not protrude its forked tongue at
the artist who produces a commonplace painting. ¶Whatsoever you
write, or paint, or play, or sing, or build, no one will strive to surpass, or
to slander you, unless your work be stamped with the seal of genius.
¶Long, long after a great work or a good work has been done, those who
are disappointed or envious continue to cry out that it can not be done.
¶Spiteful little voices in the domain of art were raised against our own.
Whistler as a mountebank, long after the big world had acclaimed him
its greatest artistic genius. ¶Multitudes flocked to Bayreuth to worship
at the musical shrine of Wagner, while the little group of those whom he
had dethroned and displaced argued angrily that he was no musician at
all. ¶The little world continued to protest that Fulton could never
build a steamboat, while the big world flocked to the river banks to see
his boat steam by. ¶The leader is assailed because he is a leader, and
the effort to equal him is merely added proof of that leadership. ¶Failing
to equal or to excel, the follower seeks to depreciate and to destroy—but
only confirms once more the superiority of that which he strives to
supplant. ¶There is nothing new in this. ¶It is as old as the world
and as old as the human passions—envy, fear, greed, ambition, and the
desire to surpass. ¶And it all avails nothing. ¶If the leader truly
leads, he remains—the leader. ¶Master-poet, master-painter, master-
workman, each in his turn is assailed, and each holds his laurels through
the ages. ¶That which is good or great makes itself known, no matter
how loud the clamor of denial. ¶That which deserves to live—lives.

Cadillac Motor Car Co. Detroit, Mich.

Perhaps the most famous of all automobile advertisements, Cadillac's "The
Penalty of Leadership," appeared in *The Saturday Evening Post*, Jan. 2, 1915.

Toward the end of his life, Theodore McManus built a private golf course, but just as he had never learned to drive a car, he had never learned to play golf. He walked around the course for exercise and to dispel his dislike of advertising. Too much of it, he had concluded, was cheap, blatant, and tricky.

The new automotive industry produced one dominant figure. Henry Ford became its giant. He wrought sweeping and lasting changes in the social and economic structure of the United States and changed essentially the texture and pattern of life for most of its population. He also ranks with P. T. Barnum, Sir Thomas Lipton, and Cyrus H. K. Curtis, each of whom made his specific and very different contribution to the development of American advertising.

Henry Ford, born on a farm near Dearborn, Michigan, in 1863, evinced his early interest in mechanics by repairing watches and clocks at night while still a schoolboy. At sixteen he went to work in a Detroit machine shop, continuing after hours to work at watch repair for a jeweler. He left the machine shop to work in an engine shop and began trying to build a farm tractor. A few years later, after an interval back on the farm outside Dearborn, he went to work for the Detroit Edison Company as a machinist and engineer. In a shed behind his home he began to build a gasoline automobile. He completed the car, ran it about one thousand miles, sold it for two hundred dollars to build another which he drove about the Detroit streets in 1896. In 1899 he left Detroit Edison to start manufacturing cars as the Detroit Automobile Company, supported by a number of prominent Detroit citizens.

The venture was not successful, and Ford left the company in 1902. His next venture, another failure, was the Henry Ford Automobile Company. After defeating Winton in a two-cylinder car he built, Ford dropped everything else to build two racing cars, the 999 and the Arrow. The 999 was too big and too fast for Ford or Tom Cooper, a racing driver Ford knew, to handle. They sent to Salt Lake City for a famous bicycle racer, Barney Oldfield. Oldfield in 999, which weighed over 2,800 lbs. and had a wheel base of 120 inches, won a three-mile race at Grosse Pointe by a half-mile.

The publicity was enormous. It was Ford's best advertising thus far. He organized the Ford Motor Company, with himself as manager, superintendent, and master mechanic, June 16, 1903. The company began immediately to produce a whole line of cars—heavy, expensive cars selling up to $2,800, and a lighter car at $850—and to place advertising before it had one to sell. In *The Saturday Evening Post*, June 27, 1903, eleven days after the company had been organized, Ford advertised his first Model A.

BOSS OF THE ROAD
The Latest and Best

This new light touring car fills the demand for an automobile between a runabout and heavy touring car. It is positively the most perfect machine on the market, having overcome all draw-backs such as smell, noise, jolt, etc., common to all other makes of Auto Carriages. It is so simple that a boy of 15 can run it.

For beauty of finish it is unequaled—and we promise IMMEDIATE DELIVERY. We haven't space enough to enter its mechanical detail, but if you are interested in the NEWEST and MOST ADVANCED AUTO manufactured today write us for particulars.

FORD MOTOR COMPANY
689 Mack Avenue   Detroit, Michigan

"The FORDMOBILE with detachable tonneau," sold for $850.[11]

Ford had already gathered about him some of the men who remained his close associates and with him developed the Ford Company. John and Horace Dodge were making the engines for his cars. James Couzens was in charge of the

---

[11] The Cadillac runabout was being advertised at the same time in 1903 for $750, though the "new tonneau attachment" brought the price up to $850, the same as the Fordmobile.

financial end of the business. Harold Wills, who had been a bookkeeper for the Burroughs Adding Machine Company and was to become a great practical metallurgist, making important contributions to the development of the Ford car, managed the shop. With Wills, Ford began to work again on the second of his two racing cars, the Arrow. They took it—and a newspaper reporter with them—for speed trials on the ice of frozen Lake St. Clair outside Detroit and drew more publicity for Ford.

BOSS OF THE ROAD

The Latest and Best

THIS new light touring car fills the demand for an automobile between a runabout and a heavy touring car. It is positively the most perfect machine on the market, having overcome all draw-backs such as smell, noise, jolt, etc., common to all other makes of Auto Carriages. It is so simple that a boy of 15 can run it.

The FORDMOBILE with detachable tonneau, *$850*

For beauty of finish it is unequaled—and we promise IMMEDIATE DELIVERY. We haven't space enough to enter into its mechanical detail, but if you are interested in the NEWEST and MOST ADVANCED AUTO manufactured to-day write us for particulars.

FORD MOTOR COMPANY

689 Mack Avenue   Detroit, Mich.

The first Model A Ford, advertised in *The Saturday Evening Post* in 1903, sold for the same price as a Cadillac advertised that year.

Ford kept hammering away through advertising, most of it for his lighter and cheaper cars, most of it emphasizing their economy and dependability. The Ford advertisements boasted of the strong materials, efficient engines, and sound workmanship in the various Ford cars. They would furnish

reasonable speeds but not "any of those breakneck velocities
which are so universally condemned." The Ford was:

> Always ready, always sure.
> Built to save you time and consequent money.
> Built to take you anywhere you want to go and back on time.
> Built to add to your reputation for punctuality; to keep
>   your customers happy and in a buying mood.
> Built for business or pleasure—just as you say.[12]

Ford stressed the cheapness of his light car, urging that its
"exceedingly reasonable price places it within the reach of
many thousands who could not think of paying the comparatively fabulous prices asked for most machines."

By 1905 the new Piquette Avenue Ford plant had a huge,
white-lettered sign reading: "The Home of the Celebrated
Ford Automobile." Placards were placed on all freight cars
leaving the plant: "Loaded with Ford Automobiles." The
plant was turning out twenty-five cars a day.

During 1903 and 1904 Ford produced 1,700 cars; in
1906–7, he produced 8,423, almost one-sixth of all the cars
made in the United States during the period.[13] In 1905 Ford
was advertising, "Don't Experiment—Just Buy a FORD."
The illustration with the advertising showed his big Model F
spinning down the highway with five passengers, men in
chauffeur's caps and women in hats and motoring veils. "It
seats five people, climbs hills on high speed, has a roomy,
side-entrance tonneau, is light, strong, and rides like a Yacht.
Has the latitude of speed on the high gears of a $5,000 car.
Do not be deceived by 'Horse Power' TALK. Make it your
business to see what THIS car will DO."

A year later Ford was advertising the mammoth size of his
operation. A 1906 advertisement said: "We are making
40,000 cylinders, 10,000 engines, 40,000 wheels, 20,000 axles,
10,000 bodies, 10,000 of every part that goes into the car—

---

[12] Allan Nevins with the collaboration of Frank Ernest Hill. *Ford, The
Times, The Man, The Company* (New York: Charles Scribner's Sons,
1954), p. 242.
[13] Denison, *op. cit.*, p. 132.

think of it! For this car we buy 40,000 spark plugs, 10,000 spark coils, 40,000 tires, all *exactly alike.*"

"Watch the Ford Go By" was a Ford advertising slogan as early as 1907.

Ford, with a growing reputation gained through racing and production, was still trying to reach both the luxury trade and the mass market he envisioned. In 1905 he offered a Model N, a light, four-cylinder car at $500, but in 1906 and 1907 he produced his heavy, expensive, six-cylinder Model K. Somewhere along the line he decided to risk everything on the light, low priced car, "The Universal Car," as he dubbed it, which would make the automobile available to almost everyone, supplant the trolley and the bicycle as the ordinary means of transportation, and really become the car of the people. The result was production of his first Model T in 1908.

This was the Ford, the tin lizzie, the flivver, the jitney, the light, high, homely, imperishable model he was to produce, virtually unchanged, by the millions for the next twenty years. It was the car that was to make Ford a multi-millionaire, a world figure, and a legend. Fifteen million Model T's were produced and sold before the changeover to the Model A in 1928. The first advertisement made it clear what the car was to be. "Our purpose is to construct and market an automobile specially designed for everyday wear and tear— business, professional, and family use . . . a machine which will be admired . . . for its compactness, its simplicity, its safety, its all around convenience and—last but not least—its exceedingly reasonable price."

Such was the Ford paid advertising. There were other invaluable advertisements for which no money was paid. Ford always preferred free publicity to paid advertising, strove for every bit of it he could get through devices of many kinds, and used it shrewdly. From 1903 to 1911 the Ford Motor Company fought the strangling Selden Patent.

George B. Selden, a Rochester, New York, lawyer, who never built a practical car, had applied for a patent on a projected gasoline motor vehicle in 1879. He applied and reapplied for sixteen years, finally obtaining a patent in 1895. Selden thereupon declared his exclusive right to manufacture or license the manufacture of gasoline automobiles. Many of the early companies acceded, obtained a Selden license and, for competitive purposes, formed themselves into the Association of Licensed Automobile Manufacturers. Included in the twenty-six members of the A.L.A.M. were Stevens-Duryea, Pope, Winton, Franklin, Cadillac, Peerless, Autocar, Oldsmobile, Haynes-Apperson, Pierce-Locobile, Packard. Selden and the Association claimed: "No other manufacturers or importers are authorized to make or sell gasoline automobiles, and any person making, selling, or using such machines made or sold by any unlicensed manufacturers or importers will be liable to prosecution for infringement."

This contention was stated in an advertisement headed "Notice to Manufacturers, Dealers, Importers, Agents and Users of Gasoline Automobiles" that appeared in 1903, just as the Ford Motor Company began to produce its cars. Ford replied with a comparable advertisement denying the validity of the Selden claims and guaranteeing protection to dealers, importers, agents and users of gasoline automobiles. The Ford advertisement read in part:

> We are pioneers of the GASOLINE AUTOMOBILE. Our Mr. Ford made the first Gasoline Automobile in Detroit and the third in the United States. His machine made in 1893 (two years previous to the granting of the Selden patent November 5, 1895) is still in use. Our Mr. Ford also built the famous '999' Gasoline Automobile, which was driven by Barney Oldfield in New York on July 25, 1903, a mile in 55.4-5 seconds on a circular track which is the world's record.

Ford led the fight against the Selden patent, getting all the free newspaper publicity he could, advertising in paid space at the same time the accomplishments of the Ford car and its maker's intent.

> Henry Ford's idea is to build a high-grade, practical automobile, one that will do any reasonable service, that can be maintained at a reasonable expense, and at as nearly $450 as it is possible to make it, thus raising the automobile out of

the list of luxuries, and bringing it to the point where the average American citizen may own and enjoy his auto-mobile. . . . The Ford Motor Company are doing it, and as a result thousands of people will own a good car this year where otherwise it would have been impossible.

Ford hired an old circus press agent, Leroy Pelletier, as advertising manager. Pelletier may have been responsible for some of this Ford copy, sensible, practical, addressed to the ordinary man. He was, said *Motor Age* in 1907, ". . . fairly charged with nervous energy, plausible . . . hospitable, in-gratiating, and likeable to a degree and resourceful, far be-yond the average. Even the great Barnum himself would have found him a valuable assistant."[14]

"Nobody Mortgages his House to Buy a Ford" was another slogan while Ford was fighting the Selden patent. The fight, reported continually in the newspapers for eight years and reinforced by this kind of advertising, made Ford a popular hero. He was a champion of the people against "the interests," a Rooseveltian trust-buster. It followed in the public mind that his cars were all he claimed for them. The Selden Patent fight ended in 1911, when Ford won on appeal. It was triumph in a competitive struggle for Ford, and a de-cision which freed the entire automotive industry from a legalistic restraint.

"Our best advertising," Ford happily declared, "is free advertising."[15] He got the kind he liked most from the Ford jokes which he relished, collected, and even promoted. Leroy Pelletier is said to have written some of them.[16] There were thousands of these Ford jokes. They were told everywhere, printed in paper-bound pamphlets, sold on trains, and at news-stands. They mocked, but they were affectionate. Know what Ford is going to do now? Paint his cars yellow so that dealers can hang them in bunches like bananas. A woman sent the Ford factory a collection of tin cans. They sent her

[14] Quoted by Nevins, *op. cit.*, p. 345.
[15] Big Bill Knudsen remarked dryly that Ford had a very keen sense of advertising, Nevins, *op. cit.*, p. 503.
[16] *Advertising Age*, June 10, 1946.

back a new Ford and five cans that were left over. Ford has shaken hell out of more people than Billy Sunday. Why is a Ford like a motion to adjourn? Because it's always in order. Owners of Cadillac, Pierce-Arrow, Peerless, and Packard cars were said to carry Fords in their toolboxes to pull them out when they got stuck in the mud.[17]

In 1920 on his private railroad car with Edison, his son Edsel, and Edsel's wife, en route to Muscle Shoals, Henry Ford told a reporter that he had a collection of fifteen thousand of these Ford jokes and intended to publish them some day. His favorite was one which told of a Model T Ford's going full speed for some eighty miles with no gasoline in the tank. The owner was astonished but a knowing gas station attendant explained that the car had been traveling on its reputation.[18]

Ford got his greatest free advertising when on January 5, 1914, he suddenly announced that as a way of profit sharing he would pay a minimum of $5 for an eight-hour working day. The Ford Motor Company had earned $20 million in 1913. The announcement created a sensation. It brought droves of applicants to his Detroit plant. It made Ford a national and international figure. He was attacked as a Utopian idealist. Cynics accused him of operating from shrewd self-interest. The sentimental lauded his generosity. Ford made copy everywhere. The newspapers were filled with stories of his life and achievements, his cars, his factories, his spreading interests. The advertising volume of the move was inestimable.

Ford's skating, his folk dancing, his love of old music were all played up. The mass production techniques he had put to use in his building of cars, his adaptation of the assembly line to the manufacture of automobiles, and his improvements of the first crude method to the point of perfection became

[17] Mark Sullivan, *Our Times* (New York: Charles Scribner's Sons, 1932), Vol. IV.

[18] Manuel Rosenberg, "The 20th Century's First Ten in Advertising Development," *The Advertiser*, January, 1950.

world wonders. Ford himself was looked upon as a wizard,
like Edison, a sage whose advice was sought on every problem, even those about which he knew nothing and pretended
to know nothing. With Thomas Edison he started a campaign against the cigarette, distributing millions of copies of
a pamphlet, "The Case Against the Little White Slaver."
Cigarette advertising proved stronger than Edison and Ford
combined. Ford made pronouncements on government. He
attacked the Jews. He and a strange crew sailed for Europe
December 4, 1915, to "get the boys out of the trenches before
Christmas," a venture that brought him ridicule enough to
have leveled a smaller figure. Ford denounced history as
bunk, but he had made and was making history of his own.
He made it again in 1915 with what has been called a master
stroke of advertising.

He announced—in 143 newspapers in 51 cities—that if
the Ford Company could make and sell at retail 300,000 cars
that year, every buyer would receive a cash rebate of from
forty to sixty dollars. The company spent only a little over
six thousand dollars for an advertisement that made every
Ford buyer anxious to see that more Fords were sold. The
300,000 were sold, and purchasers got their rebate.[19]

Henry Ford created and destroyed. He created the cheap,
light car, the virtually indestructible Model T. He made the
automobile a possession for the many instead of the plaything
of the few. He revolutionized transport and travel, the way
of life in the city and on the farm. He believed in work, believed in making more work for more men, possibly, as Mark
Sullivan has pointed out, with some dim realization that mass
production could be fed only by mass purchasing power.
More than any other one man—Olds, Durant, even the Duryeas—he created the vast American automotive industry. He
brought the idea and practice of service as well as manufacture into car making. He was the benefactor of the millions
who found convenience and pleasure in his Model T automo-

[19] Charles T. Brownell, "Boom Days in Advertising the Model T," *The
Adcrafter*, December 10, 1940, p. 101.

biles. He did more than anyone else to create the American road, joining cities and towns, farms and villages, making car travel possible, supporting the business and social life of the road that did not exist until the coming of the automobile.

It was other things he destroyed. A craftsman himself, he destroyed through mechanization the pleasure a man could take in his work. His standardizing processes stamped sameness into American life at the same time that they helped stamp fine craftsmanship out of existence. He uprooted people from their traditions and usages. He built museums to house relics of the past he had done so much to destroy and re-created villages to display at least a reasonable facsimile for a time of the simplicities he had known as a boy and had valued. The most modern of pioneer industrialists and the most successful became a saddened antiquarian. Over the fireplace mantel of the mansion he built for himself he had carved the old motto: "Chop Your Own Wood and It Will Warm You Twice," but Ford had made a world in which few men could swing their own axes.[20]

Whatever he did and how, Henry Ford did it all to the loud accompaniment of insistent advertising and in the glare of all the publicity he could focus on his activities. He advertised in newspapers and magazines, in trade papers, on billboards and car cards, in manuals, folders, circulars and in the *Ford Times* which carried the gospel to Ford dealers every month. He used the Selden Patent fight, the *Dearborn Independent*, the Peace Ship, the Five-Dollar Wage, the rebate to Ford purchasers, the 15,000 Ford jokes, the Wayside Inn— everything that came to hand or could be gathered in.

Once the advertising manager of a national weekly complained that it was getting no Ford advertising despite all the personal publicity he was giving Henry Ford. Ford's adver-

---

[20] It is ironic that Henry Thoreau, who hated the industrial revolution and all its ways and would have seen Henry Ford as its arch-fiend, looked with satisfaction through the window of his Walden Pond cabin at his woodpile and wrote in 1854: "As my driver prophesied when I was ploughing, they warmed me twice, once when I was splitting them, and again when they were on the fire . . ."

tising man advised him to cut out the editorial tributes that made Ford think, "Why pay for it when I'm getting it free?" The magazine stopped publishing articles about Ford, and the Ford advertising came in.[21] The advertising had to go on. Ford used it to remake the world in his own image.

[21] *Rosenberg, op. cit.*

21

Repentance and Reform

IN 1900 OR 1901—it is impossible to set an exact date—S. S. McClure, inspired, discovered evil. It was the most valuable discovery he had made in his drive for mass circulation and mass advertising. Strenuous exploitation of his discovery sent *McClure's* circulation soaring, and the magazine quickly outran all its rivals in advertising volume. For a decade McClure and a stable of brilliant reporters probed every promising aspect of American business and public life. They found the United States a glorious den of iniquity and, month after month, *McClure's* emblazoned its pages with revelations and exposés of criminality and fraud, violence, corruption, and vice. *McClure's* became perhaps the most popular, certainly the most powerful, and not far from the most profitable magazine in the country. It not only overflowed with advertising richness, but also, directly and indirectly, influenced all advertising.

S. S. McClure had not had to search far to make his appalling discovery. Like any shrewd editor he seized and capitalized upon what was already obvious. He provided sensation and raised the clamor for reform when it was already apparent people wanted both. The murmurs of dissatisfaction were growing louder.

The country had been expanding so fast that no one had been greatly disturbed at how the expansion was engineered. Resources were inexhaustible. Who was robbed for the benefit of whom did not much matter while everyone, in theory at least, had an equal chance to be a successful thief. Only a fool did not pile up a fortune while he could, and few

quibbled about the means to ends that all admired. A minimum of business honesty made more sense than extravagant
insistence upon a minor virtue. Grant's administration had
made corruption accepted and expected in national politics,
and no one expected much else in city government. Boss
Tweed and his friends had simply got careless and let themselves be caught. Jay Gould and Jim Fisk were good entertainment. Who cared if the heroes of industry and finance
ruined and killed off themselves or a few of their fellows?

It was only when competition got too sharp, when suddenly resources seemed to have limits, when equality of opportunity to plunder, or get at least a small share of the
plunder, seemed suddenly to vanish that moral indignation
arose. When distribution of the spoils became too manifestly
unequal and the unsavory practices of industry, commerce,
finance, and organized labor too apparent, the rumbling and
grumblings arose to cries of exploitation. The inequity rather
than the iniquity of the situation was what bothered most men
who were aware of it at all.

McClure ran Ida M. Tarbell's "History of the Standard
Oil Company" in 1902. A full study of the company, done
with the help of its officials, it showed that the corporation
had been built through means that included bribery, fraud,
violence, the corruption of railroads and government officials,
and the wrecking of competition by any available means. The
articles created a sensation.

McClure hired Ray Stannard Baker, and the enthusiastic
young journalist began his long series of exposés of the railroads and of capital–labor relations in industry. Drawing
blueprints of the working relationship between criminals and
machine politicians, he filled *McClure's* pages with damaging
evidence against employers and labor alike. McClure sent
Lincoln Steffens to the Midwest. In "The Shame of the
Cities" and "The Struggle for Self-Government," Steffens
painted a lurid picture of graft and collusion between business and the political bosses who, whatever the form of municipal government on paper, actually ran most American cities.

In Josiah Flynt's "The World of Graft," *McClure's* exposed the big city alliance between criminals, the police, and the politicians.

The public clamored for more. This was news, exciting news, stirring news. Copies of *McClure's* were swept from the newsstands. Advertisers clamored to get into issues that were attracting such attention and achieving such circulations. Theodore Roosevelt, brandishing his big stick at the trusts and the malefactors of great wealth, leaped aboard. He sent for the *McClure's* writers, eagerly demanding more information, loudly offering his support. William Allen White praised Roosevelt in *McClure's*, condemned Boss Platt, the villain who had shunted Roosevelt into the Vice-Presidency.[1]

The cry was on now. Other magazines bayed after *McClure's*. In 1904 *Everybody's Magazine* published "Frenzied Finance" by Thomas W. Lawton, an attack on investment syndicates and the financial conduct of some of the large life insurance companies. *McClure's* raced in with Burton J. Hendrick's "The Story of Life Insurance." *Cosmopolitan* loosed "The Treason of the Senate" by David Graham Phillips, who concluded that the Senate did not represent the people at all, but the special interests who had placed most of the members in their seats. In two books, *The Cost*, 1904, and *The Deluge*, 1905, he exposed the financial manipulations in Wall Street through which the few profited and the many suffered. The collusion between the meat packers and the railroads was exposed by Charles Edward Russell in *The Greatest Trust in the World*. Upton Sinclair in *The Jungle* described the filth and horrors he found in the packing houses.

The agitation for reform mounted with every new disclosure of corruption, privilege, and cynical disregard for public welfare. Intoxicated with their unaccustomed success, journalists were urging on the riot with more and louder outcries against those they described as the power-crazed pirates

[1] Roosevelt supported the *McClure's* attacks and the whole reform movement as long as he found them useful; when, after the Senate had been attacked, he thought they no longer were, he fastened the term "muckraking" on the whole activity.

of finance, business, and industry who, with no more moral sense than brute beasts, were ravaging the country. Magazines and newspapers battened on new sensations every day and cried out for new laws to protect the helpless people. Theodore Roosevelt, riding higher than ever on the waves of popular approval, launched antitrust suits against monopolies with abandon, gusto, and all possible publicity. Governmental bodies instituted investigations into the conduct of some of the businesses attacked. Some of these, like the 1905 Armstrong Investigation of life insurance in New York, accomplished lasting results.

In all this furor of reform it was unlikely that advertising would escape attention. It had grown in the 1880's and 1890's with all the recklessness, lack of direction, and often, of responsibility, that had characterized the expansion in trade and commerce. The advertising of reputable manufacturers of branded products, backed by company name and often by guarantee, was generally truthful. Enlightened self-interest necessitated this observance by the advertiser who intended to stay in any business dependent on customer satisfaction. There was little to check the claims of other advertisers except the limitations of their imaginations or their pocketbooks. Exaggeration was expected. Fraud, deception, falsehood, and fantasy were commonplace. The penalty of succumbing to advertising allures, which mounted in almost direct ratio to the worthlessness of the product advertised, ranged from petty monetary loss to irreparable injury or even death.

The attack on advertising came where advertising was, as it had been for well over two centuries, most vulnerable as well as most successful. It was leveled at the same enemy Samuel Bowles had struck at in the *Springfield Republican* in 1831 and that Samuel Bowles II had castigated in 1864—the patent medicine. Perhaps the original complaint dates back to August, 1652, when in *Mercurius Mastix* Samuel Sheppard derided the publishers and writers of the newsbooks for all their practices, but especially for their patent medicine advertising.

Besides all Iterations, Petitions, Epistles, News at home and abroad
. . . they have now found out another quaint device in their trading.
There is never a mountebank who either by professing of Chymistry,
or any other Arts drains money from the people of the nation but
these arch-cheats have a share in the booty, and . . . he must have
a feeling to authorize the Charletan, forsooth, by putting him in the
News-book. There he gives you a Bill of his Cures, and because the
fellow cannot lye sufficiently himself, he gets one of those to do't
for him . . . just like those who being about to sell a diseased or
stolen horse in Smithfield are fain to get a Voucher who will say or
swear anything they please for sixpence. . . .

The full-scale attack came, as had the other exposés,
through the magazines. Some magazines had quite early
attempted to protect their readers from fraudulent advertising. In October, 1880, *Farm Journal* ran this notice:

Fair Play

We believe, through careful inquiry, that all advertisements
in this paper are signed by trustworthy persons, and to prove
our faith by works we will make good to subscribers any
loss sustained by trusting advertisers who prove to be deliberate swindlers. Rogues shall not ply their trade at the
expense of our readers, who are our friends, through the
medium of these columns. Let this be understood by everybody now and henceforth.

Not to be outdone, the stout, little *Rural New Yorker*
printed this:

A Square Deal

We believe that every advertisement in this paper is backed
by responsible persons. We use every possible precaution
and admit the advertising of reliable houses only. But to
make doubly sure, we will make good any loss to paid subscribers sustained by trusting any deliberate swindler, irre-
sponsible advertisers, or misleading advertisements in our
columns. Any such swindler will be publicly exposed.

The *Rural New Yorker* made good its promise and used editorial space to expose frauds attempted on its readers.[2] Other
agricultural papers followed with similar guarantees: *Farm*

[2] H. J. Kenner, *The Fight for Truth in Advertising* (New York: Round
Table Press, Inc., 1936).

Life in 1897, *American Agriculturist* in 1900, then *Farm & Fireside, Kimball's Dairy Farmer,* and the *Progressive Farmer.*

In 1892 Cyrus H. K. Curtis had announced that *Ladies' Home Journal* would no longer accept any patent medicine advertising. In 1904, at the height of the muckracking movement, the *Journal* launched a bitter campaign against the entire patent medicine industry. Bok hired Mark Sullivan, a recent graduate of Harvard Law School, to unearth all the damning evidence he could and published Sullivan's reports as they came in. As Samuel Bowles II had done forty years before, Bok attacked the religious papers for accepting and publishing the advertising of harmful nostrums. He accused the Post Office of laxity in distributing advertising that was in reality, he said, obscene matter. He exposed some patent medicines as containing no less than 40 per cent alcohol and showed that others, though not so labeled, contained poisonous drugs. As a woman's magazine, the *Journal* singled out a woman's remedy for special attention.

Lydia E. Pinkham had first put her Vegetable Compound on the market in 1876, advertising it then as "A Sure Cure for Prolapsus Uteri, or Falling of the Womb . . . Pleasant to taste, efficacious and immediate in effect. It is a great help in pregnancy and relieves pain during labor . . . For all weaknesses of the generative organs of either sex. It is second to no remedy that has ever been before the public and for all diseases of the kidneys it is the Greatest Remedy in the World."

Mrs. Pinkham died rich and famous in 1883, and the newspapers duly noted her passing, yet the Pinkham company kept her picture in its advertising and continued to proclaim: "Mrs. Pinkham in her laboratory at Lynn, Mass., is able to do more for the ailing women of America than the family physician. Any woman, therefore, is responsible for her own suffering if she will not take the trouble to write Mrs. Pinkham for advice."

Ladies' Home Journal reproduced these advertisements, together with a photograph of Mrs. Pinkham's gravestone which showed that she had been dead for more than twenty years. It charged that the letters trusting women wrote their

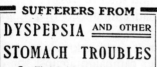

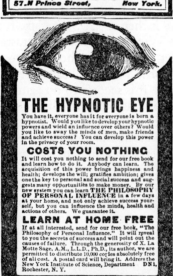

Patent medicine advertising bloomed noisomely even in the leading literary

monthlies and sophisticated journals of the 1890's and early 1900's.

deceased benefactress were opened, snickered over, then sold
to compilers of mailing lists for five cents each. It was the
advertising methods, not the medicine, which was condemned.

While all this was going on, other magazines of less fas-
tidiousness continued to run Pinkham copy which, though it
did not feature the founder's picture nor urge women to
write, put forward other claims for the Vegetable Compound
with almost obscene skill. *Ainslee's* carried this masterpiece.

BEWARE OF MORPHINE

Mrs. Pinkham Asks Women
To Seek Permanent Cures and
Not Mere Temporary Relief from Pain

Special forms of suffering lead many women to acquire
the morphine habit.

She has (symptoms) she cannot bear to confide to her
physician, for fear of an examination, the terror of all sensitive, modest women.

The physician, meantime, knows her condition but cannot
combat her shrinking terror. He yields to her supplication
for something to relieve the pain. He gives her a few
morphine tablets, with the very grave caution as to their use.
Foolish woman! She thinks morphine will help her right
along; she becomes its slave!

A wise and generous physician had such a case; he told his
patient he could do nothing for her, as she was too nervous
to undergo an examination. In despair, she went to visit a
friend. She said to her, "Don't give up; just go to the nearest
druggist's and buy a bottle of Mrs. Lydia E. Pinkham's Vegetable Compound. It will build you up. You will begin to feel
better with the first bottle." She did, and after the fifth
bottle her health was reestablished. . . .[3]

Certainly Pinkham's was not alone in exploiting this profitable market. It was merely the best known and most successful. One competitor, Brown's Vegetable Cure for Female
Weaknesses, advertised by Sears, Roebuck in 1905, cured a
longer lists of ailments, disorders, diseases, and symptoms

[3] Quoted by Quentin Reynolds, *The Fiction Factory* (New York: Random House, Inc., 1955), p. 133.

(including a dragging sensation in the groin, sparks before the eyes, hysteria, temple and ear throb, a dread of some impending evil, morbid feelings, and the blues) than any competitor had been able to amass.

While the attack of the magazines and some newspapers on patent medicines increased in fury, the same 1905 Sears catalogue devoted twenty pages of small type to scores of patent medicines. It offered a cure for gonorrhea, "Injection No. 7 Cures in One to Five Days. . . . A French specific having a great reputation abroad as a reliable cure for all troubles of the urinary organs in either male or female." Sears had its own White Star Liquor Cure which a wife could put into a husband's food or drink without his knowledge. It also had its cure for drug addiction. The use of narcotics had spread during the Civil War and seemed to have grown steadily. The Sears' Cure would "Completely destroy that terrible craving for morphine and opium in those who are victims of the deadly habit of taking these poisonous drugs, and free them from their bondage, restoring their health and making them feel like living again . . ."[4]

The religious and farm papers, many of them in chronic financial straits and dependent on the bounty of quacks, could not afford to indulge in ethical niceties. Some of the choicest patent medicine advertisements appeared in their pages. One manufacturer was so sure the ingredients in his nostrum would bring customers back again and again that he offered the first bottle gratis in *Farm and Fireside*, January 15, 1901.

> A trial bottle of this marvelous household remedy will be sent free, postpaid, to any reader of this paper who will send us their name and address. The curative powers of this remedy are the wonder of the medicinal world. It gives instant relief and permanently cures Rheumatism in all its forms and stages of development, Sciatica, Backache, Neuralgia, Gout, Consumption, Dyspepsia, Asthma, Hay Fever, Catarrh, Croup, Liver and Kidney Troubles, Sleeplessness, Nervous and Neuralgic Headaches, Scrofula, Eczema, Earache,

[4] David L. Cohn, *The Good Old Days* (New York: Simon and Schuster, Inc., 1940), p. 221.

> Toothache, Heart Weakness, Paralysis, Creeping Numb-
> ness, etc. It purifies the blood, builds up a weak stomach,
> makes kidney trouble disappear, dispels headache, renews
> heart action, eradicates scrofula and eczema, instantly stops
> malaria, cures consumption, cleanses the system of all blood
> diseases, and is the only known positive cure for the most
> horrible of all afflictions, Rheumatism.

The manufacturer had discovered the advertising truth that
if a thing is worth saying once, or even if it is not, it is worth
saying several times.

All the patent medicines did not paralyze, blind, or kill.
There are apologists who, not without reason on their side,
have defended their widespread sale and use at the time.
Medical science had advanced little from the days of Hip-
pocrates or Galen. There were often no physicians in rural
communities, and those in many towns were ignorant and
untrained.

There may have been some virtue in some of the patent
medicines, and others were relatively harmless. They provided comfort, whether actual or imagined, and palliation for
minor pains. Some of the tonics and bitters, mostly alcoholic,
made life seem a little brighter. Men and women who had
not yet discovered that they were underprivileged and frustrated and knew only that they felt bored and dispirited
sluiced them down and obtained a satisfaction, both spirituous
and psychological, from drenching their dulled insides. Who
would find fault with sarsaparilla? The nostrums that claimed
to cure cancer and tuberculosis, the barely disguised narcotics,
the undisguised aphrodisiacs and vicious cure-alls, were another matter.

Collier's, as well as *Ladies' Home Journal*, was pouring
broadsides into these in 1905 and 1906. It ran "The Great
American Fraud" by Samuel Hopkins Adams, a *New York
Sun* reporter who had muckraked earlier for *McClure's*, blast-
ing at newspaper and periodical advertising of the patent
medicines. When Mark Sullivan turned up more evidence
than *Ladies' Home Journal* could use in its campaign, Norman
Hapgood published it in Collier's as "The Patent Medicine

Conspiracy against the Freedom of the Press," and added Sullivan to the *Collier's* staff. The conversion of the young lawyer into a crusading journalist, who became a Washington correspondent and political columnist, finally a social historian, was thus complete.

What *Ladies' Home Journal* and *Collier's*, with Dr. H. W. Wiley, then chief of the U.S. Department of Agriculture, on their side, were fighting for was passage of food and drug legislation which would drive many of the patent medicines from the market and put an end to the fraudulent advertising of them all. They won their battle with passage of the Food and Drug Act of 1906, the "Wiley Laws," and with legislation in the various states. They certainly did not scotch patent medicines, but they did bring about their exclusion from the pages of many periodicals, which no longer dared run advertising that had met with such outcries of public disapproval. They forced all the manufacturers of proprietary remedies to tone down their claims. Few longer dared to advertise that their products cured anything. The most they could claim was that their medicines relieved certain pains and discomforts, and they were obliged to list the ingredients their nostrums contained.

Patent medicines are still advertised loudly and insistently, particularly on television, where, hourly or more often, the manufacturers of headache remedies, laxatives, sedatives, vitamin admixtures, and comparable preparations laud their wares with all the adjectives within the law and all the claims that can squeeze past official scrutiny—and discount the claims of rival preparations with the same nice verbal and dramatic dexterity.

The rich and powerful patent medicine manufacturers and the quacks who preyed on human weakness and hope were merely the most notorious purveyors of fraudulent advertising. They had strong competition from other ambitious entrepreneurs who filled the newspapers, the magazines, and the U.S. mails with their false or misleading claims. One ingenious benefactor used the mails to offer a Potato-Bug Eradicator for ten cents. Those who answered his advertisements received two neatly whittled pieces of pine wood, together with explicit directions to place the potato-bug exactly between the two sticks of wood and press them together. Chagrined purchasers automatically became agents for the manufacturer, who did very well until a humorless Post Office Department, empowered by the Fraud Order of 1872, issued a cease-and-desist order against him.[5]

Fraudulent financial advertising came under bitter and deserved attack in 1904 when it was estimated that large-space newspaper advertising of wildcat stocks schemes, of ambitious proposals to open fantastically rich but nonexistent mines or to develop nonexistent lands, and of get-rich-quick enterprises of all kinds, had mulcted the greedy of Boston and New England alone of nearly $500 million in ten years time. Fortunes were promised those who would invest in sure things, always described as "well-advertised," in glowing prospectuses that covered solid pages of newspapers. As soon as he had garnered sufficient cash from his willing victims, the promoter would simply disappear and not be heard of again until he came forth with some scheme more grandiose than the last and reaped another easy harvest. Newspaper publishers stood accused in many instances of knowingly accepting false advertising of this kind.[6]

Stirred by such attacks, and like the magazines well aware that the value of their advertising space depended upon public confidence, the newspapers took protective action. In 1903 the Scripps-McRae League of Newspapers appointed a censor of all advertising in papers of the chain with power to scrutinize all copy submitted and reject the objectionable. About a half-million dollars worth was refused the first year.[7] The *Chicago Tribune* and the Philadelphia *North American* attacked quacks and frauds; the *New Orleans Item*, the *St. Louis Star*, the *Cleveland News and Leader*, the *Detroit*

[5] Macgregor Jenkins, "Human Nature and Advertising," *The Atlantic Monthly*, September, 1904.
[6] "Swindling and Newspaper-Advertising," *The Atlantic Monthly*, August, 1904.
[7] W. G. Bleyer, *op. cit.*, p. 417.

Times did the same. Many of the large newspapers quietly began to censor their advertising pages. The *New York Times*, which had long barred disreputable advertising, offered a hundred-dollar reward for information leading to the conviction of anyone using its advertising space to defraud. The *Financial World*, the *Outlook*, the *Literary Digest* and other periodicals all ran exposés of financial frauds.

In 1896, at the suggestion of the advertising and publicity manager of Vantines, long a famous oriental shop, New York advertising men had grouped themselves into the Sphinx Club. The purposes of the club were largely social, and its monthly dinners at the old Waldorf-Astoria were festive affairs. It was sharply reminded that it should have more serious interests when, in 1903, John Adams Thayer, advertising manager of the *Delineator*, rose and scored fraudulent advertising of many kinds, lacing his talk with choice examples.[8] From that point, the movement for reform became a central issue with advertising men themselves. The Associated Advertising Clubs of America, formed in 1905, took up the campaign, which did not really get under way until a few years later when the organization, under the new name of the Advertising Federation of America, came out firmly and righteously for honest advertising. The livelihood of these men was at stake, and they knew it. Some, undoubtedly, were motivated by an idealism that gave fire to their practical interests. They enlisted the aid of the advertising trade press, and soon *Printers' Ink*, founded by the advertising agent and patent medicine fancier, George P. Rowell, was in the van of the fight.

The Federation met in convention in Boston in 1911 and declared for ethical advertising. A code was drawn up. "Truth in Advertising" was adopted as a slogan. Vigilance committees were formed in the various advertising clubs represented. Immediately after the convention, the vigilance committee of the Advertising Club of New York and John Irving Romer of *Printers' Ink*, who had covered the conven-

[8] H. J. Kenner, *The Fight for Truth in Advertising* (New York: The Round Table Press, Inc., 1936), p. 12.

tion, got to work. Romer began to publicize the campaign in
Printers' Ink and retained a New York lawyer to draw up a
model state law penalizing false and misleading advertising.
Printers' Ink published the model statute in November, 1911.[9]
The statute read:

Any person, firm, corporation, or association who, with intent to
sell or in any way dispose of merchandise, securities, service, or anything offered by such person, firm, corporation, or association, directly or indirectly, to the public for sale or distribution, or with
intent to increase the consumption thereof, or to induce the public
in any manner to enter into any obligation relating thereto, or to
acquire title thereto, or an interest therein, makes, publishes, dis-
seminates, circulates, or places before the public, or causes directly
or indirectly to be made, published, disseminated, circulated, or placed
before the public, in this state, in a newspaper or other publication,
or in the form of a book, notice, handbill, poster, bill, circular,
pamphlet, or letter, or in any other way, an advertisement of any sort
regarding merchandise, securities, service, or anything offered to the
public, which advertisement contains any assertion, representation or
statement of fact which is untrue, deceptive, or misleading, shall be
guilty of a misdemeanor.

At this time only New York and Massachusetts had laws
forbidding fraudulent advertising. *Printers' Ink* and the Advertising Federation went to work to push through adoption
of the model statute in other states. In 1913 it was introduced
in the legislatures of fifteen states. It first became law in
Ohio, where it was vigorously supported by the various advertising clubs. About ten days later it was adopted in Minnesota, then, somewhat modified, in Pennsylvania. Within a
few years, thirty-seven states had enacted the statute or variations on it. The advertising clubs lobbied everywhere for
the new order of things, and their vigilance committees—
which in 1915 became The Better Business Bureau—saw to it
that violators of the code were prosecuted.

Perhaps the most influential contribution made by a publisher during the whole campaign for honesty in advertising
came in 1910 when Cyrus H. K. Curtis published *The Curtis
Advertising Code*. From the beginning Curtis had exercised

<hr>

[9] *Ibid.*, p. 27.

strict control over the advertising in both *Ladies' Home Journal* and *The Saturday Evening Post*.[10] The *Post* was the country's largest and most powerful weekly magazine. It was, par excellence, the national advertising medium. In addition, Curtis himself was one of the country's largest advertisers. Curtis had a large stake in the reliability and public repute of advertising and he was in a position to make his dicta heard and observed. *The Curtis Advertising Code* said this:

Our first consideration is the protection and welfare of our readers, and our second consideration is so to conduct our advertising columns as to command the confidence of our readers and lead them to a greater dependence upon the printed message. This is the keynote of Curtis policy . . .

. . . it is our purpose to protect both our advertisers and our readers from all copy that is fraudulent or deceptive and, what is perhaps equally important, we are prepared to protect honorable and legitimate advertisers against unfair competition . . .

Under "Censorship of Copy" *The Curtis Advertising Code* laid down these rules:

1. We exclude all advertising that in any way tends to deceive, defraud, or injure our readers.
2. Extravagantly worded advertisements are not acceptable.
3. "Knocking" copy is not acceptable—that is, copy which points out the *inferiority* of competitors' goods in contrast with the *superiority* of the advertiser's.

[10] Many stories are told to illustrate Curtis' complete belief in advertising. To the mystification of the building attendant, the soap he placed in the washroom of his employer's office kept disappearing. For several days he kept replacing the lost soap. Finally he told Curtis about it. "Oh," Curtis told him, "I've been throwing them away. They weren't advertised."

When Joseph M. Hopkins started in 1906 to solicit advertising for *Printers' Ink*, he called on Cyrus Curtis who was both a regular reader and a consistent advertiser in the advertising trade periodical. Hopkins suggested that Curtis appoint someone with whom he could talk so that he would not be taking up the publisher's valuable time. As Hopkins told the story many years later in *Printers' Ink*, October 29, 1948, Curtis swung around in his chair and said, in effect, "Young man, I can hire men to conduct the editorial affairs of my magazine and to look after the circulation satisfactorily. But the *promotion* of the business is a matter I feel it is my duty to attend to myself."

4. Medical or curative copy is not acceptable.

5. Advertisements for alcoholic liquors are not acceptable.

6. We do not desire the advertising of mail-order houses doing a general merchandise business. . . .

7. Advertising in which installment plan selling is incorporated is not encouraged and must be carefully investigated before being accepted.

8. Advertising of an immoral or suggestive nature is not allowed, and representations of the human form are not acceptable in any suggestive negligee or attitude. . . .

9. It is desired to maintain in our advertising columns the same tone and atmosphere that prevail in the editorial sections.

10. "Blind" advertising or advertising which in purpose and intent is obscure or misleading is not acceptable.

11. Answers to advertisements cannot be sent in care of our publications.

12. Advertisements in our columns must not include editorial quotations from our publications . . .

14. Advertising for the purpose of obtaining boys or girls as agents is not acceptable.

15. The word "free" must not be used unless the article is actually free . . .

19. Speculative real-estate advertising is not acceptable.

In addition to these general rules, special rules were stated for *Ladies' Home Journal*. It would not publish any advertising of alcoholic liquors, tobacco, playing-cards, or securities. *The Saturday Evening Post* would run no advertising for highly speculative securities. Though it would take no liquor advertising, it would accept tobacco advertising, except for cigarettes.[11]

Curtis had already inaugurated another important reform. In 1901 he took a considered step which helped to regularize the practice of advertising, a step which helped change the structure of the advertising agency, transforming it from a space brokerage into an organization serving the interests of both publishers and advertisers.

In an effort to abolish rate-cutting, commission cutbacks, and various other means ranging from the furtive to the piratical by which the agents competed with each other for lucrative advertising contracts, The Curtis Publishing Com-

---

[11] *The Curtis Advertising Code* (Philadelphia: The Curtis Publishing Company, 1912).

pany in May, 1901, issued its first agency contract. It bound Curtis to pay the advertising agency a commission of 10 per cent on the cost of all space it sold in Curtis magazines, plus a 5 per cent discount for cash payment. It obligated all advertising agencies to charge their clients the full published rate for all advertising space used in *Ladies' Home Journal* and *The Saturday Evening Post*. The Curtis agency contract read:

> Gentlemen: In acting as your agent for the placing of advertising in the *Ladies' Home Journal* and *The Saturday Evening Post,* for which we are now allowed a commission of ten per cent, we hereby agree to maintain your *full card rate,* less the regular cash discount of five per cent for payment before the first day of month following date of bill.
>
> We further agree not to quote any price for advertising in the *Ladies' Home Journal* or *The Saturday Evening Post* at less than the full card rates at that time in effect, and should this agency, or any of its solicitors or connections, accept business and violate this agreement, either by direct cut in price or by allowance in any form, we will, upon satisfactory proof of same, pay you the full card rate for the business on which cut or allowance has been made—subject only to the regular cash discount. . . .
>
> It is understood and agreed upon our part, that, should this agreement be violated a second time, we are to be dropped from the list of agents for the *Ladies' Home Journal* and *The Saturday Evening Post.* . . .
>
> We further understand and agree that ten per cent added to your net rate to us is a cut in your rate, and further that the five per cent discount for cash cannot be allowed to an advertiser, unless that advertiser pays us as promptly as we must pay you to obtain it. . . .
>
> Very truly yours,
>
> ———————
>
> In consideration of the above agreement being accepted and signed by you, The Curtis Publishing Company hereby agrees that it will not accept any advertising, either direct or through any of its agents, at other than the card rates at such time in force, and that it will not, under any condition or circumstance, allow the agent's commission to any advertiser.
>
> ———————
>
> President
>
> The Curtis Publishing Company

In effect, the Curtis contract recognized that the advertising agency performed a useful service for the publisher. Under this agency contract, Curtis paid the agency to bring new advertisers into his magazines and to encourage old advertisers to use more space. At the same time, the contract made it impossible for one agency to offer financial advantage to an advertiser purchasing space in *Ladies' Home Journal* or *The Saturday Evening Post,* and it took the publisher out of competition with the agency in selling Curtis space. Most important for the development of the advertising agency as a service organization, the Curtis contract forced the agents to solicit business on the grounds of offering superior service in the preparation of advertising copy and illustrations, in marketing advice and general business counsel. By recognizing the usefulness of the advertising agency to both magazines as advertising media and to advertisers who were in need of advice and assistance in bringing their products to public notice, the Curtis contract did much to establish the agency as a necessary and reputable unit which accomplished a specific function in the complete advertising transaction.

Only the strongest publishers and publications could take such a stand, and Curtis was not always able to enforce the provisions of the contract. Weaker publishers continued, perforce, to countenance price-cutting and to pay extortionate commissions.

When in 1919 Cyrus Curtis, who by then dominated magazine publishing in the United States, announced that The Curtis Publishing Company would pay recognized advertising agencies a commission of 15 per cent on all acceptable business sent to its magazines, he further strengthened the agency position. The Curtis Company, he reiterated, would pay no commission to any agency which rebated any part of the commission.

Talking to the Advertising Club of New York, January 23, 1956, Bruce Barton, one of the founders of the Barton, Durstine and Osborn advertising agency and when he spoke board chairman of the later BBD&O, said that in making this move Curtis "lifted the advertising agency out of the

gutter of price cutting in which it had been struggling. . . .
On that day the advertising agency became a business to
which a man could give his life with full self respect."

In 1914 the Newspaper Division of the Associated Advertising Clubs of the World produced "Standards of Newspaper Practice." These declared it the duty of publishers to
protect the newspaper reader and the honest advertiser from
deceptive or offensive advertising, to sell newspaper advertising on the basis of proved circulation, to maintain uniform
advertising rates, to accept no advertising which threatened
public welfare. These standards were endorsed by leading
newspapers across the country.[12] In the same year the *New
York Tribune*, daring what the radical agriculturist Wilmer
Atkinson had risked in *Farm Journal* thirty-four years before,
guaranteed its readers against loss through patronage of
Tribune advertisers. It began investigating the practices of
its advertisers and barred one of the large New York department stores which it found guilty of misrepresenting its
merchandise.

Another move in the direction of greater honesty in advertising—one which affected the internal operation of advertising rather than its external appearance and effect—came
with the establishment, also in 1914, of the Audit Bureau of
Circulations. For the first time, an advertiser could obtain an
actual, verified count of the circulation of a newspaper or
magazine. He no longer had to depend on the mythical
approximations of publishers or the guesses, weighed as their
interests dictated, of the advertising agents.

These various attempts of advertising to clean its own
house were real, earnest, and reasonably effective. As yet
no one has successfully legislated all fraud and chicanery out
of advertising, any more than anyone has been able to stamp
them out of other departments of human life. They have, as
others have noted over the centuries, a certain staying power.
Yet advertising was chastened, disciplined, and emerged an
improved and more dependable instrument through the re-

[12] Bleyer, *op. cit.*, p. 418.

forms forced upon it, mostly by its own adherents and practitioners, in the first decade of the twentieth century. Whatever their motives, and they were not all dictated by understandable self-interest, the reform was necessary. It was made
necessary not only through obvious and flagrant abuses, but
also by the dawning realization that advertising was a major
force that could no longer be allowed to rage out of all
control.

Advertising was everywhere. Seemingly, it affected everyone. "So important an element has advertising become,"
Macgregor Jenkins wrote in the *Atlantic Monthly*, September, 1904,

that it enters more or less directly into every modern business, it
enlists in its army of promoters men of large means and ample learning . . . The great mass of the business is done along legitimate lines,
and is of positive benefit to the public. Manufacturers vie with one
another to put upon the market articles of merit and usefulness at a
low cost in order to secure a share of the enormous sums spent each
year by the American people for the necessities of life.

The newspapers and magazines were filled with advertising. It was advertising which supported them; advertising,
many claimed, which controlled them. The countryside
from New York to Chicago looked like one giant billboard.
Since the mid-1890's electric advertising signs had made
Broadway at night one of the spectacles of the New World.
The Hudson River night boats for Albany and Troy turned
their great searchlights on billboards along the shore to delight their passengers.

Advertising, people were beginning to realize, not only
sold goods, kept factories running, supplied the home with
staples and equipped men and women with luxuries undreamed of a few years earlier, but also affected morals,
manners, customs, and the very spirit of the times. Advertising affected those who bought advertised goods. It affected
as well those who did not buy, but simply noticed—could
not help noticing—the brand names, the pictures, the proffered delights, the sharp reflections of life as it was being lived
about them.

There was bad in all this. There was also good. The writer of a serious article in *Collier's* pointed out what to him was one of the goods.

It is safe to say that one of the most powerful of moral influences being exerted today is the constant repetition of the guarantee clause in advertisements. It inculcates the idea, as nothing else can, that this is an age of guaranteed transactions; and it is easy to see that its influence may extend not only to forcing men to concede the guarantee plan in their business on account of competition, but to instilling in them the moral principle upon which it is founded. Thus they are led, by this influence, not only to be honest externally, but actually to become honest at heart.[13]

The taste of the millions in dress and house furnishings was being influenced by the advertising of clothing and of rugs, furniture, pictures, and other household goods. That was obvious. Less obvious, but apparent to the same *Collier's* writer in 1909, was the fact that advertising, through its constant repetitions, developed in people the very spirit of enterprise it exhibited. Advertising imbued men and women with "the idea that this is an age of enterprise, and that one must be enterprising even to hold one's own."

People were very conscious of advertising in the first decade of the twentieth century. It was a marvel they talked about, wrote about, read about. Some men, another *Atlantic* writer pointed out, were born to advertising; others had it forced upon them. He used King Edward VII and the Siamese Twins as examples of those born to be advertised. The notorious and their families and the excessively rich had it foisted on them. It had all happened within twenty years with the multiplication and diffusion of the printed page and the cheapening of the processes of pictorial reproduction.[14]

Another thoughtful observer commented on the significance of all the advertising which, he said, had become the most conspicuous and characteristic feature of American life in 1909. After noting the pervasiveness of advertising, that

[13] Waldo P. Warren, "By-Products of Advertising," *Collier's*, February 6, 1909.
[14] Edward Sanford Martin, "Advertisement," *The Atlantic Monthly*, January, 1909.

it had invaded all fields and every medium of distribution,
Frederick Dwight suggested why it was necessary, and commented upon the direction in which advertising had developed. "This is not," he wrote in the *Yale Review*,

a day of strong affections, of bitter partisanship, of unflinching ad-
herence. It is a time of independence, of tepid preferences, of facile
change; constant advertising is necessary to prevent customers from
drifting easily away. . . . If a new product is to be placed upon the
market, however meritorious it may be, a very large fraction of its
direct cost must be added almost inevitably to provide for advertising
it, if the venture is not to be a failure.[15]

Advertising, Dwight saw, had established itself as a necessary accessory of business. Once the handbill of the trades-
man, or the beseeching cry of the hawker, it had reached out
and taken under its control undertakings that only a few
years before no one would have thought of connecting with
it. The evolution of advertising had paralleled the growth of
the country. It was addressed to the great middle class, and
its concern was to impress the name of the advertised article
as gently and as firmly as possible in the minds of everyone
it could reach: ". . . advertisements more than almost any
other utterances are addressed to the public, are framed to
appeal to the greatest number. Not to the poorest, for they
have no money, nor to the wealthiest, for they are not interested."

Implicit in Dwight's argument is what he did not state, for,
of necessity, he used the jargon of his own day, not that of a
half-century later. Advertising grew with the growth of
democracy in the United States. It can function only in a
democracy. It must appeal to the ruling majority whose tastes
and inclinations must be wooed and satisfied. Dwight thought
that in 1909 advertising was doing this basic job well. "The
course of development has been from servility to dignity,
from hysteria to calmness, from narrowness to breadth. The
controlling force has been an intelligent interpretation of
what would please and attract the average person."

[15] "The Significance of Advertising," *Yale Review*, August, 1909.

22

The Role of Advertising
in World War I

ONE HARDLY SURPRISING result of all the reforms attempted
and achieved—for most reform movements give invaluable
publicity to the object of the attack—was to deepen the
penetration of advertising into the whole social and economic
complex of the United States in the early years of the twentieth century. Advertising was warped firmly into the woof
of commerce and the community. It became so notoriously
honest that it was generally recognized that advertising was
respectable. Only the constitutionally disapproving could
longer cavil and the most reactionary, timid, or impecunious
manufacturers refrain from using it.

Even those who objected to some of the more noisome
manifestations of advertising recognized its compensating virtues. In 1904 a critic who pointed out that P. T. Barnum had
been right in his appraisal of the public was willing to admit,
". . . advertising has built up great businesses, has renewed the
activities of decaying communities, and worked many social
and commercial benefits."[1] Another observer who, as others
have done before and many, some vehemently, have done since,
took advertising to task for desecration of outdoor beauty
spots, began his complaints by admitting that advertising
could not be suppressed and that even he could not and would
not suppress it. Advertising was producing too many direct

[1] Macgregor Jenkins, *op. cit.*

345

and indirect benefits.[2] Mark Sullivan, who had been one of the leaders in denouncing the vicious advertising of the patent medicine industry, was equally emphatic in listing the benefits of advertising, not merely to business through the direct sale of merchandise, but to the public and to the arts. Advertising had given the country the modern magazine. It had given the public the larger and more complete newspaper. It supported literature by providing the novelist with a remunerative market when his work was published in serial form in one of the periodicals, and these same authors could now reach millions of readers where, when their work appeared in book form alone, they could reach but a few thousand at most.

The magazines as advertising media had found the short story well adapted to their use. They developed the short story in a way that it had never been developed before. The market offered by the magazines encouraged scores of competent short-story writers, some of them producing work of high literary excellence, where earlier the United States had produced only a handful of writers—Poe, Hawthorne—who excelled in the form.[3] Advertising was a patron of art as well as of literature, paying direct commissions to artists like Frederic Remington, Maxfield Parrish, Jessie Wilcox Smith, and Charles Dana Gibson. The manufacturers of soaps, breakfast foods, clothes, and cars had become, through advertising, patrons of the arts, and the public benefited.[4]

It was the extravagances of outdoor display that was causing wrinkled noses and pained outcries. Objections to this kind of advertising were not so much on moral as on aesthetic grounds. Not all the ugliness was the work of the billposter and sign painter—the snipes, tackers, and daubs, as the trade called them. The desecration of the countryside and the

[2] Charles Mulford Robinson, "Artistic Possibilities of Advertising," *The Atlantic Monthly*, July, 1904.

[3] James Branch Cabell, who was a contributor, spoke of *The Saturday Evening Post* as the great American weekly which printed fiction among its advertisements.

[4] Mark Sullivan, *Our Times*, Vol. 4, (New York: Charles Scribner's Sons, 1932).

cities by these artists was deplored, but the ingenuity and
humor of certain other advertisers was even worse.

There were wagons on the streets and roads brightly
painted over with signs, gongs ringing to attract attention,
drawn not by horses but by ostriches. Box kites carried advertising into the sky. In a theatre or at some other public
gathering lines of bald-headed men were seated, each carrying
one letter of a brand name on his shining pate. The sides of
circus elephants and camels were rented out for signs advertising headache powders or chewing gum. Advertisements
were painted on the sails of boats that tacked back and forth
before crowded beaches. Advertising hats and caps were
distributed at parades and worn by small boys for weeks
afterward. Someone invented a device which could project
an advertising message on clouds as high as three miles in the
sky. Pulitzer used one to advertise his *New York World*, a
newspaper which had outstripped all its rivals in advertising
volume. Tarrant's Seltzer Aperient planned lines of advertising buoys running up and down the Atlantic and Pacific
coasts and for five hundred miles along the course of steam-
ships bound for Europe.[5]

Billposting was one of the oldest forms of advertising.
Honest John Donnelly had plastered the country for P. T.
Barnum to promote Jenny Lind's visit. When the International Bill Posters Association of North America was
founded in 1872, billboards were already an American commonplace and already had drawn down the ire of critics.
Public opinion forced the removal of some signs and managed
to force some legislation through that checked the worst
offenses, but outdoor advertising was too useful and economical a medium to be controlled easily. Philadelphia-New
York trains ran through almost a solid alley of billboards as
they left and entered the two cities. *Scribner's,* May, 1907,
appealed to farmers not to sell or rent the space to the outdoor

---

[5] *Printers' Ink,* July 28, 1938, pp. 122-23. The account mentioned also the
advertising button craze of the 1890's. The advertisers' buttons carried endearing slogans such as "Yes, darling." "Is it hot enough for you?" "I'm
somewhat of a liar myself."

advertisers, but farmers liked the income. It was not, critics
complained, the idea of advertising of this kind that offended,
but the ugliness of the advertiser's attempts to shock the eye,
and worse, their predilection for the comic, the supposedly
witty, and the actually grotesque. They found it easier to be
funny than to present something which would please, though,
it was argued, a beautiful display would do its work long
after a tired comic attempt had begun to annoy.[6]

Actually, posters had improved. Developed in France by
Jules Cheret, the first had been used in England in 1871 to
advertise Wilkie Collins' romance, *The Woman in White*.
The poster had further developed in England with the work
of Aubrey Beardsley. Beardsley's black and white, aesthetic,
elongated, and unnatural but "modern" figures acquired a
great vogue in posters. Their style was imitated by American advertisers when the manufacturers of bicycles adapted
the poster to their purposes. Parrish, Louis Rhead, Bradley,
J. C. Leyendecker, and other artists of the period produced
posters, used in both outdoor advertising and for magazine
reproduction, which led to improved advertising display in
the United States.

In 1895, *L'Oeuvre Nationale Belge* held an exhibition of
advertising art in Brussels, awarding prizes to actual advertisements considered the most artistic. Soon afterward an exhibition was held in Paris. Comparable recognition for the
artistic merits of poster advertising was urged in the United
States.

A marvel had already taken place in outdoor advertising.
In 1882 W. J. Hammer constructed the first electric sign
seen in London—Miner's Theatre at 28th Street and Broadway had the first in the United States. It was quickly imitated. By 1893, Broadway was already "The Great White
Way." New York and the other large American cities began
to shine with night brilliance, dimming the moon and stars
with the names of foods, pickles, newspapers, and cigars. The

---

[6] Robinson, in his 1904 *Atlantic* article already quoted, instanced department-store window-dressing as advertising of artistic merit which pleased
instead of distressed those who saw it.

first big electric signs in New York were built on the north wall of the Hotel Cumberland at the junction of Broadway, Fifth Avenue, and 23rd Street where the Flatiron Building has stood since 1901.

The first advertisement to use this space was for "Manhattan Beach, Swept by Ocean Breezes." This was erected in May, 1892. For a long time afterward the space was used by H. J. Heinz. The name "Heinz" was lighted in a large, green pickle across the top of the building. Beneath it huge letters in electric lights spelled out the names of the mystical "57 Varieties." India relish, malt vinegar, tomato chutney, and sweet pickles got top billing. Later advertisers in the same space were Franco-American Soups, Paul Jones Rye Whiskey, and the Continental Tobacco Company. The display space was 60 by 30 feet.

O. J. Gude, who became known as the "Father of the Great White Way," pushed his efforts further north. In 1899, the two most prominent displays were at the 23rd Street location and at 25th Street and Broadway where the *New York World* had a giant electrical sign. The newspaper had paid $1,500 for its construction, paid $714 a month rental, $200 a month for electricity in summer and $250 in winter. The sign was 60 feet wide by 30 high. Stretching north along Broadway were soon other huge electric signs. A famous chariot race advertised the "Rice Leaders of the World." It took 20,000 electric bulbs flashing 2,500 times a minute to depict the action as the drivers whipped their galloping horses into a fury of speed. An equally famous sign showed playful kittens entangled in strands of Corticelli spool silk. A few years later the great Wrigley sign at Times Square was 200 feet long by 50 feet high. Tails of the peacocks in the sign were 60 feet long. The capering spearsmen were 15 feet high.[7]

The colorful electric signs that delighted city crowds made outdoor advertising acceptable to the many. The Outdoor

[7] "A Brief History of Electric Advertising Displays," *Printers' Ink Monthly*, March, 1931; Jack B. Kemmerer, "That Business of the Sign," *Nation's Business*, February, 1952.

Advertising Association of America undertook systematic reform, urging the industry to avoid offense by leaving beauty
spots unmolested and setting physical standards for "paint,"
posters, and the supports on which they were mounted. Government use of posters for many purposes during World War
I gave sanctity to the billboard.

Advertising was established and strong when World War
I broke. In England it was called into service even before
the war broke out. Great Britain's Secretary of State for
War was playing golf in the fall of 1913 with an old friend,
the founder and head of the Caxton Publishing Company,
Hedley Francis LeBas. At the time the British Army was
trying to recruit seven thousand men and having little luck.
Colonel Seeley complained of it as he and his partner sank
their putts on one green.

LeBas asked why the army did not try advertising. Seeley's
indignant retort was that they were advertising and it was
doing no good.

"Do you call that advertising," LeBas is reported to have
answered. "You print a government proclamation on a sheet
about the size of an ordinary letterhead. You stick it up in
cowsheds and police stations alongside reward notices for
murderers and you expect prospective soldiers to be interested in your six-point announcements!"[8]

LeBas explained as they hammered their way down the
next fairway. He would sell the army to men just as he
would sell tea, soap, or tobacco. He would make his readers
want to enlist. He would play on sentiment, good will,
patriotism, take full pages in the newspapers to describe the
glamor of foreign service and the delights of travel.

The result of this golfing conversation was that the War
Office asked LeBas to prepare a formal presentation of his
plan. He did this convincingly and was given a sizeable appropriation to implement it. He got the needed men for the
British army at only 57 per cent of the former cost of raising
recruits.

[8] Percy Waxman, "The Power and Cheapness of Good Advertising,"
American Magazine, March, 1916.

When World War I broke out in August, 1914, LeBas was appointed to head a committee of England's leading advertising writers. They produced all the copy and art work used in newspaper advertising and on billboards, and their advertising was given a large share of the credit for raising the army from an expeditionary force of 125,000 men to one of over three million. LeBas said that nothing had ever before so clearly demonstrated the usefulness of advertising.[9]

LeBas was called on again when the Chancellor of the Exchequer announced the first British War Loan to the House of Commons. For twelve days LeBas and his group ran full pages of advertising in the English press explaining in simple language the financial terms of the loans, the necessity for the money to prosecute the war, and the dependence for success of the drive upon the purchase of small bonds by wage-earners as well as subscription to the larger denominations. In two weeks' time, at a total advertising cost of about $180,000 the goal of $3 billion in war bond purchases was met. As the war progressed, Hedley LeBas kept government advertising for recruits and the various war loans running in 1,500 papers and on countless hoardings. Billions were raised in loans and millions of men for the service. The government used advertising to discover a million men for work in munitions plants, a million women to work on farms, and to persuade everyone in England to work harder and produce more. In the summer of 1916 Sir Hedley, knighted that year for his contribution to the war effort, could report the success of advertising campaigns of a nature and extent never before attempted by any government.[10]

The Saturday Evening Post naturally approved letting the businessmen of a nation run a war. It commented in 1918 that Sir Hedley LeBas had taught the British government the value of advertising and made advertising a national habit in England.[11]

[9] *New York Tribune*, June 12, 1915.
[10] *New York Times*, August 6, 1916.
[11] Isaac F. Marcosson, "Business-Managing an Empire," *The Saturday Evening Post*, January 18, 1918.

Before the entrance of the United States into World War I, Germany considered itself relieved of all moral and legal responsibility when it used advertising in American newspapers to warn Americans against sailing in British ships.[12] Saturday, May 1, 1915, this advertisement appeared alongside the ship schedules in the New York newspapers:

NOTICE

Travellers intending to embark on the Atlantic voyage are reminded that a state of war exists between Germany and her allies and Great Britain and her allies; that the zone of war includes the waters adjacent to the British Isles; that, in accordance with formal notice given by the Imperial German Government, vessels flying the flag of Great Britain or of any of her allies, are liable to destruction in those waters, and that travellers sailing in the war zone on ships of Great Britain do so at their own risk.

Imperial German Embassy
Washington, D. C., April 22, 1915

The *Lusitania* sailed the same day. She was torpedoed without warning by a German submarine and sank eleven miles off the Irish coast on May 7 with loss of 1,198 lives, including 124 of the 159 Americans aboard. Germany's triumph dealt Wilsonian neutrality a severe blow. Emotionally, a large part of the United States was at war, the press and many advertisers were anticipating America's formal entry into the conflict.

[12] Lucy Maynard Salmon, *The Newspapers and the Historian* (New York: Oxford University Press, 1923), pointed to this as evidence of the stature which advertising had achieved by this time and made this significant comment *re* the ad-less newspapers which some reformers had urged as a remedy for the evils of which it accused advertising and the press. Such a newspaper, she said "would deprive society of the most flawless mirror of itself and the historian of the most unimpeachable evidence at his command." The ad-less newspaper would carry the seeds of its own dissolution "not because 'the advertisements pay for the news,' but because news is ephemeral, while advertisements fundamentally record the mainsprings of human action." *P-M* proved the point a few years later that newspapers which have tried to run without advertising have either failed or been forced to accept it. In 1955 *The Reader's Digest* proved the same point true for popular magazines.

Leslie's Weekly Illustrated News for October 19, 1916, was practically a wartime sheet. Its cover featured a French poilu in a Flanders trench. A double spread covered the German U-Boat war with special attention given to the landing at Newport of the German U-53. Lieutenant Commander Hans Rose of the submarine was shown being greeted by Captain Robinson of the United States Navy to whom he entrusted a letter to be posted to Count von Bernstorff, the German ambassador to the United States. Obligingly, the crew of the submarine posed on deck so that Commodore James of the Newport base could take some snapshots. Off Nantucket, on his way back to work, Lieutenant Commander Rose sank four British ships, one Norwegian, and one Dutch by way of demonstration. The U.S. Navy picked up the survivors.

More pictures in this issue of *Leslie's* covered General Black Jack Pershing's punitive expedition into Mexico. There were shots of U.S. soldiers in camp in Texas, of armored cars in use at Fort Bliss, and of Y. M. C. A. trucks unloading 1,000 New Testaments and 100,000 sheets of writing paper for the men. Shots of more troops departing for the border showed soldiers leaning out coach windows in the Union Station in Washington to kiss their girls good-bye. It was all to become more and more familiar.

The advertising had the same air of war. The inside front cover was an advertisement for the Packard. The government had purchased over $2¼ million-worth of chainless Packards in six months for use on the Mexican border. The first order had been for 27, the latest for 330. "In all, re-orders now total 3,650 per cent. The largest number of motor trucks of any one make bought for U.S. Army use are dust-proof, chainless Packards." Other truck manufacturers pushed hard too in this issue of *Leslie's:* Buda, White, Continental, Federal, Waukesha. Passenger cars and motor oils were advertised as well, but the back cover in color was faithful Nipper listening to "His Master's Voice."

Two things happened in advertising as soon as war was declared in 1917. Many advertisers quickly canceled all their contracts and declared they would do no further advertising during the war. Many manufacturers had been selling the larger part of their output to the Allied countries. The likelihood was that now they would have little or nothing to sell the civilian public. Some manufacturers, dependent on foreign markets for materials they could no longer get, could not carry on their regular businesses. A few were moved by moral reasons; they felt it wrong to exploit the war in advertising. Others reasoned that it was uneconomical to advertise when they had nothing to sell, and one went so far as to send out a proclamation saying that if advertising to create more business did not cease, the country was headed for disaster. Cutbacks in advertising were the order at first. *Printers' Ink* and the rest of the trade press fought against this attitude all during the war, and paid advertising actually increased.

The other immediate happening was that representatives of the advertising agencies and the advertising media formed themselves into a group and offered their services to the Council of National Defense. As the welter of wartime agencies and administrations which quickly sprang up were reshuffled and renamed, the group became the Division of Advertising of the Committee of Public Information headed by George Creel, editor of the *Rocky Mountain News*. Its services were not sought immediately. Government officials, particularly army chiefs, believed in orders and edicts, not in persuasion through advertising. The advertising men, England's example before them, persisted, and soon proved the efficacy and efficiency of advertising in selling ideas, persuading to action, in effect, controlling the population. Their victory was not complete. The government did not buy advertising as England did. It took and used all that it could get free, and it got a lot before the war was over. Creel believed that use of direct advertising by the government in paid space would be more direct and economical, but could not convince his superiors.[13] Before the war was over, the Advertising Division had used more than $1½ million of

[13] *Advertising Age*, June 10, 1940.

donated advertising facilities, and under a plan devised by William H. Rankin in Chicago, businessmen had donated some $5 million in outdoor, newspaper, and magazine space.[14] In addition over eight hundred publishers of monthly and weekly magazines contributed $159,275 worth of space a month throughout the war, and advertisers used their own paid space in untold amount to publish wartime messages in cooperation with the various Liberty Loan Committees, the Red Cross, the Fuel Administration, the Food Administration, various divisions of the potent War Industries Board and all the other commissions, agencies, subcommittees, chests, and official or quasi-official bodies that flourish importantly during any war and fight to establish themselves in perpetuity afterward.

During World War I civilian cooperation was sought on a voluntary basis. Baruch's War Industries Board, which controlled prices of raw material, enforced a system of priorities, allocated materials to industries, standardized sizes, and generally controlled production, asked for what it wanted and got it. It had little power to issue and enforce edicts. Advertising was a help in carrying out its functions. Food was rationed entirely on a voluntary basis. Only a few items were actually in short supply because the bulk of production was being shipped to the European Allies. Advertising helped Herbert Hoover's Food Administration with its wheatless, meatless, and porkless days. Posters and magazine and newspaper space carried the message. One advertisement, which showed a U.S. infantryman charging with fixed bayonet, read:

Victory is a
Question of Stamina
Send the Wheat
Meats, Fats, Sugars
the fuel for fighters
United States Food Administration

[14] *Printers' Ink*, July 28, 1938, and *Advertising Age*, June 10, 1940.

When the draft was decided upon, advertising men felt that the idea needed all the persuasion that could be used in order to convince the American public, traditionally against conscription, to accept it. General Enos Crowder and his military advisors disagreed and would have none of it. An order was an order. The military stuck to its attitude despite intercession by the Council of National Defense. Only at the last minute was the advertising group given permission to put in motion the campaign it had prepared. At a signal, newspapers and signs across the country released:

ALL PATRIOTS WILL, ALL OTHERS MUST REGISTER

That thirteen million men were registered in one day without serious incident was credited in part to this move.

Advertising called on Columbus, George Washington, Thomas Jefferson, Benjamin Franklin, and all the other familiar symbols of patriotic tradition to sell conservation, thrift, Liberty Bonds, and to support the drives of the Red Cross and other charitable agencies. Stirring posters appeared everywhere showing emblematic eagles or romanticized fighting men, Uncle Sam, the Statue of Liberty, the Doughboy. These were reproduced in newspaper and magazine advertising, and the pictures of the smashed Uhlan helmet, the German mailed fist, the mother worrying over her soldier son, or the baby awaiting its absent father's return, or just Uncle Sam with his finger pointed, carried the messages:

I Want You for the U.S. Army
What Does "War-Time" Mean to You?
Back the Fighting Lad with the Fighting Loan
These Men Are Doing Their Part—Let Us Do Ours
What Will Protect You If These Are Defeated?
One Hundred Million Americans Must Enlist to Win the War
Bonds Are Not a Burden but a Blessing

There were mammoth parades during World War I. Mary Pickford and Douglas Fairbanks exhorted to the purchase of Liberty Bonds. There were bands and an unashamed appeal to patriotism. An idealistic people believed—for the reform movement still had some years to go—that they were actually "making the world safe for democracy." The advertisements of manufacturers and merchants were filled with pictures of men marching away to war, of laughing sweethearts, and appealing children—and of product tie-in claims.

Kodak took full pages in color in *The Saturday Evening Post* during the war to urge people to cheer up the boys in camp and overseas by sending them snapshots from home. They also suggested the folks at home send cameras to the men and "Ask your Soldier Boy or Sailor Boy to send pictures to You." Economy Renewable Fuses were "At Work for the Flag!" Beaming, smooth-shaven soldiers and sailors announced that the Army and Navy had declared for "Ever-Ready" razors. Republic Tires were performing "A Real Service to the Nation." Haynes automobiles were "War-Time Models," with no frills.

U.S. Tires were shown on American ambulances with shells bursting over them in No-Man's Land. Sunshine Biscuits were baked "In absolute compliance with war-time regulations." Everyone was "Stepping on to Victory" on Cat's Paw Cushion Rubber heels. Sellers Kitchen Cabinets helped "Conserve the Woman-Power of America." War materials had the right of way on all railroads, but there were no delays, advertisements announced, for businesses which used Bethlehem Motor Trucks.

Uniformed soldiers cried happily that "Aunt Jemima Rings the Bell with Me!" This was when they were not gathered around a camp fire listening to kindly Velvet Joe extolling the virtues of Velvet Tobacco, indulging in Prince Albert, "The National Joy Smoke," or, face smeared by battle grime under their battle helmets, smoking a White Owl Cigar. Every officer, as text and pictures showed, needed both a Gruen pocket watch and another on his wrist. The thrift slogan was translated into "Let's All Save—$51 on the Oliver Typewriter."[15] Pepsodent disclosed that the real enemy was film on the teeth.

[15] Thrift, since the 1930's deplored by experts as uncooperative and antisocial, was then considered a virtue.

All the opportunists were not manufacturers. A full-page advertisement in *The Saturday Evening Post* in 1918 was a vigorous appeal "for everyone to join hands and to destroy the Liquor Traffic forever." Its sponsor, the Strengthen America Campaign, had a New York headquarters and the blessings of The Federal Council of Churches of Christ in America. Pepsodent had been wrong. The real enemy was not film on the teeth. The Campaign isolated another villain. It quoted Lloyd George: "We are fighting Germany, Austria, and Drink—the greatest of these deadly foes—is Drink." The Campaign begged for just one $50 Liberty Bond to help fight its battle—which it won before the year was out.

The automobile manufacturers, their production of cars for civilian use limited by their work for the armed forces, could boast of real accomplishments during the war, but they were careful to keep their names and wares before the public. Haynes advised: "Please order your Haynes now. Half of the big Haynes factory is now at work for Uncle Sam." Saxon warned, "There will not be enough Saxons to go around this spring." Paige declared the automobile as utilitarian a necessity as the telephone. "It is standard field equipment of every aggressive businessman, and to employ it is not merely good judgment but a PATRIOTIC DUTY as well." The Selden Truck advertised: "It is essential that the business of the nation move forward—that back of our iron-hearted men in khaki and the big guns at the front will be prosperous industries to provide foods, equipment, and ammunition to WIN THE WAR." Reo warned solemnly of shortages of material. "We cannot be sure how long it will be possible to procure material to our own specifications . . . in common with all other automobile manufacturers, we may be compelled in the near future to accept as good as we can get. . . ."

The American Tobacco Company was faced with both a predicament and an opportunity when in April, 1918, the government requisitioned the entire output of its Bull Durham, together with that of Liggett & Myers Duke's Mixture, for the armed forces. Percival Hill, American's president, immediately put out a four-column advertisement which he had printed in newspapers across the country.

> Our Government has requested that we put at the disposal of the War Department our entire output of the 'makings'—Bull Durham Tobacco. . . .
> And we have complied fully, gladly. . . .
> We have been sending immense quantities of 'Bull' to our men at the front, and at the same time trying to supply consumers at home. But now we are asked to give *all* our output—36,000,000 sacks, 2,000,000 pounds, 100 carloads of 'Bull' Durham every month. . . .
> It means that the Government has found that *our fighting men need the 'makings.'*. . . If 'Bull' is a necessity to you here, in the peaceful pursuit of your daily life, how much greater its necessity to those splendid Americans who have gone to fight for *you*—to *win* this war for *you*. I know that you will think of them as I do—only of them. . . . And I know you will not forget the little muslin sack—gone for the present on its mission of hope and inspiration to our boys in the trenches.
> 'Bull' will come back, with ribbons of honor. Have no fear.

This became the theme. Newspaper advertisements and car cards in every large city carried the story. "So-long, but not Good-Bye" said Old Bull himself. "Never fear," the advertisements comforted, "he'll be back with medals of honor."

Despite all the public and private advertising, the trade was worried. Magazine advertising increased from $26,643,385 in 1914 to $35,093,398 in 1916, to $44,628,806 in 1917, $48,643,563 in 1918, then catapulted to $78,025,145 in 1919, the first full peace-time year, but the fear was expressed all through the war that it might slacken, and the warnings were grave.[16]

Printers' Ink, June 6, 1918, headed a full page with the announcement in large type: "Germany Gloats Over Decrease in American Advertising." The page carried two quotations from the enemy press.

April 26, 1918, the *Berlin Tageblatt* had said:

[16] *Advertising Age*, March 2, 1942. The figures were attributed to a study made by the Crowell-Collier Publishing Co.

If the despised Yankee nation thinks they are going to win this war and force Germans out of foreign markets, there is nothing to indicate this sentiment in their local and foreign advertising. Many of the advertising agencies have closed their doors through lack of patronage. Their much-talked-of captains of industry have cancelled advertising everywhere. Germany and German merchants have increased their advertising space in neutral markets and at home. . . .

The *Berlin Lokal Anzeiger*, April 20, 1918, had been equally exultant. It said a prominent Buenos Aires advertising agency had announced that 83 per cent of U.S. advertisers had canceled their contracts and that all U.S. papers had suffered linage losses. "In other words, the war has terrorized the American nation, but not the Germans, for a perusal of their periodicals will show the manufacturers still advertise even if they have not the goods to deliver, but with the idea of keeping their name before the public. . . ."

Bruce Bliven, then a *Printers' Ink* editor, contrasted, March 2, 1918, the dull pamphlet output of the Committee on Public Information with the lively work done by the volunteer groups "along advertising lines." There was some point to Bliven's contrast. Courtland N. Smith, riding a Long Island coach after a visit to the office of a client, got the idea for what became probably the most famous advertisement of World War I. As soon as he reached his desk he sketched the design and wrote the slogan used in the second drive for the Red Cross—"The Greatest Mother in the World." Arthur Kudner wrote another poignant appeal for the Red Cross.

Early in the war Herbert S. Houston, Chairman of the National Advisory Board, cited Herbert Hoover's campaign for the relief of Belgium as demonstrating the fact that while "publicity gives information, advertising spurs to action."[17] He quoted the banker Festus J. Wade as saying, "It is my belief that advertising will be the prime factor through which our government will appeal to the American people in many situations during the war." The advertising man and the banker proved good prophets, but others were already shrewdly looking ahead.

[17] "Advertising and Victory," *World's Work*, August, 1917.

Eight months before the end of the war a writer in *The Outlook*, after noting the difficulties under which manufacturers worked during the war and their inability to supply their normal markets, warned in modern terms of the dangers of advertising cessation:

> Our manufacturers must keep the public informed of their present and future plans and must help that public not to forget. A manufacturer may be loaded up with war orders, but that is no reason why he should jeopardize his post-war market by allowing people to forget his existence. It is due to both the public and himself to issue a reasonable amount of advertising "news" in order to keep the established merit of his goods before the public. . . .
>
> There is another strong reason for advertising now for after-the-war effect. This lies in the tremendous addition to capital investment and plant capacity for war purposes. What is to become of these great industrial plants after the war unless they are devoted to the manufacture of new products? And if this is done a market for these products must be prepared in advance by persistent advertising.[18]

A few large advertisers fell out during the war. Among them were Pearline, Pears' Soap, Sapolio, and Sweet Caporal Cigarettes. The advertising fraternity likes to think that these disappeared because they ceased to advertise; the likelihood is that commercial plans and accidents were basically responsible. Most major advertisers kept hard at it, the automobile manufacturers, Kodak, and particularly Wrigley's Chewing Gum, which spent great sums tying down the American habit which grew wondrously during the tense war years. Some new advertisers actually began large-scale activities during the war—Lucky Strike, Eversharp, Pepsodent, Del Monte.

Advertising performed still one more public service as the war ended, at least was put to new use to sway public opinion. Will H. Hays, then Chairman of the Republican National Committee, called on Albert Lasker in June of 1918. They wanted an advertising man to make their sick party well, and there was a patriotic duty to be performed. Persuaded, Lasker allowed Hays to take him to Oyster Bay. Theodore Roosevelt, clad in khaki, shirt, breeches and riding

[18] "War-Time Business and Advertising," *The Outlook*, March 6, 1918.

boots, met them at the front steps, put his arms around Lasker's shoulders, and said, "They tell me you are America's greatest advertising man."[19]

Hays and Roosevelt wanted to put propaganda to work to mend the Republican Party, which had been split by the Bull Moose movement in 1912 and defeated again in 1916, and were intent on discrediting Wilson's avowed internationalism. Roosevelt explained to Lasker that peace was about to come and that Wilson intended to drag the United States into European affairs. He had to be stopped. Lasker, who believed that Europe was blighted, decayed, and evil, and that George Washington's stern advice against America's entering into foreign entanglements should be zealously observed, pitched delightedly into this new kind of advertising.

He utilized all his salesman's skill on behalf of the beliefs he shared with Roosevelt, Hays, William E. Borah, and Hamilton Fish. As the war drew to a close, Lasker went to Washington and fought with propaganda and advertising to defeat the party which had just won a great war. A Republican House and Senate were elected. Lasker then threw his energy and craftsmanship into backing Hiram Johnson for the Presidential nomination, not, as he wrote proudly in 1925, with the belief that Johnson could win it, but that he would show so much strength in the primaries that the Republican Party would be forced to commit itself against the League of Nations.

Under Lasker's direction, advertising and propaganda convinced the many. The traditional isolationism of the United States was preserved. Henry Cabot Lodge and his adherents won when, in 1919, the Senate rejected the Versailles Peace Treaty. Warren Gamaliel Harding was nominated and easily elected in 1920. Like Roosevelt, before him, Harding put his arm around Lasker, promised that he would never let the United States get involved in the affairs of wicked Europe either, and made him chairman of the United States Shipping Board.

[19] Lasker tactfully but truthfully replied that no one could claim to be that as long as T. R. was alive. *The Lasker Story*, p. 31.

23

Advertising Unlimited
—the 1920's

ADVERTISING CAME TRIUMPHANTLY out of World War I. It was better, it was bigger, it was reputable. It had proved its ability to sway people's opinions and govern their actions. It had sold ideas and regulated human conduct. It had been used effectively by governments. Advertising broadsides had been fired by both sides in warfare between unions and employers. Streetcar companies and railroads had pleaded their cases with the public through advertising. Passionate advertising was employed by both in a hotel waiters' strike, a harbor strike, a dispute between actors and theatre managers, another between milk companies and their drivers, another which involved battling factions of the graft-ridden building industry.

Everything in the United States seemed to emerge triumphant and stimulated out of World War I. The country had proved itself in world conflict. Its industrial and armed might, brought late into the war, seemed to have been decisive. The United States might or might not have saved the world for democracy, but it had acted effectively as a nation. It felt strong, powerful, and pleased with itself. Little of its energy had been expended. It plunged headlong and a little bewildered into all the extravagance of the vital 1920's.

People had money late in 1918, and they wanted to spend it. Wartime scarcities had aggravated their appetites. Prices soared as they fought to buy. It was a sellers' market, and advertisers made the most of it. The first flurry over, there was a slight depression in 1921 and 1922. Prices dropped as money tightened. Advertisers got down to the business of selling again. Recovery was quick. Prosperity came swiftly, then boom.

The period from the end of World War I until the stock market crash of 1929 was a period of extremes, of cynicism and enthusiasm, of reckless optimism and romantic despair, of flaming youth and the lost generation, of impatience with everything that was old and a fever for what was new. It was the period of the bobbed-haired flapper and John Held's cartoons, of the sharpies and the "finale hoppers," of T. S. Eliot's *The Waste Land* and the early novels of Hemingway, of *Main Street* and *Babbitt*, of the discovery and exploitation of sex, of bathtub gin, companionate marriage, and Rotary. Greenwich Village was so self-consciously wicked it hugged itself in ecstasy; the Algonquin wits were dazzled by their own brilliance; Edna St. Vincent Millay sang the vitality and weary disillusionment of the flapper in her lyrics, and Vachel Lindsay happily thumped out his booming verse.

Jazz was the tempo and Texas Guinan's "Hi-ya, Sucker!" was the cry. H. L. Mencken gleefully attacked the Booboisie and puritanism, and Professor Stuart Sherman came stiffly out of Illinois to fight doughtily in puritanism's defense. Dr. Coué and Dr. Freud were accepted with indiscriminate enthusiasm. Lytton Strachey slew Queen Victoria to the cheers of the critics, and biography went sadistically iconoclastic. Nobody knew what it all meant or cared very much. You could make a fortune on margin, and any conflicts could be solved in speakeasy liquor and the wail of the saxophones. It was a kind of innocent orgy, a nearly ten-year-long saturnalia that opened with Harding's confident "Return to Normalcy" and closed with the suicides of the financially ruined in 1929. Cynical disillusion, super-salesmanship, Rudy Vallée, "Strange Interlude," and—"Yes, We Have No Bananas!"

Advertising was a part of most of it. It surged forward in a breakthrough as the war ended. Total advertising expenditures, which had sagged to $1,468,000,000 in 1918, leaped to $2,282,000,000 in 1919, almost touched the three billion dol-

lar mark in 1920, fell off slightly for two years, reached
$3,099,000,000 in 1925, and soared again to almost $4 billion
in 1929. Advertising was more than respectable now. It was
glamorous and exciting. It pictured life as people wanted to
see it. The glossy advertisements in the slick magazines were
more accurate to peoples' ideas of themselves than the duller
editorial pages of most periodicals.

Wartime industry had proved that America could produce
more than enough of everything. High wartime wages had
put money into the hands of people who had had little before,
and they wanted all the luxuries once considered solely the
natural possessions of the rich. The workman yearned for
and got his silk shirt, and the worker's wife thirsted for the
clothes, the scents, the allure of the woman of fashion. Industry produced in profusion. Now it was for the salesman
to persuade. Selling, for the first time, began to be looked
upon as almost as important as production. Advertisers raced
for markets. The high-pressure salesman became the darling
of business and the pattern of the successful American man.

The nineteen-twenties, as Frederick Lewis Allen wrote,
saw the canonization of the salesman as the brightest hope of
America.[1] Salesmen met in conventions in New York, Chicago, Atlantic City, in any city which could attract their
aristocratic patronage, to admire each other and be admired,
to regale each other with stories of the big sales they had
landed, to sing sales songs written especially for their bibu-
lous celebrations, to pep themselves up to bring in even more
and larger orders for locomotives, soap, or bobby pins. Bruce
Barton, Amherst-educated son of an Oberlin preacher as well
as agency man, wrote a book to prove that Christ himself
had been both a salesman and an advertising man. Seriously,
Barton described Christ as a business executive, told how he
had founded modern business and the advertisements he had
used to establish it.[2] The public made the book a best-seller.

[1] Frederick Lewis Allen, *The Big Change* (New York: Harper & Bros.,
1952), p. 139.
[2] Bruce Barton, *The Man Nobody Knows* (Indianapolis: Bobbs-Merrill
Co., Inc., 1924).

Salesmen purred in the warmth of popular approval. Glenn Frank, publicity man and widely read newspaper columnist as well as president of the University of Wisconsin, wrote: "I suspect the most important man in the world today is the good salesman . . . the art of civilization is largely the art of salesmanship. Nothing of permanent value has come down to us from the past save by the grace of good salesmanship on the part of somebody."[3]

The size of *The Saturday Evening Post* almost doubled after World War I, to two hundred pages in many issues. Large space, dominant illustrations, compelling copy, took the place of more modest appeals for public notice, approval, and purchase. More care was expended on the writing and appearance of advertising in many publications than on the editorial pages of the magazine. Advertising took on a new and shining splendor. There was no need for him to glorify advertising, Lorin F. Deland wrote in *Harper's* as early as March, 1917. Advertising did not need it. The qualities of good advertising, he thought, were, first, imagination; second, knowledge of human nature; third, more knowledge of human nature.

Advertisers in the 1920's proved they had all three qualifications and many more. They urged everybody, and few needed the encouragement, to keep up with the Joneses and then to go one better than the Joneses. They told women they could be as glamorous as any beauty queen they pictured, and men they could be as successful as any millionaire if they would just buy—buy almost anything. They invented new and strange diseases that people could avoid by using the correct toothpaste. They warned people they were giving social offense by failing to purchase and use courses in correct English or deodorants guaranteed to make you unutterably ineffable or the president of a corporation. Freed by the new mores, advertisers could mention all that had been unmentionable and exploit what had been hidden behind blushes of shame.

[3] Quoted by Raymond Rubicam in *Publishers Do Not Fix the Cost of Space* (privately printed; New York: The Maia Press, 1930).

The advertising man, the *New Republic* pointed out in 1919, was the acknowledged genius of America. There was no longer need for him to conceal his awareness that he was the cornerstone of the newspapers and the magazines. Democracy had made him a god.[4] With comparable irony, which yet had to acknowledge the facts, the *Nation* insisted that the serious writing in American newspapers and magazines was in the advertisements rather than in their editorial content. The advertisement of an automobile company was "The Truth that Embodies All Truth." A cement company offered an essay on "Dependability." An insurance company's advertisement was "The Employer Who Upholds the Race, the Fourth of a Series on the Story of Industrial Justice."[5] Toward the end of the period, a more skilled critic, George Jean Nathan, in his *American Mercury*, thought that some earlier advertising perhaps had been more effective in catching his eye and selling him its products by simpler devices, but wrote seriously, "The profession of advertising . . . has made enormous strides in the direction of intelligence, good-looking copy, and public persuasion." Its advance, he thought, had been noteworthy.[6]

Whatever else it was or was not, the advertising of the 1920's was colorful, ingenious, often spectacular, and sometimes incredible. Almost anything could be sold and was. The advertising agencies rose gloriously to positions of unchallenged power. Appropriations were large, campaigns ambitious, enthusiasms feverish. The magazines had developed high-speed four-color printing, and advertisers and agencies used it extravagantly. New products were developed, taken to market, and established in a fraction of the time it had previously taken.

Advertising changed much of the thinking of people in the 1920's and many of their habits. It disseminated ideas,

[4] S. N. Behrman, "The Advertising Man," *New Republic*, August 20, 1919.

[5] "Deep Stuff," *Nation*, July 3, 1920.

[6] George Jean Nathan, "Advertising," *American Mercury*, December, 1929.

good or bad, and some of them took hold. It utilized the new war-born freedoms to ignore what some called prudery and others good taste. It played on hopes and fears; preyed on ignorance; dazzled with the new and vaunted sophistication of the time. Pyorrhea, dandruff, undie odor, athlete's foot, underarm hair, body odor, intestinal toxicity, colon collapse came in with renewed automobile enticements and elegant luxury advertising. Cigarettes and dentifrices vied with each other in enticing to new delights. Cars identified themselves with beautiful women and toilet papers with social failure or success. Publicity-conscious celebrities proffered rapt testimonials for everything from toilet soap to brassieres, cigarettes, and courses in etiquette.

Some of the first advertising stemmed directly from wartime experience, with manufacturers striving to consolidate gains made and throw open larger markets. Immediately after the war Harvey S. Firestone decided to extend the market for truck tires. He visualized the motor truck as a new, war-proved, vital means of goods transport, and used advertising of all kinds to hasten the change from which all truck-tire manufacturers would benefit, Firestone getting its share of the profits. In January, 1919, Firestone inaugurated a series of full-page advertisements in national weekly magazines. The advertisements were designed to instill the lessons learned from the military use of motor trucks. A Firestone advertisement in *Collier's*, January 25, 1919, read:

> When the French line stood at the Marne, the truck began to receive the recognition it deserved. . . . People realized, all at once that the motor truck was essential and vital in our transportation and therefore a basic part of our living.
>
> Like good roads, motor trucking should interest every man, woman, or child. Both are basic elements in lowering the cost of distribution, saving products now wasted, opening up resources heretofore untapped. . . .
>
> Ship by Truck. Let us make this the slogan of a new business era.

"Ship by Truck" became the chant in a two-year campaign on which Firestone spent more than two million dollars. He sent a fleet of loaded trucks out of Akron through the South. Publicity men in attendant cars interviewed mayors, fire chiefs, and police officials along the way. In each town lectures were given on the economy of motor truck haulage.

The army was persuaded to dispatch the First Army Transcontinental Truck Convoy from Washington, D. C., to San Francisco. Sixty-five vehicles and three hundred men, with Lieutenant Colonel Dwight D. Eisenhower second in command, made the hazardous trek over a route advocated by the Lincoln Highway Association. The Lincoln Highway had not yet been built. The army convoy had to carry road and bridge-building equipment along with it. Some of the army trucks equipped with solid rubber tires bogged down. Those equipped with Firestone pneumatic tires, loaded with more of the same for delivery in San Francisco, sailed through. Firestone and the army did a good job of selling both the need for new highways and Firestone tires.

The company devised a national Ship-by-Truck–Good Roads Week, obtaining the valuable endorsement of such men as William G. McAdoo and Bernard Baruch. Mammoth parades were staged in cities large and small. A motion picture was made and released. Sixty-seven bureaus were set up in various cities to publicize advertising that became a national movement. A Highway Education Board was established to award an annual college scholarship to the winner of an essay on good roads. Warren G. Harding presented the first award at the White House in 1921.[7]

Every step of the campaign was attended by display advertising, newspaper, magazine, and motion picture publicity. The campaign made news. It was instrumental in the passing of a Federal Highway Act which made the Bureau of Public Roads of the United States Department of Agriculture liaison agency with the various states to develop a coordinated highway system.

[7] Alfred Lief, *The Firestone Story* (New York: Whittlesey House, McGraw-Hill Book Co., Inc., 1951).

This was advertising of the scope and kind that was to dominate in the 1920's. All-out, hard-driving, intense, nation-wide, it was realistic, progressive, far more reputable than some campaigns for other products, praiseworthy in its in-telligent display of enlightened self-interest—and effective for Firestone.

A two-page spread for Firestone in *The Saturday Evening Post*, July 8, 1919 showed the front wheels of a huge truck just reaching the crest of a hill as the rear wheels of the truck ahead of it started down the other side. The legend in large type was simply:

Half the Truck Tonnage of America is Carried on Firestone Tires

Firestone had begun to make carriage tires in Akron in 1900, then developed and sold pneumatic tires for automo-biles, for electrics and then gasoline cars and trucks.

This was an established business which had boomed dur-ing World War I. Out of the war came other products and new habits hardly known until then. One alert opportunist, guided by his own taste, developed a business that influenced millions and made his advertising slogan a catch phrase of the period. One Robert B. Wheelan returned from World War I convinced that the daily exercises he had done to music under officer direction were a good thing, and he determined to carry the habit into civilian life. He found it dull and a chore. It was, he decided, the music that was lacking. This led to the idea that exercise set to music on phonograph records would work, and that others beside himself might enjoy them. He approached Walter Camp, Yale football coach, and arranged to use the famous trainer's "Daily Dozen" on a royalty basis.

Wheelan picked out suitable music, barked out his com-mands in a drill sergeant's voice, and had the whole recorded. He plunged his entire capital of $1,000 into one big adver-tisement in the New York Sunday newspapers. The response was immediate. People really wanted to be healthy if it did not hurt too much.

Wheelan in partnership with Nelson Doubleday began manufacture of sets of "Daily Dozen" records at twenty dollars the set. He sold three-quarters of a million sets the first year and spent a quarter of a million dollars in advertising. His magazine advertisements showed Walter Camp in his World War I officer's uniform directing exercises. They told "How Walter Camp Put Joy into Living." Couponed magazine advertisements directed readers to order directly from Health Builders, Inc., Garden City. Wheelan and Doubleday had trouble manufacturing enough sets to fill the orders. Advertisements showed contrasting photographs of the same man old and gray, then black-haired and vigorous after taking his "Daily Dozen." "An Old Man at 40—Young at 41!" Men, women, and children cavorted and leaped to the records. Doing your "Daily Dozen" became synonymous with all calisthenics.

The cigarette, like the wrist watch for men, came into its own during World War I. The British "fag" had become a wartime fixture even before the entry of the United States into the conflict. Army life and wartime tensions fastened the cigarette habit on to millions of men, and the cigarette, which had accounted for only 5 per cent of expenditures for tobacco in 1904, overtook the cigar and pipe tobacco in sales. There were thousands of brands of cigarettes, mostly local in distribution, and many of them manufactured by the original American Tobacco Company, founded in New York by J. B. Duke in 1890, or its subsidiaries. There were few blends. Most cigarettes were of Virginia or Turkish tobacco. Favorites were Meccas, Ziras, Sweet Caporals, Richmond Gems, Helmars, Murads, but no brands dominated. None had a substantial national market.

Tobacco had always been a strong advertiser. The first display tobacco advertisement in the United States is said to have been run by Peter and George Lorillard in the *New York Daily Advertiser* May 27, 1789. The advertisement showed an Indian smoking his pipe while leaning on a hogshead of tobacco. The copy was for cut tobacco, ladies' twist, pigtail in small rolls, snuff, and other varieties "warranted as

good as any on the continent." Pierre Lorillard, of the next
generation, had his snuff and cigar mill in the upper Bronx.
He believed in advertising and kept it up long before the
larger tobacco combines were formed. As early as 1868, he
was doing a business of between $4 million and $5 million
annually, and was reputed to have built up a fortune of $20
million through advertising his snuff and tobacco.

Sweet Caporals were pushed with "Ask Dad, He Knows."
Card pictures of actresses, baseball players, and prize fighters
were enclosed as premiums with some cigarettes, and people
collected them as they had the earlier advertising trade cards.
Small boys traded one Jack Johnson for a Fitzsimmons and a
Gentleman Jim Corbett or a Christy Mathewson. Some of
the Turkish cigarettes used miniature oriental rugs as premiums, though the slogan for Meccas was not as oriental.
"Where was Moses when the light went out? Groping
around for a pack of Meccas." Lord Salisbury was "the only
100 per cent pure, all-Turkish tobacco that sells for as little
money as 15 cents for Twenty, TWENTY, TWENTY Cigarettes."

Cigarettes had not only to battle each other, but also to
rebut attacks made by reformers who, in those days, condemned cigarettes not on physical but on moral grounds.
Ford's 1914 attack had been violent. He held press interviews reviling cigarettes, said that almost all criminals were
inveterate cigarette smokers and that he would hire no one
who smoked cigarettes. His pamphlet quoted Edison who
said: "The injurious agent in cigarettes come principally
from the burning paper wrapper. It has a violent reaction on
the nerve centers, producing degeneration of the brain cells,
quite rapid among boys. Unlike narcotics, this degeneracy is
permanent and uncontrollable." John Wanamaker, Marshall
Field, the W.C.T.U., and Connie Mack all allied themselves
with Ford. Their protests made the front pages of the newspapers, but World War I displaced them and wartime cigarette smoking was the answer to their arguments.[8]

[8] William E. Richards, *The Last Billionaire* (New York: Bantam Books,
1956).

All the cigarette advertising to this time and all the attacks were as nothing compared to the advertising war for market domination by a single brand which was soon to come. It really began with the introduction in 1914 of Camels, a blend developed by the R. J. Reynolds Tobacco Company as a national brand to compete with local favorites. At the suggestion of N. W. Ayer & Son, the advertising agency handling the account, the new cigarettes were pretested, without advertising, first in Cleveland, then in other cities. Repeat orders proved the public liked them. Full-scale advertising was then begun with a teaser newspaper campaign in cities across the United States. The first advertisement was "The Camels are Coming!" The second advertisement was "Tomorrow There Will be More Camels in this Town than in Asia and Africa Combined." Then came, everywhere:

CAMELS ARE HERE!

Magazines and outdoor advertising were added to the Camel schedule. While a sign painter was at work on a Camel sign a man walked up and asked him for a cigarette. The sign painter gave him a Camel. The man thanked him, lighted his cigarette, inhaled, and said, appreciatively, what, after the painter reported it, became one of the best known slogans in cigarette advertising:

I'D WALK A MILE FOR A CAMEL

Within four years Camels was the leading brand of cigarette. It was time for the competition to do something about it.

In 1911 the Supreme Court had held the "Tobacco Trust" —the American Tobacco Company—a combination acting in restraint of trade, and had broken it up into the American Tobacco Company, Liggett & Myers, and Lorillard, making three large advertisers where there had been only one before. American Tobacco controlled thousands of brands of tobacco, cigars, cigarettes, snuff, chewing tobaccos, plug, twist, fine cut, and cheroots. It owned the great Bull Durham, which had been a favorite smoking tobacco of Longfellow, James Russell Lowell, Thomas Carlyle, to whom Lowell had

THE STORY OF ADVERTISING

introduced it, and Lord Tennyson. J. B. Duke had always pushed Bull Durham, a favorite with cigarette smokers who rolled their own. As far back as 1907, Percival Hill, who succeeded Buck Duke as president of the company, had contracted for a year's use of the advertising space on the outside of the horse-drawn Fifth Avenue buses in New York.

Signs, 6 to 8 feet long and 3 feet high, depicting the great bull in full color and in all his roaring bullishness, appeared suddenly on the buses. Fifth Avenue was horrified. The Municipal Art Society charged desecration and vandalism. Guardians of morals were outraged by the nearly life-size pictures of what was all too obviously a bull. The driver of the first bus captured was arrested. The driver was freed, but the case went all the way to the Supreme Court before Bull Durham was banished from Fifth Avenue. It was the best kind of advertising, as was the wartime confiscation of Bull Durham and Duke's Mixture by the War Department.

The trouble was that men had had enough of rolling their own. They wanted machine-made cigarettes. Hill tried to push Bull Durham as being like sugar in coffee. Men were advised to add a pinch to their favorite pipe tobacco, but it was obvious now that cigarettes were taking over in tobacco sales.

Percival Hill brought his son George Washington Hill, a Williams College sophomore, into the business. At twenty-five, young Hill, super-salesman, an uninhibited advertising man, began the big brand era at American Tobacco. He decided to pit one American Tobacco brand against Camels and chose Lucky Strike, a name first registered for a tobacco in 1871. Charles Penn developed the blend for the Lucky Strike cigarette at the American Tobacco plant in Brooklyn. Young Hill inspected the operation, sniffed the pleasant odors as he passed by the cigarette making machines, and returned to New York. "There's something in that process of Charlie Penn's," he told his father in New York, ". . . he cooks it, cooks the tobacco." Percival Hill was unimpressed. All tobacco was heated in processing. A cigar man came in to ask

These happy tourists made the fearsome San Francisco to Los Angeles trip in less than 21 hours in 1905. Traffic was lighter then than now.

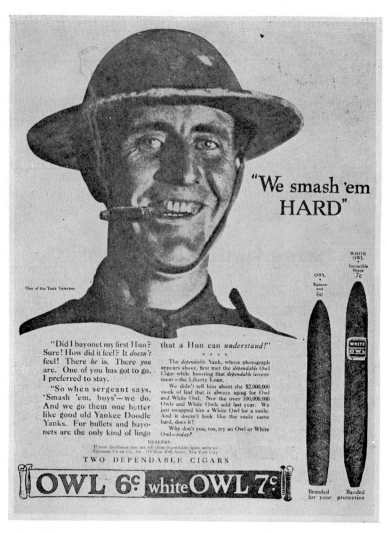

The bloodthirsty propaganda of World War I was echoed in this advertising hymn of hate. This cigar-smoking doughboy expressed the approved attitude.

the senior Hill a question and the younger Hill asked him a question. "What do you have that is appetizing to which heat is applied?" His morning toast, the cigar man said. Percival Hill seized on his answer. "That's it—it's toasted." It became the Lucky Strike slogan:

It's Toasted[9]

The idea was first injected into advertising in January, 1917. A cut showed a piece of bread, speared on the familiar toasting fork of the time, being held over a fire. The toasting process was held up as a new principle in cigarette making. It was claimed that it held the Burley flavor in cigarette form. The advertising campaign was tremendous. Within eighteen months the sales of Lucky Strikes were nearly six billion a year.

By 1925 when planes were writing "Lucky Strike" across the skies in letters a mile high, cigars, chewing tobacco, pipe tobacco, snuff, and all the other forms of tobacco had given way to the domestic blend cigarette, and a handful of brands controlled the market. American Tobacco sold 17.4 billion cigarettes that year, 13 billion of them Lucky Strikes; Reynolds sold 34 billion Camels; Liggett & Myers over 20 billion Chesterfields. These three brands already had 82 per cent of the entire U.S. market.[10]

By this time A. D. Lasker was working with Hill, urging him on, driving the annual American Tobacco advertising appropriation up from $600,000 or $800,000 to $20 million a few years later. According to Lasker, Camels and Chesterfields were away ahead, and Lucky Strike really on the way out when he took over. He actually told Percival Hill and his son at their original luncheon meeting at the Vanderbilt Hotel in New York that he intended to run the account up to $5 million within two or three years. Then he doubled and redoubled the ante, making another fortune out of his 15 per

[9] *"Sold American!"* (New York: The American Tobacco Company, 1954), p. 53.
[10] *Ibid.*, p. 58.

cent commissions on the gigantic account and taking a large share of the credit for the Lucky Strike achievement.[11]

Together or between them—for the egotistical Lasker and the domineering, impetuous George Washington Hill were at odds as often as they were agreed—the advertising man and the tobacco man, both legendary figures of advertising now, created and engineered a revolution in cigarette smoking.

In 1904 a woman had been arrested for smoking a cigarette in an automobile on Fifth Avenue. It was a press sensation and almost a scandal when Irene Castle was discovered smoking a cigarette in the Pompeian Room of the Seneca Hotel in Rochester two years later. Murad and Helmar had shown women in their advertising in 1919, but they were oriental women in costume, so there was no imputation that American women were lost to sin. There had been a girl in the advertising of Player's, the English cigarette, for some years, but, again, she was a foreigner of whom little better could be expected. Many younger women were smoking, but in the privacy of their own homes, seldom publicly, though society women might affect the habit as evidence of their European sophistication.

It was Chesterfield that broke the barrier with a now famous advertisement which first appeared on a poster in 1926. A man and woman were shown seated at night on a moonlit river bank. The man was lighting a cigarette, the girl coaxing, "Blow some my way." It was a daring move to exploit a whole new market which could easily double the sale of cigarettes. There was a tremendous, anguished outcry to which women who wanted to smoke paid no attention at all. It simply meant for many that they no longer had to hide their indulgence, and to more that they could now countenance and enjoy what had been socially dangerous to attempt before.

Chesterfield led, though Lasker, who was annoyed when his wife could not smoke publicly in a Chicago restaurant, was not far behind. He urged on Hill the fabulous profit

[11] "Personal Reminiscences of Albert Lasker," *American Heritage*, December, 1954.

possibilities in breaking down the prejudice against women's
smoking. It took little persuasion. In a few years time the
two men changed the smoking habits of half the population.
Lasker got opera stars to testify in American Tobacco advertising that they smoked Lucky Strikes to protect their precious voices. He says he used practically all the women in
the Metropolitan Opera Company for this purpose in one
advertisement or another. Economically, he paid them nothing. They got the publicity. Schumann-Heink, the first diva
to announce in public print that she smoked cigarettes, got
too much publicity. A number of her concert engagements
were promptly canceled.

The Methodist Board of Morals cried out that the tobacco
trust was ruining the health of young mothers and coining
the blood of babies into dividends. The head of the International Society of Christian Endeavor warned, "Womanhood
is being exploited for trade." Hill increased his advertising
appropriation, and Lasker spent it with enthusiasm.

Then George Washington Hill had the inspiration of his
flamboyant career. He told the story in his own words.

> I was riding out to my home, and I got to 110th Street and Fifth
> Avenue; I was sitting in the car and I looked at the corner and there
> was a great big stout lady chewing gum. And there was a taxicab—
> it was in the summertime—coming the other way. I thought I was
> human and I looked, and there was a young lady sitting in the taxi-
> cab with a long cigarette holder in her mouth, and she had a very
> good figure. . . .
> But right then and there it hit me; there was the lady that was
> stout and chewing, and there was the young girl that was slim and
> smoking a cigarette. "Reach for a Lucky Instead of a Sweet." There
> it was, right in front of you.[12]

Lasker says he had the idea at the same time, because the
candy manufacturers were advertising against smoking, and
that when he went to Hill with it, Hill pulled out of a desk
drawer a slip of paper with written on it, "Reach for a Lucky

[12] *"Sold American,"* p. 75. In 1913 American Tobacco had tried giving
away a bar of candy with each pack of Lucky Strikes purchased.

Instead of a Bonbon." He argued with Hill and got "bonbon" changed to "sweet."

It became the most useful of all the Lucky Strike slogans as well as the most notorious. It tied cigarette smoking to diet, to women's desire for a slender figure, and convinced millions more than the "precious voice" advertisements had persuaded. Lasker changed these now so that opera stars testified they protected their voices by smoking Luckies and their figures by reaching for a Lucky. Film actress Constance Talmadge advised: "Light a Lucky and you'll never miss sweets that make you fat," and the rest of the copy hammered away at the theme from every angle:

> Instead of eating between meals . . . instead of fattening sweets . . . beautiful women keep youthful slenderness these days by smoking *Luckies*. The smartest and loveliest women of the modern stage take this means of keeping slender . . . when others nibble fattening sweets, they light a *Lucky*.

> Lucky Strike is a delightful blend of the world's finest tobaccos. These tobaccos are toasted—a costly process which develops and improves the flavor. That's why *Luckies* are a delightful alternative for fattening sweets. That's why there's real health in *Lucky Strikes*.

> For years this has been no secret to those who keep fit and trim. They know that *Luckies* steady their nerves and do not hurt their physical condition. They know that *Lucky Strikes* are the favorite cigarette of many prominent athletes who must keep in good shape. They respect the opinions of 20,679 physicians who maintain that Luckies are less irritating to the throat than other cigarettes.

Lasker and Hill did not believe in understatement. They emphasized one theme, then backed it with every claim they could devise. Both believed in inspirational copy, in the emotional appeal. Lasker is said to have paid one of his copywriters a ten-thousand-dollar bonus for "So round, so firm, so fully packed, so free and easy on the draw."[13] He and

[13] "Indelible Mark on Advertising Left by Lasker, Agency Pioneer," *Advertising Age*, June 9, 1952.

Hill worked over all the Lucky Strike copy, deleting, changing, polishing. Lasker wrote no copy himself, but considered
himself a great editor of advertising copy. So did Hill.[14]

"Reach for a Lucky Instead of a Sweet" drew agonized
protests from the confectioners as well as squeals from the
moralists.[15] It was finally supplanted by other Lucky Strike
slogans—"LS/MFT," the auctioneer's rattling cry ending in
"Sold American!" and "Smoke the Smoke the Experts Smoke"
—but not before Lucky Strike cigarettes were outselling
their competitors and American Tobacco earnings had risen,
according to Lasker, from about $12 million a year in 1926
to about $40 million in 1930. George Washington Hill, whom
even the official American Tobacco Company history described as "raw, brash, impatient," and, more mildly, as "this
dramatic personality," was a man almost obsessed with his
mission of selling Lucky Strike cigarettes. He worked with
the conviction that he was performing a great social service
as well as building up the fortunes of the tobacco empire.

The advertisers of soaps were as busy, as strident, and as
ingenious as the tobacco companies. Soap was sold for magical qualities no one had dreamed it had. The advertising drive
was directed against the emotions. This soap or that would
make you beautiful, socially acceptable, desirable; failure to
use it would mean premature old age, social ostracism, and
other named or suggested evils. About the only claim that
was not made was that soap would clean anybody or anything.

[14] Said Lasker: "Hill was a particular pain in the neck because he thought
he was an advertising genius, and he wasn't . . . Take that monkey business of wearing a hat all the time, and spitting on the desk." *Ibid*. Hill's
opinions of Lasker were probably no more flattering. Most of the Lucky
Strike advertising ideas, Hill testified in a court suit in 1938, were his.

[15] Once before a tobacco advertising slogan had been based on advising
consumers to select one pleasure instead of another. In 1901, A. Lewis, who
described himself as "Dispenser of Havana Incense as an Aid to Better
Living," had advertised, "Buy a B.C.M. cigar instead of a drink." He had
raised a difficult point for the moralists, who had to decide whether tobacco
or liquor was the worse evil, but managed to offend brewers, distillers, and
saloon keepers just as the later Lucky Strike slogan offended the candy
makers.

In the 1890's the John H. Woodbury Dermatological Institute of New York and Boston, ran quarter-page magazine
advertisements featuring a man's head as trademark, presumably that of the moustached institute head himself, and
headed in heavy black type:

PERMANENTLY

   REMOVED

      WITHOUT PAIN

Eczema	Superfluous Hair
Pimples	Red Nose
Dandruff	Wrinkles
Freckles	Black Heads
Moles	Birth Marks
Warts	Oily Skin

Woodbury's was "The largest establishment in the world
for the treatment of the Skin, Scalp and Complexion. Nervous and Blood Diseases. Over 3,000 diseases and imperfec-
tions of the skin treated by Regular Registered Specialists
who adapt the treatment to individual conditions." In small
type at the bottom of the advertisement John H. Woodbury
was acknowledged as the inventor of Woodbury's Facial
Soap for the Skin, Scalp and Complexion.

In later full page magazine advertisements Woodbury
guaranteed to remove moles, liver spots, and wrinkles, and
to correct projecting ears by setting them back close to the
head, but stressed his facial soap. "If Beauty is only skin deep,
we can make you beautiful."

This was the appeal that worked, so in 1906 Woodbury
dropped his institute to promote his soap. The J. Walter
Thompson Company took on the account. Agency and advertiser pioneered and triumphed with a slogan that touched
the quick of the times when early and daringly they began
to advertise in *Ladies Home Journal* with the open sex appeal
of "The Skin You Love to Touch." Out of the crude, cure-
all advertising of the Woodbury Institute in the 1890's
sprang, through the magic of advertising, one of the glamor
campaigns of the 1920's.

In 1911 the B. J. Johnson Soap Company of Milwaukee had sought out Lord & Thomas for help in advertising their Galvanic laundry soap. The agency persuaded them to advertise instead a little-known toilet soap of small distribution which the company also manufactured. It was known as Palmolive. The Lord & Thomas men liked the sound of the name. Someone suggested that Cleopatra had probably used palm and olive oils. Another was sure that Roman beauties had used them. They would sell Palmolive as a beauty soap. They did, and so successfully, that, according to Claude Hopkins, in 1927 Palmolive was the leading toilet soap in the world. Seen everywhere in the 1920's in seductive advertisements featuring beautiful women was "Keep that Schoolgirl Complexion."

Palmolive did not stop with the toilet soap. It added a shampoo and a shaving cream. To advertise the shaving cream Lord & Thomas conducted research in advance. They listed all the qualities they found men wanted in a shaving cream, then advertised that Palmolive had them all and several more.

Nine out of ten film stars were using Lux Toilet Soap for their priceless smooth skin. One after another, they testified earnestly, so that even women who were not film stars could be as beautiful as they.

Another soap eschewed appeal to the feminine desire to be beautiful or the bisexual allure of sex. For Lifebuoy, Lever Brothers and its advertising agency made a momentous and horrifying discovery, one so fearsome it could be mentioned only by the initial letters of two frightful words. The letters were "B.O." Printed in staring letters or mouthed in a foghorn growl, they warned people of the fate awaiting man, woman, or child who failed to use Lifebuoy.

> Never again that humiliating embarrassment. A healthful glow of perspiration no longer destroys her charm with a hint of unpleasant odor. . . . Baths help, but their effect is soon gone unless Lifebuoy is used. Lifebuoy's antiseptic lather penetrates each pore and removes every trace of odor-causing waste . . . your body stays sweet, fresh, immaculate all day. . . . Not a substitute for cleanness but cleanness itself.

Soap advertisers were determined. If they could not charm the obdurate into beauty, they could frighten them into cleanliness. There had been a war. The 1920's was no world for the sensitive. Privacy was a public matter now. The least the public could do was stop looking and smelling like ordinary human beings.

At first the public quailed, and some even rebelled until they were sternly taught the uselessness and absurdity of such behavior. In 1919, the J. Walter Thompson Company, an early leader in the advertising of toilet soaps and cosmetics, dared collision with another taboo. It began deodorant advertising with Odorono. An advertisement headed "Within the Curve of a Woman's Arm" showed a woman in a man's embrace, her arms upraised. The body copy was a "frank discussion of a subject too often avoided." It pointed out that, "There isn't a girl who can't have the irresistible loveliness of perfect daintiness." Fastidious women wanted to be absolutely sure, and Odorono was so simple, so easy, so sure. Many women "have found they could not trust their own consciousness, they have felt the need of a toilet water which would insure them against any of this kind of underarm unpleasantness. . . ."

When the advertisement was run in *Ladies' Home Journal*, two hundred readers cancelled their subscriptions. Publishers begged the agency to stop running the offending copy. When they learned that he had written the advertisement, several women told James Webb Young they would never speak to him again. The furor seems incredible when by the middle 1920's frankness had so permeated advertising that dozens of deodorants were being advertised, and full pages of women's magazines carried advertising for feminine hygiene products as well as for cosmetics, beauty creams, and articles of intimate apparel. In 1927 Lysol Disinfectant showed in full color in *Ladies' Home Journal* a worried mother in negligée bending over her disconsolate young daughter, saying softly: "Read this little book *carefully*, dear . . . It explains things so much better than I can." The booklet, the copy carefully explained, had been written by a woman physician.

Some tooth pastes offered matchless beauty. Manufacturers of other dentifrices gave you a choice. You could brush with their concoction and be irresistible, or you could take the horrifying consequences. Pepsodent took the smiling approach. It had not been doing well. Its original promoter, who had got the formula from an invalid seeking health in Tucson, was despondent. Claude Hopkins bade him be of good cheer. In a book on dentifrices, he found the phrase "mucin plaque." This, Hopkins decided, was "film on teeth." In full and double page magazine advertisements, he promised its prevention, removal, and utter radiance for those who brushed with Pepsodent. He had Pepsodent a national best seller within a year. By 1927 it was being advertised in seventeen languages in fifty-two countries, and succeeding everywhere. Besides his Lord & Thomas earnings from the account, Hopkins made a million dollars on Pepsodent. He bought a share of the business for $13,000, collected $200,000 in dividends, then sold his share for $800,000.[16]

Ipana, horrified, discovered a condition even worse than Lifebuoy's B.O. Instead of promising pulchritude, it threatened whimpering men and women with the terrors of pyorrhea and presented the infallible diagnosis—pink tooth brush. There was only one prevention, only one way out after the first telltale tint on the bristles of the brush. You could be saved only by gum massage and frequent, lavish use of Ipana.

It was difficult to be sure, safe, beautiful, unoffending, prosperous, or even keep up with all the rewards you were supposed to achieve and the misfortunes you were supposed to shun. There was hardly time during the day and night to take all the correspondence courses which would guarantee you business success, the other courses that would insure your social popularity, use all the dentifrices that would make you irresistible, drive a better car than your neighbor, eat enough yeast to make you healthy and radiant, have a film-free smile, full consciousness that you were offending no one through

[16] Claude Hopkins, *op. cit.*

B.O. or failure to use the proper underarm deodorant. "Are
you too guilty of this sin against beauty?" asked the full-page
advertisements of a powder puff manufacturer. There was
the awful chance you might be. "Must you hide your skin
under a concealing coat of cosmetics?"—but the next page
said you were supposed to!

The incredible was followed by the fantastic. In 1879,
following on the work of Pasteur and Lord Lister, a Dr.
Joseph Joshua Lawrence, working in a small office and
laboratory in St. Louis, developed an antiseptic which he
called "Listerine." He had purchased the ingredients for the
product from a drug store in which one Jordan Wheat Lambert worked as a clerk. Lambert arranged with Dr. Lawrence
to sell the new mild germicide on a royalty basis, and "Listerine" was registered as a trademark August 2, 1881.

Until 1914 it was sold only by prescription. Jordan Lambert pushed its sales by hiring young college-bred salesmen
dressed in black frock coats, top hats, and Ascot ties to call
on doctors and druggists, impressing them with the dignity
and worth of the product which had been named after the
great Lord Lister and accepted by the medical profession in
the United States and abroad.

In 1922 Gerard B. Lambert, son of Listerine's proprietor,
was $700,000 in debt. His four brothers, by right of birth,
were all vice presidents of the Lambert Pharmacal Company.
He went to the company and demanded to be put on the
payroll. He was made general manager. In that capacity he
decided to boost Listerine sales and sent for a representative
of the company's advertising agency. Two men, Milton
Fuessle and Gordon Seagrove, were sent down from Chicago.
Lambert closed the door after they had entered and announced
that none of them would leave until they had an idea for
pushing Listerine. "How about bad breath?" he asked.[17]

An employee was sent for a book of newspaper clippings.
One from the British *Lancet* mentioned "halitosis." Lambert

[17] Gerard B. Lambert, "How I sold Listerine," *Fortune*, 1956. The full
account was later published in book form as *All Out of Step* (New York:
Doubleday & Co., 1956).

leaped upon it. Listerine for halitosis! He hurried downtown, bought a picture of a girl for $2.50, and wrote the first
advertisement at home that night. The poor girl had everything her little heart could desire but she was getting no-
where. She had halitosis and didn't know it.

Lambert and the agency tested the advertisement. It
worked. Listerine was then spending $100,000 a year on
advertising. Lambert proposed spending an additional $5,000,
cumulatively, each month. He would resign if the advertising did not show an additional profit every month of at least
$5,000. By 1927, Lambert was able to pay off his $700,000
debt in full. By 1928 the Lambert Pharmacal Company was
spending $5 million a year in advertising, and there was no
need for Gerard Lambert to resign because he was not showing additional profits. The profits were pouring in.

He and Fuessle went to New York and as Lambert &
Feasley opened their own advertising agency to handle the
Lambert account. Fuessle was president, but Lambert owned
all the stock. They had a wonderful time. Lambert tells how
they would sit sipping gin in Fuessle's office until they got an
idea. They would outline their advertisements on any scrap
of paper, rush out to a photographer to get pictures taken for
the advertisement, run it unretouched to show just how halitosis affected an otherwise attractive woman. Sometimes,
Lambert says, they spread a sheet of tin on the office floor
and amused themselves by playing the harmonica and clog
dancing while their advertising inflamed the world.

Even Your Best Friend Won't Tell You

The advertisement spread uneasiness like the rumors of a
plague. How could you know whether or not you had bad
breath? People shriveled into themselves in shame and horror.
They were palsied with fear. Anyone could be heinously
guilty and never know.

Often a Bridesmaid, But Never a Bride

Lambert threatened young women with a fate worse than
B.O., pyorrhea, undie odor, and underarm offense combined.

Flappers crept along apprehensive and despairing, in the looming shadows of threatened spinsterhood. So that was the reason! For some it was a revelation and a release. A trip to the nearest drug counter, and everything would be all right again, marriage and bliss assured. But could you ever be sure? Your best friends wouldn't tell you. You could see the man shrinking away from the girl in the picture, or the girl, nose wrinkled in dainty distaste, trying not to show her repugnance as the handsome young man came toward her. There was one way perhaps. Children were cruel and notoriously honest.

If You want the Truth, Go to a Child!

Lambert played games with his advertising. He could afford to, and somehow he always won. He would do no advertising for three months, assuming the terrified populace still trembled. Then he would start again, increasing the expenditures until he reached $600,000 in the third month. He let men and women live unmolested for a time, then, just as they felt they were safe again, began with a new series of terrifying truths. Even that worked. Profits went up another million dollars.

The *American Mercury* was at the height of its power, Mencken was hurling derision in every direction, tearing down false idols, massacring superstitions, thrashing the booboisie, murdering traditions, scoffing at everything and everybody, then setting up the empty bottles and demolishing the dead Indians too. Lambert offered the gander some of his own sauce. He told Mencken he would take full pages of advertising every month for a year in the *American Mercury* if he could say what he pleased, even to the extent of ridiculing Mencken himself. Mencken agreed, and Lambert used the iconoclastic sophomore's bible of the 1920's to sell more Listerine to the doubly bedeviled populace.

In November, 1927, the *Mercury* was fat with 112 pages of solid advertising. Kuppenheimer had the second cover, Steinway the third, Lucky Strike the fourth. Inside, one full page of black and white with a double rule border was an essay by Gerard B. Lambert.

Ego

We have been wondering lately a lot about these brilliant writers such as Mr. Mencken and the contributors to his irritating little green book. All of them, while taking a crack at the world in general, seem so definitely sure they are right. In their comprehensive diatribes they reflect a self-confidence which is amazing. Surely they must be in error on some little thing now and then.

In our simple way, we have always been mystified by the apparent fact that infallible judgment and correct thinking seem entirely confined to those fortunate individuals who have been endowed with the talent for brilliantly expressing their own opinions.

We often wish that we might obtain one of these patronizing fellows to write our advertisements for Listerine so that we could get the same reflection of authority over to the great American Boobery.

LAMBERT PHARMACAL CO.
St. Louis, Mo., U.S.A.

Even without the assistance of "one of these patronizing fellows," Gerard Lambert was getting his ideas over to the great American Boobery rather well.

In 1891, W. F. Young, Inc., began the manufacture and sale of a horse liniment, Absorbine, for use in treating equine lameness, spavins, and bruises. The veterinary liniment was a success, but the company founder, proud of his accomplishment, grew impatient with his son's penchant for toying with chemicals instead of paying what the father considered proper attention to business. He said so with emphasis and expletive. The son made conclusive retort. He devised Absorbine Jr. for use on people. As the horse population declined and the human rose, it proved by far the more valuable embrocation. There was every excuse for the son's placing the mysterious intials P.D.F. after his facsimile signature on the label of every

bottle. The initials did not, as many surmised they did, indicate some little known doctoral degree. They stood for
"Pa's Damn Fool!"

Twice inspiration blessed the marketing of Absorbine Jr.
It was sold at first only as a "liniment with antiseptic properties" for use on sore muscles, sunburn, and insect bites. In
1911 an executive of the Young company read an article in
the *Literary Digest* on the prevalence of trench foot among
Americans. He decided to test the effectiveness of Absorbine Jr. in dealing with trench foot. Absorbine Jr. passed the
tests handsomely, and the company began to advertise its
product for its hitherto unsuspected properties. An initial
advertising appropriation of ten thousand dollars was set, and
the schedule went into *Munsey's, Everybody's,* and the *Outlook.*

This was before the second inspiration that shot W. F.
Young's annual advertising expenditure up to a half-million
dollars by 1940. It came when Edwin, Wasey & Jefferson
discovered that the itching, burning, paining feet that had a
large part of the American public squinching up its toes and
scratching with digging fingernails was really "athlete's foot."
It was a wonderful designation. People who might have
flinched at admitting to sweaty feet, ringworm, chilblains, or
a half dozen other unpleasant sounding foot discomforts,
could feel rather proud of suffering from athlete's foot. It
suggested heroic and muscular endeavor, a risk dared and a
penalty exacted for the active life. "Athlete's foot" caught
on immediately. It became one of the most popular of the
advertising-discovered diseases. The nation learned about athlete's foot and what to do for it. Sales of Absorbine Jr.
soared. The W. F. Young plant in Springfield, Mass., had to
be enlarged as people flocked to drugstores for relief from the
uncomfortable and highly contagious foot condition they
learned about in vivid copy and illustrations.

The advertising for the pungent smelling, green liniment
was forthright and graphic.

"Feet soaked in perspiration are targets for ATHLETE'S
FOOT." The top of an encasing shoe was cut away in illus-

tration to show a male foot steaming and smoking as athlete's foot bit and burned its way in.

"Cracks between your toes are DANGER SIGNALS." A hand pried apart the tormented toes to discover the cracked and pealing skin. "Drench them at once with Absorbine Jr."

"ABSORBINE Jr. kills Athlete's Foot Fungi on contact."

In winter, Absorbine Jr. copy quieted to talk of "cold weather joints" and the uses of the liniment for muscular aches and pains. In summer back came the athlete's foot copy with the blistering pavements, the shoes that were a hotbed of infection, the wet socks, the feet soaked in perspiration, the soggy skin, the red and itchy toes. "Athlete's foot germs breed in this perspiration—feed on the dead skin." If you did not already have athlete's foot, your toes began to itch and burn as you read, and Absorbine Jr. throve as horses' gift to man.

Many advertisers sold products, ideas, and prejudices very successfully in the 1920's. They also imbedded one welcome idea and fastened down a practice which has characterized domestic economy in the United States ever since.

In the 1840's Cyrus McCormick originated installment selling with his Virginia Reaper. He had his agents deliver the reaper to farmers in the spring, asking only a small deposit, the remainder of the price to be paid for out of returns from the fall harvest. Isaac Singer began to sell his sewing machines to women in 1856 on an installment purchase plan. These were durable articles, an expensive piece of agricultural machinery, and a proportionately expensive household device. The time-payment plan for such products was as acceptable as a mortgage on the home. Indulgence in installment purchases for other articles was frowned upon for many years. Originally the big mail-order houses sold for cash only. Automobile manufacturers had been incensed when Maxwell began to sell its cars on a partial purchase plan.

Pulpit and press opinion was largely against installment selling and buying. In 1909 *Ladies' Home Journal* inveighed against the practice in an article entitled "A Trap for the

Newly Married." It was possible to buy sewing machines, pianos, clothes, and jewelry on time payments, but it was unwise. You were always in debt. You risked losing your possessions through being unable to keep up your payments. "The installment plan of buying goods . . . is a far-reaching evil; it bears heavily on the poor and the people of only moderate means, the wages of salary earners and the small business people, and it entraps the young at the very beginning of their married life. . . ."

Ten years later advertisers had changed all that. Primarily it was high-pressure salesmanship and the spreading desire to own an automobile that caused that change. The Spartan way of getting only what you pay for or saving until you could purchase and enjoy a luxury did not appeal to a people bent on pleasure and getting it in a hurry, nor did it appeal to manufacturers and advertisers who were intent only on piling up sales, beating their competitors, and putting to shame their sales records of last year, month or week.

Installment selling gained impetus with the automobile and with the development and offering for sale of every new electrical appliance; and they were being invented and advertised fast in the 1920's. By 1927, it was estimated that consumers had actual possession and use of over $4 billion in unpaid merchandise.[18] The significance of this is that advertising by this time was reaching successfully not only for people's cash but also for their future income. To keep the flow of goods spilling out of factories into the laps of consumers, it was necessary to take a lien on the individual's future earning capacity as well as to rake in the fruits of efforts already made.

Few demurred. It was better to have an automobile, a washing machine, an electric refrigerator, and later a radio and then a television set than to do without during lean years while you tried to stifle envy of your neighbor and endure the ignominy of your announced poverty. How strongly advertising has fastened down the practice and how established

18 *Printers' Ink*, July 28, 1938, p. 340.

a part it now is of American life is indicated by figures released by the Federal Reserve Board in April, 1956, showing
that outstanding installment consumer credit was then $28.3
billion. Automobiles, homes, and almost everything in them
can be and are bought on the installment plan, consumers
using what is actually owned by the banks, renting where
once they were more apt to own or do without. The advertising clamor of "No Money Down," "Credit Terms," "Nothing to Pay Until ——," "Liberal Trade-Ins," and all the rest
got its start and strong impetus in the advertising of the
1920's.

"They laughed when I sat down at the piano . . ." This
was advertising for a course of instruction, but you had to
have the piano too. How could you buy the beautifully
illustrated furniture unless you had a house to put it in, or
have any of it—now—unless you got it all on credit? How
could you drive a car, any of them, and in the advertisements
they were all compelling, unless you could get it on time?

One of its oldest practitioners was one of the most active
in high-pressure installment selling in the 1920's. In 1925
Singer machines had been sold on time payments for nearly
seventy-five years. Singer had eight thousand salesmen and
eighteen hundred retail stores, one in every city of any size
around the world, each shop marked with the familiar red
capital "S." There were Singer machines in half the homes
of the United States, and children learned their letters from
Singer A.B.C. cards. Yet the company had done little national
advertising. It began.

Lynn Sumner, Singer's advertising agent, devised a sales
stunt and advertised it in all the large women's magazines.
"FREE! 100 NEW SINGER ELECTRICS in Exchange
for the 100 OLDEST SEWING MACHINES!" The advertisement urged women to fill in and return to Singer a
coupon giving the age of their sewing machine, regardless of
make, and its serial number.

Immediately a Singer salesman called to verify the information. His spiel was already memorized: ". . . we cannot
tell whether you have won until all the entries are in and the

100 winners determined. Meanwhile, why be deprived of the use and enjoyment of this beautiful modern Singer which may be awarded to you some time this coming fall? I have here a guarantee certificate. I am authorized to deliver to to you at once one of these new electrics, allowing you a liberal credit . . ."[19]

An ancient advertising dodge was rejuvenated to a vitality it had not enjoyed in its first use. Testimonial advertising became as exaggerated as life itself was in the 1920's. It came in with the soaps, lotions, and breakfast foods. Soon it was being lavished on cars, motorcycles, typewriters, yeast, hair tonic, storage batteries, deodorants, razor blades, fountain pens, and scores of other commodities. With the eagerness of newly made converts at a prayer meeting, celebrities pressed to testify to their exclusive use of one brand of cigarette or coffee, soap or automobile.

Opera stars, society women, prize fighters, baseball players, explorers were all available at a price. They like the publicity and the fees. Enterprising gentlemen got up lists of celebrities who would for a consideration endorse everything from life insurance to burial vaults. Hearing aids and watches, tobaccos and lipsticks competed for and with the names of the famous. Women who did not smoke at all testified earnestly that they smoked only a given popular brand. Men who could hardly write their names swore they would use only a specified pen. According to Roy S. Durstine, who reported the incident in "Twelve Cylinder Critics," *Forum Magazine,* January, 1928, an agent appeared on Madison Avenue selling a list of names of people "unbelievably prominent in the world's corridor of fame," who would endorse nearly any product at five thousand dollars per testimonial. Motion picture stars did business wholesale, lending their names indiscriminately to fifty or sixty products, if that was all they could corral. One shampoo got the names and faces of forty film actresses into one advertisement.

[19] G. Lynn Sumner, *How I Learned the Secrets of Success in Advertising.* (New York: Prentice-Hall, Inc., 1952), p. 120.

When Charles A. Lindbergh made the first solo flight of the Atlantic Ocean, May 20, 1927, he testified to the excellence of the fountain pen he carried. A bank hastened to point out in an advertisement that he carried a draft on its Paris branch. The makers of steel used in building the "Spirit of St. Louis," the makers of the spark plugs used in its engines, and the refiners of oil explained how they had all contributed to the success of the flight. The War Department announced in its recruiting advertising that the Army had trained Lindbergh.

The appeal of testimonial advertising was universal. A man liked to think that he and General Grant wore the same shoes; a woman, that she and Mary Pickford used the same face powder. Little girls were thrilled to eat the same cereal that made Shirley Temple beautiful or Jane Withers famous. If a cowboy hero announced that he fed his horse on just one brand of oats, small boys clamored for it. Testimonial advertising provided association with the great and near great. People thrilled to the hero and heroine worship granted them by the testimonial advertising.

The truth of many of the testimonials was suspect. It was proved that some were false. It was common knowledge that the endorsements were bought and paid for. The Federal Trade Commission passed a ruling against the use of testimonials unless the advertisements containing them stated that a fee had been paid to the endorser whose name was used. The Better Business Bureau published a recommended code saying that testimonials should be honest, sincere, and reliable. None of this made much difference.

A London department store published letters by Bernard Shaw, H. G. Wells, and Arnold Bennett, together with pictures of the popular writers, saying that they could not and would not lend their names to product endorsements. The advertisements worked as well as if the novelist and playwright had testified with the same earnestness as Douglas Fairbanks or Ty Cobb. A mattress manufacturer used testimonials and photographs of Henry Ford, Guglielmo Marconi, Shaw, and others, presumably in praise of his products.

The letters actually were in favor, not of the mattress, but of sleep. A few years later, the world-famous Dionne Quintuplets, who earned about a half million dollars through endorsing a variety of products, advised people at some length to use only the same soap used on their sensitive skins, the one soap that was made with Gentle Olive Oil. The Quintuplets were two years old at the time.

Alarmed, the advertising trade press inveighed against "tainted testimonials," as *Printers' Ink* called them. A survey made by Batten, Barton, Durstine and Osborn discovered that testimonials lacking in good faith not only destroyed the effectiveness of the device, but also injured all advertising. Stanley Resor, president of the J. Walter Thompson Company, which resurrected the testimonial in the 1920's and used it extravagantly in the advertising of its soap, cosmetic, and lotion clients, defended the practice: "People like to read about other people. Sincere testimonials are a tonic for readers."[20]

Testimonial advertising was misused and abused before the 1920's ended, but the public did not seem to mind greatly. Identification with the great or the glamorous, preferably the glamorous, was reward enough; a little obvious falsity was not too much to pay. Tests showed testimonial advertising effective. People noted the advertisements more than those not embellished with the names and the pictures of the great and, presumably, bought the products they recommended. It was the advertisers who took fright, or perhaps the device just wore itself out. Its use fell away, but certainly did not disappear. The testimonial has been a tried and proven advertising success for too long, and is still a mainstay of radio and television advertising.

Not all the advertising of the 1920's was exaggerated, devious, or strident. Conservative advertisers, modest in their claims, but persistent, established items that have long since been staples of American life. Insurance companies, paper makers, steel corporations, food processors and packagers, appliance manufacturers, and others etched their names on

[20] Roy S. Durstine, *This Advertising Business* (New York: Charles Scribner's Sons, 1928), p. 61.

the public consciousness with quiet, consistent advertising. Even a product for which, as for cigarettes, cosmetics, and what are now called "proprietary medicines," advertising is perhaps the chief expense, took the quiet way of the constant reminder, repeated often and virtually everywhere, to achieve a market dominance that has seldom been matched.

In 1886, in Atlanta, Dr. John S. Pemberton concocted the original Coca-Cola syrup. For less than three hundred dollars he sold a one-third interest in the soft drink. By 1891 Asa Candler, a wholesale druggist, had acquired control and was developing the business which he sold in 1919 for $25 million.[21]

Twenty-five gallons of the Coca-Cola syrup were sold the first year. In the same year, $46 was spent for advertising. At the time there were just eight soda fountains in Georgia. One of the earliest Coca-Cola advertisements was an oilcloth streamer for pinning to drugstore awnings. It read simply, "Delicious and Refreshing." This, though the wording has been changed slightly, is the only claim the Coca-Cola Company has ever made—that its product is refreshing. It has been using "The Pause That Refreshes" since 1929.

The familiar red and white Coca-Cola signs, the familiar script in which the name is written are known everywhere in the United States and in many places around the world. The familiar Coca-Cola bottle is shown in the advertising which always shows the drink in the company of pleasant people; in the 1920's it was often in company with an attractive girl in white seated alone on a drugstore stool. The company's advertising has developed the conviction of the superior quality, taste, and the social acceptance of Coca-Cola. It is directed to everybody everywhere, for everybody is a potential Coca-Cola drinker. The advertising, two wars during which it traveled with American troops, the ubiquitous Coca-Cola signs, the distinctively shaped bottle, and the drink itself, have built the international "Coke" empire.

[21] H. B. Nicholson, "Host to Thirsty Main Street," Address before Newcomen Society of England, Christmas Honors Luncheon, New York, 1953; *Advertising Age*, April 2, 1956, report of address by Felix W. Coste, Washington, D. C.

Coca-Cola is sold from the Arctic to the Cape of Good Hope. It is popular in North and South America, Europe, Asia, Africa. People order it in French, Italian, German. "Coke" is the same word in any language or dialect. Stories are told of foreigners landing on American soil, seeing a familiar sign, and exclaiming with surprise and pleasure that "Coke" is sold in the United States too. To them it looks like home. The names of Schweppes, Guinness, and Bovril loom large on Piccadilly Circus hoardings. Just as large and just as natural is the Coca-Cola sign that stands with them. The Coca-Cola Company, a continuous advertiser throughout the 1920's, spends millions of dollars annually advertising in practically all media. This advertising maintains the happy situation in which, internationally, Coca-Cola is simply an omnipresent fact of human existence.

More in tune with the spirit of the 1920's, with the emotional extremes and the excitement, the extravagant testimonials, the miraculous tooth pastes, the sex appeal and the soaps, were the advertisements for one automobile that somehow managed to suggest all the sex, the romance, and the excitement of the decade.

As the man who assembled the car and wrote the advertisements credited with changing the whole direction of automobile advertising tells it, he was dancing one night at a Cleveland country club when a girl asked him why he did not build a swanky roadster "for the girl who loves to swim and paddle and shout . . . and for the boy who loves the roar of the cut-out."[22]

Edward S. Jordan leaped at the suggestion. A designer had allowed him to glimpse a car which Flo Ziegfeld had had built for Billie Burke. The custom car gave him the idea for the racy looking roadster with slanting windshield, crown fenders, vanity case, dashboard clock, the sporting lines and accessories, that became the Jordan "Playboy." Jordan had a chassis designed, got aluminum bodies from Buffalo, ordered precision parts, dressed the car up to its very boot and saddle bag, and was off. He had more than a new car. He had a

[22] Edward S. Jordan, *The Inside Story of Adam and Eve* (Utica, N. Y.: Howard Coggeshall, Inc., 1945), p. 12.

new way of selling cars—to women. He would sell his automobile not on the basis of its mechanical excellence, but on the promise of romance.

He broke the glorious excitement in *The Saturday Evening Post.* "We might as well tell it. The secret will soon be out. It's a wonderful companion for a wonderful girl and a wonderful boy. . . . A girl who loves to swim and paddle described it to a boy who loves the roar of the cut-out. So we built one just for the fun of doing it . . . stepped on it . . . and the dogs barked, and the chickens ran. . . ."[23]

Then came one of the most famous of all automobile advertisements. It appeared in *The Saturday Evening Post*, June 23, 1923. A Playboy (Jordan had named his car from Synge's *Playboy of the Western World*) sped along the top of the page, a girl at the wheel, mountains in the background. A cowboy on his pony galloped alongside, swinging his Stetson in the wind. The picture spelled speed, exhilaration, romance. The advertisement read:

Somewhere West of Laramie

SOMEWHERE WEST of Laramie there's a broncho-busting steer-roping girl who knows what I'm talking about. She can tell what a sassy pony, that's a cross between greased lightning and the place where it hits, can do with eleven hundred pounds of steel and action that's going high, wide and handsome.

The truth is—the Playboy was built for her. Built for the lass whose face is brown with the sun when the day is done of revel and romp and race.

She loves the cross of the wild and tame.

There's a savor of links about that car—of laughter and lilt and light—a hint of old loves—and saddle and quirt. It's a brawny thing—yet a graceful thing for the sweep o' the Avenue.

Step into the Playboy when the hour grows dull with things gone dead and stale.

Then start for the land of real living with the spirit of the lass who rides, lean and rangy, into the red horizon of a Wyoming twilight.

[23] *Ibid.,* p. 15.

This was "poetry," sentimental, rhetorical, illogical, and irresistibly flattering. You could not tell whether the Playboy rode on wheels or wings, whether it was made of metal or the substance of a Zane Grey idyll. Car and girl were identified, and both were desirable. Jordan sold two thousand Playboys his first year at a net profit of five hundred dollars on each car. That was just the first million dollars. No talk of horse-power, cylinders, speed, differentials, or miles per gallon, but "Heigh-ho for the open road! . . . and you'll greet the rising sun in El Dorado." There was more poetry for Jordan. "We *did* make a lot of money *awfully fast.*"[24]

In 1916 the Maxwell, over the protests of Buick, Cadillac, and Reo and with the disapproval of the entire automotive industry, had featured a "Pay As You Ride" slogan in its advertising and sold for a 50-per-cent down payment. Even the introduction of installment selling did not save the car. Walter P. Chrysler bought the slipping company and Theodore McManus brought it back temporarily to life with advertising that featured the car as the "good Maxwell."

In 1923, McManus took on a new campaign. *The Saturday Evening Post* of December 8, 1923, carried a column of type down the center of an unillustrated full page. It introduced someone named Walter P. Chrysler (a footnote explained that the name was pronounced as though spelled Cry-sler) as one of the commanding figures of the motor car industry and promised that a full account of his abilities and accomplishments would appear in the next week's *Post*. It did, and a full page advertisement in *The Saturday Evening Post*, December 29, 1923, announced the new Chrysler car available in four models—sedan, touring car, brougham, and roadster. The announcement was repeated the next week, then every two weeks until prices of the new cars were divulged in the *Post* for March 1, 1924.

The Chrysler advertising was a phenomenal success. The car-conscious 1920's responded avidly. The old Maxwell,

24 *Ibid.*, p. 50.

now the new Chrysler, reached twenty-seventh place in automobile sales in 1924 when Chrysler used twenty-seven pages
in the *Post*. Chrysler ran forty-eight pages in 1925 and
reached eighteenth place. He used seventy-six pages in 1926
and announced in March, 1927 that the Chrysler car was now
fourth in sales in the United States. A year later it was third.

No one was more surprised than Walter Chrysler. A rail-
roader and mechanic, he had disdained advertising and announced emphatically that he thought it an economic waste.
He was, he said, primarily a manufacturer and one who believed in building up a business through making such a product
at such a price that its sale would be insured. He discovered
that advertising enabled him to reach markets in a fraction of
the time it would have taken otherwise, and publicly re-
canted. The Chrysler, he declared, was an advertising as
well as an engineering achievement.

The efforts of Chrysler and even of Edward Jordan paled
besides those of a far greater advertising man. Chrysler was
well under way. Jordan, having skimmed the rich cream of
his market, was already beginning to liquidate the Playboy
when Henry Ford stole the show.

The Model T was done. The Ford plant had been closed
down for almost a year. Ford dealers had been left with
nothing to sell. A number of them had failed. It was possible that Henry Ford himself, now nearly 65, was through.
There was a rumor that the man who had stubbornly refused
to modernize his ungainly, high-wheeled, black automobile
was making a new car, but no one was certain until Ford
admitted it in May, 1927. He would say no more. He was
experimenting. If the experimenting was successful, if the
new car was right, the public would be told. Deliberately,
a wall of secrecy was erected about the operation.

Ford publicity, carefully engineered at every step, built
up the secrecy and suspense. Only a drop of news was
allowed to leak out from time to time, mostly as unverified
rumor. Newspapers reported that even the name of the new
car had not been decided upon. It might be the Linford, a

cross between the sleek Lincoln and the old tin Ford. It might be the Edison. Name plates were being secretly manufactured somewhere in Detroit or nearby or far from Detroit, but no one knew where.

August 2 the new car was announced as an actuality. Henry Ford, it was admitted, was testing it daily on roads near the Dearborn laboratory. Its speed was terrific, but even if you glimpsed the fabulous car, it would do you no good. Its working parts had been camouflaged under a Model T body. Then, the body removed, it was reported that the mystery car was being driven daily about Wayne County. The Ford Motor Company promptly announced that this was not yet the finished car. The spectacular new Ford was not yet perfected.

One newspaper published what purported to be a picture of the new car, snapped from behind a concealing barricade. All Ford would say was, "We've got something. We've got something good." His advertising men kept feeding the public tantalizing bits of information. Ford and his son Edsel were now taking the car out every day, subjecting it to strenuous tests over rutted roads, through sand, bouncing it along the ties over railroad rights of way. Ford announced again that he did not believe in paid advertising. He cared only about perfecting his new car. The publicity was peaked to a climax. Then, December 2, 1927, the mammoth newspaper advertising campaign planned by N. W. Ayer & Son was touched off.

The first advertisement of a four-day series run in two thousand newspapers at a cost of about $1,500,000, was a full page of text headed:

IMPORTANT FACTS ABOUT
The New Ford Car
Complete details of the new model will be available this FRIDAY in this city

Henry Ford signed the dignified and factual advertisement which said, in part:

> The new Ford has exceptional beauty of line and color. It is,
> in every respect, a new and modern car, designed and
> created to meet modern conditions. . . . The new Ford has
> unusual speed and power. It will do 55 and 60 miles an hour
> with ease and has run 65 miles an hour on road tests. . . . The
> new Ford car embodies the best results of experience in mak-
> ing 15,000,000 automobiles. We consider it our most im-
> portant contribution thus far to the progress of the motor
> industry, to the prosperity of the country, and to the daily
> welfare of millions of people.
>
>   Henry Ford

The second day's advertisement described the Model A.
Specifications of the car were released on the third day. On
the last day the first picture of the mystery car was published
and its price announced.

Simultaneously in every American city and in many cities
abroad the Model A was placed on public exhibition. Publicity and advertising had whipped public interest to a frenzy.
Hundreds gathered trying to peer through a Ford dealer's
windows in New York at three o'clock in the morning before
the day of the unveiling. By nine o'clock police reserves had
to be called out to control the pushing and pulling crowds.
Some 150,000 struggled that day to see the first car shown in
Detroit. In some places, schools and factories were closed so
that children and adults could descend on the Model A,
which newsboys hawked as if it were a war or national disaster. In England special trains carried avid enthusiasts to
London where a fee was charged for the viewing. Millions
saw the car the first day.

Celebrities strove to be the first to buy and drive a new
Ford. Ordinary people tried to do the same. The Ford
Motor Company was besieged with requests for preferential
delivery. Within a few weeks 800,000 Model A's had been
ordered. "Mr. Henry Ford," said the Springfield (Massachusetts) *Union*, "takes his place as the master showman of all
times." Editorially the Chicago *Post* described Henry Ford
as a dramatist. "No writer of plays ever succeeded more
completely in concealing the denouement, the great and
thrilling climax, than Mr. Ford has succeeded in keeping the

secret of his latest contribution to the traveling facilities of a hither-and-thither age."[25]

"Be Nonchalant—Light a Murad," halitosis, B.O., "Body by Fisher," and Somewhere West of Laramie; Pink Tooth Brush, athlete's foot, yapping testimonials, the blindfold test, the grave warnings, and the thrilling promises!—this was the 1920's, and this was advertising as the world spun faster than it had ever spun before, and the straw men marched stiffly through the days of their unmeaning, and the "It" girls danced, and hardly any money down, and life was so unbearably exciting everything was bound to end in magnificent calamity and promptly did.

[25] Quoted by George W. Cecil, "When Ford Introduced the Model A," *Advertising & Selling*, September, 1943, p. 46.

24

A New Medium—
The Debut of Radio

RADIO CAME IN 1920 as a miracle and a delight. It was not envisioned or planned as an advertising medium. Advertising happened to radio. It fastened itself to the miracle over the protests and expressed distrust of radio pioneers and the initial distrust of the advertising press.

Guglielmo Marconi first succeeded in transmitting a wireless message a short distance in London in 1896. In December, 1901, seated tensely in a room of an old barracks in St. Johns, Newfoundland, he heard, first faintly, then more clearly, the letter "S" broadcast across the Atlantic in Morse code from London. Over a Marconi high-power station erected on Cape Cod, Massachusetts, President Theodore Roosevelt broadcast a message to King Edward VII of England, January 19, 1903.[1] Those were the beginnings.

Experimentation continued. Enthusiastic amateurs sat before wireless receiving sets they had built themselves, straining to hear sounds hopefully broadcast by the visionary inventors. Wireless progressed to the point where it could transmit the human voice and sounds other than key signals. In 1913 Prince Albert of Monaco steaming toward New York on his yacht cheerfully broadcast music from a wireless piano while still 150 miles out, and the sound was picked up as far

[1] Frank A. Arnold, *Broadcast Advertising* (New York: John Wiley & Sons, Inc., 1933).

403

inland as the Great Lakes region.[2] In 1915 the Naval Radio
Station in Arlington, Virginia, sang out with "Hello, Hawaii,
How Are You?" and was heard in San Francisco and Hono-
lulu.

David Sarnoff is credited with proposing in 1916 a system
of radio broadcasting much as it came to exist. At the time
a young employee of the Marconi Wireless Company, he
wrote a memorandum to the officials of the company suggesting erection of a radiotelephone transmitter with a range
of from twenty-five to fifty miles and the manufacture and
sale of "radio music boxes," arranged for several wave lengths
which the listener could control by pushing a button or turning a switch. "The idea," he wrote, "is to bring music into
the house by wireless." Purchasers of the sets, Sarnoff pointed
out, could listen to concerts, lectures, and recitals. As an
afterthought, he added, "baseball scores could be trans-
mitted." Sarnoff estimated the selling price of the "radio
music box" at $75 and thought that sales of a million might
be expected in three years.[3]

This same year, Station 2ZK in New Rochelle, New York,
began to broadcast music an hour each day. November 2,
1920, Westinghouse KDKA began with a broadcast of the
Harding-Cox election returns and soon afterward began daily
broadcasts of varied entertainment at specified times. WJZ
in Newark broadcast its first program October 5, 1921. The
first broadcasting license was issued to WBZ in Springfield,
Massachusetts. The American Telephone and Telegraph
Company opened WEAF in New York, July 25, 1922 and
began broadcasts of the New York Philharmonic Orchestra
and of music direct from the stage of the Capitol Theater in
New York, William Rothafel (Roxy), its manager, exulting
"I nationalized the Capitol Theater in one day!"[4] WEAF

[2] Orrin E. Dunlap, Jr., *Radio in Advertising* (New York: Harper & Bros.,
1931), p. 15.

[3] Frank Folsom, "Adventures in Marketing," Address at Harvard Graduate School of Business Administration, October 23, 1947.

[4] William Peck Banning, *Commercial Broadcasting Pioneer* (Cambridge,
Mass.: Harvard University Press, 1946), p. 114.

broadcast the first act of *Wildflower*, a musical comedy. For weeks afterward the theater was sold out and sale of popular numbers from the show in both sheet music and on phonograph records shot up.

WEAF had been built by A.T.&T. with the idea of commercial operation. In July, 1922, it announced that it would rent time at a hundred dollars for ten minutes to business firms and organizations. The unfavorable reaction was immediate.

Dr. Lee De Forest, inventor of the three-element vacuum tube which made radio possible, was an early critic of what he heard as crude radio advertising. He said he had learned as early as 1919 that direct broadcast advertising did not always build good will. He said later,

I have consistently condemned the practice as perverse, pernicious, reflecting on the good name of radio, and distinctly retarding its development. The good will carefully built up by the entertainment part of the program could be swiftly turned to ill will by clumsy salesmanship. Such advertisers are not clever salesmen; they are stupid, uncouth "sandwich men" who have found this door of sudden entrance into the privacy of the home. . . .[5]

WEAF tried to avoid wrath like this by starting very carefully. It permitted only "indirect" advertising. There could be no sales pleas or product mention in the program itself. A firm could merely identify itself as the sponsor of a program. Despite this discretion, the advertising community was affronted. *Printers' Ink*, April 27, 1922, proclaimed: "Any attempt to make the radio an advertising medium . . . would, we think, prove positively offensive to great numbers of people. The family circle is not a public place, and advertising has no business intruding there unless it is invited." *Printers' Ink* had not changed its mind when, February 8, 1923, it talked about the A.T.&T.'s experiment with WEAF. It admitted the fine quality of the station's programs. It noted the company's insistence on subtle advertising announcement and its prohibition of bald sales claims, but said,

[5] Dunlap, *op. cit.*, pp. 2, 4.

"The plan is loaded with insidious dangers. . . . We are opposed to it on much the same grounds that we object to
'readers' or press agent dope or any other kind of disguised
publicity that inveigles people to read it on the ground that it
is news."

Radio Broadcast, July, 1922 demanded to know whether
the public wanted the ether used for such purposes. *Radio
Dealer*, July 22, 1922, urged its readers to write to their Con-
gressmen protesting the use of radio for advertising.

Instead, the public was listening, first with crystal sets
and headphones, then with battery-powered one-bulb sets.
Plug-in all-electric sets were being demanded and were on
their way. There were over two million radio sets in use in
1922, and people listened fascinated to entertainment, music,
drama, news, and sports in their own homes. WEAF's first
commercial broadcast was on August 28, 1922. It broadcast
the first football game, Princeton *v.* the University of Chicago,
from Stagg Field, Chicago, using long-distance telephone
lines, on October 2. The first Capitol Theater Overture
came November 19. In June, 1923, it broadcast a banquet
to British visitors to the Associated Advertising Clubs of the
World from the Hotel Pennsylvania in New York. It broadcast the heavyweight championship fight between Dempsey
and Firpo from Boyle's Thirty Acres in Jersey City, the 1923
World Series from Yankee Stadium and the Polo Grounds, and
on December 6, 1923, over six stations, President Coolidge's
message to Congress.

Radio had begun as entertainment, and the contention of
many was that it should continue as it had started. Various
schemes to pay for what had been freely broadcast but which
it was obvious could not be scattered gratis forever were proposed. Municipalities were urged to underwrite radio entertainment on a civic basis. A plan was put forward to tax
manufacturers, jobbers, and retailers of the swelling radio
industry. The proposal was made to tax receiving sets. One
scheme was to make each receiver a coin box on the model
of the quarter gas meter. WEAF, despite the protests and

the arguments, went serenely ahead with the idea and practice of commercial sponsorship, the station filling unsold time
with what later came to be called sustaining programs.

The first advertiser to buy and use time over WEAF was
the Queensboro Corporation, developer of Jackson Heights
in Long Island City. This was the first in a series of fifteen-
minute announcements by the corporation. Tidewater Oil
and the American Express Company bought time for similar
series. Gimbel Brothers, New York department store, was
the first firm to sponsor a program. It was sent over the air
from a studio built in the store, operated by WEAF tech-
nicians and talent, and open to public observation. Browning
King, Inc. became the first company to sponsor a WEAF
program designed for its exclusive presentation.[6] By December, 1922, WEAF had thirteen program sponsors. The Sunday talks of Dr. S. Parkes Cadman the station itself sponsored.
At Christmas it broadcast carols sung by two thousand employees of American Telephone & Telegraph.

The station maintained its rigid rules. No samples of
merchandise could be offered. Description of a can or
container, even naming its color for purposes of identification in a retail outlet, was forbidden. There were no
plugs, no "commercials," as the term came to be used. Such
a policy deterred many possible advertisers, but soon there
were the Ipana Troubadors, the Gold Dust Twins, the Silver-
town Cord Orchestra, the A. & P. Gypsies, and the Happiness
Boys. Advertisers named their programs after their product
or corporate name to establish their sponsorship and extract
what meager publicity they could from the programs for
which they paid.

Graham McNamee, a church singer who had played professional baseball and hockey, was hired in 1923 and became
the most famous announcer of the decade. Ernest Hare and
Billy Jones, the Happiness (Candy) Boys, began in December, 1923, as radio's first comedy team. The National Carbon
Company, one of the first manufacturers to pay for radio

[6] Banning, *op. cit.*, pp. 90, 107.

time, began with its Everready Hour in December, 1923. Its advertising agency claimed it presented the first drama on the air, the first stage show, the first sound effects, the first man-in-the-street program, the first book adaptation, the first paid "guest stars."[7]

The pattern of radio was being rapidly established—music, news, variety shows, comedy, sports. The radio became newspaper, magazine, theater, concert hall, vaudeville—and advertising. It was competition for every other advertising medium and every other form of entertainment.

"If a speech by the President is to be used as the meat in a sandwich of two patent medicine advertisements," warned Herbert Hoover, then Secretary of Commerce, "there will be no radio left."

Nobody paid much attention. The trick was to tune in KDKA, WEAF, WBZ, or General Electric's WGY, Schenectady, or any station you could get, the further away the beter. The thrill was in bringing in sound from a distance, in sitting in your own living room in Brooklyn and hearing a man in Hoboken, Chicago, or Cincinnati. Whether the man was playing a violin, giving the weather, singing, or selling soap made little difference. You heard, instantaneously, what another man or woman hundreds of miles, perhaps a thousand miles, away was saying and doing. It was the mystery and the marvel that fascinated. The contagion spread rapidly, from a few thousand enthusiasts to millions. The telephone lost its standing as a miracle; the phonograph was discarded. People breathed, ate, slept, and listened to the radio, often performing the first three functions perfunctorily so they could concentrate on the last, sitting up late at night to battle the static and the squeals and roars from the atmosphere, straining to hear fragments of distinguishable human sounds from the darkened ether.

Manufacturers raced into production to meet the demand for sets. Technical advance was rapid as they competed for the rich market. Programming kept pace. In an incredibly

[7] *New York Herald Tribune*, April 29, 1957, p. 8.

short time the public knew, intimately in their own homes, glamorous figures of the great world, musicians, actors, politicians, announcers who became family friends, and hordes of vaudevillians who, driven from the stage by the motion pictures, descended hungrily on the new medium. John Philip Sousa, Jessica Dragonette, Graham McNamee, Harry Lauder, Dr. Cadman, Eddie Cantor—the list was long and swelling, and to it was added, as soon as he got out of Yale, the golden name of Rudy Vallee, who brought crooning, his saxophone, Joe College, and male sex appeal to radio when he was paid by Herbert's jewelry store in New York for his first broadcast. Vallee had to pay his first handful of Connecticut Yankees out of the eighty dollars he received. With all of this came advertising, more and more of it. Advertising was firmly established as part of the whole before the first elation of uncritical public acceptance of radio had ended.

Understandably worried, the American Newspaper Publishers Association, meeting in convention in 1925, warned solemnly: "Broadcast advertising, if it becomes more specific in nature, is likely to create a reaction on listeners which will be unfavorable, rather than a help to the advertiser. Radio fans are beginning to resent the dissemination of the lower forms of radio advertising through the ether lanes."[8] The Association declared that results from radio advertising were intangible, that listeners would turn off what they did not like, that radio advertising was far too expensive to warrant the expenditure. The newspaper publishers were too late.

The discretion observed in radio advertising by WEAF was soon abrogated by many stations and by many advertisers. As transported by the possibilities of the new medium as the public was by the entertainment it offered, advertisers were eager to experiment. The appeal of the human voice, tested for centuries by barkers and pitchmen, opened manifold advertising possibilities. Undeterred by experience, by criticism which had led to reforms in outdoor advertising and in print media, radio advertising quickly went to extremes.

[8] Banning, *op. cit.*, p. 260.

Advertising now could get deep into the privacy of the home. Carried by programs of diversified appeal, it could reach men, women, particularly women, and even children, who could be made brand-conscious as soon as they could understand speech. Advertising agency men and the advertising executives of manufacturing companies could mingle with musical comedy stars, prima donnas, celebrated comedians, in excited planning and exciting productions. There was novelty and glamor about it all, and there was a fanatically devoted audience to be reached for unimaginable profit.

The Radio Corporation of America purchased WEAF in 1926 and established the National Broadcasting Company. Columbia Phonograph opened the Columbia Network in September, 1927, with a broadcast performance of "The King's Henchmen," a narrative poem by Edna St. Vincent Millay, for which Deems Taylor wrote the operatic score. There were seven million radio sets in operation now, and American industry spent more than $4 million for radio time in 1927.[9]

The pattern and structure of the broadcasting industry were becoming established, and with them the nature of radio advertising. A new means of public communication, as important as print and more immediate, as the spoken word is more direct than the printed symbol, had sprung into being. Its exploitation posed myriad difficulties and problems but lured with infinite promise. Programs had to be matched with products, sponsors identified by as many means of sound as could be devised, units of time sale fixed, kinds of sales appeals decided upon. The indirect advertising approach was quickly discarded by most sponsors, and the blatantly direct embraced with frenzied abandon.

Most radio advertising became, as it has remained, insistent, demanding, and unsparing. Listeners were exhorted, wheedled, threatened, deafened, and numbed by repetition. It was true that the listener could switch off the commercials,

[9] *The Sound of Your Life* (New York: Columbia Broadcasting System, Inc., 1950).

but it was unlikely he would. Advertising men knew what the man or woman listening avidly to a soap opera, a baseball game, a symphony, a murder mystery, or whatever his taste dictated, would endure. Product names were spoken or sung in voices chosen for their rich inflection and hypnotic effect. They spoke stern command or coaxed seductively, and they did it again and again and again and again. The theory was established that it did no harm to annoy. Annoyance worked as well as charm, perhaps better, in piercing inattention and stamping product names and claims deep into the creases of the brain. Advertisers spent $10½ million in the attempt in 1928.[10]

Two classes of advertisers began to dominate early in radio. Radio became the mass appeal medium for products of low price and frequent purchase: cigarettes, cosmetics, tooth pastes, canned foods, cereals, mouth washes, soft drinks, and patent medicines. These articles were purchased by people of all kinds and purchased throughout the year. The public needed nuisance reminders of the existence and virtues of each brand, and the regular pattern of radio matched this advertising need for repeated, familiar messages. Manufacturers of these products became the characteristic radio advertisers, using strident appeals, urgent messages, brassy theme songs, and later inane ditties. The object of the advertiser was to make the product name as familiar to the child as the Lone Ranger and Tonto, as familiar to the adult as Moran and Mack—"The Two Black Crows"—or the voice of the instructor calling out the setting-up exercises every morning from the tower of the Metropolitan Life Insurance Building.

The other class of radio advertisers sponsoring network programs were the large manufacturers of durable goods, from automobiles to major and minor household appliances. Theirs were usually programs of substantial and dignified content, and their advertising was kept more modest and restrained in tune and temper with the entertainment.

[10] *Ibid.*, p. 11.

Radio covered the Presidential election of 1928, and the public heard the voices of Al Smith and Herbert Hoover. Ted Husing, the sports announcer, described the arrival of the Graf Zeppelin over New York. Bing Crosby crooned his way in. A little later came the rapid-fire, brassy omniscience of Walter Winchell and the insinuating voice, both waspish, wheezy, and caressing, of Alexander Woollcott as "The Town Crier." People—and millions more were tacking up aerials and proudly installing receivers and loudspeakers in their living rooms—took them and their tooth pastes and all the rest into their families.

Without complaint, the public accepted certain conventions imposed by the new medium. The news came by courtesy of cigars, sports events by way of razor blades or beer, mystery and comedy with foodstuffs, the higher culture through network sponsorship or that of some heavy industry, cowboys with cereal, crooning with salad dressing and cheese, dance music from almost anybody. Blandly, the public countenanced surprising shifts and agreed to identify with cream whip the clown, singer, or hero of vaudeville which last week it had identified with cigarettes, watches, or nail polish. It reviewed with calm the defection of sponsors and performers' facile transfer of loyalty and persuasive sincerity from automobiles to ice creams.

The public took radio in stride at a time when everyone was hurrying. People accepted with complete equanimity the pushing back of the walls of their homes to world horizons and, without protest enough to bar their way, the clamoring push of salesmen for products of all kinds into their living rooms and boudoirs. Instead of reading advertising if and when they pleased in magazines and newspapers, on car card or billboards, they knew its din from "Cheerio" in the morning to the last adult bedtime story at night. They tolerated, if they did not enjoy, the enforced intrusion as inevitable, seeing it as the price they had to pay for heady pleasures. By 1930 more than half the homes in the United States had radios. There were fifteen million radio homes for 27,980,000 American families. Advertisers spent $40 million that year for broadcast time alone, and probably as much more for talent, in a medium which had not existed just ten years before.

When program and talent costs were added to the time charges, radio advertising was expensive. Advertisers wanted proof that their expenditures were justified. Rating systems had to be devised to find out which programs were listened to most, which least, which most earnestly and faithfully, and which were neglected or ignored. The assumption that program ratings were correlated with commercial effectiveness, led to the rise and fall of stars, some waning almost as they waxed, a Jack Benny, a Kate Smith, an Eddie Cantor, later a Charlie McCarthy waxing perennially. Some shows were dropped while others which proved their popularity went up for competitive bidding. Commercials were tested by give-away offers which brought in the sacks of mail for which programs, stars, advertising agencies, and advertisers hungered. There was much at stake. Radio audiences were measured in the multi-millions where other media reach hundreds of thousands or at best a mere handful of millions. The competition of radio led to more and more intensive research and promotion by publication media, to defensive research, and to hard promotions by the networks in selling time. The advent of radio in the 1920's stimulated all advertising activity.

It did more than that. As radio greatly enriched human life, it added time to space in advertising. It gave advertising the human voice and the emotional appeal of drama, both fictional drama and the drama of the passing scene. It took advertising where advertisers had always striven to get it, directly into the home. Radio infiltrated defenses once virtually impregnable. All this was a gain of fundamental importance. There was more, and this was the essential difference. For the first time advertising had a medium which it controlled. In newspapers and magazines, editorial matter was distinct from advertising. The better publications observed strict lines of division between editorial content and advertising, jealously guarding the editorial integrity which gave the magazines and newspapers their individual distinctness and their repute. In radio, the advertiser selected and often, through his advertising agency, the station, a programming bureau, or the work of his own staff, concocted the editorial background for his advertising. As radio advertising progressed, the effort was to make foreground and background one, to fuse entertainment and advertising into one unit of sales impact, using announcer or entertainer as salesmen as well as lure.

"What have you done with my child?" Dr. Lee De Forest asked the National Association of Broadcasters unhappily in 1946; ". . . you have sent him out on the street in rags of ragtime, tatters of jive and boogie-woogie to collect money from all and sundry for hubba hubba and audio-jitterbug. You have made of him a laughing stock of intelligence, surely a stench in the nostrils of the gods of the ionosphere. . . ."[11]

Advertising did more than fasten itself to radio over strong early protest. It took practical control of a new and flexible instrument for mass exploitation, and in the years between 1920 and 1930 made it a major advertising medium of stature it had taken other media centuries to develop. Its later decline and transformation were almost as rapid.

Unhindered by competition in kind, radio burgeoned in the 1930's and through World War II. Radio saturated the public consciousness. It crackled with the reporting of disasters, with kings' renouncing thrones to marry commoners, with the explosiveness of wars, piqued with gossip, convulsed with the wit of wooden dummies, lulled with contented hours. Radio was big-time, big names in industry, big network programs, big budgets, and big stars. It developed personalities as well known and made them as affluent as those of what, during the same period, was fabulous Hollywood. Singers, news commentators, comedians, band leaders,

[11] Quoted in "The Revolt Against Radio," *Fortune,* March, 1947.

public figures, and assorted entertainers held the national spotlight every night before audiences of many millions.

Bing Crosby was first cheese, then a make of radio. Bob Hope was tooth paste. For years Fibber McGee and Molly were a brand of wax. Burns and Allen were coffee; so were Edgar Bergen and Charlie McCarthy. Ed Wynn was gasoline; so was Lowell Thomas. Jack Benny was a gelatine dessert. Fred Allen, Boake Carter, "Amos 'n Andy," Bob Burns, Edwin C. Hill, "Henry Aldrich," Walter Winchell, Arthur Godfrey, Lanny Ross—the names were many, the money was much, and the number of advertised products was more. Some programs remained with one product for years. The Lone Ranger, Tonto, and Hi-Yo, Silver! rode always for cereal. "One Man's Family," which began in April, 1932, and is still on the air, though shifted from an evening to an afternoon hour in 1957, was at various times cooking oil, tobacco, foods, yeast, and a medicinal preparation.

Radio soared for about twenty years, reaching its peak as an entertainment and advertising medium in the years immediately following the close of World War II. It was struck hard by television by 1948. Stars, programs, personalities, and even operating personnel deserted to television. Radio lost nearly 70 per cent of its evening audience to the spectacular new medium. Annual network advertising volume fell from $210.6 million in 1948 to $71.2 million in 1956.[12] If not dead, radio as a major medium seemed at least moribund. Yet total expenditures in radio held up, peaking at $624.1 million in 1952, falling only to $570.7 million in 1956.[13] Monetary inflation accounted for some of this, as in all postwar advertising figures, but the increasing use of spot and local radio was actually responsible for total radio's survival, then resurgence.

Instead of dying, radio transformed itself in the 1950's. It could not compete with television for the giant shows, costly dramas, and gaudy spectaculars. It could not recapture

---

[12] *Printers' Ink*, "Advertising Guide to Marketing for 1958."
[13] *Ibid.*

the vast and vastly enraptured evening audience, glued now to their television screens, or the big, free-spending national advertisers. It turned instead to more modest programs and to many small advertisers. Radio began to feature what had been its filler material, using news and music as its staples and seeking sectional and local rather than national advertisers.

Disc jockeys spin their patter and their platters around the clock on the newer radio. The listener has his choice of jive, rock 'n roll, jazz, progressive jazz, dixieland, boogie-woogie, pop, semi-pop, pop-pop-pop, classical, modern, and not as modern as all that, almost any time of day or night almost anywhere on his radio dial. News and weather come in more detail and at more frequent intervals, all with fat interlardings of more and more frequent commercials. The short news program once sponsored by a single large industrial advertiser has grown to have a half dozen or more smaller sponsors, stores, automobile dealers, local services, and the manufacturers or purveyors of low-cost, fast-turnover merchandise.

Radio sold itself to these more numerous smaller advertisers as the natural mass medium for reaching women with daytime soap operas to which they could listen as they went about their household chores, for reaching teen-agers with their dependable crazes for novelty rhythms and fads in music, and for reaching consumers in the remaining non-television homes. The manufacture of small transistor radios and the increasing use of car radio aided in the resurgence of radio entertainment and advertising. The very high cost of television time and production aided by driving a few large advertisers back into less expensive radio network programs.

25

The Combined Assault
on Advertising
in the 1930's

THE STOCK MARKET crashed October 29, 1929. With unbelievable suddenness the flamboyant activity, attitudes, and
temper of a decade crashed with it. The feverish speculation,
the reckless abandon, the cynicism, sophistication, and the
eager gullibility flashed into smoking ruin as panic gripped
the country. The financial debacle was followed by unnum-
bered personal tragedies as fortunes and modest homes alike
were swept away. Hysteria drove out reason. Banks closed,
businesses failed. Markets collapsed as buying power vanished. Industry faltered, then ground almost to a halt. Unemployment, hardship, and hunger settled in coldly for a
long stay.

Advertising was toppled from the peak of $3,426,000,000
which it reached that year. Advertisers tumbled over each
other to cancel their schedules. Some, their factories already
closed, had nothing to sell. Others saw no one to sell their
products to. Many, seized by the contagious and palsying
fear that was paralyzing business, wanted only to block the
escape of more money. Advertising expenditures dropped
almost a billion dollars in a year's time, falling to $2,607,000,000
in 1930, dropping nearly another billion to $1,627,000,000 in
1932, and reaching their lowest point, $1,302,000,000 in 1933.

Advertising recovery was very slow. Not until after World War II did advertising regain, in 1946, its approximate level of seventeen years before.

Not only did advertising suffer precipitous decline during the depression, but it also suffered sharp and sustained attack. Business and industry, it was felt, had failed the country. Angry and frightened, people loudly accused them and the banks for having ruined them. Somehow, something or everything had treacherously reneged on the golden promises of millennium for everyone tomorrow, or, at latest, by noon the day after. Instead, people were jobless and scrambling desperately for relief, even for sign of alleviation of the undeserved horrors they were enduring. Public figures competed with each other in promising the quick return of prosperity, but only fresh disasters and a new weight of hopelessness came. There had to be a villain. Advertising as the public voice of industry and business was obvious and accessible to attack. Advertising had been used to urge people to expenditures they could not afford, to lure with false promises, to lull into false security. Advertising was to blame, and shrill cries arose for its annihiliation.

This was a very different attack from that made on advertising earlier in the century. Then, false and misleading advertising had been assailed. Corruption in advertising had been uncovered, and reform measures had been instituted. This time the entire economic system of which advertising was seen as vociferous, raucous, and treacherous part, was under attack. Competitive enterprise which used advertising for its own purposes was the root disease, but advertising was a virulent symptom which had to be cut and pruned away before the basic malignancy could be treated.

The attack on advertising came from two quarters, from articulate customers organized into self-constituted vigilance committees and from government. The object of the attack was not to reform advertising but to discredit it entirely, to force it out of existence or render it impotent through government control.

The consumer movement seems to have had its beginning in 1916 with the formation of a National Consumers' League, an organization which issued white lists of manufacturers whose labor programs its founders approved and whose products were therefore worthy of purchase. The movement got a new and sharper start with the publication in 1927 of *Your Money's Worth* by Stuart Chase and F. J. Schlink. This was an onslaught on advertising, accused of falsity and deceit, and on all the super-salesmanship of the lush period. Chase and Schlink, as defenders of the helpless consumer against the machinations of competitive business, formed the Consumers' Club, an organization to protect the innocent buyer against the wily seller. In 1929 the Consumers' Club became Consumers' Research, Inc., with F. J. Schlink as president and headquarters in Washington, New Jersey. The group were social planners of politically socialist tendencies whose strategy was to attack, bitterly and sometimes hysterically, everything they disapproved of. At the time, this meant almost everything in sight.

In 1932 Schlink and Arthur Kallet, secretary of Consumers' Research, published *100,000,000 Guinea Pigs*. The book, which became a best seller, was an attack on all advertising, in particular an exposé of food and drug advertising. The public, avidly seeking a scapegoat for all its troubles and confusion, was shocked and pleased by the revelations of adulteration, misrepresentation, and quackery. The fierceness of the attack and the hatred of advertising manifested by the authors was exciting. Facts went unquestioned. The book did not intimate, nor did the public recognize, that many of the cases cited were old and outdated, and that few were typical of the practice of national advertisers of repute. It was a listing of lurid crimes in tabloid style, with indignation paraded and castigation loudly administered.

So successful and profitable was *100,000,000 Guinea Pigs* that the formula was quickly repeated by members of the Consumers' Research group and imitated by others anxious to capitalize upon a popular trend. In 1934 came *Skin Deep* by

M. C. Phillips (Mrs. F. J. Schlink); in 1935, *Eat, Drink and Be Wary* by F. J. Schlink; in 1935 *Partners in Plunder* by J. B. Matthews, a vice president of Consumers' Research, and R. E. Shallcross.

There were truths and partial truths in all these books. There were also distortions. The fanaticism and malevolence were as apparent as their ballyhooed sympathy for the mal-treated consumer. General Motors, Henry Ford, the du Pont interests, various public utilities, Coca-Cola, the cos-metic, canned food, and drug industries virtually *in toto*, were speared, tormented, and despatched.[1]

In the midst of its evangelical ministry, its shrill denuncia-tion of the profit system, and its advocating of some more ideal political and economic arrangement, Consumers' Re-search was stricken by internal dissension. When three of them were discharged and officials of Consumers' Research refused to recognize a union of office workers, employees of the organization went on strike. The strike was noisy and bitter. The complaint was made that while some of the workers received less than fifteen dollars weekly, Mr. and Mrs. Schlink received eleven thousand dollars a year from what was widely advertised as a nonprofit, product-testing organ-ization. The organization's officers, who had been loud in their pro-labor claims, refused to arbitrate with the workers and demanded and got police protection from their fellow idealists. The disaffected employees thereupon withdrew from Consumers' Research and formed their own competing organization in New York. With Colston E. Warne, an

---

[1] The same methods, motives, and even the same incriminating case his-tories appeared in a flood of such books which appeared as book publishers hastened to try for a share in the profitable sales. The revelations, rancor, and bitterness were sure-sale material in the depression years. They were sensational books, often with sensational titles. Arthur Kallet produced *Counterfeit* in 1935, a compilation of exposés of advertised articles from Consumers' Research publications. Ruth de Forest Lamb brought out *American Chambers of Horrors*, an account of death-and-destruction deal-ing foods and drugs, in 1936. James Rorty dedicated *Our Master's Voice* in 1934 to Thorstein Veblen ". . . whose 'conscientious withdrawal of efficiency' may yet accomplish the burial of the ad man's pseudo-culture, which this book contemplates with equanimity."

Amherst College economist, as president, the Consumers' Union of the United States was formed in 1936. Immediately it took a full page advertisement in the *New Republic* to state its case and its purposes.

Originally formed to attempt a fair settlement of the strike at Consumers' Research, the Association turned its attention to a new organization when it became clear that there was no hope of bringing about its original purposes through appeal to the directors of Consumers' Research. . . . The strike emphasized the need for a pro-labor consumer organization, functioning on a broad social base, democratically controlled, and serving especially the worker, the low-salaried employee, and the housewife.

The inconsistency of using advertising to state its case was not apparent to the promoters and founders of the new organization. In fact, both Consumers' Research and Consumers' Union have vigorously promoted their activities since the inception of the movement. Complaining at first that standard advertising media were closed to them, they depended largely on direct mail advertising and on advertising and promotion in their own bulletins.

Consumers' Research issued bulletins giving the results of tests made on advertised products to determine whether or not they lived up to advertising claims. It also issued an Annual Cumulative Bulletin to subscribers. Product information was disseminated only on the subscriber's pledge to keep the data confidential. Statements signed by F. J. Schlink as "President and Technical Director" during the 1930's emphasized the nonprofit aspects of the work, and repeatedly asserted the complete integrity of the organization. Subscribers were urged to send in newspaper and magazine clippings, circulars, labels, catalogues, anything which might lead to the uncovering of more and more lurid advertising evils.

"Recommended," "Intermediate," and "Not Recommended" were the labels affixed to products by Consumers' Research after they had been tested. All these opinions, it announced in its advertising matter, were impartial, authoritative, and expert. The organization's intent was only to guide

the consumer through the jungles of glibly presented conflicting claims, the flattery, sex appeal, and exaggeration purveyed by advertisers. Consumers' Research was against all
lies and half truths—hardly an assailable position.

In *Introduction to Consumer's Research* issued from Washington, New Jersey, F. J. Schlink urged subscribers to send
in the names of those who could be approached with a Consumers' Research sales talk and, if they signed the confidential
pledge, enrolled as subscribers. There was something of the
enticement of a secret society about the whole. Subscription
forms with "Please pass these blanks along to a friend"
printed on them were supplied in profusion. All income,
the officials stated, came from the sale of the Bulletin, special
bulletins, books, and reprints, but, Schlink suggested, "a few
subscribers voluntarily contribute additional sums of from
one dollar to twenty-five dollars a year."

Consumers' Research pushed its services for gifts at Christmas or on other occasions, just as the strictly commercial
magazines do, and, again like the commercial press, began to
offer a *Consumers' Digest with Teacher's Manual and Study
Outline*. The *Digest* was advertised as a "popularly priced,
popularly written magazine," composed of releases from the
United States Bureau of Standards, Federal Trade Commission reports, and papers by college and university research
workers rewritten by the experts of Consumers' Research.
Consumers' Research was itself a shrill advertiser.

Its offshoot and bitter rival, Consumers' Union, promoted
itself with equal vigor and self-confidence as "A Nonprofit
Testing Organization for Consumers," urging itself on the
public as its subscribers' Bureau of Standards. Like the parent organization, it broke down the results of its product
testing into three classes, but called them "Best Buy," "Also
Acceptable," "Not Acceptable." It began to issue the *Consumers' Union Buying Guide*, describing it as "a far better
guide to intelligent purchasing than any other ordinarily
available to the consumer . . . it gives the consumer the satisfaction of having his buying choices determined by technical

tests rather than by the cleverness of an advertising copy-writer, or the ingenuity of a manufacturer in making a shoddy product look like a good one."

Both the depression-born testing agencies operated on the assumption that all advertising was fraudulent, charged with deliberate intent to cheat the impaled consumer-victim. Companion assumption of the self-appointed critics was that they alone were capable of discriminating between the good and the bad. They stood in resplendent altruism as champions of the weak and ignorant, and almost in awe of the social service which their own critical intelligence was performing in protecting the uncritical masses from maltreatment by manufacturers and advertisers. Convinced of its David-Goliath mission, Consumers' Union pushed its wares with the same sales devices used by its arch-rival parent, boasting of the number of its subscribing families, of the number who received its services as gift subscriptions from discerning friends, urging subscriptions in one appeal in the 1930's as an "easy, inexpensive way of wishing their best friends a Merry Christmas and twelve months of intelligent help with their buying problems."

At a time when the forerunners of the later supermarkets were being set up in warehouses to get food cheaply to people without the costs of retailing display and service, when George Washington Hill had resurrected Bull Durham with, "Roll Your Own and Save Your Roll. Now 5 Cents," the testing agencies and their reports found a ready hearing. Most people knew a desperate need for economy. They wanted to feel that they had been cheated and bilked into their misfortunes. They needed satisfaction for basic physical wants and not, just then, the psychological satisfactions purveyed by the advertisers of the 1920's. The various consumer reports appealed actually not so much to labor and the general public as to the academic intellectuals already, and with good reason, offended by the extravagant claims, bad taste, and basic vulgarity of much of national advertising. It was not so much that reason had been offended as that sen-

sibilities had been insulted. Teachers—not, generally, of
economics, though some of the critics had pretentions to
economic training—read and approved the bulletins, passed
the critical attitudes and the information on to students.
Cynicism about advertising became popular.

The other basic attack on advertising was much more
formidable and had more lasting effects.

Advertising, in the view of its honest and articulate critics
in the 1930's, was extravagant and wasteful. It did not increase the consumption of any product but simply divided
the market among many brands. It added to the cost of the
article advertised, and the cost was paid by the long-suffering
consumer. Advertising was wasteful as well as vulgar and
confusing. A hundred shoe manufacturers competed to shoe
the public, where one manufacturer might, conceivably and
economically, supply all the shoes needed, freeing thousands
of people for other useful work. True, advertising supported
the means of public communication, but many of the newspapers, magazines, and radio programs were not worth supporting. Instead of being a social good, as its proponents
claimed, advertising, as these critics saw it, was an unmitigated
social and economic evil.

Among those who shared these opinions were men whom
Franklin D. Roosevelt called to Washington and placed in
positions of public power when he became President in 1933.
These men, drawn mostly from the academic world, formed
the so-called "Brain Trust," which rose to prominence in the
early days of the New Deal when the adminstration was
turning every effort toward national economic recovery.

Roosevelt sought the aid of advertising early. June 15,
1933 he wrote the president of the Advertising Federation of
America: ". . . I wish you would say that I hope the high
standards which have made good advertising an economic
and social force of vital importance to us all will be continued. Your cooperation will be valuable to the restoration
of improved levels and flow of trade. It will also help business and industry return to better times. By doing these

things you will be serving your country and your government."

When the National Recovery Administration was placed
in motion later in the year, General Hugh S. Johnson, appointed by Roosevelt to head the vociferously publicized
movement, which it was hoped would restore order out of
economic and social chaos, wrote this letter to leading manufacturers and advertisers throughout the United States.

Sept. 29, 1933

Aggressively promote your products to the public.

There is no longer any reasonable doubt that the public is
beginning to shop again and to look toward replacements for
its worn-out possessions.

American industry must help the public find the goods it
needs.

The modern method is advertising. The American public
looks to advertising for news of good merchandise and good
values.

There has never been a time when the public was so alert
for news as now. Events have moved so rapidly that people
would be completely ignorant of what is going on if they
did not closely follow the press.

This tremendous public interest in news can be capitalized
by American industry. And the way to do it is to place the
news about a good value or a good product side by side with
other news of the world.

There can be little doubt that these letters were suggested
and probably prepared for their impressive signatures by interested advertising men. They bear the earmarks of propaganda, but they became official when they were signed and
published. They spoke government approval of advertising,
but governments have seldom found consistency a required
virtue. The Brain Trust had other plans for advertising.

The group included outspoken proponents of a planned,
government-controlled economy in opposition to the competitive system of free industrial enterprise, which they were
convinced was an outmoded system whose collapse had
brought economic ruin to the country. Rexford Guy Tugwell, a Columbia University economist, who had been ap-

pointed an Assistant Secretary of Agriculture, was an avowed and vocal advocate of planned economy and an enemy of what he saw as the culpable inefficiencies of the competitive system. His announced sympathies and those of his fellows were for the laboring man who, they promised, would thrive when released from the thralldom imposed on him by capitalistic corporations and placed under the guidance, instruction, and control of the state. In *Our Economic Society and Its Problems,* Tugwell, with Howard Copeland Hill, had pilloried advertising as a social waste and quoted Stuart Chase in support of his views. Tugwell had described advertising as too often only an aspect of the entire profit-seeking system which he decried, and ridiculed the waste and extravagance of advertising which merely attempted to turn sales from one company to that of another making a product identical in value.

June 12, 1933 Senator Royal S. Copeland of New York, a physician who had been a public health official, introduced in Congress Bill S.1944. Written largely by Tugwell, it was "A BILL to prevent the manufacture, shipment, and sale of adulterated or misbranded food, drugs, and cosmetics, and to regulate traffic therein; to prevent the false advertisement of food, drugs, and cosmetics, and for other purposes."

The Tugwell Bill called for compulsory grade labeling. It required drastic permit control of all canning plants and the use of a U.S. label legend upon payment of fees. Section 9a of the bill defined false advertising. It read: "An advertisement of a food, drug, or cosmetic shall be deemed to be false if in any particular it is untrue, or by ambiguity or inference creates a misleading impression regarding such food, drug, or cosmetic." The bill proposed to substitute government grade labeling, at the expense of the packer, for advertised brands. This was to be applied to foods, then to drugs and cosmetics. All authority for enforcement of the provisions of the bill was to be vested in the Secretary of Agriculture. At the time this was Henry Wallace. Severe penalties were provided for violations.

The packers and canners immediately protested certain provisions of the Tugwell Bill, though it was generally agreed that some new legislation was necessary to extend the power of the original Wiley Law which had gone into effect in January, 1907, and the McNary-Mapes Amendment of 1930, which had provided for a minimum standard for canned food and use of a special label on products which did not conform to this standard. The other industries involved also protested the extreme measures and the extent of government control outlined in the proposal.

The advertising community was more deeply alarmed. They saw in the Tugwell Bill an attempt at far-reaching control of advertising by a man who had made no secret of his desire to see advertising fettered if it could not be abolished. Tugwell, they believed, was trying for dictatorial powers in a move which would place all food, drug, and cosmetic advertising under the absolute power of the Secretary of Agriculture. Advertisers and the advertising media were particularly concerned that the phrase "an advertisement . . . shall be deemed to be false if *in any particular* it is untrue . . ." was open to wide interpretation by any court. Any advertisement could be misread or have read into it ideas and impressions which no advertiser had intended. The wording of the proposed bill seemed to be purposefully vague in order to hamper or injure advertising by leaving it open to fair or unfair attack.

Others besides advertising men saw the threat and protested. Governor Alfred E. Smith, who was, of course, a political opponent of Roosevelt at the time—and there were political aspects to the question—said:

The Tugwell Bill . . . goes a long way beyond simply amending and putting teeth in present laws. The author himself has stated . . . that what he aims at in his bill is not just reform but a revolution in the whole theory governing this field. He regards advertising as largely waste, and he thinks that Government should take a hand in limiting costs to the ultimate consumer by cutting out the advertising middle man. He also believes that Government control of industry will inevitably take the place of mere regulation, that the Government is competent to exercise such control. . . .

Advertising men made it clear in various hearings conducted on the bill that they were fighting not merely an advertising restriction but a socialistic theory which struck at the foundations of the traditional American economy. It was obvious that government control of industry, as Tugwell visualized it, would mean the end of advertising as an activity. This time advertising was fighting for its very existence against the idea of the planned economy, the welfare state.

Tugwell advocated price control and the limitations of profits as a part of social planning. He believed, it was evident to advertising men, in using whatever legal methods could be devised or stretched to suit his ultimate ends. In *The Industrial Discipline* and other writings he had said he considered three things necessary to a sound economy: higher prices to raw material producers, higher wages to labor, lower prices to consumers. He had described advertising as all "more or less an attempt to escape the necessity of honest market expansion through decreased prices. . . . It is doubtful whether nine-tenths of our sales effort and expense serves any good social purpose."

In Senate hearings, spokesmen for the advertisers and media contended that manufacturers of canned goods had created, through their advertising, great markets for food in cans. Before this time people had considered canned foods poisonous. The advertisers had convinced the public of their wholesomeness, created large markets for farm products, and contributed to social good. If advertising of canned goods were curtailed or abolished, markets would decline, growers as well as canners suffer, publishers of advertising media be deprived of income needed to support vehicles of public communication, and the general public would suffer in the end.

"There is no popular demand," a magazine publisher's representative said in Senate hearings on the Bill, "to curb the great advertisers. . . . Their brand names are household words." Food advertising had "got the cat out of the cracker barrel." It had converted the public from "insanitary" bulk foods to packaged foods. Advertising had not always been impeccable, but its standards had improved. It could be credited with producing exceptional factories and some of the finest kitchens in the world. "No person is compelled to buy advertised products. The great American public of its own free will and accord gladly and enthusiastically buys advertised products because advertised products give excellent values at reasonable prices."

One form of advertising had already been killed by government action. Public sentiment during the depression was almost violent against banking and finance. Hurried through both houses of Congress and signed into law by Roosevelt, May 27, 1933, the Securities Act made financial men directly responsible for claims made in advertising statements. It imposed drastic liabilities on directors and officers of companies issuing or underwriting securities. The law operated to make financial advertising practically nonexistent—and to stop the flow of badly needed capital into industries as companies feared floating new issues under the law. The Securities Act was not a temporary measure but a permanent law. What little financial advertising could continue became and has remained a matter of announcements only, and these bore such self-defeating safeguards as: "This announcement is not an offer to sell or a solicitation to buy these securities." "This advertisement appears as a matter of record only." It had happened to finance. It could happen to any business enterprise, or to all business.

The fight was really not between food advertisers and a proposed restriction. It was, as the combatants knew, a fight between a form of government and an economy in which advertising was possible and the planned economy of a socialistic state in which it could not exist. Advertising won an important victory when the Tugwell Bill was defeated on the Senate floor May 16, 1934. A much modified Copeland Bill, known as the Federal Food, Drug and Cosmetic Act, and satisfactory to business and advertising, was passed in 1938. Royal S. Copeland died a week before Franklin D. Roosevelt signed the bill into law.

Advertising did not demolish the threat and, later, the
actuality of the welfare state, which came into being during
the 1930's. It did something to keep it within the control of
a democratic form of government which retained competitive industry, advertising's principal client.

It was ironic that while the New Deal was utilizing advertising to the full to promote its confusion of recovery programs and administrations, other government forces were
scheming valiantly for its abolition. It was also ironic that
idealists and ideologists, with great publicity, fought and bled
in Washington, D. C., Washington, N. J., and New York,
N. Y., for the consumer, who did not want particularly to
be bled for. It seemed that the self-described "consumer
leaders," the Tugwell economists in the Brain Trust, and their
fellows were really not as concerned about the abused consumer as they were about the planned Utopia of a govern-
ment-charted economy which, automatically, they would
direct.

The combined forces gained some of their ends. Labor,
though the coming war helped more than their agitation, got
more money. More government restrictions were placed on
business. An intrenched bureaucracy, self-perpetuating, was
firmly established. The consumer, who seldom wins, did not
get the promised lower prices. The consumer leaders produced, advertised, and successfully sold publications which
satisfactorily disseminated their ideas. The members of the
Brain Trust maintained themselves in positions of influence
and some prestige for a time. They failed to supplant competitive private enterprise with state control.

Assuming that the patent absurdities of advertising were
not patent at all, the delighted critics of advertising, intoxicated with their new discovery of age-old sins and silliness,
blind to possible virtues, pleased a large part of the public
which, in those depression-starved years, was badly in need
of solace. Advertising, as by nature it always is, was brazenly
out in front where it could be seen and shot at. It made an
easy and popular target. It would make a wonderful sacrifice

to the demon of the depression. The critics shouted it down with loud shouts. Possibly because advertising, both the impulse to its creation and use and the impulse to hear and sometimes heed it, is too deeply imbedded in human nature, they did it little harm.

26

Advertising's Counter-Attack

THE ATTACKS ON advertising in the 1930's had two direct results. One was the placing of further restrictions on advertising excesses and the arming of police bodies. The other was the formulation of advertising's defenses.

The Federal Trade Commission had been set up in 1915 to enforce prohibitions of unfair methods of competition in interstate commerce. The powers of the FTC were broadened by the Wheeler-Lee Amendment of 1938, which prohibited dissemination of any false or misleading advertising. The other federal bodies with power to regulate advertising to some extent are the Food and Drug Administrations, the Federal Communications Commission, the Securities and Exchange Commission, the Alcohol and Tobacco Tax Division of the Internal Revenue Service, and the United States Post Office, which can exclude obscene matter and the advertisements of lotteries and fraudulent schemes from the mails.

Most powerful and most zealous of them all is the Federal Trade Commission. The worst case histories from their files were used as lurid exhibits by authors of the sensational anti-advertising books of the 1930's. Current proceedings are always given wide press coverage. Court judgments resulting from suits brought by the FTC have been used often to condemn, sometimes to support, advertising effort.

After Ipana had been using them for nearly fifteen years, the FTC ordered the company to stop running its "pink toothbrush" advertisements in which the tooth paste was held up as protecting the gums from the dangers of a soft-food diet. It allowed Ipana to continue with its "Smile of Beauty" slogan, regarding this as a legitimate advertising claim. An investigation of the advertising of the American Tobacco Company brought out the fact that 50 out of 440 people who claimed to smoke Lucky Strike cigarettes exclusively did not smoke at all. American was enjoined from claiming that Lucky Strikes were less irritating to the nose and throat than other cigarettes and that they were preferred, two-to-one, by independent tobacco experts. It was allowed to continue with "It's Toasted," as the claim was considered an accurate description of part of the cigarette manufacturing process.[1]

The FTC in earlier findings against the makers of Camels and of Old Gold cigarettes had decided there was no significant difference in the amounts of nicotine, acids, and throat irritants in any of the leading cigarette brands. Old Golds had claimed, on the basis of laboratory findings reported in an article in *The Reader's Digest*, July, 1944, that it contained less irritating substances. The same tests had showed that there was no considerable difference and that the difference in effect on the smoker was negligible. The judge hearing the case decided: "An examination of the advertisements . . . shows a perversion of the meaning of the *Reader's Digest* article . . . a perversion which results in the use of the truth in such a way as to cause the reader to believe the exact opposite of what was intended by the writer of the article."[2]

The largest and most persistent offenders in advertising have usually been the manufacturers of cigarettes, dentifrices, headache remedies, and other patent medicines—products which cost little to make and which must be continually advertised to sell competitively. They are, generally, the largest advertisers, in the sense that they spend a larger amount of money as a percentage of sales than the manufacturers of other products, considering advertising as a major production expense rather than simply a part of distribution.

[1] *New York Times*, June 29, 1951.
[2] Quoted by Max Geller, *Advertising at the Crossroads* (New York: The Ronald Press Co., 1952), p. 161.

At one time and another most of the widely advertised dentifrices, including Squibb's, Forhan's, Colgate's, Kolynos, Dr. Lyon's, Calox, and others, have been subject to FTC scrutiny for some of their advertising claims. Proceedings have been instituted against many of the companies and, usually, cease-and-desist orders have resulted. The makers and advertisers of many nationally advertised laxatives, headache, overweight, and cold remedies, of cures for baldness and gray hair, of antiseptics and vitamin preparations, have come in for the same unfavorable attention, usually with the same restrictive results.

The other class of large advertisers are the manufacturers of heavy durables which must be moved quickly from production lines to consumers before planned obsolescence sets in. Usually more conservative in their advertising claims, they still come under sharp FTC scrutiny on occasion. In the case of the Ford Motor Company v. Federal Trade Commission in 1941, the Circuit Court stated the case for advertising succinctly, but also generalized on part of the case against it. "Advertising goes hand in hand with volume of production and retail distribution. It operates to increase the demand for and availability of goods and to develop quickly consumers' acceptance of the manufactured products. Expressed another way, it breaks down consumers' resistance, and develops consumers' demand." The Court added, however, in specific reference to the complaint, "The average individual does not make, and often is incapable of making, minute calculations to determine the cost of property purchased on the deferred payment plan. Mechanization, industrialization, and urbanization . . . have . . . raised to the proportions of a major social problem, the protection of the installment purchaser against his own ignorance and the pressure of his need."[3]

In another case, the Court, in giving its opinion elaborated on this theme. "The law is not made for the protection of experts, but for the public—that vast multitude which includes the ignorant, the unthinking and the credulous, who

[3] *Ibid.*, pp. 6, 9.

in making purchases do not stop to analyze, but are governed by appearance and general impressions."[4]

Not all FTC investigations result in suits against advertisers. The great majority do not. Most advertising, even in the eyes of this inquisitive body, is respectable and responsible. In the year from June, 1941, to June, 1942, the FTC examined 362,827 printed advertisements. Of this number they found 18,221 which, when strict standards were applied, contained what appeared to be false or misleading representations. During the same period, the FTC found 17,925 offending advertisements among 1,000,450 radio continuities.[5]

Unfortunately, some advertisers, though it was not the eventuality planned or wished for, make FTC rulings, or the fear of FTC citation, the maximum of their morality. Others, very practically, consult the FTC in advance, much as the fearful citizen checks some of the deductions claimed on his income tax return with the inquisitorial Internal Revenue office before filing his statement. The liquor industry presented what the FTC itself described as a well-prepared and dignified series of advertisements, but the Commission frowned on the central theme of the campaign which was that liquor eases nervous tension and contributes to the drinker's feeling of well-being.[6]

As with most other human activities, it is the abuses, not the legitimate use, of advertising which are most widely publicized and lead to cries for more reform. There is a continual pressure, usually on moral grounds, to prohibit the advertising of tobacco and liquor. Some media refuse to accept one or the other or both.[7] Opponents of all advertising have proposed both the raising of postal rates to discourage publication advertising and the placing of heavy federal taxes on advertis-

[4] *Ibid.*, p. 162.
[5] Blake Clark, *The Advertising Smoke Screen* (New York: Harper & Bros., 1944), p. 18.
[6] *New York Times*, May 8, 1957.
[7] *The Saturday Evening Post* will not accept liquor advertising, though it began to accept cigarette advertising in 1930. *The Reader's Digest* will not publish liquor, tobacco, or medical remedy advertisements in its domestic edition.

ing. This taxation would be not for revenue but for punitive purposes. Actually it would diminish government revenue by shrinking the tremendous sums which government obtains through taxing the profits of businesses and the incomes of individuals, both of which depend largely on advertising.

Some adverse critics of advertising, like Stuart Chase in the 1930's, point out that many people employed in advertising might better be released for more useful employment, the criterion of usefulness depending, of course, on the prejudices of the critic. In 1949, a professor of philosophy warned that advertising halted the psychological growth of people by making them do too much wanting, especially too much wanting of things for the wrong reasons.[8]

Who is to decide which are the right and which the wrong things to want the writer did not say. The assumption that desire itself is evil has not always been accepted as philosophical truth. Advertising has few dispassionate critics. The very language they employ indicates how deeply their tastes and emotions are involved. In *The American Mind* (1950), Henry Steele Commager wrote that popular advertisements portrayed American society as "a nightmare of fear and jealousy, gossip and slander, envy and ambition." He complained that nothing was sacred to the advertiser, neither love nor marriage, religion, health, nor cleanliness; that friendship was for sale, that advancement was to be gained through deception, bribery, and blackmail. Though it is easily understandable, more of angry disgust than of judgment colors such pronouncements.

Another popular historian, though he gave advertising full credit for its social and some of its economic accomplishments, found the American citizen of the 1930's "constantly being inveigled into ill-advised expenditures, when not actually being gulled by misrepresentations. . . ."[9] Almost twenty years later, Bernard De Voto called the advertising agency

[8] Harry A. Overstreet, *The Mature Mind* (New York: W. W. Norton & Co., Inc., 1949).

[9] Arthur M. Schlesinger, *Rise of the City* (New York: The Macmillan Co., 1933), p. 198.

the principal cause of academic distrust of business. A self-confident popularizer of many subjects and a brash critic of more, De Voto admitted that advertising was aimed at mass markets, not at intellectuals, but complained that academicians who met advertising in their daily lives were affronted by fake laboratories, witch doctors, shamans and their magic.[10] Much criticism of this kind is superficial and obvious. It is obvious, too, that the critics have looked at only a small part of advertising and that the most garish and indefensible, which conscientiously screams its own offensiveness.

Certain other historians, some economists, and various literate observers of American society have likewise discovered flaws in advertising, its appeals, and its effects, but found in it also basic economic and social values which have become the standard defenses of advertising. They have been widely accepted as both a philosophic *raison d'etre* of advertising and as a practical demonstration of its worth to business and society.

The economic argument generally goes back to Adam Smith, who said in *Inquiry into the Nature and Causes of the Wealth of Nations* in 1776: "Consumption is the sole end and purpose of all production." F. W. Taussig pointed out early in the twentieth century that the productive process is not complete until goods come to market, until people see them and buy them. The quickest, easiest, and most economical way to get large quantities of goods and products to large markets is through advertising. When, as in the United States, industry is geared to mass production, it must have mass consumption to support it. Unless the great quantities of merchandise produced by manufacturing can be sold and sold quickly and profitably, mass production cannot be sustained. Employment, hence purchasing power, depends on this uninterrupted sequence of actions. Mass production and mass consumption are thus interdependent, and mass consumption, in our economy, could not exist without advertising,

[10] Bernard De Voto, "Why Professors are Suspicious of Business," *Fortune*, April, 1951.

438   THE STORY OF ADVERTISING

which stimulates purchase and sometimes actually creates markets.

Probably the best, as it is the best known and most often quoted, statement of this argument was made by Professor Neil H. Borden of Harvard in *The Economic Effects of Advertising*. Borden said:

> Advertising's outstanding contribution to consumer welfare comes from its part in promoting a dynamic, expanding economy. Advertising's chief task from a social viewpoint is that of encouraging the development of new products. It offers a means whereby the enterpriser may hope to build a profitable demand for new and differentiated merchandise which will justify investment. . . . In a dynamic economy . . . advertising . . . is an integral part of a business system in which entrepreneurs are constantly striving to find new products and new product differentiations which consumers will want.[11]

In a democratic society, where freedom of choice is the prerogative of the consumer, advertising is a means of mass communication which operates through persuasion to purchase what is produced. It is the only means of what advertising men have long liked to call "consumer education." It educates the consumer as to what is available for purchase, where, and at what price. At the same time it educates to appreciation of the material things that make for the well-advertised "American standard of living." The tutelage is never impartial. An advertiser is spending his money, considerable sums of it, to persuade the consumer to buy *his* car or tooth paste, refrigerator or cigarette, not that of a competitor, at least to obtain a share of the market in his product line. Yet it is education, and brand-biased as it may be, its effect is to arouse desire, stimulate purchase, provoke ambitions to buy, own, and enjoy.

The result is the consumption which makes quantity production possible. Whether the consumer should be so stimulated through fear, envy, avarice, greed, ambition, and the other emotions through which advertisers channel their appeals, whether desire is better or worse than the nirvana that

[11] Neil Borden, *The Economic Effects of Advertising* (Chicago: Richard D. Irwin, Inc., 1942), p. 881.

Mc Callum Silk

Y O U   J U S T   K N O W   S H E   W E A R S   T H E M

Intimate yet modestly discreet were both illustration and sentiment in the
McCallum advertising slogan of the 1920's: "You Just Know She Wears Them."

The girl in the moon is a blonde. Hoyden sex or beauty but seductively idealized and "honi soit qui . . ." in this hosiery advertisement of 1926.

comes with desire's extinction, even where the balance between the two extremes should be set, is beyond the ability of
most historians or economists, poets or philosophers to determine. Only the self-appointed critic unhampered by the
discipline of any study can be certain.

The social good that advertising accomplishes was admitted by Schlesinger in *The Rise of the City*, acknowledged
by Frederick Lewis Allen, who called mass advertising "one
of the great incentive makers" and a form of "journalistic
mass education," which he considered a purely twentieth-
century phenomenon.[12] Advertising's proponents have many
times listed and emphasized these social gains. They have
been well summed up by an English writer.

> Whatever the motive and whatever the means, it is probably true
> that commercial advertisers have done more than all the doctors, the
> scientists, the schools, and the social workers to make cleanliness
> "popular," and to impose the sanctions of social disapproval on those
> who are careless in this respect. . . . The same is true of hygiene in
> the home . . . disinfectants and insecticides, household soap, cleaners
> and polishers, toilet tissue, vacuum cleaners, mangles and wringers.
> In the use of all these and many other articles the commercial adver-
> tiser can claim to have been the most effective educator of the
> average housewife. . . . The voice of the housewife is not often, if
> ever, heard in support of the academic critics who condemn modern
> advertising.[13]

Bishop's was a modest list. Advertising brought people
quickly to acceptance and use of mechanical refrigeration, to
purchase first of radio then of television receivers, to eating
oranges, then learning to drink them as juice, to home insulation, to synthetic fibers, to airplane travel. By making mass
production possible, it brought these and other products and
services down in price to where they are within the means
of the average person. Without mass production and mass
distribution, the automobile would still be the envied possession of the wealthy, a toy, and a toy lacking the refinements

---

[12] *The Big Change* (New York: Harper & Bros., 1952), p. 223.
[13] F. B. Bishop, *The Ethics of Advertising* (London: Robert Hale, Ltd.,
1949), pp. 139-40; quoted by Geller, *op. cit.*, pp. 6-7.

of engineering and styling made possible through the markets built to absorb the products of the assembly line. Instead of raising prices to the consumer, as academic critics have long insisted, advertising, through its ability to tap a mass market, has actually lowered prices. It was estimated in 1949 that one automobile built for one person would cost fifty thousand dollars. As inflation has progressively debased United States currency, it would cost much more today. The advertising of an automobile adds about as much to its retail price as the extra cost of white-walled tires. One canner long placed the advertising charge against a can of its nationally known soup at .017 of a cent.

Advertising as a percentage of sales runs from a high of about 16.5 per cent for cosmetics and beauty aids to less than .05 per cent for insurance, according to a 1956 study sponsored by *Advertising Age* and the University of Illinois. For all but three of fifty-five product classifications studied, the expenditure was under 10 per cent. Such advertising does add to the cost of a product, but, again through making mass manufacture possible, adds little or nothing to the price paid by the consumer, who would pay a higher price for comparable nonadvertised products made in smaller quantity.

The costs of distribution—selling, including advertising, packaging, transport, warehouse, retailing—continue to mount. They have long been a subject of worried discussion, and competition has forced manufacturers and distributors to various efforts to contain them. It is often assumed that production costs are legitimate but distribution costs unjustifiable. In defense, some economists point out the unreason of this and urge that there is a value added by distribution, just as there is a value added by manufacture. The availability of products in a broad national market is a service to the consumer. A product out of reach might as well be out of existence. Advertising is one of the means by which what is made in a factory hundreds or thousands of miles away can be purchased where and when a man or woman wishes. The product is of uniform quality and of generally identical price in Texas and Maine, and, through advertising, it often carries an added quality of prestige which, in itself, is an emotional satisfaction.

Possibly, as some of the opponents of advertising noticed earlier insist, it is wrong for people to feel these satisfactions. Possibly they feel them for what can be argued are the wrong reasons. Undoubtedly the utilitarian value of many prestige articles is no greater and is sometimes less than that of comparable unadvertised products, yet the satisfaction is a reality to the small boy glorying in possession of a certain make of baseball or baseball glove, the man fly-casting with the approved rod, the woman wearing a glamorously advertised lipstick, the family driving a car cushioned deep in snob value.

By profession, advertising men are articulate and charmingly to culpably persuasive. By temperament some of the academic critics of advertising are at least equally loquacious, and often their voices are shrill with indignation. They have some reason on their side. Offensive, wasteful, and injurious advertising does exist. Yet the suspicion is unavoidable that many of those who set out to expose and correct the sins of advertising are really trying to expunge a large part of general and rather obstinate human failings. These have been susceptible of attack but proved inimical to cure for, conservatively, several thousand years. It might be pleasant if dualism could be abolished but, however defined and in whatever categories of human experience, good and evil have been in conflict for a long time. The best that either side has been able to accomplish seems to be an enduring stalemate.

27

Advertising as a Weapon in World War II

ADVERTISING THROVE DURING World War II. Advertisers had the money to splurge and they splurged. Print media managed to overcome shortages of paper. Radio had all the time there is. Advertising soared to new heights of the sublimely ridiculous, as many eager advertisers strove to capitalize on the drama and excitement of world conflict for sales purposes. It also attained new strength and prestige as a powerful instrument of government propaganda.

There was little tendency this time for advertisers to abolish or diminish their efforts for the duration. This was a larger and was probably going to be a longer war than that of 1914–18. No automobiles were being made. There were no tires for sale. Food and gasoline were rationed. So was clothing. Manufacturers of typewriters were making machine gun parts instead. Most plants, big or little, had contracts for war materiel of some kind. Some companies had little to sell the public; others had nothing. It was completely a sellers' market. People had money they burned to spend, but goods were not available for them to buy.

Despite all this, despite shortages and scarcities, advertisers who had learned the shortness of the public memory during the depression knew the necessity of keeping their brand names prominently displayed even when their branded products could not be bought. Some day the war would be over.

They wanted to retain their markets and be in a position to fight for the expanded markets expected when the war was over. Besides, much of the advertising cost little. The Treasury Department allowed a reasonable amount of advertising as a legitimate business expense and business was busy. If a company was in the excess profits bracket, the money not spent in advertising simply went to the government anyway. Such firms could advertise at a cost of about fifteen cents on the dollar.

The direction a company's advertising could take was dictated largely by its wartime situation. Some could advertise business as usual for sales as usual. Manufacturers of cosmetics and beauty aids, of some prepared and canned foods, of tobacco, and of items comparatively unaffected by the war could proceed with their normal advertising appeals. Others, the entire automotive industry, the manufacturers of farm implements, appliances and other consumer durables, their greatly expanded plant capacities entirely devoted to the manufacture of military equipment or supplies, could not. In many cases, their advertising became largely institutional, prestige and reminder advertising. Some could, with honesty and permissible pride, point admiringly to their contributions to the war effort. Many advertisers, with or without justifiable excuse, sang peans of praise for their efforts toward winning the war. Some gave the impression that they were doing it all by themselves.

Manufacturers of bolts and nuts used full magazine pages depicting bombers and fighter planes in action to show what their nuts and bolts were doing. Soft drink manufacturers ran copy which read as though the fighting troops owed all their energy and courage to drinking their beverages. Manufacturers of ball bearings, metal fasteners, wire rope, shoes, all advertised that they were comforting service men or building both battle front and home front morale. One manufacturer of air-conditioning equipment proclaimed that he had helped sink torpedoed Japanese ships because the periscope lens of American submarines had been ground and polished in an air-conditioned shop.[1] The straining for wartime tie-ins by some advertisers was marked and ludicrous. Some gave it up and admitted only that their products, lipstick, tooth paste, vitamin preparations, candy, or cola did good to everybody's morale everywhere all the time.

Boastful advertising of this kind aroused resentment and ridicule both among civilians and servicemen during the war. Men in the army and navy overseas complained when they were sent special editions of the magazines with the advertising omitted. The advertisements, they said, told them more of home than the editorial contents. They wanted to know what people at home were buying, using, and wearing, what was going on. They were bitter when they did see some of the advertising. They found advertisers' picturing of the glamor and excitement of war ridiculous and salesmanship's depicting of military scenes and personnel usually wrong and always tiresome. They did not want to be told that the peacetime manufacturer of a hearing aid or jackscrew was winning the war. The servicemen thought they had something to do with it. They were annoyed with promises of new and shinier products in the postwar world. The war was not over for them. Regular product advertising they rather liked. It looked and sounded like the world they had left and wanted to get back to. They objected to the lofty explanations of why they were fighting in some institutional advertisements and to all the attempts to twist copy for products only tenuously connected with the fight into tie-ins with the military.[2]

One advertisement was headed, "Who's Afraid of the Big Focke-Wulf?" All the bomber pilots at one combat field in ETO signed it, "*I am,*" and sent the clipped magazine page back to the manufacturer.[3]

The advertising which servicemen most approved was that run in behalf of the war effort. Almost all this advertising—

[1] Cited by Raymond Rubicam in "Advertising," in *While You Were Gone,* ed. Jack Goodman (New York: Simon and Schuster, Inc., 1946), pp. 421-46.
[2] "Servicemen's Views on Advertising," *Tide,* November 15, December 1, December 15, 1944.
[3] Rubicam, *op. cit.*

and, though it did not dominate in magazine and newspaper space or in radio time, it was the most conspicuous feature of advertising during World War II—resulted from the work of the War Advertising Council.

All advertising in Germany was under government direction and control. On Adolf Hitler's accession to power in Germany, advertising had been placed under the jurisdiction of the Reich Minister of Propaganda. Advertising was seen as a form of propaganda and therefore a government matter. A council set up within the ministry said in September, 1933: "All propaganda depends for its effect on the credence given it. All advertising must be true." It was also ordered to be dignified and moral. Goebbels had used advertising propaganda successfully, helping to establish the Third Reich through reiterated slogans, such as "A New Germany Rises from the Ashes of the Past."[4]

Britain, as it had done in World War I, bought and paid for advertising in support of the Empire's war effort. Newspaper, magazine, and poster advertising were used extensively by the War Office, the Air Ministry, the Ministry of Agriculture, and a score of other ministries including Fuel and Power, Home Security, Labour, Production, and Information. Advertising was used in recruiting and in everything from gathering binoculars for Admiralty use, to urging women to enlist in the Women's Land Army and warning that "Careless Talk Costs Lives" or suggesting, "Be like Dad, Keep Mum." Private business continued advertising in the war-shortened newspapers and magazines to keep brand names and trademarks alive, but government was by far the largest advertiser in all media.

The United States, following the same policy it had adopted in World War I, used little paid advertising. Though the Army did some recruiting in paid advertising space through N. W. Ayer & Son, Inc. and ran a large campaign for WAC through Young & Rubicam, the government said and seemed to feel that it could depend on Rooseveltian persuasion in print and in radio fireside chats to sway the

4 *Printers' Ink*, September 21, 1933.

thoughts and ideas of the population and direct civilian activities into designated wartime efforts. The publicity mills of the various government bureaus could take care of the rest.

This opinion was not shared by the War Advertising Council. An Advertising Council had been formed to serve as spokesman for advertising in defense against its attackers. The body had not got into operation when the United States entered the war in December, 1941. Quickly the group, which was composed of representatives of advertisers, the advertising agencies, and the advertising media, went into action to place the facilities and force of advertising at the disposal of the government. It began immediate cooperation with the Office of Facts and Figures, precursor of the Office of War Information. It obtained the approval of the War Production Board. Its services were quickly accepted by the Treasury. Immediately it proposed that business undertake to do what officialdom had refused, bring realization of the war and the urgency of the need for action home to the American people through advertising. Its proposal read:

> Advertising can make people
> realize what Total War means

It can *convince* the entire nation that there must be no bystanders in this war.

It can convince the country that every business and every family has a job to do.

It can paint the ghastly results of what will happen to America if we lose this war.

It can make people accept the terrific sacrifices that are coming, because it can make them understand why these sacrifices must be.

It can put zeal and fire needed to wage this war successfully into the heart of almost every American soldier, every American worker, every American business man, every American man, woman, and child.

It can make clear that in total war the fighters are not only those in the armed forces, those in our industrial plants, but all the members of every family—in EVERY HOME.

And that not until every home is ORGANIZED will the United States be fully organized for total war.

It can tell the story simply, clearly, and get the job done quickly.[5]

[5] "A Plan for business to use one of its principal tools to help win the war." (New York: The Advertising Council, n.d.).

The remainder of the pamphlet rang with enthusiasm and energy. It was an advertising call to arms. It stressed the urgency of the situation. It explained why industry should do the job, assured businessmen that government would welcome industry's help, pointing out that dozens of national advertisers were already donating their services in the promotion of the sale of war bonds, the salvage campaign, and the U.S.O. It warned that there would have to be an over-all plan to coordinate "Total Advertising" effort and presented one.

The Advertising Council

War Information Plan

This Plan Proposes:

1. That the Advertising Council shall supply facts to industry concerning basic themes the Government wishes publicized.
2. That each major industry, or a combination of industries, shall then decide which theme they prefer to promote and publicize—provided this theme has not already been adequately covered.
3. That each industry, or a combination of industries, shall then provide advertising facilities adequate to promote this theme properly.
4. That the Advertising Council, cooperating with the industry committees, shall plan, clear, and secure approval of such advertising from the government.

The Advertising Council was soon the War Advertising Council, and in essence, it operated according to the plan it initially proposed. It operated forcefully, and it operated successfully.

The War Advertising Council planned and engineered nation-wide campaigns in all media in support of war bond sales, manpower and womanpower recruitment, conservation of rubber, paper, rope, fuel, and other scarce products and materials. It recruited for WAVES, WACS, Cadet Nurses and for the Army Medical Department. It worked for Red Cross, the security of war information, the achievement of farm production goals, for homes for war workers, the use of V-mail, for forest fire prevention. It argued for proper civilian nutrition and against venereal disease. Government had but to mention a wish and advertising was for it.

In the first year of World War II, the War Advertising Council got and used a hundred times as much free advertising as was donated during all of World War I. By September, 1942, the Treasury Department alone estimated it had received free publicity that would have cost $65 million if purchased. An estimated expenditure of $11 million by advertisers, agencies, and media brought in sales of $18 billion in the second war loan drive. By mid-1943 the War Advertising Council saw an estimated $1 billion contributed in radio time and talent, and an equal amount in paid advertising in newspapers and magazines. Some 450 advertising agencies had contributed perhaps $4 million worth of time and skill. Nearly one-half of all outdoor advertising was devoted to support of government-approved war themes. By 1944 the Council had helped develop more than ninety war-theme campaigns.

Government now was enthusiastic in its praise of advertising. Its spokesmen vied with each other in effusive compliments. The President, the Secretary of the Treasury, the Secretary of Commerce, and the Price Administrator all argued the vital necessity of advertising in the United States and lauded its patriotism. The politically ambitious governor of New York insisted that he liked advertising. The Attorney General complained aggrievedly that he was in favor of advertising and always had been, but that it was hard to make some people believe him. The president of General Electric called advertising a responsibility of business citizenship. The director of the Bureau of Foreign and Domestic Commerce called for more brand-name, good-will advertising, and the Department of Commerce built and exhibited a display of public service advertisements of which it approved most. Advertising, which had so lately smarted under sharp criticism and quailed before government attack, basked in the sunlight and solace of having its good works recognized.

It was not all praise. President Harry S. Truman, late in the war, pointed out that the government was really paying for some of the donated advertising. "The cost of advertising . . . has been charged by the advertisers on their books as an expense before profits, thus reducing the amount of profit on which federal income taxes are payable. This means that much of the advertising is indirectly paid for by the government, and to the extent that government has obtained value from the war campaigns, it is entirely proper that it should pay the expense."[6]

Organized labor, reveling in its New Deal, wartime powers, was loyally derisive of advertising. It had found no good in management before, and could see none now in this display of management's patriotic advertising. The money business spent in advertising should have gone into the U. S. Treasury. Shame, labor cried. Sabotage! Its characteristically unpleasant complaints went unheard in the chorus of praise, most of it well deserved, that the work of the War Advertising Council evoked, and in the profusion and effectiveness of the war theme advertising.

Not all advertisers responded willingly to the appeals of the Council. It had to work for the cooperation of advertisers as well as work out the organization and implementation of the advertising. It issued a steady series of brochures urging advertisers to fight and keep up the fight. In one, "They've Taken Away the Sandbags," it said, "Institutional sob-sistering, industrial bragging and fatuous fol-de-rol about a postwar world are things we can do without." Advertising was urged to further efforts to justify its usefulness and integrity as a profession. The Council asked for, and many times obtained, industry-wide promotions for campaigns it sponsored.

A thousand magazines ran war bond pictures or feature material on their covers as a drive started. Entire editions of newspapers had every advertisement in them devoted to pushing war bond sales. War bonds were advertised by advertisers in space for which they paid or by newspapers and magazines in space they donated or on radio time donated by

---

[6] Quoted in "Review of Ad Status Under War Conditions," *Advertising Age*, September 4, 1950.

the networks or stations. Even wrappers on diapers were used to promote war bond sales. Advertisements prepared by McCann-Erickson and paid for by the American Iron and Steel Institute worked for the salvage of scrap metals. Kenyon & Eckhardt ran campaigns for the savings of fats and grease for the glycerine-producing industries who paid the advertising costs. Newell-Emmett did posters and pamphlets for the Army, Navy, and FBI, warning that "Loose Talk Costs Lives." Young & Rubicam hammered away for war bonds. Other advertising agencies did as much, lending their men and talents to the war effort.

At one period of the war WAVE recruit quotas were not being met. The Navy appealed to the War Advertising Council. The Council used research to find out why girls enlisted and why they did not. Advertising was based on the results of this research. Sample advertisements with pre-researched appeals were then sent to four thousand advertisers. The appeals appeared everywhere. WAVE enlistments doubled. The Public Health Service could not get enough volunteer cadet nurses. A Council task force went to work, devised advertising, broadcast copy for advertisers' use and the quota of sixty-five thousand cadet nurses was more than reached. Efforts of the War Advertising Council resulted in helping establish twenty million gardens, which the U.S. Department of Agriculture reported produced eight million tons of food.

The Council was asked to help combat inflation. Twelve advertising agencies turned out 72 full-page advertisements, then picked the twelve best. These were sponsored by 492 magazines with a total circulation of 91 million. Life insurance companies took the lead in the anti-inflation campaign. The Council produced a symbol familiar during the war, a hand thrusting prices down and the slogan: "Help US Keep Prices Down."

The Council responded to an Army appeal to get ten times as many women to enlist in the Women's Army Corps. It worked with the Army to heighten morale in the Army Medical Department and to get soldiers to take care of their equipment—"Take care of your equipment and your equipment will take care of you."[7]

Advertisers sometimes gave all their space or time to supporting wartime causes and campaigns or divided the advertisement between product or institutional advertising and the war effort. The magazines not only gave space, but the Magazine Publishers of America also used donated space themselves for such wartime messages as "Use it up . . . Wear it out. . . . Make it do . . . or do without!", a slogan devised by the Council, or "See that prices go no higher. . . . Be a saver—not a Buyer!" The newspapers printed daily and radio spoke hourly reminders of the war. What advertising did was help make the civilian population of the United States inescapably conscious of the actualities of war which, unlike the people of other embattled countries, they could not see, hear, and fortunately did not have to endure.

Besides participating in actual war theme campaigns, national advertisers used their regular advertising for propaganda purposes, working war themes into their copy and display.

B. F. Goodrich urged people to conserve tires: "Hitler Smiles When You Waste Miles."

H. J. Heinz proclaimed the "Land of the Free—To Serve!"

The major oil companies combined to urge: "Get in the Scrap! Bring your scrap rubber NOW! Take your old tires, garden hose, hot water bottles, etc., to any gasoline dealer."

Pabst Brewing raised its glass in a toast. "To the Jap Navy —Bottoms Up."

Todd Shipyards depicted itself as "Battle-front U.S.A."

U. S. Steel said, "It's a good thing we spent $600,000,000 in the hard depression years." Expansion of plant and facilities enabled the corporation to produce as it was producing for the war.

Westinghouse listed many answers to the question, "What Can *I* Do to Help Fight the War?"

[7] Don Wharton, "The Story Back of the War Ads," *Reader's Digest,* July, 1944, from an original article in *Advertising & Selling.*

"Idle words make busy subs! Keep it under your STET-SON."

The Meat Institute printed recipes for "Making the Most of Meat."

Green Giant Peas told victory gardeners how to grow peas in their own gardens.

Bell Telephone urged people to stay off the long-distance wires so that servicemen could get their calls through.

Revere Copper and Brass advertisements showed a soldier amputee. "Lend a hand . . . he gave one."

The New York Central showed a military stretcher case being loaded aboard a Pullman. "Bedroom 'B' is Taken."

New England Mutual called for blood donors. "Will *YOU* Give a Pint of 'Life Insurance'?"

Greyhound Bus, in cooperation with the Office of Defense Transportation, advertised to discourage unnecessary civilian travel.

Hawaiian Pineapple asked, "Can You Pass a Mail Box with a Clear Conscience?" Wartime mail boxes, as the one pictured in its N. W. Ayer advertisement, bore the stenciled legend: "Buy War Bonds & Stamps."

Eastman Kodak showed a uniformed girl being admired by her parents. "We feel awfully good about Mary's joining the U.S. CADET NURSE CORPS."

Hiram Walker showed a B-24 heavy bomber flying across the ocean. "How to make a letter hustle overseas. SEND IT V-MAIL."

Perhaps the most famous of all wartime advertisements, quoted, reprinted and chosen in various lists of best advertisements was "The Kid in Upper 4," a New York, New Haven & Hartford Railroad magazine advertisement prepared by the Wendell P. Colton agency. The advertisement showed a youthful G.I. awake in his berth at exactly 3:42 a.m. Obviously he was shipping out. He is thinking wistfully of things he has left, his girl, the taste of hamburgers, his dog, and wondering about the strangeness into which he is going. The advertisement concluded:

If you have to stand en route—*it is so he may have a seat.*
If there is no berth for you—*it is so that he may sleep.*
If you have to wait for a seat in the diner—*it is so he . . . and thou-sands like him . . . may have a meal they won't forget in the days to come.*
For to treat him as our most honored guest is the least we can do to pay a mighty debt of gratitude.

Such were typical of the best; most, in fact, won wartime advertising awards, and there were many more. Another ad-vertisement did not win an award, but it was refreshing among the many, particularly during the early part of the war, which made absurd claims for the wartime importance and value of their products. One advertiser of cosmetics got impatient. He could go no more. "It won't build morale, it won't preserve our way of life, all (our) lipstick will do is make you look prettier."[8]

As some of those cited, many commercial advertisements during World War II offered nothing for sale. Some, a novelty in advertising, even urged people not to buy the ad-vertiser's product, even when he had it to sell. Before the war was over an estimated one billion dollars of press space and radio time alone had been given for use in support of govern-ment-approved wartime campaigns, and an inestimable amount in the time and skills of advertising executives, copywriters, artists, layout men, and radio talent. This advertising proved its effectiveness in bond selling, salvage drives, recruiting of nurses, merchant seamen, and industrial workers. It spread ideas which a government at war wanted spread, and the ideas took hold. Advertising proved its usefulness not in selling goods but in affecting opinion and provoking actions, in organizing, regimenting, to an extent controlling millions of people. Cooperating with twenty-seven government agen-cies and departments, The War Advertising Council stage-managed more than a hundred home front campaigns.

These totals in terms of time and money expended, in num-ber of newspaper and magazine advertisements devoted

[8] Quoted by Rubicam, *op. cit.*

wholly or in part to war purposes, and in hours of radio time donated and used, are impressive. The voluntary cooperation of advertisers, advertising agencies, and advertising media, whether motives were altruistic, sprang from enlightened self-interest, or were mixed, was likewise remarkable. More significant was the fact that advertising showed its force and proved its effectiveness when used consciously and skillfully for propaganda purposes on a national scale. It operated at high governmental level, enjoying sensations of power and official approval not previously experienced nor easily relinquished.

28

The Modern
Advertising Agency

AN ADVERTISING AGENCY may be one man, with or without a
typist or an office boy. He needs no capital or plant, though
he may be happier if he has petty cash available for unavoidable minor expenses and more comfortable if he has a chair
to sit on and a desk or table to work at. To be in business
he needs a minimum of one account. Even if he has no more,
he will be a busy man. What he is expected to do is solicit
and capture the account, plan the client's advertising, write
the copy, create the ideas for illustrations and have them
accepted, then executed, place the advertising in the most
effective media, collect space or time costs from the advertiser, pay the media, and plan and help the advertiser carry
out merchandising and promotion schemes based on the advertising. He is expected to be familiar with his advertiser's
entire production and distribution operation, to know or be
able to dig out the facts which will answer the advertiser's
every question, defend the advertising strategy he has proposed, and show cause why the advertiser should not take the
business away from him and give it to some other agency. For
all this, he will charge the advertiser nothing. Instead, he will
extract from the newspaper or magazine publisher, or from
the radio, television, or outdoor organization with which he
has placed the advertising, a commission, usually 15 per cent,
on the cost of the space or time, and an additional allowance,
usually 2 per cent, for cash payment of the bill.

Most advertising agencies are somewhat larger than the one described. There is more often two, three, or a group of men with adequate clerical assistance and office space both large enough to work in and pretentious enough to impress prospective clients. Usually the agency has more than one account, though a half-dozen large accounts are usually more profitable than a half-hundred smaller ones. The work done by one harried and distracted man in the one-man agency is now shared by others and, in the larger agencies, broken down by departments or operating units.

Terminology and titles may differ from agency to agency. The "account executive" in one agency may be simply the "contact man" or representative in another, simply a vice president without designated portfolio in another, but his function is the same. There is usually a media, a copy, and an art department. There may be several if an account is large enough to warrant the grouping of all these services about the man or group of men in charge of it; there may be but one large plans, media, copy, and art department in agencies where all accounts are handled as house accounts. The differences lie in internal organization of the agencies, not in the functions they perform for advertiser and publisher, and in the amount or quality of service they find necessary to give their clients in order to keep the business. Usually the amount is large and the quality at least high enough to pass hard scrutiny, for the advertising agency business is fiercely competitive and highly volatile.

There are something over five thousand advertising agencies in the United States.[1] They range in size from the mythical but not impossible one-man, one-account agency to the giants —the J. Walter Thompson Company; Young & Rubicam; Batten, Barton, Durstine & Osborn; N. W. Ayer & Son, Inc.; McCann-Erickson; Benton & Bowles; Kenyon & Eckhardt; Leo Burnett Co.; Ted Bates & Co.; Foote, Cone & Belding. These are among the leading advertising agencies in terms of billings, the amounts of advertising they place for clients and

[1] *Census of Business, 1954*, United States Department of Commerce.

for which they bill the media. Some of them bill well over $200 million a year, the least of them about $75 million. In 1956, thirty-four advertising agencies each billed $25 million or more, and seventy-seven advertising agencies were each responsible for $10 million or more in advertising.[2]

Leviathan among the giants in terms of billing and in the international scope and breadth of its operation has long been the J. Walter Thompson Company.

In 1916, after forty-eight profitable years as an aggressive agent, J. Walter Thompson sold his business to Stanley Resor, who had worked for him for eight years, first in Cincinnati, then in New York, and to Charles Raymond, manager of the Thompson office in Chicago. Thompson was sixty-nine. His billings had reached $3 million a year, and he did not think advertising could go much further. Raymond's holdings were soon purchased by Henry Stanton of Procter & Gamble and James Webb Young, who had worked for the business book and magazine publisher, A. W. Shaw, in Chicago. This group, with Helen Lansdowne, who had worked with Stanley Resor at Procter & Collier, Cincinnati house agency for Procter and Gamble, and whom Resor married in 1917, made the J. Walter Thompson Company the very model of the modern advertising agency.

Thompson's is by far the world's largest advertising agency. It is world-wide in its operations. At last count, it had offices in New York, London, Buenos Aires, Sao Paulo, Rio de Janiero, Santiago, Antwerp, Johannesburg, Cape Town, Bombay, Calcutta, Sydney, Melbourne, Port Elizabeth, Durban, New Delhi, Nairobi, Paris, Frankfurt, Madras, Tokyo, Manila, Chicago, Detroit, San Francisco, Los Angeles, Hollywood, Seattle, Montevideo, Washington, Montreal, Toronto, and Mexico City. It has had others, and it will have still more as they are needed. The company has perhaps five thousand employees, a half-hundred vice presidents. Its executive offices with their Spanish grille work, period furniture, each room an individual unit of decor, are as well known as the

[2] *Advertising Age*, February 25, 1957.

company's Lexington Avenue address. It has a long list of "blue chip" accounts: Kodak, Edison, Ford, Swift, Sylvania, Schlitz, Standard Brands, Kraft Foods, New York Central, Quaker Oats—foods, metals, railroads, powerful industry and trade associations, banks, a rich cross-section of American business and industry. Many large accounts, Pond's, Libby, McNeill & Libby, Lever Brothers, Kodak, Johns-Manville, Owens-Illinois, Scott Paper, Shell Oil, Ford, it has served for many years.

Yet Thompson's is rather more than a compilation of its components and appearance. It has made itself a synonym for dignity, even sedateness, and a Bank-of-England manner in its advertising approach. It is most proud, perhaps, of its thoroughness. Thompson executives like to say that the company loses itself in the business of its clients. It studies and investigates every phase of the client's business, production, packaging, distribution, pricing, competition, before presenting its advertising proposals. J. Walter Thompson merges itself so closely with the client's plans and problems that the agency almost loses its identity. This is deliberate. At Thompson's it is never "the agency did," but "the advertiser did." Thompson infiltration of the client's business, consultation, painstaking preparation of the groundwork, make the statement reasonable. They also make the final preparation of copy and display what Thompson executives like to call it, a detail—an inevitable outcome of all the work that has gone before.

J. Walter Thompson is very conscious of the mission and accomplishments of advertising. It believes that advertising can and does affect war, peace, religion, morality, the major conditions of life and human attitudes toward it. It believes that advertising creates, then fulfills, new human needs, and that Thompson advertising for soap chips and flakes, cosmetics, electric refrigerators, processed cheese, disposable tissues, vitamins, and automatic washers and home insulation has changed human habits. It believes that "Advertising raises the standard of living through education to new desires, habits, and incentives to work . . . leads to the actual improvement of the products themselves through the constant search for new and compelling advertising themes . . . cuts distribution cost through lessening selling resistance."[3]

Thompson's insists that in the United States advertising has become "the greatest single means for mass communication, information, and persuasion, which has ever been seen in any society, anywhere, at any time." James Webb Young wrote: "No man or woman who can read or hear—even those who boast that they never read advertising—can fully escape its impact. Any anthropologist who attempted to describe our culture with advertising left out, would, I suggest, be as near-sighted as one who left corn out of the story of the Mayas—or the camel out of that of the Bedouin tribes."[4]

The J. Walter Thompson idea is that an advertising agency is simply people, creative people working closely with advertisers to produce effective sales results. Methods used vary by product, account, and situation. Stanley Resor, who believes in appeal to consumer emotions, began to use testimonial advertising strongly for Pond's in 1924, modernizing a centuries-old but always useful device.

Thompson's got Scott Paper as a client in 1927. The paper company was then producing 2,800 brands of toilet tissue of various quality. Thompson's persuaded Scott to discontinue many and to concentrate on two. Scott Tissue was continuously advertised, reached a volume market. Through the expenditures of millions of dollars the price fell steadily from the original thirty-five cents a roll until the consumer was paying less than a quarter of that amount. Thompson's feels that it helped institute packaged cereals, thus all packaged foodstuffs, and believes its Ford advertising imbedded the idea of the two-car family in the American consciousness, just as the use of soap chips and flakes instead of bar laundry soap grew of its advertising of Lux.

[3] "J. Walter Thompson Company," *Fortune*, November, 1947, p. 206.
[4] James Webb Young, *Some Advertising Responsibilities in a Dynamic Society* (New York: J. Walter Thompson Co., 1949).

Thompson's—and the innovation is usually credited to the imagination, drive, and copywriting skill of Mrs. Stanley Resor—borrowed magazine editorial treatment and applied it to advertising. The agency made greater use of pictures, of color, and of copy as brightly written as that appearing in the text of the general mass magazines and the women's periodicals. Advertisements were made more attractive and more readable. Products were personalized through the use of testimonials and pictures of the celebrities introduced. Thompson's pioneered in the use of fine art in advertising, assigning noncommercial artists to painting scenes about the Maxwell House in Tennessee, romanticized as the birthplace of the coffee that is "good to the last drop," and continuing with the magazine reproduction of paintings in later Maxwell House campaigns. Thompson's brought Edward Steichen into commercial photography for Jergen's Lotion and commissioned the work of Yousuf Karsh.

The agency matches creative activity of this kind with fact-finding research in marketing and advertising with which to bulwark its account solicitations and support the distribution efforts of its clients. Marketing research on a continuing basis is generally understood to have started with the publishers of advertising media, who used it to promote the sale of space and to provide a service to advertisers. The Curtis Publishing Company began to do work of this kind in 1911. Charles Coolidge Parlin was hired, devised the term "commercial research," and began the study of markets through asking questions of manufacturers, jobbers, retailers, and then of consumers. He undertook a comprehensive study of the market for agricultural implements in 1911, followed that with an analysis of department store lines in 1912, and in 1913 attempted what was probably the first census of distribution. This was a study of all cities above fifty thousand population to estimate the volume of department-store, dry goods, and what was then called "ladies' ready-to wear" business. It was in one of the reports of these early studies that Parlin phrased an advertising maxim so often repeated that it passes for established truth. "The consumer is king. His preference is law, and his whim makes and unmakes merchants, jobbers, and manufacturers. Whoever has his confidence, controls the mercantile situation. Whoever loses it is lost."[5]

Among the advertising agencies, the J. Walter Thompson Company pioneered in research of many kinds. In 1923 its Cincinnati office conducted what the agency believes to be the first qualitative study of magazine circulation ever made. Issued as "A Study of Magazine Circulation in Cincinnati, Ohio," it was a detailed analysis of the subscription circulation of forty-four national magazines in the metropolitan area which produced information not previously obtainable about readers by sex and occupation. For the first time an advertiser had some idea of what kind of prospects his magazine advertising was reaching. The Curtis Publishing Company duplicated the study in Cleveland, verifying the methods and results. Since these beginnings, Thompson's has been among the agency leaders in developing and using research of many kinds in the selling and servicing of its accounts.

The agency hired a professor of marketing from the Harvard Business School to become its director of research in the 1920's; and, to study the consumer and what responses he could be conditioned to give to the right sales stimuli, added the behavioristic psychologist, J. B. Watson, to its staff. It issues periodic studies of population trends, production, consumption, living standards, and consumer purchasing powers, analyzing the various economic factors to provide business with market indicators for use in advertising planning.

The agency is elaborately equipped to do the thorough job it considers characteristic of its efforts. In 1939 it instituted its Consumer Panel of five thousand U.S. families corresponding in geographical location and by social factors with the family population of the United States. These families report monthly in diary form on what brands of a long list of products they purchase and give information

[5] *Department Store Lines, Including Textiles* (Philadelphia: The Curtis Publishing Co., 1912).

about their expenditures for other products and services as
the agency requires. Thompson's, one of the few advertising
agencies which completely produces a major, night-time television show, though it exerts considerable control over scores
of others purchased for advertisers, maintains a completely
equipped closed television circuit. Agency men and clients
may sit before receivers in the two-story conference room at
the Thompson offices and watch experimental commercials
from the Thompson television studios a few blocks north on
Lexington Avenue.

What any advertising agency has to offer is talent, ideas,
business judgment, fact-finding resources, imagination, and
creative skill. Differently ordered as they may be internally
by specializations, which invariably overlap, and fronted by
facades ranging from the consciously opulent to the deliberately austere, they must all, more than most other forms of
business, depend finally upon and survive by the abilities of
their personnel. Essentially, all advertising agencies offer the
same services, or purport to. How well or how ill a given
agency performs its advertised functions stems directly from
the temperaments and intelligences of the men and women
who form the agency. Differences among advertising agencies must be largely differences in people, differences in emphasis and approach to the work they all attempt.

In most years, Young & Rubicam is the second or third
largest advertising agency in terms of billing. It does for its
accounts just what J. Walter Thompson or any other large
agency does for its clients. The structure, purpose, and performance of all the large agencies is closely similar, but it is
not identical. There are distinctions enough perceptible to
advertisers for, roughly, one thousand accounts to switch
from one advertising agency to another in any given year.
What differences there are between top agencies such as
J. Walter and Y. & R. emanate generally from the personalities of agency founders and principals.

Unlike J. Walter Thompson, which can trace its history
back to 1864, Y. & R. dates back only to 1923 when two

young men, one a copywriter, the other an account man employed by the N. W. Ayer agency in Philadelphia, were walking across nearby Independence Square at the lunch hour. They decided to form their own advertising agency and did, starting, as John Orr Young recalls, literally on a shoestring. Their first account was for the "Quick Tipper," a kit for making your own shoestrings by pinching a tip of metal on whatever length of lace you wished.[6]

The basic idea of the two men was to emphasize two advertising ingredients in their work, more knowledge of the consumer and greater skill in copy and display. The first big business they captured was the difficult Postum account. Postum, which had been on the market and advertised for twenty-nine years, was not doing well. Many people, Young and Rubicam discovered through research, had tried Postum and disliked it. They expected it to taste like coffee, which it did not. Some thought of it as an invalid's drink. There were other prejudices to remove. Having discovered the pertinent facts, the swaddling agency started out to break down these prejudices and to design a campaign which might induce people to try and perhaps get to like and continue to use Postum for the qualities it had.

They devised a magazine campaign, using *The Saturday Evening Post* as the spearhead to get national circulation paralleling distribution of the product and to reach a selective audience of potential customers. The campaign stressed the healthfulness and wholesome flavor of Postum. Some magazines had banned Postum copy because of previous advertising attacks on coffee. Comparison was avoided, but Postum was recommended for those troubled by sleeplessness. Appeals were directed to businessmen, nurses, older boys and girls, especially to the housewife who was told exactly how Postum's Carrie Blanchard prepared the drink at the Battle Creek plant. Advertisements urged people to try the "thirty-day test," with the first week's supply offered free. Local

6 John Orr Young, *Adventures in Advertising* (New York: Harper & Bros., 1948).

newspaper advertisements, booklets, and folio promotions to
grocers were used to supplement the national magazine advertising. In 1925, only two years after two daring young
men had, with mingled elation and fearfulness, embarked on
their own, the Postum campaign brought Young & Rubicam
the Harvard Award for a national advertising campaign
"most conspicuous for the excellence of its planning and
execution."

Success with Postum and Harvard's recognition led to
their obtaining other lucrative accounts of the General Foods
Corporation and the accounts of other large companies—
Borden; Johnson & Johnson; Parke, Davis; Spalding; and
Cluett, Peabody. In 1926 the agency moved from Philadelphia to New York. First Young was president, then Rubicam.
They concentrated on soliciting a few large accounts, on
which they could afford to expend full service, rather than
many small ones. John Orr Young left the agency, and it was
from the copywriter Raymond Rubicam that the agency got
its tone and imprint.

Rubicam had been a creative man from the beginning. He
had been a reporter on Philadelphia newspapers before joining the staff of the F. Wallis Armstrong agency. As an Ayer
copywriter he had devised advertising slogans which are still
in use—"The Instrument of the Immortals" for Steinway
pianos and "The Priceless Ingredient . . ." for Squibb's.
While Rolls Royce automobiles were still being assembled at
the old Stevens-Duryea plant in Chicopee, Massachusetts, he
had coined, "No Rolls Royce Has Ever Worn Out." One of
Raymond Rubicam's intentions when he and Young founded
Y. & R. was to make it an agency in which creative men
would have as great a voice in policy and receive as much
recognition for their work as account men and executives.

The accent was on creative imagination. As Raymond
Rubicam phrases it, "Y. & R. tried to develop the art of being
interesting to the highest possible degree consistent with
honesty and integrity." His reiterated advice to his people
as the agency grew was to let the best idea win. It did not

matter whether the idea stemmed from a copywriter, from an account representative, from a research man, or from an office boy. It was as important to recognize a good idea as to originate one. What the group worked toward in its advertising planning, Rubicam says, was truth imaginatively presented, the "interpretive presentation." Young & Rubicam advertising became distinguished for its creativeness but, like Thompson's, it sought solid facts on which to base its fancies.

Rubicam and Young in the early days of the agency hired a former Ayer man, who was then on the circulation staff of a New York newspaper, to head their merchandising work, paying him more than either partner then drew from the firm. One man was made responsible for all agency solicitation. Account executives did not solicit. Marketing analysis became part of their service on each account. In 1932, in a search to find out more about consumers, Rubicam hired George Gallup from Northwestern University, where he was teaching, to head the agency's research. Gallup's first job with the agency was an analysis of both the editorial and advertising content of what were then the six leading women's magazines. He analyzed five thousand advertisements in the women's publications in an effort to find out which were read, which were not read and why. He analyzed the general magazines in the same way. Rubicam took the findings and actually held night classes to teach his copywriters, art men, and other creative workers the significance and advertising use of what this research had uncovered.

Gallup went on to conduct Y. & R. research into reading and not-reading, copy-testing, and marketing. Gallup and Y. & R. devised research methods which they applied in hundreds of studies, work which influenced the development of research in the independent testing and rating organizations with which advertising now abounds. In 1948, 10 per cent of the thousand employees Young & Rubicam had at that time were employed in research.[7] Research became an in-

[7] John Crichton, "Y. & R. Hails 25th Milestone," *Advertising Age*, May 24, 1948.

tegral part of the Y. & R. program, but it did not, as it does
in some agencies, dominate. It was used to complement and
support the creative approach which became the hallmark of
the agency. The idea was to "know more about the public
and put that knowledge into the hands of writers and artists
with imagination and broad human sympathies."[8]

Like Thompson's, Y. & R. claims credit for certain advertising innovations. It was the first agency to integrate the
radio commercial and have it delivered by the talent as a
part of the show; the first to use comic sequence techniques
and characters in Sunday comic supplements for advertising
purposes; the agency which at the request of the U. S. Treasury during World War II devised a combination withholding tax receipt and simplified federal income tax return form.[9]
Y. & R. claims to have been the first agency to produce a
home-economics radio program shared by several clients; the
first to check sponsor identification and the registering of
selling points in all its radio advertising. Like Thompson's
and other of the important agencies, Y. & R. have brought the
work of well-known painters, photographers, and cartoonists
to the public in print advertising and glorified various performers and personalities on radio and television programs
purchased or concocted for their clients.

Rule of thumb in the trade is that any agency billing $10
million or more yearly is equipped and staffed to give complete advertising service to any client. Competition has
tended to erase the differences among the strong, long, and
well-established agencies. As one develops new techniques
or procedures that prove of value, the others imitate or adopt
it. Though, for a season, one may become known as a "research agency" or, through some spectacular campaign, an
"idea," an "art," or a "copy" agency, lines of distinction have
become blurred. The fully formed agency is apt to be less
conspicuous in many ways than its clamoring rivals, though

[8] Quoted by Nathaniel A. Benson, "Raymond Rubicam—A Close-up,"
Forbes, February 1, 1944.

[9] Whether any or all of these have contributed greatly to the gaiety of
nations or the increased palatability of advertising is debatable.

distinctions of prestige and sometimes actual performance, difficult to describe but generally acknowledged, remain.

N. W. Ayer & Son, Inc., which in the nineteenth century did much to establish the agency as a recognizable entity and to bring about its recognition as a part of the complete advertising structure, early acquired a reputation for integrity through the work of F. Wayland Ayer himself. Over the years there has accrued to Ayer a dignity and stability commensurate with its rich experience. It has represented some of its clients, Steinway, International Correspondence Schools, American Telephone & Telegraph, Hanes Knitting, and Atlantic Refining, for nearly or more than a half-century. Foods, fabrics, watches, beverages, cigarettes, automobiles, airlines, steel, tools, toiletries, meat, and gasolines and oils are among its product accounts. Among others, its magazine campaigns for De Beers Consolidated Mines, Ltd., and its radio and television coverage of sports for Atlantic Refining are notable in many ways. In annual billings, Ayer is always well up among the top ten agencies.

Like the other large advertising agencies, Ayer likes to refer to its assorted talent, its teamwork, its supervision, its careful staff recruitment and training, its meticulous planning, research, media selection, marketing, and merchandising. All the facilities of its Philadelphia office are at the disposal of its branches in other cities and are used on behalf of all Ayer clients. Beyond all this, Ayer has, perhaps, two distinguishing assets.

The first is Ayer's policy book. This statement is open to any advertiser and to any Ayer employee. A prospect or an Ayer typist as well as the agency's executives knows exactly where the house stands on questions of agency practice. Ayer will not take competing accounts. It will not hire account executives from outside the organization because they control accounts which they can deliver to Ayer. The other Ayer operating principles are recorded and published for all to read. Ayer is owned by more than fifty active employees, the stock so assigned as to give desired importance to the various departments and to align management authority. That fact, too, is published.

Ayer's other distinguishing property is its financial resources. These, Ayer believes, are greater than those of any other advertising agency. This financial strength permits complete implementation of stated house policies, the maintenance of a large and able staff, and the expenditure of large sums in research investigation or comparable study from which no immediate profit is expected.

Within the limits set by their size and resources, all of the other five-thousand-odd advertising agencies in the United States operate much as J. Walter Thompson, Young & Rubicam, and N. W. Ayer & Son operate. The differences lie in the scale on which the work is conducted, the quality of the work produced, emphases and tendencies dictated by the character of the agency's personnel, and the requirements and idiosyncrasies of their particular advertisers.

There are, of course, other aspects to advertising agency operation. The advertising agency has been gloriously pilloried, burlesqued, and satirized in popular fiction and humor. The attention is a measure of the importance which the advertising agency has attained since the days of Volney B. Palmer, Pettingill, and Rowell. The advertising man has become the hero that the newspaperman was in fiction and drama earlier in the twentieth century, and, though there is undoubted truth in many of the accusations of the novelists, their presentation is about as accurate to the whole of advertising agency activity as the melodramatic descriptions of their predecessors were to the city rooms of the metropolitan dailies.

There is much that is ridiculous in the advertising agency, much that is spurious and meretricious. The agencies exist to capture and sell ideas, not pure or disinterested ideas, but ideas cunningly conceived to persuade, convince, and sometimes delude. All the research in which the agencies indulge is not for finding useful facts. It is an amassing of abracadabra in almost direct proportion to the felt insubstantiality of the basic effort of the advertising agency. The advertising agency needs the support of "science" in its dealing with elusive things—the minds and emotions of consumers and the tantalizing incertitudes of the arts of persuasion.

When John Orr Young and Raymond Rubicam left Ayer, they decided they would solicit no Ayer accounts for a year. Such ethics are not typical. Over-scrupulosity is not an agency vice. When Lou Wasey left Lord & Thomas he told Lasker he would take only the accounts he had brought into the agency or else he would take all those he had worked on. Lasker, he says, settled on his basis. Wasey took Robbins & Meyer, Musterole, Dr. Edwards' Olive Tablets, and other patent medicines to the agency he formed.[10] New agencies have been formed by the deft transfer, sometimes, in the opinion of the bereft, the outright stealing, of accounts. To avoid this, the stronger advertising agencies set up their accounts so that their full servicing necessitates all the resources of the agency.

"The biggest thing the ablest advertising man may justly claim for himself is that he is a fairly successful opportunist," one advertising agency man wrote in 1929.[11] It would be hard for many modern advertising men, immersed in a demanding activity of whose importance they are convinced, to agree with this appraisal. The American Association of Advertising Agencies, known to most as the "Four A's," founded in 1917, exists as much to convince advertising men as the lay world that the advertising agency has a social and economic *raison d'etre* transcending mere opportunism.

The advertising agency system is always under discussion,

[10] *Advertising Age,* January 2, 1956. Wasey believed in the profitable advertising of patent medicines and early conducted original research that justified his belief. While riding on a train through the Midwest, he noticed the unbroken snow between many farmhouses and outhouses and decided there was enough constipation in the country to justify considerable advertising expenditure for cathartics. Conversation with another expert, the founder of Cascarets, confirmed his suspicion. "Mr. Wasey," the other told him earnestly, "the whole world is constipated."

[11] Howard W. Dickinson, *Crying Our Wares* (New York: John Day Co., Inc., 1929), p. ix.

often under attack. Many are perplexed and some annoyed by the historically developed anomaly that the agency works for the advertiser but is paid, in the form of commission, by the advertising media. Periodically this method of advertising agency compensation comes up for review and, generally acrimonious, discussion. Some large advertisers would prefer to conduct their advertising through "house agencies" which they could operate and control, a method not now permitted, or to buy advertising space and time direct from the media at standard discounts from published rates, than pay the agency for its work.

The agencies, of course, defend the present system under which they augment their commission income by charging the advertiser for a variety of special services. In general, the media uphold the advertising agency system, which magazine publishers did much to develop. They believe it to their advantage to deal with advertising agencies responsible for the preparation and delivery of copy and for billing and payments. They know that the advertising agencies work continually to obtain new business by which both profit and encourage advertisers to use more time or larger space with greater frequency.

In 1955 the Department of Justice brought an antitrust suit against the advertising business, using the Four A's and five media associations as defendants. A year later the Four A's signed a consent decree, by which the agencies agreed not to insist as a group on maintenance of the 15 per cent commission and other standard methods of agency compensation. Individual agencies were not enjoined from doing business on these standard terms; thus, the result of the suit and its conclusion brought little or no immediate change in the situation. In 1956 the Association of National Advertisers authorized a new study of advertising agency compensation. It reported in 1957 after sampling opinion in 1,806 of the 3,300 advertising agencies listed in the *Standard Advertising Register*, 3,795 advertising managers, 2,107 media men, and 1,012 men in executive positions in business. The large majority proved to be in favor of retaining the present advertising agency system of payment at the still standard 15 per cent commission.

There are probably as many fools, bores, dillettantes, rakes, and deviates in the advertising agency business as in any other, industrial, commercial, or subsidized. Perhaps there are a fraction more in proportion, because an atmosphere at least tainted with creativeness is apt to draw more nonconformists, talented or self-deceived, than might be attracted to the offices of a certified public accountant. There are sedate dignitaries and stuffed pomposities in advertising agencies, just as there are unfettered exhibitionists in the clergy, law, medicine, or the army and navy. The strong competition in the advertising agency simply exhibits itself differently than in the State Department or on the faculty of a two-century-old New England college. None of these other institutions has yet convincingly demonstrated exclusive possession and enjoyment of hypocrisy, nepotism, lechery, or culpable charm. The advertising agency has shown that it can use some of these too—and the agency has repeatedly shown that its influence, good or bad, is often stronger and more pervasive than that of these other institutions which compete for public attention and approval.

There is little philosophical profundity about the ordinary advertising agency. Actually there is little enough in the average college faculty, government department, or profession. When inspiration or pure intellect does add a fact or idea, both rare, to the little hoard of hard-won human knowledge, it does not happen in the advertising agency. Yet if the fact or idea—soap, cigarette, or democracy—needs selling, and most of them do, the advertising man can sell it quickly, deftly, and efficiently. He does not have to understand it, though if he does, so much the better.

If he is good, the advertising agency man's wits are as nimble as a gambler's fingers. His guesses are swift correlations of complex experience, usually those of others. He has speed, superficiality, and facility, the articulateness to set the ponderous in swift motion. He is as human as professional cynicism will allow, as innocent sometimes as childhood, as wise as age, sometimes as senile as dotage—and he loves it. He can be an actor, just as the politician always, the doctor often, and even today's hero-scientist sometimes is. He can even learn to tolerate dullness, if it is that of a prospect, already checked in Dun & Bradstreet, with a large advertising appropriation that he can be encouraged to double next year and quintuple the year after.

The advertising agency is seldom dull. It is edged with bright challenge and dark with frustrations. The contact man has charmed the difficult client. Research has sampled, questionnaired, and solemnly tabulated. The campaign has been ordered. Creative talent, sick with depression for days and about to give up, has a sudden inspiration. It slashes down slogan and copy. Art sketches in pictures and layout. The committee, plans board, executive group—whatever a given agency calls it—sits in critical session. They look, listen, and beam. Then one frowns a little. "That's wonderful, Bill! It's perfect! Still—What do you think, Webster?" Emboldened, the agency psychologist says it won't work. The sociologist disagrees. He says it will be a dilly for the masses. Research reports flatly that it will be anathema to the classes and dilly to nobody. The changes start. After the sixteenth, the whole is shown the client in a full-dress presentation.

The client loves it, though he changes slogan, copy, and layout back to what they were before the agency critics improved it. He says the psychologist is an ass and the sociologist a nasty man too. The campaign goes into the newspapers, the magazines, radio, and television. It works like two dillies and no anathema at all. The triumphant client watches his sales curve soar and demands to know why the agency could not have come up with something as good as this which, by this time, he is convinced he originated and executed all by himself.

It does not always happen this way, but the pattern occurs with variations often enough to make life in an advertising agency very interesting. Sometimes, despite all the skill and wisdom employed and the sums expended, the recalcitrant consumer, who doesn't like economists anyway, decides to prove obdurate and save his money instead of spending it. Regretfully, the indignant advertiser is forced to change agencies.

When he was in Bowdoin College, Nathaniel Hawthorne decided that he did not want to become a doctor and live by men's ills, a lawyer and live by their troubles, or a minister and live by their sins. He became a writer. More than two hundred years before that Sir Philip Sidney had looked at the historian and seen him "laden with old mouse-eaten records, authorizing himself (for the most part) upon other histories, whose greatest authorities are built upon the notable foundations of hearsay." He looked at the philosopher and found that "one that hath no other guide but him shall wade in him till he be old before he shall find sufficient cause to be honest." It was the poet, Sidney saw, whose tales "kept children from play and old men from their chimney corners."[12] Sidney became a poet.

Under the exigencies of an economic and spiritual climate somewhat different from that of England in the sixteenth or transcendentalist New England in the nineteenth century, both Sidney and Hawthorne might well have become advertising agency men today. They might have worked in New York and slept in Westport, Connecticut, or disported themselves in less well-publicized equivalents. They might have known the mingled scorn and envy of their fellows as well as the triumphs and defeats, sickening charlatanry, plunging despair, and heady sensations of power endured or enjoyed by most advertising men. Many of these, if on a somewhat lower scale, chose their work through a comparable process of elimination, coupled sometimes with distaste or ineptitude for more mundane pursuits.

Though one chose to write in prose, Sidney and Hawthorne were poets who responded to a fascination. The

---

[12] *Apologie for Poetrie* (1595).

same fascination draws and holds many advertising men. "The advertising agency business," one successful and highly placed agency man explained rather helplessly, "is very fascinating, very lucrative and very dangerous. I wouldn't— I couldn't—do anything else." Despite all the research and the other trappings of business-like solemnity, the advertising agency uses all the communication arts and available media to convey and exert something of this same fascination. Partly through deliberate plan, partly, it sometimes seems, because they are the kind of men and women they are, they use their imagination and craft to produce advertising that will disarm, disable, imbue with whatever desire or conviction they wish. That they fascinate so well is a measure of the excellence of their performance, or, some say, their reprehensible and dangerous skill.

29

The Newer Advertising

AFTER WORLD WAR I came radio. After World War II came television, but television showed none of radio's original diffidence as an advertising medium. It was advertising's from the start. The public, devoted to radio and the motion picture, looked on television not so much as another miracle as a natural development which added sight to sound and, as naturally, brought radio programming and the radio commercial with it. Television sprang full-blown into both eager public acceptance and the favor of advertisers. It gripped the imagination of both and grew with fever speed. Quickly, television became to radio what $64,000, soon quadrupled by mounting excitement and ballooning inflation to $256,000, is to the $64, which simpler audiences once found almost unbearably exciting as the fantastic give-away on a radio quiz program.

Television has a history almost as long as that of radio. A German scientist patented a device for transmitting pictures by wireless in 1894. French scientists used the word "television" in 1909. The first television apparatus was demonstrated in 1925. In 1927 the first experimental television program was sent from Washington, D.C., to New York. WGY, Schenectady, put on the first television drama in 1928. By 1937, there were seventeen experimental television stations in operation in the United States, and the new medium made its formal American debut at the New York World's Fair in 1939, when both the National Broadcasting Company and Columbia Broadcasting were on the air for two or three hours a week. World War II interrupted experimentation and delayed both the manufacture of receiving sets and the erection of transmitting stations, but hastened technical development.

The first television network was formed when WRGB in Schenectady was joined to WNBT in 1939. The presidential conventions of both parties were telecast from Philadelphia in 1940, and a coaxial cable made network coverage of the convention of 1944 possible in the Philadelphia, New York, and Schenectady areas, but the great burgeoning did not come until the close of the war. In 1944, when only a few thousand sets were in operation, large advertisers began their use of the medium: Cluett, Peabody, U. S. Time, Carter's Underwear, Lifebuoy, *Reader's Digest,* Commonwealth Edison, Nash Kelvinator, Botany, Hudnut, Atlantic Refining. Football games, weather, news, and kitchen advice were all on the air. Before the end of 1948 there were three million television sets in use, and programs were diversified and practically continuous. Set ownership vaulted to eighteen million by the middle of 1952 when there were 110 commercial transmitters in operation. Advertising and people's delight with the newest and most fascinating entertainment made ownership of a television set as necessary as possession of a car and an electric refrigerator. It became a social obligation.[1] By 1956 there were thirty-seven million television families in the United States listening to telecasts from some 450 stations, and television was on its way to the virtually universal coverage of American homes which radio has.

[1]An advertisement for television sets, run in November, 1950, in 502 newspapers in 358 cities, broadcast, and used in other media, got even more attention than the advertiser wished. In it a newspaper authority on child guidance explained that children who did not have a television set in their homes were ostracized by their companions and so ashamed they could not even tell their cruel and thoughtless parents. The advertisement was castigated as scare selling and as undermining the sacred parent-child relationship. The National Education Association, the Newspaper Guild of New York, the Methodist Church, Mrs. Eleanor Roosevelt, and Americans for Democratic Action made outraged protest. The Federal Trade Commission demanded and received the written promise of the manufacturers of television sets that they would never again use such a child appeal, then commended them and the advertising agency involved for their prompt display of remorse.

Here was the mass audience sought by many large advertisers. Undeterred by the expense of television time and high production costs, the manufacturers of convenience goods and durables, the same groups which had used radio for the same purpose, seized on television and for much the same reason. People had been radio enthusiasts. They became television addicts. Audiences could be counted in multiples of millions. They could be reached in their own homes, and they could be reached by sight as well as sound, by animated cartoon as well as singing commercials. Lulled into stupor by hours of westerns, soap opera, and crime drama, or excited to attention by football, Congressional investigations, or coronations, they were in a state of helpless receptivity and assailable through the eyes as well as the ears.

The blatant commercials of radio were considered too modest for television. Television advertising became and has remained untrammeled in insistence, frequency, and repetition. More commercials are crammed into a half-hour program than ever radio dared. Multiple sponsorship, encouraged by the high cost of television advertising, and the enthusiastic sale and extravagant use of spot advertising, throttle programs and fray the nerves of those viewers who have not yet developed the numbness which is their only defense.

Television advertising has developed as mass advertising, and much of it seems to have reverted to the methods of the medicine-show pitchman of patent medicine days. In fact, proprietary remedies are among the loudest and most characteristic television advertisers. With television, a part of advertising seems to have swung full circle back to the shouting barker of the fair, wheedling, cajoling, clowning, enticing. Thanks to the wonders of electronics, the pitchman is in the house visibly as well as vocally and almost in the flesh. The fastidious may writhe, but the television commercial is selling soap, cereals, medicines, cigarettes, cosmetics, and beer to the millions by the billions. Television advertising did not exist before World War II. By 1957 advertisers were spending above $1½ billion annually in television time, talent, and production costs.

In print media a distinction is observed between advertising and editorial matter. An advertisement announces itself as an advertisement. In television, advertising attempts to merge itself with the entertainment, announcer, actor, salesman, or glamorous salesgirl slipping glibly into the commercial as part of the program. The dividing lines between text and advertising have been erased or at least ignored. Part of the reason for this is that in many instances the advertiser, through his agency, controls the entire production. He purchases, sometimes completely stages, the entertainment as well as the television time and, within the limits set by FCC or network restrictions, can use it as he wishes. This integration of the commercial with the show, which originated in radio, is carried to extremes in the newer and far more expensive medium, whose high cost makes it imperative for the advertiser to wrest the maximum of sales value out of his expenditure.

Television has had its marked effect on competing media. Magazines have shortened, sharpened, and tried to brighten their offerings to compete for the effortless attention television requires. With variety and drama deserting en masse to television, radio, as already indicated, has been relegated largely to news, weather, recorded music, and the unceasing mechanical patter of the disc jockey.

World War II brought other changes to advertising as well as those which came with the introduction of a new and powerful advertising medium. It gave added impetus to types of advertising already extant and developed one concept that was new. The decade following the close of the war saw expanded use of various kinds of advertising research with greater emphasis upon psychological dissection of the consumer at whom all advertising is directed.

There has been a manifest increase in the advertising of manufacturers of component parts. These manufacturers, who make no products for direct sale to consumers, advertise the excellence of the materials or devices which they supply to the manufacturers of consumer goods. Dow Chemical thus advertises its plastics, American Bemberg its rayon yarns, Forstmann and Botany Mills their woolens, Minneapolis-Honeywell its controls. Du Pont not only advertises its synthetic fibers but dramatizes the importance of its research and the contributions of chemistry to human life. United States Steel advertises the importance of its steel in the industrial and consumer products which it does not itself fabricate.

The Aluminum Company of America produces aluminum and its alloys only in the raw and semifinished state, yet ALCOA advertises to the consumer the virtues of aluminum in paint, windows, roofing, weather stripping, screens, cylinders, pistons, truck and bus bodies. It shows its aluminum in use in appliances, airplanes, ships, and in plant equipment. It advertises to make known its research, the quality controls used to insure the excellence of its product. Reynolds Metal and Kaiser Aluminum do similar advertising. This indirect advertising is meant not alone to support manufacturers making consumer products of aluminum and retailers selling these, but also to gain goodwill for and approval of these companies and to enlist public support of big industry based on understanding of its contributions to public welfare and comfort.

Most so-called "institutional" advertising is of somewhat this same nature. Used heavily during World War II, when many of the advertisers had nothing to sell, its use has continued steadily. The device predates the war, for it has long been used by business organizations that function rather as quasi-public trusts, such as the telephone system and the life insurance companies, to inculcate impressions of their stability, responsibility, and efficiency. Where a business is a near monopoly or in danger of further governmental restriction on its operations, such advertising is a safeguard. All institutional advertising is designed to influence the consumer favorably in his attitude toward a company, to familiarize him with its name and mark, to build prestige and good will.

General Motors has been using institutional advertising of this kind since 1923 to acquaint the public with GM as an institution backing its automotive products with the excellence of its engineering, research, styling, and service. Basic industries, ethical drug houses, the communications industry, and the electrical companies are large users of institutional advertising. Armco Steel, Railway Express, Allis-Chalmers, Chrysler, American Cyanamid, Anaconda Copper, Boeing Airplane, Borg-Warner, Caterpillar Tractor, Ethyl Corporation, International Nickel, Owens-Illinois Glass, Parke, Davis, Philadelphia Electric, Weyerhauser Timber, are among the other large companies and regular national advertisers using institutional advertising of one kind and another. Advertising of this kind has a public-relations purpose. It is used to educate consumers, dealers, stockholders, plant communities, and even government officials whose actions may be important to the companies, in the values and services which the companies represent or perform.

This type of advertising has stemmed from social change which brought the labor unions to positions of power and strong governmental support during and immediately after World War II. Business, which once had only to make and sell its products, has been forced to defend its economic and social position and justify its existence. Once unquestioned, it has been faced with what it feels is the necessity of asking for public approval. It wants its contributions to American life understood and appreciated. It wants to be loved. Many large companies are as much concerned in their advertising now with selling themselves as with selling their products or services. They advertise to erect a favorable "image" or "profile" in the public mind, picturing themselves as public servants and benefactors, as offering advantages to their employees, as useful to the family, the community, and the nation.

Such advertising is applied where interests conflict. The Great Atlantic & Pacific Tea Company used advertising to educate the public to the issues involved in the government's antitrust suit against the company. The Bell Telephone Sys-

tem explains its employee policies and benefits, points out that
it has more than a million stockholders of all ages and occu-
pations. The American Medical Association has fought the
idea of socialized medicine in paid advertisements. The National Association of Margarine Manufacturers carried on a
long and successful advertising campaign to have federal anti-
margarine laws voided. Two wars have taught advertisers the
value of advertising for propaganda purposes, for special
pleading.

A number of manufacturers use national advertising to
support the entire industries of which they are a part. Du
Pont's "Better Things for Better Living through Chemistry"
supports the efforts of many companies besides du Pont. The
U.S. Steel advertisements sell the value of steel, not just of
what is produced by U.S. Steel itself. For many years the
medical and health advertising of the Metropolitan Life Insurance Company has supported not only Metropolitan and
the idea of life insurance, but also benefited the medical profession, pharmaceutical and dietary organizations, policy-
holders, and the general public. The company's advertising
demonstrates rather than just describes one of its contributions to human welfare. General Electric has supported the
entire electrical industry with its "Live Better Electrically"
campaign, designed to sell an idea, widen the market for an
entire industry, and to demonstrate its contribution to the
ease and comfort of American society.

Some advertisers go even further and use their paid space
and time to explain and support the only economic system
under which they can operate. Responding here not so much
to changing social conditions as to the unsettled political
state of the world, their advertising is a forceful statement of
the realities and implications of democracy as it is understood
and practised in the United States, and an attack on antagonistic systems of government. Corporations emphasize the values
making possible a society in which the manufacturer is free
to make and sell and the consumer is free to choose and buy
or refrain from buying, and contrast American freedom with

the coercion which exists elsewhere in the world and could happen here.

Since early in World War II the Electric Companies advertising program has advertised the importance to the country of the business-managed, as opposed to the government-controlled, light and power companies. These advertisements attack communism and socialism, and the socialistic and economic tendencies which threaten their existence. The railroads keep travelers aware, through advertising, that a tax imposed as a temporary wartime measure to discourage travel, continues in force, raising the price of fares. Republic Steel has used four-color magazine pages to show what freedom means in America—and to urge government to economize. Many other companies put comparable messages into their advertising or devote whole campaigns, as did the Standard Steel Spring Company, to contrasting life under democracy and socialism. In 1956 the dictator of a Caribbean country even purchased full pages in United States metropolitan newspapers to defend himself and his party against accusations that they were involved in the mysterious disappearance in New York of a Dominican national.[2]

In England advertising has been used even more extensively than in the United States and certainly more directly to promote government-sponsored or -approved ideas. Government has remained since World War II Britain's largest advertiser. In 1947–48 alone the Central Office of Information, which succeeded the wartime Ministry of Information, spent £1,693,000 in press and poster advertising and a total of £3,856,927 in all media. Whereas in the United States labor has been the outspoken foe of advertising, the British Labour government spent as much or more than opposing political parties had spent while in power.[3]

In given instances, the British government advertising has been of proven success. Between 1941 and 1951 a Diphtheria

[2] The advertisement, headed "The Other Side of the Galindez Story," a "memo from Generalissimo Rafael L. Trujillo" appeared in the *New York World-Telegram and Sun* and other newspapers, September 17, 1956.
[3] Mills, *op. cit.*, p. 163.

Immunization campaign was waged for an advertising expenditure of thirty thousand pounds. During that time the number of deaths from diphtheria fell to one-tenth of what it had been previously. It was estimated that £2 million was saved the National Health Service. Advertising has helped Britain push the export sale of British goods but obviously not stemmed the creeping decay from which England's economy seems to be suffering. That, perhaps, is a task beyond its strength. Britain spent £11½ million to build and exploit the Festival of Britain, a major advertising attempt of 1951, but recovered only £2½ million.

If advertising has been used more extensively to propagate ideas rather than just to sell products since World War II, it has also been used in public-relations manner to sell people. Once frowned upon as a weapon for use in political campaigns, though plied extensively since the campaigns of McKinley, Theodore Roosevelt, and Warren Harding, its use is now openly acknowledged. In 1952 both B.B.D. & O. and the Kudner Agency were retained by the Republican party, and Ted Bates served as the advertising agency for the Citizens for Eisenhower organization. In 1956 B.B.D. & O. and Young & Rubicam were the Republicans' advertising agencies. In accepting the nomination of the Democratic Party for president in Chicago in August, 1956, Adlai Stevenson sharply criticized the opposing party for its use of advertising to influence voters, saying: "The men who run the Eisenhower administration evidently believe that the minds of America can be manipulated by shows, slogans, and the arts of advertising. . . . The idea that you can merchandise candidates for high office like breakfast cereal—that you can gather votes like box tops—is, I think, the ultimate indignity of the democratic process."

This was a political announcement for political purposes. The Democratic Party had its agency too (Norman, Craig & Kummel) and used professional advice on presentation and promotion of its candidates. During the course of the 1956 campaign both parties expended large sums in advertising, and five giant advertisers—Westinghouse, Philco, RCA, Sunbeam, and Oldsmobile—spent $25 million on radio and television coverage of the political conventions and the November election.

The War Advertising Council reverted to civilian status as the Advertising Council after World War II but did not seek relief from active duty. Instead the Council decided to continue with its work of getting advertisers and media to contribute space, time, and effort toward what it describes as public-service advertising. It had proved the power of advertising to disseminate ideas in wartime. It was convinced that advertising techniques could be invaluable in spreading information and obtaining mass public action on matters of public importance in peace-time too. It had the further conviction that it was the responsibility of corporate business, as well as good public relations, to underwrite advertising of this kind. The Council began its promotion of advertising which it believed in the public interest. Volunteer advertising agencies were marshalled to use the magazine and newspaper space, the radio and television time, the posters, car cards, and other media contributed by business.

Advertising, confounding some of its most virulent critics, has thus displayed both its newly awakened social consciousness and its force as a means of public communication in numerous campaigns where the profit motive is either non-existent or served only very indirectly. United States Savings Bonds, better schools, forest fire prevention, organized charities, the Red Cross, slum clearance, religion have all benefitted through Council-organized public-interest advertising paid for by American business. Other advertisements have pleaded for armed forces manpower, civil defense, financial aid to education, the Ground Observer Corps and safe driving, or argued for democracy as against communism. The Council's work has won plaudits and advertisers have won recognition for their work.

In 1956 the *Saturday Review* gave its accolade to Caterpillar Tractor, Weyerhauser, General Electric, Container

Corporation, Parke, Davis, Equitable Life Assurance, and the Watchmakers of Switzerland. The magazine awarded Caterpillar Tractor, which had campaigned in its advertising for better roads, highway safety, better schools, first place for "Ever Watch a Forest Die?" The illustration for this magazine advertisement showed a tired and begrimed forest firefighter leaning against a Caterpillar tractor. The Weyerhauser advertising had urged forest conservation and tree farming to guarantee the timber supply of the future. General Electric had used its advertising to stress the needed improvement of scientific education in the United States and describe its own work in that area. The magazine in announcing its awards applauded the use of advertising for informational ends, the spread of ideas, and the advancement of the public interest as "business's response to its own awareness of its obligations."[4]

The work of the Advertising Council has accomplished much for the projects it has undertaken to promote. As it should, it has done more to raise the repute of advertising and to bring unease and discomfort to its enemies. The Council's own pamphlet advertising makes this claim: "The Council is a vital safeguard to your democracy. It upholds the use of persuasion rather than legislation to secure your cooperation in important public projects. Thus it is helping to preserve your *voluntary* way of life."

Another phenomenon observable in modern advertising, less in its public appearance than in the preparation which precedes it, is the ever increasing use of research. Research is used to locate markets, to decide on appeals, to check on the success or failure of advertising copy and layouts, to count readers, listeners, or lookers. Advertising, market, consumer, and media research have almost worn down arithmetic. Billions of decimal points have been expended to convert mysteries into clarities. The consumer has been crushed by tons of tabulations, then propped up again by new bulwarks

[4] William D. Patterson, "The Challenge of Bigness, SR's Fourth Annual Advertising Awards," *Saturday Review*, May 19, 1956.

of new statistics. He has been dissected by age, sex, income, education, politics, and bewilderments. Attempts are made to discover his preferences for everything from cuts in meats to cuts in diamonds. Investigators struggle to discover to what pleas he will react and how. They experiment endlessly to find out just how much and how often the advertising dosage can safely be increased. It sometimes seems as if cereals, automobiles, tooth pastes, cigarettes, and all adults fifteen years of age or older in the United States have been so graphed and charted that they can be cross-pollinated at will.

This is research as the term is understood and unremittingly applied by advertising agencies, advertising media, and advertisers. The techniques used are those of the census taker and the forecaster—who actually learned many of them from the market research man. Questionnaire construction, sampling, coding, tabulating, and interpreting of the results have become intricate studies in themselves. Most research results are used competitively. Advertising claims are based on research results. Advertising appropriations are sometimes made after research has shown the direction in which expenditures should be made. Media are selected partly on the basis of their research claims. Copy, illustrations, and layouts are pretested whenever possible. The results of the advertising, or the lack of them, are discovered through application of research techniques by the various rating services.

This attempt to apply scientific method to advertising, at mechanizing what has long been practised as a craft, has led to economies and efficiencies. Yet research has its limitations. It cannot estimate the actual results of advertising. It cannot be sure a product will sell or an idea take hold. Research has also taken much of the color and life out of modern advertising. The clever slogan, the advertising notable for its friendliness or humor, the aesthetic and fanciful have largely been displaced by duller efforts which research indicates will make a surer sales appeal to the greatest number. The statisticians, economists, psychologists, and sociologists who regulate the research, and can sometimes help dictate policy, have a low tolerance for imaginative treatment of any subject. They depend on proved measurements and are painfully disconcerted when the use of a black patch over a man's eye to advertise a shirt leads to sensational advertising success; they are puzzled, perhaps, when a man is seated on a white horse in his living room to advertise the whiskey he is drinking from a glass in his hand.

Research has to do with testing what has already been tried. It does not often produce ideas, except promotional ideas or ideas for more research. Its results can be used as a guide, and their logic may sway a hesitating advertiser or agency media buyer, but the experienced advertising man often has his reservations and bases his decisions on more emotional grounds. Creative advertising men are apt to distrust research, at least too much research. Raymond Rubicam considered the advertising man best equipped when he was in a state of "intelligent ignorance" for he was as apt to "reach the buyer through his head or his heart . . . spark him with humor or tragedy . . . do it with a single word, or with a page of fine type. He may lean heavily on pictures, or not use them at all. But he will do it somehow."[5] James Webb Young felt that, in the absence of exact knowledge, the advertising man has to depend on his intuitive processes, "a kind of distillation of his mother-wit." He must rely on all his almost unconscious knowledge of people of every kind and how they live, feel, and think. Lasker, Webb noted, had these intuitive processes highly developed, thus his contempt for research.[6]

The talented advertising man may not, as he need not, depend on research, but on the assumption, undoubtedly correct, that there are not many so endowed, researchers in advertising are spending more and more of their time and effort in psychological study of the consumer. Work of this kind has been going on since Walter Dill Scott wrote his first book

[5] *Publishers Do Not Fix the Cost of Space.* (Privately printed; New York: The Maia Press, 1930).

[6] James Webb Young, *The Diary of an Ad Man* (Chicago: Advertising Publications, Inc., 1944), pp. 139, 142.

in 1903, but the approach of what is now called "motivational research" is grave and its language portentous.

Motivational research attempts to discover why people behave as they do with regard to advertising. It tries to find out which advertisements awaken identification, which alienate and why, and uses psychological investigations through various tests to analyze people's feelings and emotions regarding what they buy or fail to buy. J. B. Watson had tried to chart human behavior for J. Walter Thompson in the 1920's. In the 1950's psychologists are intent on finding out why they behave in accord with or in disregard of the wishes and efforts of advertisers. They have found out some surprising facts—and offered some astounding conjectures.

Soup may be associated with man's deepest need for nourishment and reassurance. It arouses sensations of warmth and protection, is rooted possibly in pre-natal sensations of the maniotic fluid in the mother's womb. Cigarette smoking, forbidden in youth, becomes a symbol of independence of parents and provides a sense of guilt which is in itself pleasurable.[7] Henry Ford failed to realize that what people wanted in a car was what Veblen called a symbol of "conspicuous consumption."[8] Motivational researchers found that women disliked a shoe preparation because a border design on the package looked like a crawling worm. After studies, they advised an airline to stop using pictures of pretty models in its advertising and use instead pictures of middle-aged people who could afford to travel. A cigarette company was advised to stop advertising to women and concentrate its attack on men, as they smoke more. One motivational research worker concluded to his own satisfaction that contributing to charity was linked with childhood toilet training; another that adolescent girls use soap to clean themselves of dawning sex im-

    [7] Ray Cault, "Advertising's Debt to Dr. Freud," *Advertising Agency*, July, 1952, p. 98.
    [8] W. G. Eliasberg, "Freud, Veblen, and Marketing," *Printers' Ink*, February 12, 1954, p. 16. Actually Henry Ford did not do too badly with his Model T.

pulses.[9] Eight social scientists watched television all one day in a Chicago hotel in an attempt to find out what type of person was best to give commercial announcements. They found that one not too glib, not too expert, seemingly a bit vulnerable, like the ordinary listener, was best. A woman listened, they decided, more readily to a man because he was not competing with her, but she resented any male display of confidence about women's concerns. Motivational research workers tested the attitude of small girls toward home permanents. The small girls thought curly hair made them beautiful, thus loved. Too many superlatives should not be used in describing advertised products. The fear is created in the consumer that it may be too good for him, and that he will be overstepping himself in desiring it.[10]

Using the so-called "projective techniques," borrowed from hospitals where they are used with the mentally disturbed, psychologists try to find out things about consumers which they do not know themselves in order to devise new ways to catch them and keep them through advertising. In "thematic apperception" tests consumer-patients are asked to make up simple stories about simple pictures. The stories are then translated into confessions and distilled to Freudian conclusions. The respondent who admits that the picture of a tree makes him think of bird watching has given himself away as sexually frustrated. It is immediately apparent to some students of human motivation that the respondent who admits to seeing a little girl in the picture either hates his father or does not like beer. And beer, the *Chicago Tribune* discovered when it had a research organization study beer drinking, is a middle-class drink meant for unpretentious sociability which advertisers should not present in formal settings among the socially pretentious.[11]

[9] Ernest Havemann, "The Psychologist's Service in Solving Daily Problems," *Life*, January 21, 1957.

[10] *Increasing Sales through Advertising Based on Human Motivations* (Chicago: Weiss & Geller Advertising Agency, 1954).

[11] "Motivations, Why People Buy, Why They Work, How to Deal with Them," *Business Week*, reprint of articles from issues May 14-28, 1954.

Depth interviews, word association tests, ink blot experiments are all used in these studies of human motivation. Through these and other methods it has been discovered that face powder sells better in a blue than in a green box, that tan automobiles are more popular in the east than in the west, and that women refused to buy prepared coffee because they thought using it showed them lazy housewives. Some facts have been isolated, but often psychologists do not agree on the accuracy or significance of the findings the finders have found.

As little of human behavior itself is predictable, the motives for that behavior are still even more obscure. Neither eugenics nor divination have advanced to the point where either the sex of the baby or the advertising stimuli to which he will respond can be forecast with certainty, yet the application of psychology to advertising is a natural and probably useful development. Both advertising and psychology are primarily concerned with human emotions, and motivational research at least makes advertising more conscious of the fact that it deals always with people as much as with products and ideas. Currently, a widely publicized attempt is being made to exploit the docile and unsuspecting consumer. Through mechanical means, "hidden sell" is injected below the victim's threshold of awareness. Experimentation has progressed to the point where the operation has been condemned as unethical, unfair, and dangerous in its implications.

Advertising in the period after World War I was as reckless and flamboyant as the 1920's it typified. It reflected the excitement, the heedlessness, and the riotous salesmanship of the time. Except in television where it has still the thrust and raw vigor of the new, advertising has seemed more modest and restrained since World War II. The prevalence of educational and institutional advertising, the public-service and public-interest advertising, the advertising given to serious defense of democracy and the American economic system, the attempt to apply the techniques and findings of social science to advertising all indicate something of the deeply perturbed years of the mid-twentieth century. They may also indicate that in the industrial and commercial civilization of the United States advertising has attained a certain maturity. That the maturity is not too far advanced is reassuring for, as Touchstone once remarked, after ripeness comes rot. There is no indication that the vitality of advertising has been in any way lessened or even that its full potentialities have been suspected.

30

Summary and Conclusion

To BE FOR OR AGAINST advertising in the United States in these latter years of the twentieth century is about like being for or against weather. Advertising is ubiquitous, incessant, and inescapable. Its pressure is relentless. It assails the consciousness and permeates the subconscious. Advertising is part of the economic, social, and political climate. The whole American atmosphere of claims, pretentions, counterclaims, and counter-pretensions is imbued with it. If, through unhappy circumstance or the machinations of free malevolence, advertising could be distilled out and siphoned off, many people would be left disoriented and dismayed. They would have to learn a different breathing. Put structurally, the disappearance of advertising would pull the props from under main elements in the complex of our cultural structure.

Economically, advertising has become a recognized necessity. It is a key component in the marketing of goods mass produced for mass consumption. It is the quickest and cheapest way to inform large numbers of people what is for sale, where, at what price, and to persuade them to buy it. How efficiently it performs this function cannot be exactly measured. The sale of any product depends on many circumstances, its quality, usefulness, and appearance, its packaging, price, availability, the amount and kind of other sales effort made in its behalf. Advertising is just one of the marketing means, but the others could not function without it. It is almost impossible to isolate the sales results of advertising from the results of these other factors which operate to take

merchandise from manufacturer to consumer, just as it is
almost impossible to measure the total results of one advertisement or campaign. What is known is that sales mount
when advertising is increased, fall if advertising is lessened,
sometimes disappear if it is stopped. Without consummated
distribution, production for profit cannot continue. Industries slacken, fail, unemployment brings the collapse of purchasing power and, quickly, general economic dislocation.

This process becomes even more important economically
as production and productive capacity expand and as wealth
spreads. Recent studies have emphasized the greater reliance
of the economy upon advertising and provided further economic justification even of advertising appeals directed at
snobbery and self-indulgence. Industry can now manufacture
far in excess of the immediate physical needs of growing
population. Much of its effort must go into the production
of luxury items not needed for subsistence. In what is described as a luxury economy, instead of an economy of
scarcity, or as an economy of opulence, people must be persuaded to buy much that they do not actually need. In-
creasingly, psychological not physical considerations must
control desire in the United States in order to approximate
full employment and to sustain purchasing power.[1]

In such a situation the economic role of advertising becomes vital. Its persuasive power must convince people that
they must have new and strange things of which they may
never have heard. It is in this way, as advertising men proudly
claim, that advertising supports and helps continually to raise
"the highest standard of living in the world."

A Yale professor of history has indicated advertising as the
only institution we have for necessary consumer education,
for altering values, provoking new needs, for training people
to want and accept the luxuries available in profusion in the
overflowing economy of the mid-twentieth century United

[1] John Kenneth Galbraith, *American Capitalism* (Boston: Houghton
Mifflin Co., 1952), p. 107; C. H. Sandage, "The Role of Advertising in
Modern Society," *Journalism Quarterly*, Winter, 1951, pp. 31-38.

States. He describes advertising as "distinctively the institution of abundance."[2]

The difference between the older economy of scarcity and the present economy of opulence and what this difference entails was emphasized in the voluminous study of the American scene issued by the Twentieth Century Fund in 1955. Its authors unequivocally assigned advertising a key function in the new dispensation.

This constant "education of consumers" to desire products never heard of before is just as essential to the smooth functioning of an economy which is geared to turn out a steady flow of new and different products as are an adequate supply of electric energy and plentiful raw material. . . . The distribution methods which make this possible—the mail order house, the chain store, supermarket, installment buying, market analysis, national advertising, and, whether we like it or not, even the singing commercial—are as much a part of American technology as are radioisotopes and fork-lift trucks.[3]

This newer economic necessity has changed advertising from the simple, informative announcement of earlier centuries, the bold frontal attack of the 1890's, and the later strong competitive product claims, to psychological appeals of greater intensity to consumer emotions. People have more food, clothing, and shelter than many of them can use. The same culture that has given them manifold possessions has in the mass deprived them of other good things, pride and pleasure in work, creative joy, and the simplicities said to bring serenity. They want emotional satisfaction for sharper drives. Advertising panders to their hunger for these, for sex in its aesthetic, romantic, and artistic as well as its copulative manifestations, for comfort, for security, for social approbation, and to their painful thirst for self-approval. Advertising assures them that conspicuous consumption, once the privilege of the plutocrat, is now the right and even the duty of all the deserving.

[2] David Potter, *People of Plenty; Economic Abundance and the American Character* (Chicago: University of Chicago Press), p. 167.
[3] J. Frederic Dewhurst and Associates, *America's Needs and Resources* (New York: The Twentieth Century Fund, 1955), pp. 888-89.

In the end, advertising can offer only material objects for satisfaction of these needs, but often they suffice. At least possession of a prestige article, observance of a socially sanctioned superstition, or purchase of what advertising has established as correct or enviable can palliate the hungers and contribute to the consumer's feeling of well-being and success. To argue that men and women are defrauded and deluded by competitive claims which have no basis in measurable properties of the advertised object is often to argue that people should be different and feel differently, live by other standards and values than they recognize or wish to appreciate.

Advertising has given, or helped to give, people conveniences and comforts they would not otherwise have had. A long list of electrical and mechanical conveniences could needlessly be adduced. The advertising was competitive and commercial. Its intent was to sell goods, not primarily to lessen the burden of the housewife or improve the working conditions of the employed. Advertising intended to sell soap and succeeded. Its primary purpose was not to make people cleaner but to make money. It did both. Advertising money was expended to bring in huge profits to the automotive industry. It did and does, but it gave people the automobile and the kind of life the automobile has made possible. Advertising has made gum chewing, cigarette smoking, and the gulping of soft drinks as characteristic of our time as snuff taking or the chewing of betel nuts is of other times and places. For whatever ill or good, it has helped fasten these habits on a large part of the world's population. Advertising set out to market the almost accidental discovery of a Labrador fur trader named Clarence Birdseye and make profits for the processors of frozen foods, not to change American dietary habits, but it did both.

None of the material gains to which advertising can point as social accomplishments were conceived and executed with pure altruism, but their beneficial results are often indisputable. Socially, advertising has effects as penetrating and as far reaching as its economic force. Its primary effect, perhaps, is to help make possible the industrial, commercial, urban, and suburban life we live, increasing the wealth of the national community, and helping to spread the obtainable material rewards from that wealth. Certainly it has other effects. It contributes to the general stock of information and misinformation. It instills product knowledge and at the same time instills strong prejudices about products and about ideas. It strengthens the hold of the material on the imagination. It keeps desire, ambition, competitiveness sharp, and, directly or indirectly, holds these up as good. Advertising makes always for standardization, uniformity, conformity, and, often, for mass-produced mediocrity.

Inevitably the self-conscious artist and the scholar detest advertising. The expression of an individual talent or the free play of a questing mind is essentially antagonistic to a force which makes for the erasure of individual differences, the standardization of taste, and, literally, the vulgarization of all it touches. Understandably, advertising is an abomination in the sight of some of the Lord's nicest children, a stench in their nostrils, and a discord in their ears. Advertising has done much for the material good of the many, little for the artistic and intellectual hunger of the few. That already bewildered romantic, Robert Louis Stevenson, might not be surprised that advertisers have filled the world with such numbers of wonderful things, but he might be depressed that so many of them are chromium-plated, micrometer-tested, cellophane-packed, and far more alike than the peas in any pod he knew. Actually it is not advertising as advertising alone, but advertising as the most characteristic expression of the whole democratic move toward a mean of indistinction in commercial and industrial society against which the sensitive sometimes rail.

Advertising contributes strongly toward the powerful compulsions to which the mass of people in such a society respond. It erects and supports the images by which that society exists. It uses infinite combinations and permutations of appeals, techniques, and media to attack your senses, your mind, and your emotions. Its greatest weapon, perhaps, is flattery. By the simple fact of advertising, the advertiser sings his awareness of your importance. By withholding your favor, you can put great corporations out of business; by bestowing it, you can sanctify and reward the efforts of some venturesome entrepreneur.

Advertising shares with the physician and the psychiatrist the power to flatter essentially. It says that you and you only are important. How you feel, says the doctor, what you are, says the psychiatrist, what you are and do, says the advertiser, is the most important thing in my world. The advertiser asks your favor, craves your indulgence, pleads for your confidence. He exists only to do things for you, to give you prizes, and to make you happy.

We want to swallow liquids that will make us feel better and live forever. We want cars that will make us feel rich and powerful, clothes that will show the world what manner of men and women we want it to think we are. It is pleasure to buy and exhibit to friends who have what may not be quite as good or as new. Our enemies are those who have what is more expensive and even newer. It is good to own a house or a car or a gun or a bottle of scent which we are convinced is the best—or better than or at least as good as those of our neighbor. What matter if the conviction of the article's superiority and our own for buying and having it comes from advertising impressions whose appeals have been carefully selected for their psychological persuasiveness? Many of them have been.

Advertisers, or their agencies, know when you eat, when you brush your teeth, take a break, drink, and how much you drink. They know at what hour of the day or night you are hard at work, when you are relaxed. They know as much about you as they have been able to find out, and they have found out more than you know; and now they are trying to find out why you are as you are and do as you do. You may not be important to your wife, your children, your dog, or yourself, but you are important to the advertisers. They noted

the moment of your birth (entrance into the market) and
have a shrewd guess of when you will die (leave the market).
You have been surrounded by experts. You are being psy-
cho-dissected right now. There is truth in the parody which
says that:

> Freud does more
> Than Barnum did
> To make consumers
> Do as they're bid.

Politically, advertising is part and parcel of the industrial
democracy of the United States. Democracy, as it is understood and practised in America, supports the economic system of competitive private business. It encourages manufacturing initiative, widespread distribution of goods, and consumer freedom of choice. A dictatorship, with industry government owned or controlled, its production governed by the
state for state purposes, products allocated to the consumer
on plans set by the state, would have no need of advertising.
It could not permit the freedom of the individual premised
by advertising. Advertising is the instrument of competition,
not of state monopoly. Only in a democracy could advertising have developed as it has developed in the United States;
only in a democracy can it function.

The relationship is not one sided. Government in the
United States is heavily dependent upon advertising. Since
World War II, mammoth and ever-expanding government,
swelling public business which dwarfs the most gigantic of
private business operations, takes a larger share of the profits
than the owners and workers in any enterprise. It prescribes
a large share of all earnings which result from human effort;
the more successful the effort, the larger the penalty exacted.
Without competing, government profits from all industrial,
commercial, and personal competition for financial reward.
In this way, big government depends for its support not only
on the advertising done in its behalf, but also on all business
advertising. American democratic government, its demands
multiplying as it assumes more and more responsibility for na-

tional and world welfare, a government which depends solely
on the profit-making energies of its working population,
would have difficulty in existing without advertising.

In public communication, advertising performs a dual
function. It supports newspapers, mass magazines, radio, and
television. Actually, it has made them all in the form in which
they exist. It is largely responsible for their virtues and their
offenses. Advertising is the penalty paid for seeking pleasure
from reading, listening, or listening and watching. The newspaper satisfies man's curiosity about immediate events; the
magazine lures with stories and articles; radio, with music and
patter; television, with drama and vaudeville. Once the consumer rises to these bright flies, he is scratched by the hidden
advertising barbs. He may be hooked, played until exhausted,
then jerked out to flop on the bank or be gently netted and
slipped into the advertiser's creel. In this version the standard
media of public communications are used by advertisers
purely to exploit the innocent.

Fortunately it is not as easy as all that. Advertising is not
that deft, and the innocent are not that innocent.[4] The actuality is generally rather different. Often people look on advertising as part of the information and entertainment they
seek. Advertising is many times news. It may, and, if the
work of the advertising agency is good, it does arouse emotions and stir more actual thought—not enough to be dis-

---

[4] Too many testimonials by too many celebrities, too much solemn at-
testation by too many white-jacketed scientists, too many propaganda claims
by government departments, political parties, corporations, countries, labor
unions, and assorted pressure groups, have made many suspicious of all
advertising. There is another fear that sometimes grips advertising men.
Some day the sated customer, surfeited to lazy discomfort with all the
goodies he has been able to swallow and all the shiny objects he has been
able to cover with down payments, may be able to take no more. It is
not that he will be unwilling or stubbornly refuse to cooperate, but there
may be just no more of him to respond. Soggy with repletion, he may
want only to lie down and sleep it off. He'll rise and try manfully again,
but his first vigor will be gone. The fear passes when it is remembered
that there is always the fourteen-year-old to whom everything is new,
wonderful, and desirable. He is teachable and will take his place as older
consumers, their desires fulfilled and their acquisitive impulses weakened,
fall out and finally are dismissed.

turbing—than many of the stories, articles, dramas, or variety
offered by the media. It may provoke ideas, insinuate impressions, and influence decisively. In effect, advertising is in itself a powerful form of public communication. In a large
part of modern usage this has been recognized, and the force
of advertising as communication is widely applied.

The advertising of, roughly, 1885 to 1905 reflected a
world of bold enterprise and unrestricted commercial competition. This advertising was brash and full-bodied. There
was no sense yet that the world had cracked, was cracking,
or was going to crack wide open. The idea prevailed without
serious question that it was legitimate and laudable to make
money, as much as possible, in business, and certainly in advertising. Advertising was vigorous, and it was fun. The men
who plied it plied it lustily.

For good and practical as well as for idealistic reasons, advertising strove to reform itself between 1905 and the start
of World War I. It began to deny the fraudulent, delete misleading claims, and to tone down the extravagant. During
World War I advertising lent itself to propaganda use, discovering a social consciousness that it threw off quickly in
the lush 1920's. This was the period, par excellence, of reckless salesmanship, and advertising was the focal point of it.
Like many other activities, advertising sobered itself during
the lean 1930's and, when under attack, not this time just for
its sins but for its very existence, it learned discretion through
fear. It went into World War II determined to redeem itself
through good works and to prove its usefulness to the nation.
It feels that it did.

An acute social consciousness has arisen since World War
II, a prevailing concern for the rights and privileges of groups
and classes within the population, with democracy concerned
not so much with equality of opportunity, as the approved
phrase once had it, as with equality of rewards and the erasure
of social and financial distinctions. Making money is no
longer considered an unmitigated virtue. When business does
make money, it is expected to feel rather ashamed and to
acknowledge its guilt for violation of the newer social canons

by giving the money away—to labor, which will seize as much as possible anyway, to government, which will certainly take it. In this environment advertising has become self-conscious, more restrained, and sometimes even modest. It has continued with its good works, not without the consciousness, perhaps, that it needs the approval of government and the community as some assurance against repetition of the kind of attack it endured in the 1930's.

As well as being the tempered instrument of profit-seeking business, advertising has become the tool of the fund-raiser, the politician, and the zealot. Corporations use advertising not only for exhorting people to buy, but also to sue for approval. Advertising courts its own official and popular acceptance by consistently approving all that is paraded as social good. Advertising fought the welfare state bitterly. The controls it threatened to apply would have annihilated it. Advertising is enthusiastic for the welfare world, supporting the economics and philanthropies involved. With fine indiscrimination, it lauds nationalism and internationalism—as does the United States society it reflects. In the sense that it supports the spread of goods and services, advertising has always been for everybody, though the profits the advertising produced actually went to the somebodies who manufactured and distributed the goods and services. Much advertising now seems to be for everybody in every direction, for everybody to have and everybody to profit from the sale of all that goes into having. Normally, advertising supports the *status quo*. As there has been little that is discernibly static about the *status quo* since World War II, advertising supports the swift, unchanneled fluidity that has taken its place.

Advertising does most things more. It is more social-minded than the professionally social-minded, more altruistic than the practising philanthropist, more forward-looking than its own forecasters—and quite innocent, sometimes, of the implications of many of its enthusiasms. It is not the business of advertising to be critical but to be wholeheartedly in favor, in favor especially of what will contribute to its free functioning, increased acceptance, and profitable use. It sells

causes now with the same fervor with which it has sold
cereals. It uses techniques and skills, originally developed for
opening markets, for opening minds to government-approved
and socially sanctioned ideas. Advertising has gone into public service, into public communication and propaganda, with
fervor and the experience of two sizable wars and a frightening economic depression behind it. As it should, it has become the salesman of American democracy. Advertising does
by intention what it has long achieved as a by-product of its
central effort. It exerts deliberately, instead of incidentally,
its immeasurable power to create conviction.

Advertising seems to have passed through its colorful and
memorable period. The undisciplined energy it showed in
the 1890's and early in this century has vanished. The slogans
and trademarks remembered are those of yesterday. Weighted
by research and a new seriousness, some of it has become as
self-effacing as advertising can be. It is more subtle, less
spectacular, sometimes a little dull. It is more insidious, and it
is more powerful, yet in gaining outward dignity and re-
spectability it has suffered some of the same loss of indi-
viduality that it has itself inflicted on so much else in modern
life.

Few things—physical properties or ideas—disappear completely. They may be transformed, but something of them
remains. The automobile still uses the wheel. Though they
are differently understood and various things have been done
to and with them, the earth, air, fire, and water of the early
Greek cosmologists have been around for a long time. Enough
of the psychological emphasis survives from the 1920's,
enough of the economic and sociological from the 1930's and
1940's to complicate the world political preoccupations of the
1950's. Enticement and allure are old. Persuading and being
persuaded are natural, human, and usually pleasurable. They
lie near the beat of living. Over the centuries, advertising has
experienced changes in the proportioning of its ingredients,
in direction, in application, but something of the first advertisement survives in the latest, and there will be traces of it in
the last.

Selected Bibliography

"Advertisements," *The Quarterly Review*, June, 1955.
"Advertisements of 'The Times,'" *Chambers's Edinburgh Journal*, March 29, 1845.
"Advertising, the Story of," (cartograph). New York: Standard Rate and Data Service, 1944.
Advertising Age. (See text for article references.)
"Advertising System, The," *Edinburgh Review*, February, 1843.
AGNEW, HUGH ELMER. *Advertising Media*. New York: D. Van Nostrand Co., 1932.
ALLEN, FREDERICK LEWIS. *The Big Change*. New York: Harper & Bros., 1952.
ALLEN, HUGH. *The House of Goodyear*. Cleveland: The Corday Co., 1943.
ARNOLD, FRANK A. *Broadcast Advertising*. New York: John Wiley & Sons, Inc., 1933.
BANNING, WILLIAM PECK. *Commercial Broadcasting Pioneer*. Cambridge, Mass.: Harvard University Press, 1946.
BARNUM, P. T. *Autobiography; Barnum's Own Story*, ed. WALDO R. BROWNE. New York: The Viking Press, 1927.
BEHRMAN, S. N. "The Advertising Man," *New Republic*, August 20, 1919.
BENSON, NATHANIEL A. "Raymond Rubicam—A Close-Up," *Forbes*, February 1, 1944.
BLEGEN, THEODORE C. "Minnesota Pioneer History as Revealed in Newspaper Advertisements," *Minnesota History*, June, 1926.
BLEYER, WILLARD GROSVENOR. *Main Currents in the History of American Journalism*. Boston: Houghton Mifflin Co., 1927.
BOK, EDWARD W. *A Man from Maine*. New York: Charles Scribner's Sons, 1923.
BORDEN, NEIL H. *The Economic Effects of Advertising*. Chicago: Richard D. Irwin, Inc., 1942.
BOYCE, HOWARD H. "Advertising and Publishing in Colonial America," *American Heritage*, Spring, 1954.
BRITT, GEORGE. *Forty Years—Forty Millions, The Career of Frank A. Munsey*. New York: Farrar & Rinehart, Inc., 1933.
BROOKS, HENRY M. *Quaint and Curious Advertisements*. Boston: Ticknor & Co., 1886.
CALKINS, EARNEST ELMO. *"and hearing not . . ."* New York: Charles Scribner's Sons, 1946
———. *"Louder, Please!", the Autobiography of a Deaf Man*. Boston: Atlantic Monthly Press, 1924.
———. *The Business of Advertising*. New York: D. Appleton & Co., 1915.

504   SELECTED BIBLIOGRAPHY

CALKINS, EARNEST ELMO and HOLDEN, RALPH. *Modern Advertising*. New York: D. Appleton & Co., 1905.

CANTRIL, HADLEY and ALLPORT, GORDON. *The Psychology of Radio*. New York: Harper & Bros., 1935.

CHERINGTON, PAUL T. *The Consumer Looks at Advertising*. New York: Harper & Bros., 1928.

CLARK, BLAKE. *The Advertising Smoke Screen*. New York: Harper & Bros., 1944.

CLYMER, FLOYD. *Early American Automobiles*. New York: McGraw-Hill Book Co., Inc., 1950.

COHN, DAVID L. *The Good Old Days*. New York: Simon & Schuster, Inc., 1940.

COMMAGER, HENRY STEELE. *The American Mind*. New Haven, Conn.: Yale University Press, 1950.

COOK, SIR EDWARD. *Delane of The Times*. New York: Henry Holt & Co., 1916

COONS, HANNIBAL. "Bicycles Built for All," *Holiday*, July, 1948.

"Curious Advertisements," *Chambers's Journal*, October 4, 1879.

DENISON, MERRILL. *The Power to Go*. Garden City, N. Y.: Doubleday & Co., Inc., 1956.

DE VOTO, BERNARD. "Why Professors Are Suspicious of Business," *Fortune*, April, 1951.

DEWHURST, J. FREDERIC and ASSOCIATES. *America's Needs and Resources*. New York: The Twentieth Century Fund, 1955.

DICKINSON, HOWARD. *Crying Our Wares*. New York: John Day Co., 1929.

DOWNEY, FAIRFAX. *Lorillard and Tobacco*. Rev. ed. New York: P. Lorillard Co., 1954.

"Drolleries in Advertising," *Chambers's Journal*, August 24, 1878.

DUNLAP, ORRIN. *Radio in Advertising*. New York: Harper & Bros., 1931.

DURSTINE, ROY S. *This Advertising Business*. New York: Charles Scribner's Sons, 1928.

DURYEA, J. FRANK. *America's First Automobile*. Springfield, Mass.: Published by Donald M. Macaulay, 1942.

DWIGHT, FREDERICK. "The Significance of Advertising," *Yale Review*, August, 1909.

ELLISON, EDWARD. "The Story of Pears'," *Progress*, Summer, 1950.

EMMET, BORIS and JEUCK, JOHN E. *Catalogues and Counters*. Chicago: University of Chicago Press, 1950.

FOWLER, NATH'L C., JR. *Fowler's Publicity*. New York: Publicity Publishing Co., 1897.

FRANKLIN, BENJAMIN. *Autobiography*.

———. "Apology for Printers," *Pennsylvania Gazette*, June 10, 1731.

FRENCH, GEORGE. *The Art and Science of Advertising*. Boston: Sherman, French & Co., 1909.

———. *20th Century Advertising*. New York: D. Van Nostrand Co., 1926.

FREY, ALBERT WESLEY. *Advertising*. 2d ed. New York: The Ronald Press Co., 1953.

GALBRAITH, JOHN KENNETH. *American Capitalism*. Boston: Houghton Mifflin Co., 1952.

GELLER, MAX. *Advertising at the Crossroads.* New York: The Ronald Press Co., 1952.

GILLINGHAM, HAROLD E. "Old Business Cards of Philadelphia," *The Pennsylvania Magazine of History and Biography,* June, 1929.

GLASSCOCK, C. B. *The Gasoline Age.* Indianapolis: The Bobbs-Merrill Co., 1937.

GOODMAN, JACK (ed.). *While You Were Gone.* New York: Simon & Schuster, Inc., 1946.

GREER, CARL RICHARD. *Advertising and Its Mechanical Production.* New York: Tudor Publishing Co., 1940.

Greville Memoirs, The, ed. HENRY REEVE. New York: D. Appleton & Co., 1875.

HART, JAMES D. *The Popular Book.* New York: Oxford University Press, 1950.

HAVEMANN, ERNEST. "The Psychologist's Service in Solving Daily Problems," *Life,* January 21, 1957.

HEAL, SIR AMBROSE, F.S.A. *London Tradesmen's Cards of the XVIII Century.* London: B. T. Batsford, Ltd., 1925.

———. *The Signboards of Old London Shops.* London: B. T. Batsford, Ltd., 1947.

HETTINGER, HERMAN S. *A Decade of Radio Advertising.* Chicago: University of Chicago Press, 1933.

HINDLEY, CHARLES A. *A History of the Cries of London.* London: Charles Hindley (The Younger), 1884.

HOBART, DONALD M. and WOOD, J. P. *Selling Forces.* New York: The Ronald Press Co., 1953.

HOLLISTER, PAUL. "Advertising—Is It Worth What It Costs?", address, Williams College, February 6, 1940.

HOPKINS, CLAUDE C. *My Life in Advertising.* New York: Harper & Bros., 1927.

HOWER, RALPH M. *The History of an Advertising Agency.* Rev. ed. Cambridge, Mass.: Harvard University Press, 1949.

HUDSON, FREDERIC. *Journalism in the United States from 1690 to 1872.* New York: Harper & Bros., 1873.

"Increasing Sales through Advertising Based on Human Motivations," Weiss & Geller Advertising Agency, Chicago, 1954.

JENKINS, MACGREGOR. "Human Nature and Advertising," *The Atlantic Monthly,* September, 1904.

JOHNSON, SAMUEL. "Art of Advertising," *Idler,* No. XI, January 20, 1759.

JORDAN, EDWARD S. *The Inside Story of Adam and Eve.* Utica, N. Y.: Howard Coggeshall, Inc., 1945.

KENNER, H. J. *The Fight for Truth in Advertising.* New York: Round Table Press, Inc., 1936.

LAMBERT, GERARD B. "How I Sold Listerine," *Fortune,* August, 1956.

LASKER, ALBERT D. *The Lasker Story.* Chicago: Advertising Publications, Inc., 1953.

———. "The Personal Reminiscences of Albert Lasker," *American Heritage,* December, 1954.

Lasting Ideas. Pleasantville, N. Y.: The Reader's Digest Association, 1956.

LAZARSFELD, PAUL F. and KENDALL, PATRICIA L. *Radio Listening in America.* New York: Prentice-Hall, Inc., 1948.

LAZARSFELD, PAUL F. and STANTON, FRANK (eds.). *Radio Research, 1942-43.* New York: Duell, Sloan & Pearce, Inc., 1944.

LEWIS, LAWRENCE. *Advertisements of The Spectator.* Boston: Houghton Mifflin Co., 1909.

LIEF, ALFRED. *The Firestone Story.* New York: Whittlesey House, McGraw-Hill Book Co., Inc., 1951.

LIPTON, SIR THOMAS J. *Leaves from the Lipton Logs.* London: Hutchinson & Co., Ltd., 1931.

MAHIN, JOHN. *Lectures on Advertising.* Privately printed, n.d.

MARCOSSON, ISAAC F. "Business-Managing an Empire," *The Saturday Evening Post,* January 18, 1918.

MARTIN, EDWARD SANDFORD. "Advertisements," *The Atlantic Monthly,* January, 1909.

MILLS, G. H. SAXON. *There Is a Tide . . . .* London: William Heinemann, Ltd., 1954.

MORRIS, JOE ALEX. *What a Year!* New York: Harper & Bros., 1956.

"Motivations, Why People Buy, Why They Work, How to Deal with Them," *Business Week,* May 14, 21, 28, 1954.

NATHAN, GEORGE JEAN. "Advertising," *American Mercury,* December, 1929.

NEVINS, ALLAN with HILL, FRANK E. *Ford, The Times, The Man, The Company.* New York: Charles Scribner's Sons, 1954.

"Newspaper Advertisements," *Harper's New Monthly Magazine,* November, 1866.

NICHOLSON, H. B., "Host to Thirsty Main Street," address, Newcomen Society of England, New York, 1953.

O'DEA, MARK. *A Preface to Advertising.* New York: Whittlesey House, McGraw-Hill Book Co., Inc., 1937.

OVERSTREET, HARRY A. *The Mature Mind.* New York: W. W. Norton & Co., Inc., 1949.

PARTON, JAMES. *Benjamin Franklin.* 2 vols. New York: Mason Bros., No. 7 Mercer St., 1864.

PEARSON, HESKETH. *The Smith of Smiths.* New York: Harper & Bros., 1934.

POTTER, DAVID M. *People of Plenty.* Chicago: University of Chicago Press, 1954.

PRESBREY, FRANK S. *The History and Development of Advertising.* New York: Doubleday & Co., 1929.

Printers' Ink, Fifty Years, 1888-1938. New York: Printers' Ink Publishing Co., 1938. (See text for *Printers' Ink* article references.)

The Radio Decade. New York: The Radio Corporation of America, 1930.

"Revolt Against Radio, The," *Fortune,* March, 1947.

REYNOLDS, QUENTIN. *The Fiction Factory.* New York: Random House, Inc., 1955.

RICHARDS, WILLIAM E. *The Last Billionaire.* New York: Bantam Books, 1956.

ROBINSON, CHARLES MULFORD. "Artistic Possibilities of Advertising," *The Atlantic Monthly,* July, 1904.

ROWELL, GEORGE P. *Forty Years an Advertising Agent.* New York: Franklin Publishing Co., 1906.

SELECTED BIBLIOGRAPHY 507

RUBICAM, RAYMOND. "Publishers Do Not Fix the Cost of Space," address. New York: privately printed, The Maia Press, 1930.

SALMON, LUCY MAYNARD. *The Newspaper and the Historian.* New York: Oxford University Press, 1923.

SAMPSON, HENRY. *History of Advertising from the Earliest Times.* London: Chatto & Windus, 1874.

SANDAGE, C. H. "The Role of Advertising in Modern Society," *Journalism Quarterly,* Winter, 1951.

SCHLESINGER, ARTHUR M. *Rise of the City.* New York: The Macmillan Co., 1933.

SCOTT, WALTER DILL. *Psychology of Advertising.* Boston: Small, Maynard & Co., Inc., 1908.

SELIGMAN, DANIEL. "The Amazing Advertising Business," *Fortune,* September, 1956.

SMALLZRIED, KATHLEEN ANN and ROBERTS, DOROTHY JAMES. *More Than You Promise.* New York: Harper & Bros., 1942.

Sold American! New York: The American Tobacco Co., 1954.

Sound of Your Life, The. New York: The Columbia Broadcasting System, Inc., 1950.

"Stranger in America," *Edinburgh Review,* April, 1807.

SULLIVAN, MARK. *Our Times.* Vol. IV. New York: Charles Scribner's Sons, 1932.

SUMNER, G. LYNN. *How I Learned the Secrets of Success in Advertising.* New York: Prentice-Hall, Inc., 1952.

"Swindling and Newspaper Advertising," *The Atlantic Monthly,* August, 1904.

THOMAS, ISAIAH. *The History of Printing in America with a Biography of Printers and an Account of Newspapers.* 2d ed., 2 vols. Albany, N. Y.: Joel Munsell, Printer, 1874.

"J. Walter Thompson Company," *Fortune,* November, 1947.

THRALL, MIRIAM M. H. *Rebellious Fraser's.* New York: Columbia University Press, 1934.

Times, The History of The. New York: The Macmillan Co., 1935.

TIPPER, HARRY and FRENCH, GEORGE. *Advertising Campaigns.* New York: D. Van Nostrand Co., 1923.

TIPPER, HARRY; HOLLINGSWORTH, HARRY; HOTCHKISS, GEORGE BURTON; PARSONS, FRANK ALVAH. *Advertising, Its Principles and Practice.* New York: The Ronald Press Co., 1915.

TURNER, ERNEST S. *The Shocking History of Advertising.* New York: E. P. Dutton & Co., Inc., 1953.

"Undiscovered World, An," *Chambers's Journal,* April 7, 1866.

VAN DOREN, CARL. *Benjamin Franklin.* New York: The Viking Press, 1938.

WARREN, WALDO P. "By-Products of Advertising," *Collier's,* February 6, 1909.

Washington, George, the Writings of. Ed. by JOHN C. FITZPATRICK from the original manuscript sources. Vol. III. Washington, D.C.: U. S. Government Printing Office, 1931.

WATKINS, JULIAN LEWIS. *The 100 Greatest Advertisements.* New York: Moore Publishing Co., Inc., 1949.

WAXMAN, PERCY. "The Power and Cheapness of Good Advertising," *American Magazine*, March, 1916.

WEISS, HARRY B. "A Graphic Summary of the Growth of Newspapers in New York and Other States," *Bulletin of the New York Public Library*, April, 1948.

WHARTON, DON. "The Story Back of the War Ads," *The Reader's Digest*, July, 1944.

WILLIAMS, J. B. *A History of English Journalism*. London: Longmans, Green and Co., 1908.

WOOD, JAMES PLAYSTED. *Magazines in the United States*. New York: The Ronald Press Co., 2d ed., 1956.

WOOLF, JAMES D. *Advertising to the Mass Market*. New York: The Ronald Press Co., 1946.

YOUNG, JAMES WEBB. *Advertising Agency Compensation*. Chicago: University of Chicago Press, 1933.

———. *The Diary of an Ad Man*. Chicago: Advertising Publications, Inc., 1944.

———. "Some Advertising Responsibilities in a Dynamic Society," New York, J. Walter Thompson Co., 1949.

YOUNG, JOHN ORR. *Adventures in Advertising*. New York: Harper & Bros., 1948.

Index